Perspectives on Projects

Modern project management had its genesis in the field of Operations Research in the late 1940s, but today it is a much more diverse subject. It has evolved and developed a much wider range of methods, techniques, and skills that the project manager can draw upon.

Not all these skills are relevant to every project, but an assortment of them will be relevant to most. This book aims to describe for students, researchers and managers the full range of skills that project managers can use to develop their methodologies. The authors group the skills into nine perspectives, representing nine schools of project management research and theory. By attaching a metaphor to each of these perspectives, students, researchers and managers are better able to understand each approach and decide whether it is best suited to the development of a strategy for managing their project.

Perspectives on Projects builds upon the various theoretical orientations that the field of project management has developed. Featuring several case studies, drawn from a variety of settings, to illustrate how the different schools can provide different perspectives on projects, this book is an ideal text for anyone involved in project management.

Rodney Turner is Professor of Project Management at the SKEMA Business School, Lille, France. He has authored or edited 16 books, written numerous articles for journals, conferences and magazines and is editor of *The International Journal of Project Management*.

Martina Huemann is an Associate Professor at the Vienna University of Economics and Business, Austria.

Frank Anbari is Professor of Project Management at Drexel University, USA. He is a board member on several journals on project management.

Christophe Bredillet is Deputy Director General and Dean of Postgraduate Programs and Research, at the SKEMA Business School, Lille, France. He is editor of the *Project Management Journal*.

Perspectives on Projects

Rodney Turner, Martina Huemann,
Frank Anbari and Christophe
Bredillet

with contributions by Darren Dalcher,
Annegret Frank, Roland Gareis,
Pau Lian Staal-Ong, Eddy Westerveld
and Terry Williams

Routledge
Taylor & Francis Group

LONDON AND NEW YORK

First published 2010 by Routledge
2 Park Square, Milton Park, Abingdon, Oxon OX14 4RN

Simultaneously published in the USA and Canada
by Routledge
270 Madison Ave, New York, NY 10016

Routledge is an imprint of the Taylor & Francis Group, an informa business

© 2010 Rodney Turner, Martina Huemann, Frank Anbari and
Christophe Bredillet

Typeset in Times New Roman by Swales & Willis Ltd, Exeter, Devon
Printed and bound in Great Britain by CPI Antony Rowe,
Chippenham, Wiltshire

British Library Cataloguing in Publication Data
A catalogue record for this book is available
from the British Library

Library of Congress Cataloguing in Publication Data
    Perspectives on projects / Rodney J. Turner ... [et al.].
    p. cm.
    Includes bibliographical references and index.
    1. Project management. 2. Project management—Case studies.
    I. Turner, J. Rodney (John Rodney), 1953–
    HD69.P75P4758 2010
    658.4'04—dc22
    2009039075

ISBN: 978–0–415–99373–9 (hbk)
ISBN: 978–0–415–99374–6 (pbk)
ISBN: 978–0–203–89163–6 (ebk)

To the new profession of project management and the academic discipline that supports it

Contents

List of illustrations

Figures

Tables

Notes on contributors

Rodney Turner is managing partner for EuroProjex, a network of trainers and consultants in project management. He is also Professor of Project Management at the SKEMA Business School. He is Adjunct Professor at the University of Technology Sydney and Educatis University Zurich, and Visiting Professor at Henley Business School and the Kemmy Business School University of Limerick. Rodney is the author or editor of 16 books, including *The Handbook of Project-Based Management*, the best-selling book published by McGraw-Hill, and the *Gower Handbook of Project Management*. Since May 1993 he has been editor of *The International Journal of Project Management*, and has written articles for journals, conferences and magazines. He lectures on and teaches project management worldwide. From 1991 to 2004, Rodney was a member of Council of the UK's Association for project management. He is now an Honorary Fellow and Vice-President. From 1999 to 2002, he was President and then Chairman of the International Project Management Association. He also helped to establish the Benelux Region of the European Construction Institute as foundation Operations Director. Rodney is a Fellow of the Institution of Mechanical Engineers and of the Association for Project Management. rodneyturner@europrojex.co.uk

Martina Huemann is Associate Professor at the WU Vienna University of Economics and Business, where she also did her PhD. She is Adjunct Professor of Project Management at the SKEMA Business School, Lille. Martina does research on the Project-oriented Company. She is especially interested in Human Resource Management in the Project-oriented Company and in project and program management auditing as an instrument for learning and governance. She has project management experience in organizational development, research, and marketing projects. She is strongly involved in PM Professional Associations and Research Networks, as a board member of Project Management Austria, a member of the IPMA Research Management Board, a member of the PMI Research Advisory Group and facilitator of PMUni, an international network for professional education and research in process and project management (www.pmuni.net). She is a trainer for assessors and lead assessor of the IPMA Excellence Award. Martina trains and consults internationally and is a network partner of Roland Gareis Consulting GmbH. martina.huemann@wu.ac.at

Frank Anbari (PhD Project Management and Quality Enhancement, MBA, MS Engineering, PMP®, PE, and ASQ Certified Six Sigma Black Belt) is Professor of Project Management in the Goodwin College of Professional Studies at Drexel University in Philadelphia, PA. Prior to that he served as a Faculty member and past Director of the Project Management Program in the School of Business at the George Washington University in Washington, DC, and taught in the graduate programs at Penn State University, the University of Texas at Dallas, Drexel University, and for the International Institute for Learning. Dr. Anbari is co-recipient of competitive research grants from the Project Management Institute (PMI®) and IBM, and the Outstanding Research Contribution 2008 from the International Project Management Association. He has published more than 110 papers, book chapters, books, conference proceedings, and case studies. He has extensive industrial experience serving in leadership positions in US industry and taught seminars in project management, quality management, and Six Sigma method throughout North America and Europe. anbari@drexel.edu or anbarif@aol.com

Christophe Bredillet has 25 years of experience mainly in the field of Strategy, Programme and Project Management in Bank, Sport goods, and IS/IT and in Higher Education. For the past 17 years, he has been Deputy Director General, and Dean of Postgraduate Programs and Research, and Professor of Strategic Management and Programme/Project Management at the SKEMA Business School, Lille. He was Professor, Chair of Project Management and Economics at University of Technology Sydney from 2001 to 2002. Recently (2005) he has also been appointed as an External Examiner for Henley Management College (2005–2009). He is Editor of the *Project Management Journal*. He is a steering committee member of the Global Working Group Standards and a steering committee member of the international non-aligned "think tank" group, OLCI. In both research and professional domains, he is deeply involved with professional project management associations (PMI®, IPMA and APM, APM Group, ICCPM and PMAJ (Japan)). These commitments enable him to be highly aware of portfolio/programme/project management research and cutting-edge professional practice. c.bredillet@skema.edu

Darren Dalcher is a Professor of Software Project Management at Middlesex University and Director of the National Centre for Project Management. He has been named by the Association for Project Management as one of the top ten "movers and shapers" in project management in 2008 and has also been voted Project Magazine's Academic of the Year for his contribution in "integrating and weaving academic work with practice." Following industrial and consultancy experience in managing IT projects, Professor Dalcher gained his PhD in Software Engineering from King's College, University of London. In 1992, he founded and has continued as chair of the Forensics Working Group of the IEEE Technical Committee on the Engineering of Computer-Based Systems, an international group of academic and industrial participants formed to share information and develop expertise in project and system failure and recovery. He has written over 150 papers and book chapters on software engineering and project management. He is Editor-in-Chief of *Software Process Improvement and Practice*, an international journal focusing on capability, maturity, growth and improvement; editor of a major new book series, Advances in Project Management, which synthesises leading-edge knowledge, skills, insights and reflections in project and programme management and of a new companion series Fundamentals of Project Management, which provides the essential grounding in key areas of project management. He is a Fellow of the Association for Project Management and the British Computer Society, and a Member of the Project Management Institute, the Academy of Management, the Institute for Electrical and Electronics Engineers, and the Association for Computing Machinery. He is a Chartered IT Practitioner. d.dalcher@mdx.ac.uk

Annegret Frank is Partner of Roland Gareis Consulting GmbH Vienna and Managing Director and Partner of ABS (Antibiotic Stewardship) Group GmbH. Since 2005 she has been a Facilitator of the ABS platform and Project Manager of the EU project "ABS International." Since 2004 she has been a consultant and trainer at Roland Gareis Consulting GmbH and lecturer at the University of Applied Sciences Technikum Vienna and the University of Applied Science IMC Krems. Annegret is a certified Project Manager (IPMA level C). She studied International Business Administration at the University of Vienna/ BWZ, ISCTE Lisbon and University of California, Los Angeles (UCLA). annegret.frank@rgc.at

Roland Gareis is Managing Director of Roland Gareis Consulting, a management consultancy specializing in project, programme, portfolio and strategic management, with offices in Vienna and Bucharest. He is Professor at the WU Vienna University of Economics and Business and Director of their Professional MBA, "Project and Process Management." He is the author of *Happy Projects* (2005), which has been translated into several languages, and author, with Michael Stummer, of *Processes and Projects* (2008). He is editor, with David Cleland, of *The Global Project Management Handbook* (2006). He is also the founder of PMUni – an international network for professional education and research in process and project management (www.pmuni.net). Roland Gareis graduated from the Vienna University of Economics and Business and received his Habilitation at the Vienna University of Technology, in the Department of Construction Industry. From 1979–1981 he was Professor of Construction Management at the Georgia Institute of Technology in Atlanta. He was Visiting Professor at the ETH Eidgenössische Technische Hochschule, Zurich (1982), at the Georgia State University, Atlanta (1987), and at the University of Quebec, Montreal (1991). From 1986 to 2003 he was president of Project Management Austria, the Austrian Project Management Association, and from 1998 to 2003 Director of Research of IPMA-International Project Management Association. roland.gareis@rgc.at

Pau Lian Staal-Ong is a consultant in process management at AT Osborne B.V., an independent management and consultancy firm in the Netherlands. Since 1999 she has been working for principals in the areas of large infrastructure projects as well as for principals in mostly the public environment. As a business consultant she helps organizations during change processes and fulfils positions in the field of quality and risk management. At present, Pau Lian is involved in the North–South Metro Line project in Amsterdam, a new metro line that is being built in the city center of Amsterdam and should be delivered in 2017. Further she is Network Manager and member of the Executive Team on the NETLIPSE project (www.netlipse.eu), an EC-sponsored research project that focuses on gathering best practices and lesson learnt on the management and organization of large infrastructure projects in Europe. The research was completed in May 2008 with the publication of the book *Managing Large Infrastructure Projects*. She carried out ISO- and INK (Dutch version of EFQM) audits, is a Lead Assessor for the IPMA Project Excellence Award and was a lecturer on Quality and Organization at the Osborne Academy. In addition, after ten years of being a Committee Member of the Dutch Fellowship of Risk Management (GVRM), serving 2005–2008 as Chairman, Pau Lian joined the Risk Management Awards jury in 2008, yearly assessing organizations, projects, risk managers and studies (PhD, doctorate). pst@atosborne.nl

Eddy Westerveld works as a consultant and project manager in projects for AT Osborne B.V. in the Netherlands. For the past ten years he has been active both as project manager, researcher and consultant in large infrastructure and urban renewal projects in the Netherlands and abroad. His main fields of interest are the bridging of the gap between science and practice in the management of large infrastructure, and the management of complexity in these projects. Recently he has been involved as the knowledge team coordinator in a European research initiative called NETLIPSE (www.netlipse.eu). NETLIPSE is an EU sixth framework program project that was executed by eight consortium members from six European countries. The research was completed in May 2008 with the publication of the book *Managing Large Infrastructure Projects*. Eddy has recently completed his PhD thesis on the management of complexity in large infrastructure projects at the Erasmus University Rotterdam. Eddy is a specialist in project management, which is shown by his membership of the committee working on the new ISO norm on project management, his work as a lead assessor for the IPMA excellent award and his membership of IPMA in the Netherlands. In addition he is the lead author of the book *Project Excellence Model* which was published in 2002. ewe@atosborne.nl

Terry Williams is Director of the School of Management at Southampton-University, where he has been Professor of Management Science since mid-2005. He worked in Operational Research for nine years at Engineering

Consultants Yard (now part of BAE Systems), developing Project Risk Management, and acting as Risk Manager for major projects (mainly defense industry). He (re-)joined Strathclyde University in 1992 and became Professor of Operational Research (OR) and Head of Department. He continued research and consultancy modeling the behavior of major projects, both post-project review and (thus informed) pre-project risk. He was one of a team which supported post-project claims, particularly Delay and Disruption, totalling over $1.5 billion in Europe and North America. Terry is a speaker and writer on modeling in project management; he has written around 60 articles in refereed OR and Project Management journals and a book, *Modelling Complex Projects*. He is a member of a number of research networks worldwide, particularly the Project Management Institute (PMI), where he is one of the Research Members Advisory Group. He edits the Journal of the OR Society and sits on a number of other journal advisory boards. He is a PMP, PhD, Chartered Mathematician, and Fellow of the IMA and ORS. He was educated at Oxford and Birmingham Universities, UK. T.Williams@soton.ac.uk

Preface

The genesis of the idea for this book came from Gareth Morgan's book, *Images of Organization* (Sage, 1997). That book describes different metaphors for organizations, and suggests that managers should try to match their organizations to the metaphors to understand them better. He suggested that typically three metaphors would describe each organization. Managers who want to change their organizations should try to understand which metaphor currently describes their organizations, what new metaphors they want to describe them, and then try to move their organizations towards the new metaphors. We believed that the same thing could be done for projects, but because projects are temporary organizations, you don't want to change them, you just want to understand them better to choose appropriate methodologies to manage them.

Project management had its genesis in the field of Operations Research in the late 1940s and 1950s, with the adoption of optimization tools, particularly critical path analysis and bar-charts. For many people it still has not moved beyond that, and so you find people taking a very narrow perspective on their own project, and drawing on a very narrow range of approaches, methods, tools and techniques to manage it. Many people using well known software packages limit themselves to critical path analysis, bar-charts and resource smoothing. However, project management is now a much more diverse subject than that. It has evolved to develop a much wider range of tools, techniques, approaches, methods and skills that the project manager can draw on to develop a methodology appropriate to his or her project. Not all these new skills are relevant to every project, but a selection will be relevant to most. We believe that at least nine schools of research are identifiable within the field of project management, and that each school provides the project manager with a different set of methods, approaches and techniques. We suggest that the project manager can develop a methodology appropriate for his or her project, by identifying which schools are relevant, selecting appropriate methods, and compiling the methodology from these methods.

We suggest that the unit of analysis should be the project, and so the manager starts by looking at his or her project. There are (at least) nine perspectives that the manager can take on their project. The manager decides which perspectives are relevant, and selects methods from the associated schools to compile his or her methodology.

To each perspective we have attached a metaphor to help the manager understand how and why they are using the skills from the associated school. However, whereas some of Gareth Morgan's metaphors are mutually exclusive (an organization cannot be both a machine and an organism; it cannot be both a brain and a psychic prison), ours are not. For a given project one metaphor might be appropriate, or all nine. At least two will be; every project will be a chameleon, and then there will be one other. Thus we suggest that a project manager should try to match our metaphors to his or her project, decide what is important and what they want to focus on, and develop a strategy for managing their project accordingly. By matching the metaphors to his or her project, we hope the project manager can understand it better, and know what key levers they have to pull to help their project to a successful conclusion.

We start by providing an overview of the nine perspectives, and the book as a whole. We introduce memes of project management, ideas (associated with the genesis of project management in optimization theory) that are so deeply ingrained that people just do not question them, and thereby limit their conceptualization of their projects. We also introduce a theory of project management that underlies the ideas of this book. The schools themselves are fields of research, not theories, and so we need a theory as a basis for what we later discuss. We also introduce two typologies of project management that we use throughout the book. In the next nine chapters we describe the nine perspectives, and the methods, approaches and techniques that can be drawn from the associated schools. In the second part of the book we include three case studies to illustrate the use of the perspectives. The case studies are drawn from three industries – construction, computers and organizational change – and so illustrate how the perspectives can be relevant to different types of projects. The three case studies are the Amsterdam North–South Metro Line, the computerization of the London Ambulance service and the development of the sustainable use of antibiotics in nine European countries.

We would like to thank those people who have helped us with the book. There are the six other contributors – Terry Williams who contributed to Chapter 3, and the five authors of the three case studies: Pau Lian Staal-Ong, Eddy Westerveld, Darren Dalcher, Annegret Frank and Roland Gareis. We would also like to thank Judy Morton for her help in proofreading the text.

We sincerely hope that the book helps you take a wider perspective om your projects, and thereby helping you to recognize that there is a much wider range to methods, approaches and techniques to draw on in managing your projects, enabling you to adopt much richer methodologies.

Rodney Turner, East Horsley
Martina Huemann, Vienna
Frank Anbari, Philadelphia
Christophe Bredillet, Lille
September 2009

1 The diversity of projects and project management

1.1 New perspectives on project management

The management of projects is a subject is of considerable economic importance. Data produced by the World Bank shows that about one-fifth of the world's $50 trillion gross domestic product is spent on new capital formation (World Bank, 2007). The amount varies by country. The developed economies spend smaller amounts – about one-sixth of GDP in the UK and USA. The developing economies spend more to help achieve economic growth. India spends around one third of its GDP on new capital formation and China a massive 45 percent. New capital formation is almost entirely project-based and so this means that at least one-fifth of the global GDP, $10 trillion, is undertaken as projects. But companies also spend money on projects through their revenue expenditure and so the total amount of the global economy spent on projects may be closer to one third, $16 trillion. Rodney Turner, Ann Ledwith and John Kelly (2009) have shown that small to medium enterprises (SMEs) spend on average one-third of their turnover on projects. SMEs make up 70 percent of the private sector economy, so that means 20 percent of the private sector economy is spent on projects in SMEs.

Thus globally substantial amounts of money are spent on projects, ranging from large infrastructure projects to small projects in SMEs. Anyone who is aware of these figures can have no doubt about the importance of the discipline and profession of project management to the global economy. It is critical for organizations around the world to develop sound project management practice. Data produced by the Standish Group (Johnson, 2006) show on average projects are at least 10 percent late and 10 percent overspent, meaning a massive $3 trillion (at least) is wasted annually on poor performing projects, three times the amount made available by the G20 countries at their meeting in April 2009 to help support the global economy.

Modern project management as a discipline started in the late 1940s as an offshoot of optimization theory from the field of Operations Research (Hillier and Lieberman, 2002). Techniques such as critical path analysis (CPA) and bar (Gantt) charts were found to be useful to help with planning and controlling the delivery of projects. Since then a substantial amount of research has been done, expanding the range of the discipline and the tools available. However, in spite of this development, the performance of projects leaves a lot to be desired. Part of the reason for this is many organizations still do not put any effort into the development of the competence of their project managers. Many project managers' competence development comes solely from on-the-job experience, and that experience comes from working in organizations of low project management maturity. If the development of project management competence comes solely from working in organizations which themselves have low project management capability, you have to expect that the competence development of project managers will be poor. However, another reason, and the one we hope to make some contribution to solving with this book, is that in spite of all the development, many project managers do not seem to be aware that there are tools available to them other than the optimization tools of CPA and Gantt charts. There is a mythodology in project management that the only success criteria of any relevance are the wretched triple constraint of time, cost and quality, and the only tools to use are network analysis and bar charts. Project managers use famous software products where that is almost the only functionality provided, and think that is all there is to project management. We call these the memes of project management, ideas that seem to be so deeply ingrained that project managers use them without question. But there is far more to project management:

- CPA has only limited applicability, being appropriate for projects with low uncertainty and ambiguity – more sophisticated modeling techniques are required on more complex projects;
- there are success criteria other than the wretched triple constraint of time, cost and performance, which Aaron Shenhar and Dov Dvir (2007) have shown to be almost irrelevant, and the achievement of the other criteria requires different tools and techniques;
- higher level governance roles other than the project manager are required to link projects to corporate strategy, and corporate governance needs to define how projects will be delivered and controlled in the organization and create the capability to do that;
- projects involve people, and the behavior of those people and their commitment to the project needs to be managed;
- people's commitment is a price to them, and they pay that price to obtain the benefit (product) from the project, and so the project needs to be promoted to people in the place they have contact with it; it needs to be marketed;
- the project itself can be viewed as an algorithm, a process to be followed to reduce uncertainty and ambiguity, and you can follow the algorithm in a structured way to manage the reduction of uncertainty;
- as you follow the process many decisions are required to establish the project and define what direction the project will take, and as the project progresses, decisions are required to keep the project on track; the decisions need to be based on a sound business model;
- every project is different and so every project requires a different set of tools and techniques for its delivery, and not just a standard set involving CPA and Gantt charts.

These eight bullets, together with the optimization tools, illustrate that there is a range of perspectives we can take on our projects and project management. These different perspectives are supported by nine fields of research in project management, which we call schools, representing different areas of research over the past six decades. These nine perspectives, and the schools which support them, guide project managers and their teams to the selection of new and different sets of tools and techniques to manage their projects. Through this book we aim to raise our readers' awareness of different perspectives they can take on their projects, and how the nine schools which support them can then suggest a range of methods they can draw for managing projects. The nine perspectives are Optimization – representing the genesis of project management – and Modeling, Success, Governance, Behavior, Marketing, Process, Decisions and Contingency – representing each of the issues raised in the list above. Our proposal is that on any project, two, three or four of the perspectives may be relevant, enabling the project management team to paint a picture of their project and guide them in selecting a much richer methodology for the management of their projects.

In the remaining nine chapters of this part we describe each of the nine perspectives in turn. Then in the second part we present three case studies illustrating the use of the nine perspectives in practice. We have case studies from different sizes of project and different industry sectors.

In the remainder of this chapter we describe first the memes of project management. We then give an overview of the nine perspectives. We give a brief description of a theory of project management to introduce concepts used throughout the book. We also want to show that we believe there are essential elements of project management which must be addressed in the management of projects, and other tools (usually associated with the memes) which are used only because they are part of project management mythodology. We also introduce two typologies of projects to which we refer repeatedly throughout the book.

1.2 The memes of project management

Up to now the theory of project management has not been widely recognized. David Cleland and Bill King (1983; first edition published 1968) offered a theory of project management based on systems theory, and Rodney Turner (2009, first edition published 1993) offered one based on the process approach. However, this work was not widely recognized as offering a theory, and so project management has essentially remained largely atheoretical. Rodney Turner wrote a series of articles in the late 1990s (see, for instance, Turner, 1999) suggesting that project management was a profession governed more by faith than knowledge. He made a pun on the word "profession" as being either "a statement of belief in a religion" or "a paid occupation especially one involving education and formal qualifications." For many people project management is little more than a religion. Many of the tools and techniques of project management are taken as being relevant as articles of faith, not based on any theoretical principles or empirical evidence. Some of these articles of faith are so strong that it is almost heresy to contradict them, and they are repeated as mantras.

We have labeled these the memes of project management, following the work of Richard Dawkins (1976) and Susan Blackmore (1999). They identify a meme as an element of culture that reproduces itself through replication in people's minds. Richard Dawkins suggests that memes were necessary in human evolution to reproduce learning before the invention of writing, so ideas could be passed from one generation to another. They include recipes for making bread, designs for houses and clothes, and stories and legends by which other learning messages are transmitted from one generation to the next. Now that we have writing memes are no longer necessary to reproduce learning, but writing was invented relatively recently in human evolution and so we have not lost the tendency to reproduce learning through the transmission of myths and legends, and so it remains with the mythodology of project management.

The memes of project management are all associated with the Optimization School and the systems approach to project management. We hope that after reading this book you will appreciate that project management is a much richer and diverse subject, and recognize that there are a wider set of methodologies to draw on than those just suggested by the Optimization School.

The memes of project management include the following:

The triple constraint

This is the worst. Repeatedly trotted out by project managers is the mantra that project management is about delivering projects within time, cost and quality, in spite of the fact that for more than 20 years researchers have shown that project success is a more complex issue (Morris and Hough, 1987; Wateridge, 1995; Shenhar and Dvir, 2007). Rodney Turner (2009) suggests that:

- the achievement of time, cost and performance targets are just as important in a routine operations environment – in fact project managers' beloved Gantt charts were invented in that environment;
- what distinguishes projects is the need to manage risk, integration and urgency.

When discussing the theory of project management below, we suggest (in Premise 2) that the main criterion of success is the project should be of value to the stakeholders, particularly the sponsor, owner and contractors. Aaron Shenhar and Dov Dvir (2007) have shown that the triple constraint is next to irrelevant.

"If you can move a mouse, you can manage a project"

Rodney Turner and Ralf Müller (2006) report an advertisement for a project management software tool in the UK that claimed, "If you can move a mouse you can manage a project." This is an extreme version of the idea popular in the project management community that the road to successful project management is the use of the right tools and techniques. This has been the overriding paradigm in the project success literature, following the work of Jeffrey Pinto and Denis Slevin (1988). Their list of ten success factors does not include the project manager, nor his or her competence or leadership style. This meme has continued to replicate itself, in spite of the evidence presented over 20 years ago (Andersen *et al.*, 1987; Morris and Hough, 1987) that organizational and behavioral issues are equally if not more important. Rodney Turner and Ralf Müller (2006) have shown that emotional intelligence is the most significant determinant of project management success, but we wait to see whether that will break the meme. Through this book we will have another go at doing so.

If you can move a mouse, you can manage any project

A related meme is the idea that once a project manager has learned the tools and techniques, he or she can apply them to any project; that project management success does not depend on domain knowledge or having the right temperament for the type of project. There is now a wealth of evidence (Crawford *et al.*, 2005; Turner and Müller, 2006) that different methodologies are required for different types of projects and that the project manager requires different emotional profiles for different types of projects. Hence we identify the need for the Contingency Perspective.

"Ask me what PERT means"

Rodney Turner attended the annual project management exhibition in Birmingham, England, in 2006. On one stand selling software there were two young women wearing orange T-shirts, and emblazoned across their breasts were the words, "Ask me what PERT means." This is indicative of the meme that the only project management modeling tool to use is critical path analysis, CPA, or its variant, the program evaluation and review technique, PERT. One of the reviewers of the book by Andersen *et al.* (1987) asked how it could claim to be a book about project management since it didn't mention critical path analysis. That in fact was not quite true. They devoted one paragraph to CPA explaining why they didn't think it was necessary on the majority of projects and how the book focused on the organizational and behavioral issues of projects. Critical path analysis has known weaknesses, it is linear and deterministic, and does not allow for inductance, capacitance, feedback, or probabilistic branching. It is virtually useless as a modeling tool for projects. Graham Winch (2004) has suggested it is appropriate over a very small area of the governance space. Computer-based modeling is not necessary at all on simpler projects, and more sophisticated modeling is necessary on more complex projects. Terry Williams (2002) has shown critical path analysis can be positively dangerous on more complex projects. On projects with feedback loops, standard project management techniques can reinforce positive feedback loops with damaging consequences. It is to recognize the need to use more sophisticated modeling techniques on more complex projects that we have separated the Modeling Perspective from the Optimization Perspective.

There is another reason why PERT and CPA remain such a key part of project management – the software companies have invested so much in their products that they cannot afford to see their value wiped out overnight.

1.3 The nine schools of project management

There is much more to project management than this very narrow perspective. Fifty years of research has substantially broadened the subject, away from its early roots in optimization theory and the field of Operations Research. We believe a substantive element of the research can be grouped into nine schools and that these nine schools offer project managers and their teams different perspectives on their projects which they can use to take different approaches to their management. By taking different perspectives on their projects, project managers can identify essential features, and draw upon the tools, methods, and approaches of the schools of research to develop a methodology specific to their project. All perspectives apply to all projects, but on a given project two, three or four perspectives may be particularly relevant. Project managers can then turn to the schools supporting those perspectives to source the tools, methods and approaches to develop their methodology. In this section we describe the nine schools, the nine fields of substantial research, which we believe provide project managers the tools to draw on in formulating their project management methodologies.

What do we mean by "schools"?

The Oxford English Dictionary amongst several others gives the following definitions of a school: "a group of people sharing common ideas or methods; a specified style, approach or method" or "the imitators, disciples or followers of a philosopher, artist, etc." The first of these describes what we mean here by schools of project management. Various fields of research in project management have led to the development of different methods, styles, approaches, tools and techniques on which project management teams can draw to manage (and govern) their projects. The second suggests that associated with many of the schools there may be key authors who have led their development.

Other types of school

The Oxford English Dictionary gives other definitions of the word "school," which can suggest other perspectives:

- an institution for educating or giving instruction; the associated buildings;
- a branch of study with separate examinations at a university; a department or faculty;
- a group of gamblers or people drinking together;
- a shoal of fish, porpoises, whales, etc.

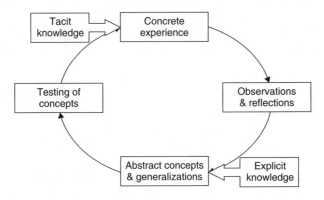

Figure 1.1 Kolb's learning cycle

The first two reflect the normal view of a school, a place of learning. In the past many project managers just obtained their competence development through on-the-job experience. That is now changing, but perhaps many more project managers could "go to school" to obtain formal tuition, either as training through short courses, or education through university masters courses. Kolb's (1984) learning cycle (Figure 1.1) suggests we obtain our competence development in two ways: through experience, giving us primarily tacit knowledge; and through tuition, giving us primarily explicit knowledge. The two reinforce each other, and both are necessary. Many project managers just rely on on-the-job experience, but now with the growth of certification programs and masters courses many are getting formal tuition as well. Ralf Müller and Rodney Turner (2007) have shown that certification does make good project managers better. In *The Republic*, Plato suggested that trades start by gaining on-the-job experience and then progress to formal tuition, whereas professions start with formal tuition and progress to on-the job experience. If project management is a profession then hopefully things have changed since Plato's time.

The last two could lead to more flippant views of schools. Perhaps on high risk projects, the project team is a "school," gambling together and drowning their sorrows in drink. And, yes, perhaps project managers wedded to the Optimization School turn their project team into a school of goldfish, blindly applying CPA, Gantt charts and the other associated ideas.

However, for the remainder of this book, we look upon a school of project management as a group of people applying common tools and methods, and developing appropriate methodologies for their projects by combining tools and methods from several schools. Each school may have lead authors strongly identified with the schools.

The schools of project management

Frank Anbari (1985) identified five schools of project management, and Jonas Söderlund (2002) seven. Christophe Bredillet (2004) conducted a co-word analysis of papers published in project management research journals and also identified seven. Table 1.1 shows the five schools of Frank Anbari, and the seven of Jonas Söderlund and Christophe Bredillet and compares them to ours. We have nine schools rather than seven because we identified two additional schools.

1   We split the Optimization School into the Optimization and Modeling Schools. There are several reasons for this. First, it is only strictly possible to optimize two parameters, whereas the Modeling Perspective aims to model more. Second, the Optimization School uses optimization algorithms (for example critical path analysis, CPA), which are not able to deal with the complicatedness and complexity of modern projects, and so we wanted to clearly differentiate between the simple algorithms that were the genesis of project management, and which still have a place on the simpler projects which represent the majority of projects, and the more sophisticated modeling techniques available for more complex projects. Third, the use of soft systems modeling is growing and that did not fall within the Optimization School. It either needed a school of its own or it needed to be part of a larger Modeling School.
2   We have identified a Process School. The work of Rodney Turner (2009, first edition 1993) and Roland Gareis (2005) has been very heavily based on a process view. However, their work has not been widely published in the academic press, so fell below the radar with the methodologies used by Jonas Söderlund and Christophe Bredillet.

We have also widened the perspective of two of the schools. We have expanded transaction costs into the full area of governance. Transaction costs point to the governance of the individual project. But we have widened this to include the governance of the project-oriented organization and its projects. We have also added

Table 1.1 The nine schools of project management and their antecedents

Nine schools	Frank Anbari (1985)	Jonas Söderlund (2002)	Christophe Bredillet (2004)
Performance			
Optimization	Management science	Optimization	Optimization
Modeling	(Contingency)	Contingency	Contingency
Contingency			
Business			
Success	Functional	Success	Success
Governance		Transaction cost	Transaction cost
Marketing		Marketing	Marketing
People			
Behavior	Behavior	Behavior	Behavior
Solution			
Process	Decision	Decision	Decision
Decision			

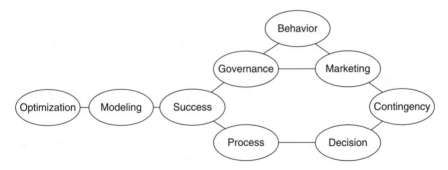

Figure 1.2 The nine schools of project management

human resource management (HRM) to the Behavior School. We could have created another new school, an HRM School, because in the field of management people do differentiate between Organizational Behavior (OB) and HRM. But for our purposes we found that they fitted well together.

Figure 1.2 illustrates the nine schools. We have grouped the schools into four sets:

- *Performance:* Three of the schools – Optimization, Modeling and Contingency – address the performance of the project, and its modeling to achieve best performance.
- *Business objective:* Three – Success, Governance and Marketing Schools – address the business objectives of the project, and management methods brought to bear to achieve those objectives.
- *People:* One – Behavior – deals with the behavior of people working on projects, and with the behavior of the project as a temporary organization.
- *Solution:* Two – the Process School and the Decision School – deal with finding a solution for the project, working through a path to reduce uncertainty and find our way to the vision for the project, and the taking and recording of decisions through that process.

Perspectives on project management

The nine fields of research suggest nine different perspectives we can take on our projects to formulate methodologies to manage them. The nine perspectives and the order they are addressed in this book are:

Optimization: The project as a machine

Project management started as an off-shoot of the field of Operations Research and optimization theory. There was a lot of work in the late 1940s in the development of optimization tools, including linear programming, quadratic programming, dynamic programming and critical path analysis, amongst others. It was recognized that critical path analysis and the associated bar-charts (Gantt charts) could be applied to the management of projects, as other tools could be applied to the management of operations. So project management and operations management were both off-shoots of Operations Research at about the same time. Initially only one parameter was optimized, the duration of the project, using the critical path method, CPM, and its extension the program evaluation and review technique, PERT, which also incorporated three-point estimating. However, cost optimization was subsequently incorporated through what was originally called the cost and schedule control systems criteria, C/SCSC, but is now called the earned value method, EVM. The Optimization School adopts a very mechanistic approach to project management, being based on the Taylorian model: that the work of human beings and their endeavors can be made as predictable as machines.

Modeling: The project as a mirror

The Optimization Perspective is very narrow, focusing on a very limited set of parameters to optimize. It is now recognized that there are many more, including scope, organization and risk. Most optimization algorithms can only cope with two parameters. With more, you need to model the system, and the best you can hope for is to "satisfice," to achieve the best in all possible worlds. Further, the techniques derived from Operations Research are very linear-rational. They work if things move in one direction and there is no divergence from plan. But projects usually don't work like that. There are feedback loops, some of them reinforcing, which come into play once there is divergence from plan. There is inductance, capacitance and resistance in the system. All of these are beyond the capacity of CPA to model. More sophisticated modeling techniques should be adopted that recognize and model the complexity of the system. Initially, mathematical modeling tools were adopted from systems theory. More recently, soft systems modeling tools have also been adopted to model the complexity of human behavior. The Modeling School holds up a mirror to the project.

Success: The project as business objective

The Optimization Perspective focuses on only three parameters to optimize: the so-called triple constraint, or golden or iron triangle of time, cost and quality (or performance). But project success is a more diverse topic, with many more possible criteria for judging project success, and many more possible factors that can influence success. There has been a development of thinking about project success. In the 1970s, people researched the tools of project management, mainly CPA. In the 1980s, people began to ask what factors might influence success, and suggested you should identify the factors first, and they would point to the tools you should use. In the 1990s, John Wateridge (1995) went one step further. He said that one needed first to identify the success criteria. Answer the question, "How will you judge the project to be successful?" These criteria will point to relevant success factors, which in turn will suggest the tools to manage the project. The Success Perspective attempts to relate the project objectives to the business objectives of the sponsoring organization, and by developing a strategy for the project linked to the strategy of the parent organization. The project becomes a business objective for the parent organization.

Governance: The project as legal entity

The project is a temporary organization created to achieve a business objective for the parent organization. That organization needs governing, and its governance needs to be linked to the governance of the parent organization. The directors of the parent organization also have to meet certain compliance requirements and so the governance of the project needs to support those requirements. Further, people and resources are assigned to the temporary organization to achieve its business objectives, and the relationships between those people and resources needs to be managed by contracts or by fiat. Under the Governance Perspective the project becomes a legal entity in its own right.

Behavior: The project as a social system

The project is a temporary organization, and so by definition involves people. It is therefore a social system. There will be behavioral issues governing the relationships between the people of that social system, as in any organization, and so the Behavior School attempts to model those behavioral relationships. We also need to care for people in the temporary organization, and their well-being, and so human resource management will be an important part of the Behavior School. Finally, the project manager needs to provide leadership to the people working on the project, and so that too is part of the perspective.

Marketing: The project as a billboard

The members of that social system, the people in the temporary organization, need to be persuaded to join the temporary organization and to support the project and its objectives. For them, the benefit provided by the project is a product, and their commitment is the price they pay for it. So the project manager must market the project to the stakeholders, promoting it in their place of work. Further the manager must seek the support of top management for the project and its objectives and for the methods adopted to deliver the project. Thus the project becomes a billboard for advertising the project and its objectives to the stakeholders and top management, and for advertising the value of project management to top management.

Process: The project as an algorithm

Returning to the Success Perspective, there is uncertainty when we start the project as to the best way of achieving the defined success criteria and how the success factors will be brought to bear. We start with a vision of what we want to achieve and we need to convert that vision into reality. To help we can adopt structured processes to provide a methodical approach to reaching our vision. As we work through the process we can solve the problem to identify best way of reaching our goal. Under the Process Perspective the project becomes like an algorithm, a structured and methodical technique for solving problems, reducing uncertainty and increasing clarity, and identifying the best route to reach our goal.

Decision: The project as a computer

As we work through the process, there are many decisions to be taken. Some will be met at the start of the project. How much will the project cost and how long will it take, is it worthwhile, and what is the best way of delivering it? Others will be met as we work through the process or algorithm. The process presents us with many potential branches and we must decide the best route to take. As we progress the project itself provides us with the vehicle to process information and take those decisions. The project becomes the computer to process the algorithm.

Contingency: The project as a chameleon

All roads lead to Rome, but to listen to the project management community you may be forgiven for thinking that one road leads everywhere. This is a consequence of the systems approach, a view that one set of tools can be used on all projects. You hear project managers say in the same breath that projects are unique, and that one set of tools works for all projects. The Contingency Perspective attempts to understand the differences between projects and to develop and adopt appropriate methodologies and competences for managing the different projects. The project like a chameleon will adapt itself to its environment, and we must adapt the color of project management to suit as well.

The order we address the perspectives in the book is a little different to the order we listed them above. We cover them more in the order your thinking evolves. First you think about optimizing your project, and in order to do that you need to model it. But to optimize and model the project you need to know how it will be judged successful and what factors will influence success. To choose the success criteria you need to know how the project will be governed, and who is responsible for it. Projects involve people and to make it work you need to develop those people and also win their support. In order to achieve our goals we need to follow due process, and create an auditable decision trail through the process. Finally, all projects are different, and so we need to develop methodologies to reflect the specific needs of our projects, and we offer the nine perspectives, and the schools of project management research that support them, providing different views to do that.

1.4 A theory of the management of projects

The schools provide perspectives on the theory of project management; they do not themselves constitute a theory. They are fields of research in project management, which fulfill at least two purposes:

1   Each provides a focus for research to enable academics to contribute to the development of the theory;
2   Each provides a perspective that helps practicing project managers better understand their projects and better enable them to apply the theory to their projects.

In this book, we are writing about the schools of project management, and the perspectives they give on the theory, but to set those perspectives in context, we do need to understand what we mean by projects and project management, and to that end we outline a theory of project management.

A theory should start with a series of premises, and from them derive essential elements and components of the item under discussion. We start with five premises and from them derive a theory of projects, project management and the management of projects:

1   The first premise defines what we mean by a project;
2   The second premise defines how the project will be of value;
3   The third premise starts by defining governance of the project and from that flows what we mean by the management of the project;
4   The fourth premise identifies that there are stakeholders in a project;
5   The fifth premise defines what we mean by different forms of multi-project organization, including the project-based organization, the project-oriented organization, programs and portfolios of projects, and so extends the theory away from projects alone to those other multi-project forms.

David Cleland and Bill King (1983) derived a theory of project management based on their systems school. They started from a series of premises, including:

1   The project organization is a temporary matrix with people drawn from across the parent organization;
2   Projects move through a life-cycle;
3   The project management process is inherently one of planning and control;
4   The project organization delivers against objectives of time, cost and functionality set outside the project;
5   Tools such as work break-down structure and critical path analysis are useful.

We believe that while their theory was an extremely useful contribution to the development of project management thinking in its early days, it contains two essential flaws.

1   The premises require the definition of terms that are not obvious – for instance what we mean by a "matrix organization";
2   Every premise makes an assumption about what project management entails or about essential tools, all of which need justifying.

The theory is then only as sound as the definition of those terms, and the assumptions that have been made. We therefore want to go back to first principles, use simple, natural language on which to base our premises, and evolve a more fundamental definition of what we mean by projects and project management, and show that many of the tools and techniques that David Cleland and Bill King assumed to be elements of project management in fact flow essentially from these simple definitions.

Premise 1: The project

The first premise defines the project (Figure 1.3):

A project is a temporary organization to which resources are assigned to do work to deliver beneficial change.

This premise is used throughout this book to define what we mean by a project. We want to emphasize that for us a project is a temporary organization. It is not a temporary task given to the routine organization, but a temporary organization with its own identity, to which people and other resources are assigned to perform a specific task. The making of a cup of tea is not a project, it is a temporary task performed by the routine organization. The critical theorists (Hodgson and Cicmil, 2006) charge that many people "reify" projects. We believe that by following our definition we do not do this. As a temporary organization a project is a social construct and so it is only as real as that construct, but people find value from creating that construct as a unit of analysis.

Let us analyze the components of Premise 1 in turn and see what elements are shown to be essential components of projects and project management.

Temporary

What do we mean by temporary? On some timescales all organizations are temporary. The oldest organization of which we are aware is the Church of Rome which

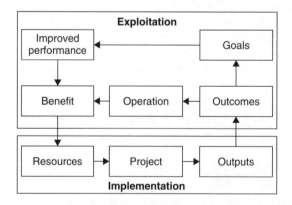

Figure 1.3 The definition of a project

is 2,000 years old. The average life of a Fortune 500 company is 50 years. On other timescales all organizations are permanent. The longest project of which we are aware from first work to eventual commissioning was the Rhine to Danube canal. Work was started by the first emperor of the Holy Roman Empire, Charlemagne, around 792, and the canal was eventually commissioned in 1992, 1,200 years later; the project outlived the Holy Roman Empire.

The answer is a matter of intent. An organization that considers itself permanent creates an organization it considers temporary, a project, to undertake a specific task on its behalf to deliver beneficial change, and when the change has been achieved the project is disbanded. There is a parent–child relationship; the parent considers itself permanent and the child temporary. The project is a social construct. The parent organization finds it useful to consider the child as a project because it aids the management of the project, the resources that will be assigned and the work they will undertake. In the process it may well reify the project (Hodgson and Cicmil, 2006), but that aids its management.

Organization

What do we mean by an organization? There are a number of different perspectives:

An association: An organization, almost by definition, is an association between people through which they work together to achieve specific objectives. The people may be what the Dutch call "natural persons" (human beings) or "legal persons" (legal entities). The Behavior and Governance Perspectives help describe the working of the organization.

As we work through the theory we identify inherent elements of project management, things which, *if* the five premises are correct, must be an inherent part of project management. We label these I, and we see the first here in Box 1.1.

Box 1.1

I   Project organization or integration management is an inherent part of project management.

A nexus of contracts: Oliver Williamson (1996) describes an organization as a nexus of contracts. Contracts are required to describe how the members of the association relate to each other. The contracts may be legal contracts or fiats, or they may just be psychological or social contracts. The Governance and Behavior Perspectives help describe the contracts (see Box 1.2).

Box 1.2

I   Project contract management is an inherent element of project management.

A vehicle for processing information: Graham Winch (2004) describes the project as a vehicle for processing information. The Process and Decision Perspectives help in the understanding of this (see Box 1.3).

Box 1.3

I   Information management and communication management are inherent elements of project management.

A system: The systems perspective of David Cleland and Bill King (1983) is a valid perspective on projects. The Nobel laureate Niels Bohr, while developing Quantum Theory, proposed the correspondence principle: that any new theory should reduce to the old theory for cases where the old theory is known to hold. We see this to be valid here, supporting both the systems approach and our new theory.

Resources

Resources can be:

* money;
* people;
* materials.

The Modeling and Optimization Perspectives can help in the modeling and optimization of the consumption of resources, the Behavior Perspectives can help in the assignment of people to the project, the Marketing Perspectives can help in persuading people to make the resources available, and the Governance Perspectives can help defining who is responsible for releasing resources (see Box 1.4).

Box 1.4

I   Cost or resource management is an inherent element of project management.
I   Human resource management is an inherent element of project management.
I   Materials management is an inherent element of project management.

Work

The work of the project is essentially unique, novel and transient, and therefore entails some uncertainty and risk. The Modeling Perspective can help in its definition and planning of the work and of the inherent risk (see Box 1.5).

Box 1.5

I   Scope management is an inherent element of project management.
I   Risk management is an inherent element of project management.

Beneficial change

The work of the project is not undertaken for its own sake, but to deliver a change, a new asset, called the project's output (Figure 1.3). But that new asset is also not delivered for its own sake, it enables us to do new things, gives us new capabilities, called the project's outcome, which when operated gives us benefit which pays for the resources consumed in the delivery of the asset. Hopefully the new capabilities will also enable us to achieve higher-level goals which lead to higher-level performance improvement. The Success Perspective help us identify the desired outcomes and goals (success criteria), and success factors that help us achieve them.

In order to deliver the desired outcomes and benefit, the new asset must perform in required ways. We need to define those requirements, make sure the asset is able to perform to deliver them, and that the benefit is actually achieved after the project. The benefits map (Figure 1.4) is a tool we will return to throughout the book which helps in that process. (See also Box 1.6).

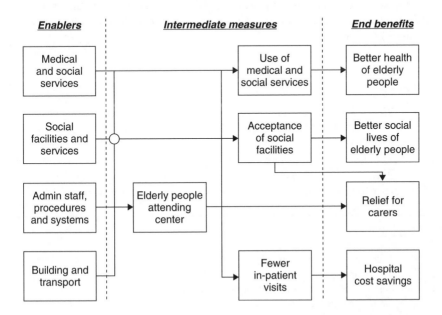

Figure 1.4 The benefits map

> **Box 1.6**
>
> I   Change management and project management are inherently related.
> I   Requirements management is an inherent element of project management.
> I   Quality management or performance management is an inherent element of project management.
> I   Benefits management is an inherent element of project management.

Now, for the first time, we see the other component of the theory. The efficacy of some of the tools can only be demonstrated by empirical evidence. In the field of project management, (and indeed in management in general), this evidence is often lacking. We label these M (for meme) and we see the first of them here, in Box 1.7.

> **Box 1.7**
>
> M   The benefits map (Figure 1.4) has been found to be a useful tool to help in project management.

Projects are fractal. Each component of a project is a temporary organization to which resources are assigned to deliver beneficial change, the delivery of a component of the output which will enable us to achieve the overall output. Thus we can decompose the project into components, and those components into their subcomponents. Indeed, we can do that for all three elements in the bottom line of Figure 1.3 (see Box 1.8).

> **Box 1.8**
>
> I   Product breakdown structure, work breakdown structure, organization breakdown structure and cost breakdown structure are three inherent tools of project management.

We can also now begin to identify several essential roles (see also Box 1.9):

> **Box 1.9**
>
> I   There are different stakeholders involved in the project, each with different objectives.
> I   Inherent roles associated with project management are the owner, the contractor, the operators and the consumers.

- *the contractor:* does the work of the project;
- *the owner:* owns the asset and receives the benefit from its operation;
- *the operators:* operate the asset on behalf of the owner;
- *the consumers:* consume the product produced by the asset and provide the revenue stream which gives the owner the benefit.

Premise 2: The value of the project

The second premise defines the value of the project:

The project provides value if the benefit is worth more than the cost of the resources consumed.

We have carefully phrased this so that the benefit may be non-financial.

Value

As Figure 1.3 illustrates, we expect the operation of the new asset (the project's output) and the new capabilities it gives us (the project's outcomes) will create benefit, and we consider that this too provides us with value if the benefit is worth more than the cost of providing the resources. Both the benefits and the costs may be non-financial. For instance, with the redevelopment of the West Coast Mainline in Britain (Hartog *et al.*, 2008), if only financial costs and benefits were considered, the cost-to-benefit ratio was 85 percent, and the project did not make a profit. But if non-financial benefits, such as economic regeneration, were considered, the cost to benefit ratio was 200 percent. Non-financial costs can include environmental impact; there are ways of evaluating these (Chen *et al.*, 2007). The Success Perspective is relevant to this discussion. The Optimization and Modeling Perspectives will help us optimize the value.

We see again that Cost or Resource Management, Requirements Management, and Benefits Management are essential elements of project management and Benefits Mapping is a useful tool.

The time value of money

The time at which we receive the benefit affects its value or worth to us. Usually the later we receive it the less it is worth. There are several reasons for this:

1   The first is from a discounted cash flow perspective – a dollar today is worth more to us than a dollar in a year's time. This reflects the interest we have to pay to borrow the money to invest in the project, the cost of capital, or the fact that if we receive the money earlier we can invest it elsewhere and receive interest on it.

2   There may be a limited time window for our product. Most of the sales for Christmas take place in the eight weeks before Christmas, so if you are two weeks late bringing the product to market you lose 25 percent of your potential sales.

3   Being first to market can help win market share. If you are late launching your product you can lose market share and so again lose potential sales.
4   In the field of events management, the event has to be launched on a particular day. If you are organizing a sports event, the Olympic Games for instance, if you are late you will earn nothing. But if you are early, the facilities will sit idle for a period of time, which again will cost you money because of the time value of money. The same holds for an artistic event, but then the asset may actually lose value if it sits idle.

Thus it is important to finish the project at or near the desired time. With an event the exact date usually has to be met. With the Olympic Games in China in 2008, because eight is a lucky number in China, the games had to start at 8.08pm on the eighth day of the eighth month, 2008. But at other Olympic Games the TV advertising has been sold, so after six years of preparation, the opening ceremony has to start to the nearest minute to suit the TV schedules. But usually time is another parameter to be balanced against the performance of the new asset and so the benefit it gives, and the cost of delivering it. Thus time is an important parameter, but one to be optimized along with others. Unfortunately, to listen to some people talk you would think the project will fail absolutely if it is one nanosecond late. The Optimization and Modeling Perspectives help model the balance between the performance of the new asset, the cost of delivering it and the time at which it is delivered to achieve the best value from the new asset (see Boxes 1.10 and 1.11).

Box 1.10

I   Time management is an essential element of project management.

Box 1.11

M   The field of Operations Research suggests that critical path networks will be a useful tool for optimizing the timescale on a project.

M   Bar charts (Gantt charts) have been shown to be a useful tool for communicating the timescale on a project to the stakeholders and for controlling it.

M   Milestone tracker charts have been shown to be a useful tool for controlling time.

M   Resource histograms have been shown to be a useful tool for optimizing the balance between resource usage and time on a project.

M   Five hundred years of costs and management accounting theory have shown that earned value management, EVM, is a useful tool for controlling the cost and the time at which the new asset is delivered, and controlling the balance between them.

We find it interesting that time management, about which many people behave as if it is the only element of project management, is the seventeenth element we have identified, and the last of the nine body of knowledge areas in the PMI® PMBoK® (2008). Now, we could have taken the first two premises in the reverse order. Premise 1 could have been that the purpose of a project is to create value by spending money to build a new asset which will deliver benefit that is worth more to us than the money spent, and then Premise 2 would be that we create a temporary organization to marshal the resources to do the work to create the asset. Then time management would have been about the fourth body of knowledge area that we met. The empirical elements also show us that we can draw on the theory from related management and business disciplines (Kwak and Anbari, 2008) to inform our understanding of project management. In the case of earned value management there is 500 years of cost and management theory to support its use. The use of critical path analysis dates from the 1940s and so the case is not so compelling. Work is required to demonstrate their efficacy and that of bar (Gantt) charts.

Premise 3: Governance of the project

The work of the resources on the project needs governing, and so Premise 3 defines what we mean by governance, and leads to a definition of project management. For a definition of governance we turn to the OECD definition (Clarke, 2004). This is intended for application to permanent organizations and other legal entities, but it can be applied to the temporary organization that is the project. There are two parts to the OECD definition: the first part defines what governance does, and is Premise 3, and the other defines the relationship between the parties to governance, the stakeholders, and is Premise 4. Premise 3 is:

Governance provides the structure through which the objectives of an organization are set, and the means of attaining those objectives and the means of monitoring performance are determined.

Objectives

Figure 1.5 illustrates a cascade of objectives, from the goal of performance improvement, down to the new capabilities desired, the project's outcomes, and the new asset that will give us those capabilities, the project's outputs. Figure 1.6 shows there are four essential governance roles associated with the definition:

The sponsor: who defines the objectives. The sponsor identifies the need for performance improvement, and that there is a change that can be made to achieve that performance improvement. The sponsor begins to draw the benefits map, and identify the potential costs and benefits of the project and therefore the value. The sponsor will also act as ambassador for the project, convincing the parent organization of the value of the benefit and thereby obtain the finance to pay the costs.

The steward: who defines the means of attaining the objectives. The sponsor is not a technical expert and so the steward identifies the work that needs to be done to deliver the asset and the resources required to do that work. The steward and the sponsor together complete the drawing of the benefits map.

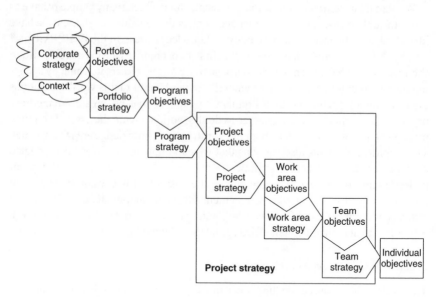

Figure 1.5 Cascade of objectives from corporate objectives to project tasks

The project manager: who monitors performance during the project. The project manager monitors the work of the resources on the project, and progress towards the delivery of the asset, the performance of the asset, and the time and cost at which the asset will be delivered to optimize value.

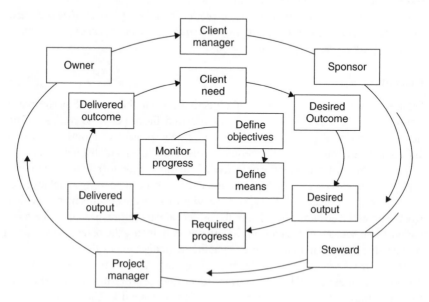

Figure 1.6 Four essential governance roles

The owner: who monitors the performance of the new asset and the attainment of the benefit. The owner owns and operates the asset, and receives the benefit from its operation, and so will source the finance to pay the cost of the project.

Many of the perspectives enlighten our understanding of these relationships, particularly the Governance, Marketing, Success, Optimization and Modeling Perspectives. Also many of the essential elements of project management already identified are identified again, particularly:

- cost management;
- scope management;
- requirements management;
- performance management;
- benefits management;
- product breakdown structure;
- stakeholder management;
- time management.

But we also identify three new inherent elements (see Box 1.12):

Box 1.12

I   Inherent roles associated with project management are the sponsor, steward, project manager and owner.
I   Project appraisal is an inherent element of project management.
I   Project finance is an inherent element of project management.

Life-cycle

Premise 3 also implies the existence of the project life-cycle and management cycle. Premise 3 itself is a very simple three-stage life-cycle:

- define the objectives;
- define the means;
- do the work and monitor progress.

Premise 3 when combined with Premises 1 and 2 leads to the five stage life-cycle we are more familiar with (Turner, 2009):

- *concept:* the possibility of performance improvement is identified;
- *feasibility:* the feasibility of the concept and its potential value are proven;
- *design:* the means is defined – the asset is designed and the work required for its delivery identified;
- *execution:* the work to deliver the asset is done and progress monitored;
- *commissioning:* the work is finished, the asset commissioned, the new capabilities and benefit attained.

Premise 3 and Premise 1 together also identify the management cycle (PMI PMBoK, 2008; Turner, 2009):

- *plan*: the work to deliver the project's objectives is planned;
- *organize*: the resources required to do the work are identified;
- *implement*: work is assigned to the resources;
- *control*: the work is monitored and controlled to achieve the desired performance.

In addition to the perspectives identified above, the Process and Decision Perspectives now enlighten our understanding of governance. The Behavior Perspective is also relevant for the design of the project organization and relationship with the human resources.

In addition to the essential elements of project management already identified from Premise 3, several more of the previous elements are identified, particularly:

- project organization or integration management;
- human resource management;
- materials management.

But further essential elements are identified (see Box 1.13):

Box 1.13

I   Life-cycle is an inherent element of project management.

I   The project life-cycle, from identification of the potential for change to achieve performance improvement to the delivery of the performance improvement, is an inherent element of project management.

I   The management process – through which the work of the project is planned, the resources identified, work assigned to the resources and progress monitored and controlled – is an inherent element of project management.

I   Project management is the means by which the work of the project to achieve the project's objectives is defined, monitored and controlled to ensure the project's objectives are attained and that it performs as desired.

What we mean by project management itself is almost an afterthought.

Premise 4: Stakeholders

The second part of the OECD definition of governance defines the relationship between the organization and its stakeholders:

Project governance defines the relationship between the project manager, sponsor, owner and other stakeholders.

The Behavior and Marketing Perspectives enlighten our understanding of this premise, and it re-identifies stakeholder management as an essential element of project management.

Premise 5: Multi-projects

No projects take place in total isolation, and we can identify several forms of multi-project management. There are at least four sub-premises here:

The project-based organization is one in which the majority of products made or services delivered for customers are against a bespoke design

– therefore it must adopt projects to perform its operation processes (Turner and Keegan, 2001).

The project-oriented organization is one which

- *opts as a strategic choice to use projects to perform its operational processes;*
- *adapts its culture, operational and management processes to support that choice;*
- *and views itself as project-oriented* (Gareis, 2005).

A portfolio is a set of projects which use common resources (Turner, 2009).

A program is a set of projects contributing to a beneficial change which cannot be delivered by a single project on its own (Turner, 2009).

The Governance Perspective enlightens our understanding of Premise 5 (see Box 1.14).

Box 1.14

I   Program management is an inherent element of the management of projects.

I   Portfolio management is an inherent element of the management of projects.

I   The governance of the project-based or project-oriented organization is an inherent element of the management of projects.

Thus we have identified 24 inherent elements for the theory of project management, and six tools which we believe to be useful, but the efficacy of those tools can only be proven by empirical research. By and large that empirical research has yet to be done.

1.5 Two typologies of projects

We end this chapter by describing two typologies of project management to which we refer throughout the book.

Levels of difference

Another mantra of project management is that projects are unique. In fact, Rodney Turner (as the main author of the English edition of Andersen *et al.*, 1987) may be as responsible for this as anybody else. While it is correct that projects are unique, no two projects are identical, that is in fact the case for all organizations, whether temporary or permanent. No two organizations are the same. Contingency theory is just as important for the management of routine organizations as the Contingency Perspective is for the management of projects. However, it is useful to recognize that some projects are more different than others. The management of projects involves much more uncertainty than the management of a routine organization. Even though the routine organization may be different from all others, within the routine organization you try to do the same thing day after day. If you can do the same thing day after day this will reduce or even eliminate uncertainty. It is the same with projects. The more you can find elements of your projects that are similar to elements of other projects you have done in the past, the more you can reduce uncertainty. That leads to the first typology of projects, which recognizes levels of differences between projects. It suggests four project types ranging from the familiar to the completely unknown:

Runners: These are very familiar projects, done repeatedly. They almost count as batch processing. Routine processes can be used.

Repeaters: The organization has done projects quite similar to these in the past. The majority of elements of the project are very similar to things done in the past, with a small number that are new and unfamiliar. There is knowledge in the organization about how they should be managed, which the project team can draw on during the project start-up process.

Strangers: The organization has never done a project like this before, but there are many familiar elements. We would classify the construction of the Channel Tunnel between England and France as this type of project: it wasn't the first undersea tunnel ever built; it wasn't the first time a high-speed railway line had been put in a tunnel; but it was the first time that such a tunnel had been built between England and France. There were many familiar elements to draw on but the overall project was completely novel.

Aliens: The organization has never done anything like this before. These projects are high risk. You may try to identify familiar projects, and if you cannot, seriously consider not doing the project. However, many projects like this are mandatory, brought on by a change in legislation, and so the organization has no choice but to do them.

Levels of uncertainty in product and process

The second typology is an idea developed by Rodney Turner and Bob Cochrane (1993): that you can judge projects by the level of uncertainty in the project objectives (the goals), that is the beneficial change in Premise 1, or in the methods of achieving the objectives, that is the work and the resources to be used in Premise 1. Uncertainty in the goals tends to lie within the remit of the owner and sponsor and uncertainty in the methods within the remit of the steward, the project manager and the contractor. This leads to four types of project (shown in Figure 1.7). Rodney Turner and Bob Cochrane associated these four types with the four traditional elements of earth, water, fire and air.

Type 1 Projects: are those for which both the goals, and methods of achieving those goals, are well defined. These are typified by engineering projects. Because

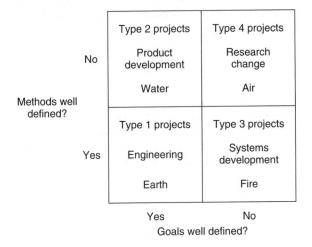

Figure 1.7 The goals and methods matrix

the goals and methods are both well defined, it is possible to move quickly into planning the work to be done, and so you will find in engineering projects an emphasis on activity-based planning. These are earth projects built on solid foundations, solid earth.

Type 2 Projects: are those for which the goals are well defined, but the method of achieving them is poorly defined. These are typified by product development projects, where we know the functionality of the product, but not how it will be achieved. Indeed, the point of the project is to determine how to achieve the goals. Now it is not possible to plan activities, because the project will determine them. Hence we use milestone planning, where the milestones represent components of the product to be delivered. These are water projects. Water flows downhill but may cut the channel as it goes.

Type 3 Projects: are those for which the goals are poorly defined, but the methods well defined. These are typified by information systems projects. When Rodney Turner started to work as a consultant in project management, it amused him when people from the information systems industry talked about project management, as all they talked about was life-cycles and phases. The goals and methods matrix explains why. On these projects, to get the users to say what they want is difficult, to get them to hold their ideas constant for any length of time is impossible. All people have to hold on to is the definition of the life-cycle. Hence on information systems projects you use milestone planning, where the milestones represent the completion of life-cycle stages. These are fire projects; be careful you don't get burnt.

Type 4 Projects: are those for which both the goals and methods of achieving them are poorly defined. These are typified by research or organizational change projects. The planning of these may use soft systems methodologies (see Chapter 3), and the plan itself will again be milestone-based, but the milestones will represent gateways, go/no-go decision points, through which the research project must pass or be aborted. These are air projects; they can't be held.

References

Anbari, F.T., 1985, "A systems approach to project evaluation," *Project Management Journal*, **16**(3), 21–26.

Andersen, E.S., Grude, K.V., Haug, T. and Turner, J.R., 1987, *Goal Directed Project Management*, Kogan Page/Coopers & Lybrand, London.

Blackmore, S., 1999, *The Meme Machine*, Oxford University Press, Oxford.

Bredillet, C.N., 2004, *Theories and Research in Project Management: Critical review and return to the future*, Thèse de Doctorat, Lille Graduate School of Management (ESC Lille), France.

Chen, Z., Li, H., and Turner, J.R., 2007, "Managing the environment," in Turner, J.R. (ed.), *The Gower Handbook of Project Management*, 4th edition, Gower, Aldershot.

Clarke, T. (ed.), 2004, *Theories of Corporate Governance: The philosophical foundations of corporate governance*, Routledge, London.

Cleland, D.I. and King, W. R., 1983, *Systems Analysis and Project Management*, 3rd edition, McGraw-Hill, New York.

Crawford, L.H., Hobbs, J.B. and Turner, J.R., 2005, *Project Categorization Systems: Aligning capability with strategy for better results*, Project Management Institute, Newtown Square, PA.

Dawkins, R., 1976, *The Selfish Gene*, Oxford University Press, Oxford.

Gareis, R., 2005, *Happy Projects!*, Manz, Vienna.

Hartog, M., Baker, S., Staal-Ong, P.L. and Westerveld E., 2008, *Managing Large Infrastructure Projects: Research on best practice and lessons learnt in large infrastructure projects in Europe*, AT Osborne, Utrecht.

Hillier, F.S and Lieberman, G.J., 2002, *Introduction to Operations Research*, McGraw-Hill, New York.

Hodgson, D. and Cicmil, S., 2006, "Are projects real? The PMBoK and the legitimation of project management knowledge," in Hodgson, D. and Cicmil, S. (eds), *Making Projects Critical*, Palgrave Macmillan, Basingstoke, 29–50.

Johnson, J., 2006, *My Life Is Failure: 100 things you should know to be a successful project leader,* Standish Group International, Boston.

Kolb, D.A., 1984, *Experiential Learning: Experience as the Source of Learning and Development*, Prentice-Hall, Englewood Cliffs, NJ.

Kwak, Y.H. and Anbari, F.T., 2008, *Impact on Project Management of Allied Disciplines*, Project Management Institute, Newtown Square, PA.

Morris, P.W.G. and Hough, G., 1987, *The Anatomy of Major Projects: A study of the reality of project management*, Wiley, Chichester.

Müller, R. and Turner, J.R., 2007, "Project success criteria and project success by type of project," *European Management Journal*, **25**(4), 298–309.

Pinto, J.K. and Slevin, D.P., 1988, "Critical success factors in effective project implementation," in Cleland, D.I. and King, W.R. (eds), *Project Management Handbook*, 2nd edition, Van Nostrand Reinhold, New York.

Project Management Institute, 2008, *A Guide to the Project Management Body of Knowledge (PMBOK® Guide)*, 4th edition. Project Management Institute, Newtown Square, PA.

Shenhar, A.J. and Dvir, D., 2007, *Reinventing Project Management: The diamond approach to successful growth and innovation*, Harvard Business School Press, Boston.

Söderlund, J., 2002, "On the development of project management research: Schools of thought and critique," *Project Management: International Project Management Journal*, **8**(1), 20–31.

Turner, J.R., 1999, "Project Management: A profession based on knowledge or faith?," Editorial, *International Journal of Project Management*, **17**(6), 329–330.

Turner, J.R., 2009, *The Handbook of Project-Based Management*, 3rd edition, McGraw-Hill, New York.

Turner, J.R. and Cochrane, R.A., 1993, "The goals and methods matrix: Coping with projects with ill-defined goals and/or methods of achieving them," *International Journal of Project Management*, **11**(2), 93–102.

Turner, J.R. and Keegan, A.E., 2001, "Mechanisms of governance in the project-based organization: The role of the broker and steward," *European Management Journal*, **19**(3), 254–267.

Turner, J.R. and Müller, R., 2006, *Choosing Appropriate Project Managers: Matching their leadership style to the type of project*, Project Management Institute, Newtown Square, PA.

Turner, J.R., Ledwith, A. and Kelly, J.F., 2009, "Project management in small to medium-sized enterprises: A comparison between firms by size and industry," *International Journal of Managing Projects in Business*, **2**(2), 282–296.

Wateridge, J.H., 1995, "IT projects: A basis for success", *International Journal of Project Management*, **13**(3), 169–172.

Williams, T., 2002, *Modelling Complex Projects*, Wiley, Chichester.

Williamson, O.E., 1996, *Mechanisms of Governance*, Oxford University Press, New York.

Winch, G.M., 2004, "Rethinking project management: Project organizations as information processing systems?," in *Innovations: Project Management Research 2004*, Project Management Institute, Newtown Square, PA.

World Bank, 2007, *Little Data Book*, International Bank for Reconstruction and Development/The World Bank, Development Data Group, Washington, DC.

Part I
The nine perspectives

2 Optimization

The project as a machine

2.1 The genesis of modern project management

Modern project management had its genesis as an offshoot of the field of Operations Research in the 1940s and 1950s. There was an explosion of the development of optimization theory and associated algorithms during and immediately after World War II with the development of techniques such as linear programming, dynamic programming, and quadratic programming (Gass and Assad, 2005). Among these were tools for network analysis: the critical path method (CPM) and the program evaluation and review technique (PERT). CPM and PERT were tools in the right place at the right time. There was a substantial growth in the number of large projects being undertaken at that time, driven by the recovery after World War II, including the Marshal Plan, and by the arms and space races. People were looking for tools to help with these large projects, and CPM/PERT were readily available.

The fields of modern operations management and project management both grew out of Operations Research at that time. People were aiming to improve performance of production, logistics and projects, and many of the optimization tools of Operations Research were found to be very useful for that. Both of the modern fields of operations management and project management have continued to develop their mathematical and systems side to improve decision making in operations, supply chain and project management. But as we shall see in the remainder of this book, whereas the field of operations management has not advanced much beyond the application of optimization algorithms to production and logistics processes (Slack *et al.*, 2006), project management has widened considerably, often adopting ideas from other fields of management (Kwak and Anbari, 2008).

The initial idea of project network methods was to optimize the duration of the project and the associated cost using mathematical modeling techniques based on CPM/PERT. Bar charts (Gantt charts), developed in the early 1900s by Henry Gantt for production scheduling, are easily produced as a by-product of CPM/PERT, and so were adopted during the 1950s and the 1960s (Archibald and Villoria, 1967). Subsequent developments included resource allocation and leveling, project crashing, Graphical Evaluation and Review Technique

(GERT), Critical Chain, Theory of Constraints, and the application of Monte Carlo Simulation.

In the 1950s, the US military also developed the idea of breakdown structures, including product breakdown structure (PBS), work breakdown structure (WBS), organization breakdown structure (OBS), and cost breakdown structure (CBS). In fact what they initially called WBS was more of a PBS. They combined these into the Cost Control Cube, which was at the heart of their cost and schedule control systems criteria (C/SCSC). This subsequently grew into the earned value method (EVM) (Fleming and Koppelman, 2005). This is now being enhanced to include, amongst other things, the concept of earned schedule.

In the 1960s, Martin Barnes developed the concept of the triple constraint – that the aim of project management should be to optimize the balance between the duration of the project, its cost, and the quality standards achieved. This third is sometimes expressed as the performance of the project's product. Techniques for optimizing quality have also been added to project management, and they are now being extended to include Six Sigma. This concept of the triple constraint, sometimes called the iron triangle or (in Europe) the golden triangle, is at the core of project management as taught and practiced by many professionals.

This school is very Taylorian in its approach. The project is treated as a machine that, once defined, will be very predictable in its performance. The project is treated as a system that can be mathematically defined and analyzed, and which will behave in very predictable ways. An important early work was the textbook by David Cleland and Bill King (1983, first published in 1968), in which they set out a theory of project management based on this view that the project is a system to be optimized. This textbook had a substantial influence on the early development of modern project management and the Optimization School. The textbook by Harold Kerzner (2009, first published in 1979) can be considered the main textbook for this school. Its title reflects what the school is about: the use of a systems approach to planning and controlling the project, to model and optimize its outcome.

In this chapter we describe optimization of the project. We describe CPM/PERT and some of their variants, EVM and its recent extensions, Lean Six Sigma method, and the optimization of project performance, as represented by the triple constraint, including quality (and other relevant parameters).

2.2　Tools for optimizing project outcomes

We start with tools adopted to plan the project's timeline. These tools are primarily designed to plan and optimize the project's outcomes, especially time, but as we shall see also apply to cost, resource usage and project value. They can also be used to track progress, but that is almost an afterthought.

Optimizing time, cost and value

The triple constraint, one of the memes of project management, suggests that we should optimize the balance between time, cost and quality, but there are

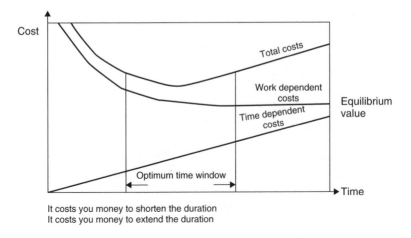

Figure 2.1 Minimizing project cost

alternative suggestions about what we mean by "quality." We may mean the finish of the project's output as specified in the specification, but more usefully we should optimize the balance between time, cost and the performance of the project's output – the value of the project. Rodney Turner (2009) shows that there is a project duration that minimizes the cost of the project. There are two types of cost on a project, those which are work dependent, and those which are time dependent (Figure 2.1). With the time-dependent costs the longer the project takes the larger they are. With the work-dependent costs, at longer timescales they are constant; one person takes 100 days, two people take 50 days, five people take 20 days, but it is always 100 person-days of work. But if you try to do the work too quickly, inefficiencies occur: ten people may take 12 days and 20 people take seven days. The work-dependent costs increase at shorter timescales. Thus, adding the time- and work-dependent costs, there is a timescale which minimizes the cost of the project. However, that is not necessarily the time that maximizes the value of the project. The returns from the project can be smaller the later the project is completed (Figure 2.2). This can be because of the time value of money, or a limited market window for the product produced by the project's output (Section 1.4). Alternatively we may need to take longer over the project to achieve the result we want. There is an apocryphal story about research done in Australia into projects finished five years previously, where every project that had finished on cost and time was judged to be a failure. In their hurry to finish on cost and time the project managers had sacrificed functionality. Thus there may be yet another time that maximizes the value of the project. The aim of project optimization should be to adjust the duration of the project, its cost, and forecast revenues to optimize the value of the project. We start by considering the tools that came directly from the field of Operations Research.

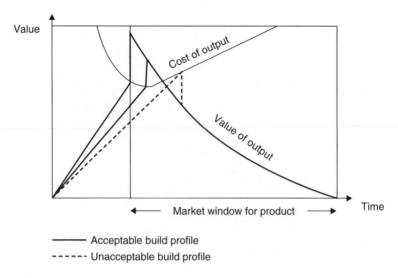

Figure 2.2 Maximizing project value

Critical path method

The critical path method (CPM) was originally developed in 1957 by Joseph Kelley and M.R. Walker working at DuPont, by adapting networking theory from Operations Research (Kelley and Walker, 1959). They were attempting to find the optimum (minimal) cost duration of a project whose activity durations were treated as fixed. The technique is also known as critical path analysis (CPA), Arrow Diagramming Method (ADM), Activity on Arrow (AoA) network or the IJ method (because each activity in the network is known by the number of its start and finish node). A year later John Fondahl, working at Stanford University, developed the alternative version, the Activity on Node (AoN) network (Fondahl, 1961), also called the Precedence Diagramming Method (PDM). John Fondahl showed that his technique could model network logic more effectively. The ability to incorporate leads and lags was particularly powerful. However, his work remained ignored until about 1973. But the PDM is now much more popular than the ADM. B. Roy, working for the Metra Group in France, had developed a similar technique a few years before called the Metra Potential Method (MPM) (Roy, 1959), but this was never adopted. Network techniques are used throughout the world in the management of projects (Gass and Assad, 2005). Figure 2.3 is an activity on arrow network and Figure 2.4 is the corresponding precedence diagram. (The data for this network is contained in Table 2.1.)

In the network techniques, a forward pass analysis is performed through the project network to calculate the earliest date by which each activity can start and finish, known as the early start and early finish dates. The early finish for the last activity

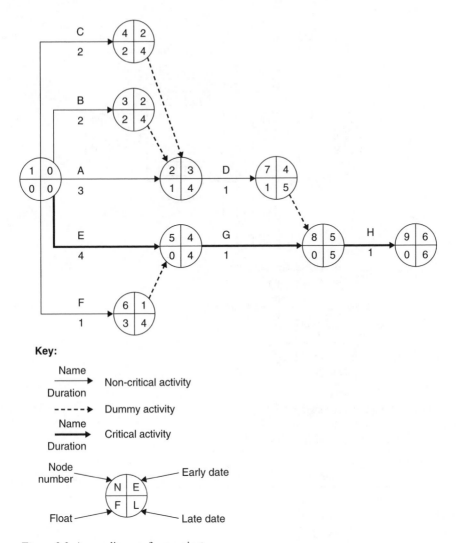

Figure 2.3 Arrow diagram for a project

is assumed to be the duration of the project. A backward pass analysis is also per-formed to calculate the latest date by which each activity can finish and start and not delay the project, known as the late finish and start dates. For most activities the late start and finish are later than the early start and finish. The difference is known as the float, or slack, the amount by which each activity can be delayed and not delay the project (as calculated by the forward pass). Because it is assumed that each activity has a fixed duration, and the activities occur in a determined sequence, there is a unique, deterministic result for this process.

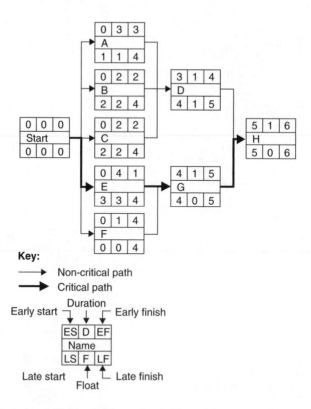

Figure 2.4 Precedence diagram for the project in Figure 2.3

Table 2.1 Data for the network in Figure 2.1

Activity name	Preceding activities	Duration (months)	Analyst (days)	Programmer (days)
A		3	24	0
B		2	24	0
C		2	16	16
D	A, B, C	1	0	12
E		1	0	4
F		4	16	0
G	E, F	1	12	8
H	D, G	1	4	8

Necessarily, in a project scheduled to finish at the earliest possible time, there is at least one path through the whole project with zero float, and this is known as the critical path (hence the name of the technique), and is the path that determines the project duration. However, a flaw in the technique is it tends to cause people to focus their attention on that one path, whereas there may be other paths of very small float, which because of estimating errors may in fact be the ones that actually determine the project duration. The nearly critical paths may involve higher risk as we shall see later.

When combined with resource loadings, as we describe shortly, CPM can be used to schedule the resource usage on the project, and optimize the balance between time and cost. Indeed it was to that aim that Joseph Kelley and M.R. Walker first developed the technique.

CPM can be very useful for scheduling the work and resources on very large projects. On large projects, it is difficult to keep track of everything that is going on without computer support, and CPM does that very effectively. However, it assumes that activity durations are fixed, and that the logic is linear and deterministic. Activity D follows C, follows B, follows A. When A is finished, B starts and so on. CPM does not allow feedback, capacitance or inductance. Nor does it allow probabilistic branching: when B finishes, A may be repeated, or B, or C may start, or D with different probabilities. Thus it is very effective at helping in the planning and scheduling of large projects, and in tracking projects, as long as the project is expected to be linear and deterministic, and as long as it performs as expected. However, if the project does not perform as expected, and in doing so there are feedback loops, then the technique breaks down, and in fact, as Terry Williams (2002) has shown (see Chapter 3), its use can cause the project to diverge even further from plan. Projects tend to involve ambiguity and uncertainty and in this way differ from routine operations which are much more linear and deterministic, and so the optimization algorithms work much better there (Slack *et al.*, 2006).

We do not fully describe how to do network analysis. Nobody does it by hand on a real project. If the project is large enough to require critical path analysis, it is large enough to require computer-aided support, and so the analysis is done by the computer. Indeed the emphasis of the approach has now changed. Whereas initially it was used to calculate the end date of the project, now people tend to impose the end date and use the computer system to show where logic is violated, and work on massaging the network to eliminate the violations. This is known as *what-if analysis*. So the systems tend to be used to find out how the project can be achieved within the desired timescale, rather than work out what the timescale is.

Program evaluation and review technique

The program evaluation and review technique (PERT) was developed independently a year after CPM by the US Navy Special Projects Office and its consulting firm of Booz, Allen, and Hamilton. PERT was successfully applied to the Polaris Project, a huge, complicated, weapon system development program developing the first nuclear submarine (Archibald and Villoria, 1967). The essential difference between PERT and CPM is that PERT uses three estimates for the duration of each activity, the most likely, the most pessimistic, and the most optimistic. This is known as *three point estimating*. Using a weighted average of these three numbers it is possible to estimate an expected duration for each activity, and a variance on the duration. From these it is possible to work out several things for the project (Anbari, 2002; Kerzner, 2009; Project Management Institute, 2008; Turner, 2009):

- The best and worst case scenarios, though in fact it is usually highly unlikely that either of these extremes will ever be attained.
- The expected duration for each path through the project. The one with the longest duration will be the critical path, but other paths may have very similar expected durations and any could turn out to be the one that actually determines the duration of the project. The expected durations for each activity will usually be greater than the most likely durations used by CPM. Thus the expected duration of the project calculated by PERT will be greater than the base estimate calculated by CPM.
- The variance of the duration of each path through the project, and thus realistic estimates of the shortest likely and longest likely duration of each path. Thus you can work out a range of durations for each path, and hence of the overall project, along with their associated probabilities. In the process you may find that whereas one path has a shorter expected duration than the critical path, it has a much larger variance, and is therefore more likely to be of longer duration. Thus you can highlight that as a path requiring as much if not more attention than the critical path to reduce the variance in its duration.

With the power of computers back in the 1950s when PERT was developed, it could take several days to perform Monte Carlo simulation on a large project, as the computer had to perform the forward and back pass on the network several thousand times. Thus Monte Carlo simulation was theoretically possible, but extremely slow. PERT provided a much quicker way of conducting probabilistic analysis on a large project. However, with the power of modern computers, Monte Carlo simulation can be conducted in minutes rather than days, and gives much more accurate results. Thus PERT has been overtaken by Monte Carlo simulation and is no longer really necessary. In spite of that, it is still beloved by many people.

Graphical Evaluation and Review Technique

A variant of CPM called the Graphical Evaluation and Review Technique (GERT) was developed by Alan Pritsker working for NASA on the Apollo program (Pritsker, 1966). It is a stochastic network analysis technique that allows for looping, conditional branching, and probabilistic treatment of the relationships between project network activities. As an example, a drug trial or a software test may have varying results and may have to be repeated several times with changing probabilities for various branches, some of which may not have to be performed at all (Kerzner, 2009; Pritsker, 1966). GERT has never proved popular with most project managers because it requires substantial computing power.

Bar charts

CPM and PERT are not very good at visually representing the schedule, and so bar charts are used for that purpose (Figure 2.5). Bar charts are also known as Gantt

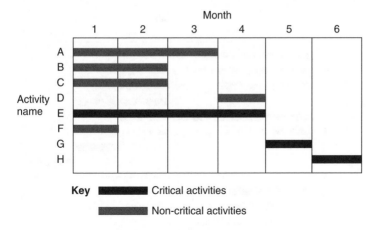

Figure 2.5 Bar (Gantt) chart for the project in Figure 2.3

charts, named after their original developer, or perhaps a piece of jargon adopted in a vain attempt to turn project management into rocket science. The bar chart shows the activities of the project as rows, with horizontal bars showing when the work will be done. Henry Gantt, its inventor, was a protégé of Frederick Taylor, the father of scientific management. He developed what he called the daily balance chart while working for the Frankford Arsenal in 1917. He developed the chart as a tool for planning daily production and the available resources. This tool was extremely effective for planning routine production. "Nothing could be simpler, yet at the time nothing of its kind could have been more revolutionary in the area of production control" (George, 1968). However, the tool as originally developed was of little use for project management because it did not show the logical dependencies between the work flows on the project. The logical dependencies are not so critical in routine production. It was not until it was combined with CPM that the bar chart became the useful project management tool it now is.

The initial inadequacies of the bar (Gantt) chart were overcome in a tool called the harmony graph, developed by Karol Adamiecki (1931). This is essentially the bar chart rotated through 90 degrees with time drawn down the page and the activities in columns, with a very clever means of showing the interrelationship between the activities. However, this work was overlooked in the field, and with the invention of CPM, the weaknesses in the bar chart as a tool for project management were overcome. Now the logical dependencies could be handled in the network, and the bar chart used to represent the results of the network analysis, showing when the work will be done.

Increasingly more sophisticated versions of the bar chart have been developed. It is common to use color to differentiate between critical and non-critical activities, as shown in Figure 2.5. (Figure 2.5 is the bar chart for the project in Figures 2.3 and 2.4 scheduled by early start.) It is also possible to show the amount of float an

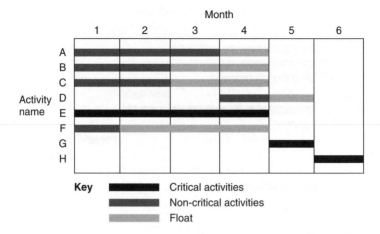

Figure 2.6 Bar (Gantt) chart with float

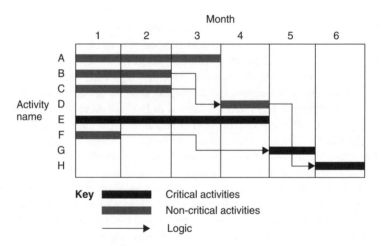

Figure 2.7 Bar (Gantt) chart with logic

activity has (Figure 2.6). (We have met critical and non-critical activities and float when we discussed the CPM.) When bar charts are combined with CPM, the logic can now be incorporated onto the bar chart (Figure 2.7) achieving what Karol Adamiecki tried to achieve with his harmony graphs. These versions of the bar chart are all planning tools. The tracked bar chart (Figure 2.8) is a control tool. Now two bars are shown against each activity. One is the plan, the other is actual and forecast dates. The chart shows the date of the report, and dates in the past are actual, while those in the future are forecast. Showing both the planned and actual dates helps maintain control because you can compare them both. Before the 1980s it was common just to show actual dates, but control was lost because when the project became delayed it was not known by how much.

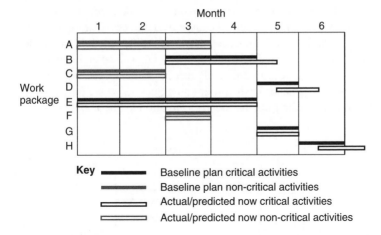

Figure 2.8 Tracked bar chart

Resource smoothing

CPM as first developed by Joseph Kelley and M.R. Walker (1959) had the aim of optimizing resource usage on projects. It is possible to add resource usage to all the activities in the network, and then ask the computer to work out the total resource usage by time. This can be presented in a form known as a resource histogram (Figures 2.9 to 2.12). Predicted resource usage can be compared to resource availability, and if there is a violation, the project can be rescheduled to eliminate the violation. The computer system can usually do this automatically but it is often a good idea to maintain some management control. Figure 2.9 is the project in

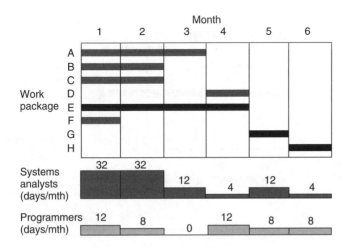

Figure 2.9 Resource histogram for the project in Figure 2.3 scheduled by early start

Figure 2.3 scheduled by early start. If there is only one analyst then there is a 50 percent overload in months 1 and 2 (one person can work about 20 days per month). Figure 2.10 is the same project scheduled by late start. The problem has been shifted to months 3 and 4. Figure 2.11 shows a feasible schedule where the analyst only has to work two or three days overtime a month. However, in Figure 2.11 there is a peak in the use of the programmer. Figure 2.12 shows a solution where we have smoothed out the demand for the programmer, assuming we only have access to half a programmer's time, but this creates a violation for the analyst again. With this

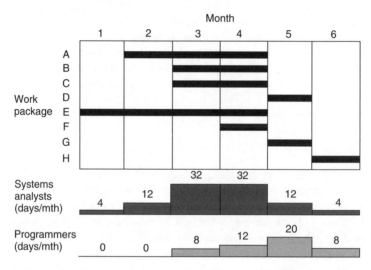

Figure 2.10 Resource histogram for the project in Figure 2.3 scheduled by late start

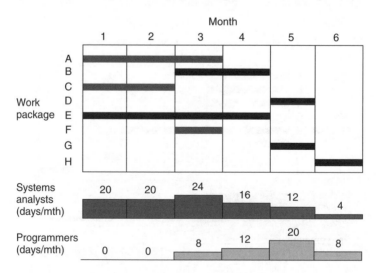

Figure 2.11 Resource histogram for the project in Figure 2.3 scheduled by analyst priority

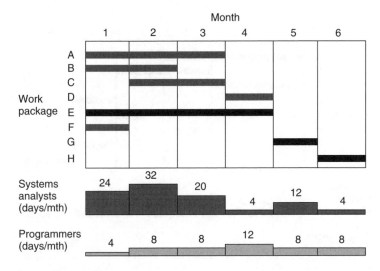

Figure 2.12 Resource histogram for the project in Figure 2.3 scheduled by programmer priority

simple project it is not possible to find a solution that satisfies the constraint for both analysts and programmer.

The reason why it is a good idea to maintain management control is that if left on their own computer systems can produce silly results. In order for the computer system to do the smoothing you have to give it a rule to choose one activity over another and one resource over another for priority when doing the smoothing. Once you have given the computer a rule it will apply it absolutely and without question. That is what can lead to silly results.

Critical Chain and Theory of Constraints

The Critical Chain and the Theory of Constraints were developed by Eli Goldratt (1997). The Theory of Constraints is applied to modify the project schedule, after CPM analysis is conducted, to account for limited resources (Goldratt, 1997; Leach, 2004; Project Management Institute, 2008). There are three essential additions or differences from CPM:

1   A second critical path is identified, resulting not from the logical dependencies of the activities, but from the rate at which a scarce resource can perform the activities it needs to do. This second critical path is known as the critical chain and does not necessarily follow the same path as CPM logic. Figure 2.13 shows the critical chain through Figure 2.11.
2   Rather than calculating the duration of the network using the most likely duration of each activity as in CPM or the expected duration as in PERT, the duration is calculated using the median duration, that is the duration with a 50

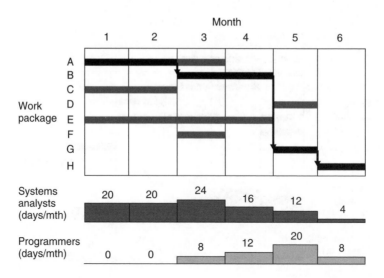

Figure 2.13 Critical chain through Figure 2.11

percent chance of being achieved. Typically the most likely duration has something like a 40 percent probability of being attained and the expected something like a 60 percent probability, so the median lies somewhere in between, and thus the duration of the project as calculated by the critical chain, before resource constraints are taken into account, will lie somewhere between that calculated by CPM and that calculated by PERT.

3   Rather than assigning float to each activity, float is assigned to each path through the network. Buffer activities are built into the network where two paths join, representing the difference between the shorter and longer duration paths. Thus each activity is planned to take the median duration, and float is managed through the buffers.

CPM, PERT and Critical Chain compared

We saw above that CPM, Critical Chain and PERT calculate different durations for the project, assuming that the duration of individual activities are the most likely, median or expected values. PERT also calculates minimum and maximum durations based on the variances of the durations of the individual activities and different paths through the project. Another flaw of CPM is it does encourage people to think that there is just a single possible duration of the project, with one critical path, whereas PERT shows us that there is a range of possible outcomes depending on the uncertainty of the outcome for individual activities. PERT provides guidance to the range of possible outcomes.

These different outcomes have different chances of being achieved. What those different likelihoods are depends on the range of uncertainty of the outcomes of the individual activities. However, PERT assumes that the distribution for the individual activities is the beta distribution. In that case the most likely outcome for the activities (as used by CPM) has a 40 percent chance of being achieved, the median outcome (as used by Critical Chain) by definition has a 50 percent chance of being achieved, and expected values (as used by PERT) have a 60 percent chance of being achieved. However, these probabilities do not translate into equivalent probabilities for the whole project. What you tend to find is that the overall duration of the project as calculated by CPM using the most likely values typically only has about a 5 percent chance of being achieved. On the other hand, the expected duration for the project as calculated by PERT typically has about a 60 percent chance of being achieved. The duration, as calculated by the Critical Chain using the median values, lies somewhere in between.

PERT was the best that could be achieved on large complex projects with the computing power of the 1950s. But in the modern world we would like a more accurate indication of what the range of possible outcomes for the project is, in terms of both the duration and cost, and an indication of the probability that both the duration and cost will be less than certain values. Monte Carlo simulation helps provide those better assessments.

Monte Carlo simulation

Monte Carlo simulation was first developed by physicists working on the Manhattan Project, particularly Stanislaw Ulam, Enrico Fermi, John van Neumann and Nicholas Metropolis (Gass and Assad, 2005). The name is a reference to the Monte Carlo casino where Ulam's uncle would borrow money to gamble. Rather than using a single-point estimate for the value of key variables, a probability distribution is adopted. For a project this will typically be for the time or cost or both of key activities. The project network is then run a large number of times, typically somewhere between 1,000 to 10,000 times. Each time it is run, a random number is drawn for every parameter with a variable value to choose a value for that

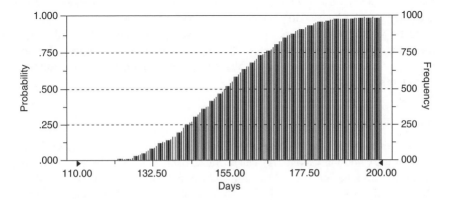

Figure 2.14 Cumulative probability distribution of the duration of a project

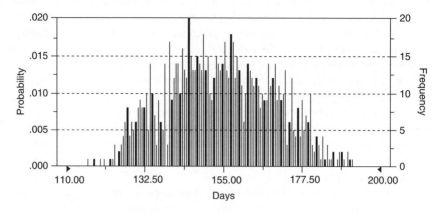

Figure 2.15 Point-wise probability distribution of the duration of a project

parameter for this run based on the probability distribution of that parameter. The total duration and cost of the project is calculated using those values. The system then counts how often the calculated duration and cost of the project falls within certain ranges and so can calculate the probability that the duration and cost of the project will fall within those ranges. The system can thereby calculate the point wise and cumulative probability distributions for the duration and cost of the project (or any other parameter of interest). Figures 2.14 and 2.15 show the cumulative and point wise probability distributions for the duration of a project calculated using Monte Carlo analysis. (See Anbari, 2002; Kerzner, 2009; Project Management Institute, 2008; Turner, 2009.)

2.3 Earned value management

The tool we have met up to now are primarily aimed at planning the project. In many people's minds they are associated with planning time, though as we have seen they can also be used to plan the rate of use of resources and cost, and to optimize the balance between time and cost. We now turn our attention to tools which are primarily used to track progress. The name, 'earned value', suggests they are used to track cost but in fact they can also be used to track time by expressing time in cost terms.

Background and development

A basic form of the earned value management method (EVM), sometimes referred to as earned value analysis (EVA), can be traced back to industrial engineers on the factory floor in the late 1800s (Fleming and Koppelman, 2006; Kim *et al.*, 2003). However, the basic concepts of comparing planned unit cost to actual unit cost, and planned units of production to actual units of production, derive from cost and management accounting, and so have been in use for hundreds of years. Around 1967, EVM was introduced by agencies of the US federal government as an integral part of the cost/schedule control systems criteria (C/SCSC) and was used in large acquisition programs. EVM has been widely and successfully used in projects associated with the US federal government. Use of EVM in private industry and support by popular project management software packages have been rapidly growing in recent years.

To encourage wider use of EVM in the private sector, the US federal government decided to discard C/SCSC by the end of 1996 and turned toward a more flexible earned value management system (EVMS) with simplified terminology. The American National Standards Institute (ANSI) and the Electronic Industries Alliance (EIA) published guidelines for EVMS in 1998 which were revised subsequently (2007). Starting in 2000, the Project Management Institute (2008) used the simplified terminology and provided the generally accepted formulas for EVM. Details of the method were provided in *Practice Standard for Earned Value Management* (Project Management Institute, 2005) and in other sources (Anbari, 2002, 2003; Humphreys, 2002; Kemps, 2007; Kerzner, 2009; Turner, 2009).

There has been a high degree of acceptance of EVM among current and past users of the method. They tend to agree that EVM can improve cost, schedule, and technical performance of their projects. Non-believers in EVM claim that the method is hard to use, that it applies primarily to very large projects, and that they do not need it (Fleming and Koppelman, 2006; Kim *et al.*, 2003). Turner (2009) does show how the technique can be simplified while retaining its essential features for smaller projects. Interest in EVM is growing globally, particularly in the public sector, with notable progress in Australia, Japan, Sweden and the UK.

Elements of earned value management

EVM integrates three critical elements of project management: scope management, cost management, and time management. It requires the periodic monitoring of actual expenditures and the amount of work done (expressed in cost terms). It compares the amount of work done to the plan to determine time performance. The original version of earned value does this in volume of work terms: is the amount of work done today more or less than we had planned to do today? A modern enhancement does it in time terms: by when had we planned to have done this amount of work and are we ahead or behind schedule? EVM also compares how much we have spent to what we planned to have spent to do the work we have done to determine cost performance. In order to make these comparisons EVM calculates cost and schedule variances, along with performance indices for project performance management. Based on these figures it forecasts date and cost of project completion and highlights the possible need for corrective action or re-planning. EVM uses the following project parameters to evaluate project performance (Figure 2.16).

Planned Value (PV): This is the scope plan for the project. It is the cumulative amount of work planned to have been done on the project up to a given day expressed in cost terms. It is the approved budget for completing the work planned

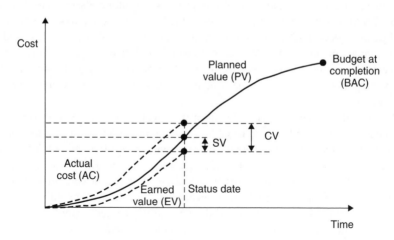

Figure 2.16 Elements of earned value management

so far, and so is the cost baseline for the project. It was previously called the base-lined cost of work planned (BCWP) or the budgeted cost of work scheduled (BCWS).

Budget at Completion (BAC): This is the total amount of money expected to be spent on the project, and so is the value that PV is planned to reach on the last day, the planned cost at completion. There are in fact a number of figures that can be used for the planned cost at completion, but the three key ones are the base cost, the target cost and the sanction cost. The base cost is the raw estimate of the project, without allowance for risk, and has a low chance of being achieved. The target cost is the base cost with a contingency allowance for risk, and it is common to use a fig-ure with a 60 percent chance of being achieved. The sanction cost is the amount of money that the parent organization has budgeted to spend on the project in their capital budget or annual expenditure plans, and so is the true "budget" for the proj-ect. It typically has an 80 percent chance of being achieved. The difference between the target cost and sanction value is client contingency or tolerance. Depending on whether the BAC is based on the base target or sanction cost, the PV (and EV) should include contingency and/or tolerance accordingly.

Actual Cost (AC): This is the cumulative actual cost spent on the project so far. The PV is the plan of work to be done, and so AC should include all accrued cost on the work done, and not just invoices paid. So AC is the actual spent and accrued cost and not just the actual spent cost. AC was previously called the actual cost of work complete (ACWC) or the actual cost of work performed (ACWP).

Earned Value (EV): This represents the amount of work done up to a point in time, expressed in cost terms. It is expressed as the amount that was planned to have been spent on the work that has been completed up to this point. EV was previously called the baselined cost of work complete (BCWC) or the budgeted cost of work performed (BCWP).

There are two ways of calculating EV. One is to sum the EV of all the elements of work performed so far. To calculate the EV for a given element of work, the planned cost is multiplied by an estimate of the percentage completion. It is easy to estimate the percentage completion for an element of work that is complete (it is 100 percent), but it is usually a subjective assessment if the work is still in progress. This is one weak point of EVM. The EV for the project is the sum of the EV for all the work elements. The other way of calculating EV is to subtract all the work yet to be done from BAC. To calculate the work remaining for an element, multiply the planned cost by the percentage remaining. It is easy to calculate the percentage remaining for work not yet started (it is 100 percent); for work in progress it is 100 percent minus the percentage completion, and suffers the same problem we have just mentioned. The first way of calculating EV is the more normal approach, and if the estimate remains unchanged the two approaches give the same answer. However, the second approach allows us to re-estimate the work remaining and so gives better control. It is called *forward looking control*, and we can adjust our future plans based on our experience so far.

We said that the BAC may be based on the base cost without contingency, the target cost with contingency, or the sanction cost with risk and tolerance. Depending on which is used the PV and EV will include contingency and tolerance accordingly. If the project manager monitors progress against the base cost, the project will probably become quickly overspent. Thus it is good practice for the project manager to monitor cost against the target cost, and so BAC, PV and EV should include contingency. However, rather than assigning contingency to each work element there will at the start of the project be a single contingency pot shown being spent throughout the project. Where a risk or issue does not occur, the PV and EV for an element of work will be calculated using the base cost. But as risks and issues occur, money will be transferred from the contingency pot to the PV and EV of the element of work where it occurred; that is, contingency will be consumed. It can also be a good idea for the project manager to produce a second EVM report for the client, and there the contingency pot will include both contingency and tolerance. The same transfers will be made from the contingency pot to the PV and EV of the work elements as risks and issues occur, but the project is more likely to be underspent at the end and the contingency pot is less likely to be fully consumed.

We said that BAC, PV, AC and EV are expressed in cost terms. That may be in terms of actual money, in any currency. Or it can be in terms of units of work performed or volume of work performed. For instance you may just want to monitor the amount of labor used, and so they may be expressed in hours or days of work done. Or you may want to monitor a particular type of work, so it may be expressed as meters of pipe erected, or lines of code written.

We have suggested above that the calculations are done for the project as a whole, but BAC, PV, AC and EV can be calculated for any element of work to determine progress on that element of work. However, we said in Section 1.4 that projects are fractal, and so each element of work is like a mini project in its own right, and we will continue to talk about applying the technique to a "project."

Project performance measurement

Cost performance on the project is determined by comparing EV to AC. AC represents what has actually been spent and accrued to do the work so far, and EV what was planned to be spent to do the work so far and the difference shows whether the project is overspent or underspent. Schedule performance is determined by comparing the EV to the PV. PV shows the amount of work that was planned to have been done (expressed in cost terms) and EV the amount that has been done. By comparing the two we can estimate whether more or less work has been performed than should have been done, and so whether the project is ahead or behind schedule. We do these comparisons by calculating variances.

Variances

The following formulas are used to calculate the variances:
The cost variance (CV) is a measure of cost performance:

$$CV = EV - AC$$

The schedule variance (SV) is a measure of schedule performance:

$$SV = EV - PV$$

Variance percentages

The following formulas are used to calculate the variance percentages:
Cost variance percent (CV%):

$$CV\% = CV/EV$$

Schedule variance percent (SV%):

$$SV\% = SV/PV$$

In the above formulas, 0 indicates that performance is on target. A positive value indicates good performance. A negative value indicates poor performance.

Performance indices

The following formulas are used to calculate performance indices:
Cost performance index (CPI) is a another measure of cost performance:

$$CPI = EV/AC$$

The schedule performance index (SPI) is another measure of schedule performance:

$$SPI = EV/PV$$

In the above formulas, 1.0 indicates that performance is on target. More than 1.0 indicates good performance, and less than 1.0 indicates poor performance. It is easy to show that:

$$CPI = 1/(1 - CV\%)$$

and

$$SPI = 1 + SV\%$$

Forecasting of project outcome

Project management is primarily concerned with decisions affecting the future. Therefore, forecasting is an extremely important aspect of project management. EVM is particularly useful in forecasting the cost and time of the project at completion, based on actual performance so far using the above calculations:

Forecasting of cost at completion

The forecast of the cost of the project at completion goes by several possible names:

- the forecast cost at completion (FCC);
- the estimate at completion (EAC);
- the cost estimate at completion (CEAC).

The forecast cost remaining also goes by a couple of names:

- the forecast cost remaining (FCR);
- the estimate to complete (ETC).

ETC and EAC are the terms suggested by PMI (2005, 2008). There are two ways of estimating ETC. The first assumes that the remaining work will be performed according to the original plan:

$$ETC = BAC - EV$$

The second assumes that we will continue to over- or under-spend at the same rate:

$$ETC = (BAC - EV)/CPI$$

EAC can then be calculated as what we have spent so far plus what we have left to spend. The first calculation for ETC gives us (Turner, 2009):

$$EAC = AC + BAC - EV = BAC + CV$$

The second calculation for ETC gives us (Anbari, 2003; Project Management Institute, 2008; Turner, 2009):

$$EAC = AC + (BAC - EV)/CPI = BAC/CPI = BAC \times (1 - CV\%)$$

The Variance at Completion (VAC) gives an indication of the estimated cost under-run or over-run at the end of the completion of the project:

$$VAC = BAC - EAC$$

In this equation, 0 indicates that the project is forecast to be completed on budget. A positive value indicates a forecast under-run. A negative value indicates a forecast over-run.

Extensions to EVM: Forecasting of completion time and the earned schedule

In its basic form, EVM was not used to estimate the time to completion or forecast end date. However, simple extensions to EVM have been developed to use EVM data for that purpose (Lipke *et al.*, 2009).

Earned schedule

Unfortunately the terminology in this area is not fully agreed as it is in EVM, so we are going to use the following terminology:

Schedule at Completion (SAC): This is the original planned (baselined) completion date.

Planned Duration (PD): This is the original planned duration of the project.

Start Date (SD): This is the start date for the project.

There is an obvious relationship between SAC, PD and SD:

$$SAC = SD + PD$$

Earned Schedule (ES): This duration from the beginning of the project to the date on which the PV should have been equal to the current value of EV. On the EVM chart (Figure 2.17) it is the date the horizontal line through the current value of EV intersects the PV S-curve.

Actual Time (AT): This is the duration from the beginning of the project to today's date.

From these two we can calculate a time variance and a time performance index. The time variance (TV) is another measure of schedule performance measured in time terms and not cost terms:

$$TV = ES - AT$$

If this number is negative the project is behind schedule and if it is positive it is

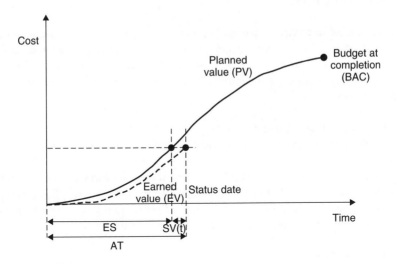

Figure 2.17 Elements of the earned schedule

ahead of schedule. This is sometimes called the schedule variance (time), SV(t), but that name could lead to possible confusion with schedule variance. The time variance percent (TV%) can be calculated as:

TV% = TV/ES

We can also calculate a time performance index (TPI):

TPI = ES/AT

This is sometimes called schedule performance index (time), SPI(t), but again there is a possible risk of confusion with SPI. As with SPI, if TPI is greater than 1.0, the project is ahead of schedule, and if it is less than 1.0, the project is behind schedule. As with SPI:

TPI = 1/(1 – TV%)

Forecasting of completion time

The forecast of time at completion also goes by more than one name:

• the forecast time at completion (FTC);
• the time estimate at completion (TEAC).

This is the forecast duration of the project. The forecast end date – forecast schedule at completion (FSC) – is:

$$FSC = SD + TEAC$$

The fact that the forecast cost at completion is just called the estimate at completion (EAC) and not the cost estimate at completion (CEAC), whereas the forecast time at completion has to be called the time estimate at completion (TEAC) underlines EVM's primary focus on cost control. The forecast time remaining also goes by a couple of names:

- the forecast time remaining (FTR);
- the time estimate to complete the remaining work (TETC).

The simplest way to calculate TEAC is based on the time variance (TV). As with forecasting cost at completion we can either assume that there will be no further delay to (or speeding of) the project, or that the rate of doing work will be maintained for the rest of the project. The first assumption gives us:

$$TEAC = PD + TV$$

The second assumption gives us (Lipke *et al.*, 2009):

$$TEAC = PD/TPI = PD \times (1 - TV\%)$$

TEAC can also be calculated using the SPI, but the calculations are more complicated. It depends on whether the project has reached the planned completion date and whether it is ahead or behind schedule. If the date is earlier than SAC and the project has not yet finished:

$$TEAC = PD/SPI = PD/(1 + SV\%)$$

After the SAC is reached, SV tends towards and concludes at 0.0 and SPI tends towards and concludes at 1.0 when the project is completed. Hence, using SPI for schedule forecasting after the SAC is reached would lead to erroneous results. Therefore, we define the Expected Accomplishment Rate (EAR) as the average accomplishment rate per time period from the status date to the completion of project or work package. Then:

$$TEAC = AT + (BAC - EV)/EAR.$$

When past schedule performance is a good predictor of future schedule performance, EAR would be equal to the average Actual Accomplishment Rate (AAR) per time period to date, which can be obtained by dividing EV over AT: EAR = AAR = EV ÷ AT. Then:

$$TEAC = AT + (BAC - EV) \div AAR.$$

The time variance at completion (TVAC) gives an indication of the estimated amount of time that the project will be completed ahead or behind schedule:

$$TVAC = PD - TEAC$$

In this equation, 0.0 indicates that the project is expected to be completed on schedule, a positive value indicates that the project is expected to be completed ahead of schedule and a negative value indicates that the project is expected to be completed behind schedule.

Statistical forecasting

EVM and ES have been integrated with statistical confidence limits to derive the range of probable outcomes for the project final cost and duration (Lipke *et al.*, 2009).

2.4 CPM and EVM compared

Many professionals use network analysis, such as CPM/PERT for schedule forecasting and EVM for cost forecasting. However, these methods have different underlying assumptions. CPM and PERT are primarily planning tools, whereas EVM is primarily a monitoring and control tool. CPM and PERT generally assume that future performance will parallel the original plan, unless changes are made to the original plan time, logic, resources, or cost. CPM and PERT initially assume that problems or opportunities that affected performance in the past will not occur in the future and that past performance is not a good predictor of future performance. The assumption generally associated with EVM is that past performance is a good predictor of future performance, that performance to date will continue into the future, and that efficiencies or inefficiencies observed to date will prevail to completion. Which of these assumptions and related forecasts will materialize depends greatly on decisions and actions taken by the project manager, the project team, and the organization.

It is advisable to ask work package managers and functional managers to review cost and schedule mathematical forecasts and to provide their own subjective forecasts for their own work areas. Both mathematical forecasts and subjective forecasts could be included in project performance reports. This effort highlights performance deviations for work area managers, encourages them to consider appropriate, timely actions, and incorporates their detailed knowledge of performance in their own areas, which may not be evident from the mathematically forecast values.

Forecasting in project management may well be a self-defeating prophecy, and that may be good for the organization ultimately. Large deviations usually attract management's attention and result in corrective action. Small deviations are usually left alone. By quantifying and highlighting such deviations, bar charts, project network analysis techniques, and EVM help focus management's interest on projects or work packages that need the most attention. As a result, these tools support effective management of projects and work packages collectively and enhance management of the enterprise's project portfolio. Using these techniques consistently to forecast project outcomes provides a uniform approach to project reviews, builds confidence in the project outcome as time progresses, and enhances management's ability to take corrective actions and make appropriate decisions concerning the project (Anbari, 2003).

2.5 The Lean Six Sigma method

The Six Sigma management method is a project-driven management approach intended to improve an organization's products, services, results, and processes by continually reducing errors and defects throughout the organization. It is a business strategy that focuses on improving the understanding of customer requirements, business systems, and financial performance (Kwak and Anbari, 2006). Six Sigma aims at reducing work process variation, working smarter and making processes and results better. Lean Six Sigma starts with a subset of the Six Sigma method by reducing the emphasis on some statistical tools, in particular the treatment of the Design of Experiments. Then Lean Six Sigma integrates that subset with lean principles derived from industrial engineering aimed at improving work process flow, eliminating waste, improving efficiency, improving productivity, and making processes faster. The Lean Six Sigma method expands and enhances the concepts developed and applied in Total Quality Management (TQM) or similarly in Continuous Quality Improvement (CQI), and integrates them with lean concepts. Thus Lean Six Sigma can be said to include the following (Anbari, 2005):

- TQM (or CQI); and
- additional data analysis tools; and
- stronger customer focus; and
- productivity improvements; and
- financial results; and
- project management; and
- senior executive leadership.

Project management and Lean Six Sigma are generally addressed in the literature as separate subjects. Thus, there are two concurrent waves affecting management thinking and using organizational resources: project management and Lean Six Sigma. However, it appears that management researchers in each of these two areas are rarely aware of the progress achieved in the other area, although both approaches are aimed at enhancing the overall performance of organizations. Frank Anbari (2005) suggests that in the formulation and implementation of its strategy, an organization needs to carefully integrate the following two goals to enhance its competitive position:

1   The planning and introduction of innovations, new products, services, results, processes, operations, systems, and technologies to enhance organizational effectiveness, efficiency, competitive position, and customer satisfaction.

2   The maintenance and improvement of current products, services, results, processes, operations, systems, and technologies used for delivering the organization's products, services, and results to its customers.

The first goal can be carried out as coordinated innovation projects and programs, guided to their completion by project and program management methods, tools, and techniques. The second goal can be pursued through quality management methods, business systems improvement initiatives, and the current Lean Six Sigma method

There are strong relationships between project management and Lean Six Sigma beyond their common aim of enhancing organizational performance and their concurrent demands on scarce resources of the organization. Lean Six Sigma uses some project management tools and techniques in its implementation of project-by-project business process improvement. Quality, and as such Lean Six Sigma, plays an important role in project management as an important parameter with strong interactions with other critical project parameters, such as scope, time, and cost. Lean Six Sigma strives to achieve a heroic success rate of 99.99966 percent, which is a maximum of 3.4 defects per million opportunities (3.4 DPMO). Clearly, some of the metrics used in Lean Six Sigma to pursue near perfect performance may not be achievable or even measurable in individual projects. However, the approach and concepts advanced by Lean Six Sigma could provide important insights to the management of projects in general and may be of particular interest to those involved in managing projects in high reliability organizations (HROs) such as those conducted in the aerospace and pharmaceutical industries and other highly critical settings.

2.6 Is that all?

For many people, the answer to this question is, "Yes!" A reviewer of the first English edition of *Goal Directed Project Management* (Andersen *et al.*, 1987) questioned how this book could be about project management because it did not address CPM at all. That was not strictly true. That book had one paragraph saying why the authors thought that CPM was not important for the sort of projects that were described in the book, and how the book was focusing more on behavioral issues. Some people see project management as a sub-set of operations management. For some, project management is just one chapter in a book on operations management, and that chapter primarily describes CPM/PERT (for example see Slack *et al.*, 2006, and Heizer and Render, 2008).

Popular computer systems support CPM, resource leveling, bar charts, and sometimes EVM. Often they do not help in the management of quality, because that is considered to be qualitative and not mathematical. The importance of factors beyond those that can be calculated mathematically or depicted graphically has been acknowledged by pioneers of optimization techniques. However these techniques are generally not designed to handle such factors.

Further, the assumption behind the Optimization School is that the project will behave predictably, like a machine. But that is not the case. First, there are people involved, and as they would say in Yorkshire, "There's nowt so queer as folk!" But there are also risks involved. Not everything is entirely predictable; the project can be held up by the weather, or technology may fail to act as predicted. These all can cause diversions from the plan. There can be feedback loops within the project, and if these are self-reinforcing, the diversions can become worse. Further there can be delays in the system which build in capacitance, and relationships which build in inductance. CPM, which is very linear and deterministic, can handle none of these. CPM is very useful for analyzing large but simple projects, and predicting the duration of the project if things go according to plan, and to conduct "what-if" analysis on things that can be controlled, but it is not a modeling tool for the behavior of the project under ambiguity, uncertainty, feedback, capacitance and inductance. And it is certainly not very good at modeling the behavior of people. Herbert Simon, recipient of the Nobel Prize for Economics in 1978, argued that the goal of optimizing the best choice needs to be replaced with the goal of "satisficing" decision-makers' aspirations (Simon, 1955). Thus, to consider multiple project objectives and constraints, human behavior, unpredictable factors, and feedback loops, all of which are becoming increasingly common in projects, we need to adopt more sophisticated modeling techniques.

References

Adamiecki, K., 1931, "Harmonygraph," *Przeglad Organizacji* [*Polish Journal of Organizational Review*].

Anbari, F.T., 2002, *Quantitative Methods for Project Management*, 2nd edition, International Institute for Learning, New York.

——, 2003, "Earned value project management method and extensions," *Project Management Journal*, **34**(41), 12–23.

——, 2005, "Innovation, project management, and Six Sigma method," *Current Topics in Management*, **10**, 101–116, Rahim, M.A., and Golembiewski, R.T. (eds), Transaction Publishers, New Brunswick, NJ.

Andersen, E.S., Grude, K.V., Haug, T., and Turner, J.R., 1987, *Goal Directed Project Management*, Kogan Page/Coopers & Lybrand, London.

American National Standards Institute (ANSI)/Electronic Industries Alliance (EIA), 2007, *ANSI/EIA-748-B, Earned Value Management Systems,* American National Standards Institute, Washington, DC.

Archibald, R.D., and Villoria, R.L., 1967, *Network-Based Management Systems (PERT/CPM)*, Wiley, New York.

Cleland, D.I., and King, W.R., 1983, *Systems Analysis and Project Management*, 3rd edition, McGraw-Hill, New York.

Fleming, Q.W. and Koppelman, J.M., 2006, *Earned Value Project Management*, 3rd edition, Project Management Institute, Newtown Square, PA.

Fondhal, J.W., 1961, *A Noncomputer Approach to the Critical Path Method in the Construction Industry*, Department of Civil Engineering, Stanford University, Stanford, CA.

Gass, S.I. and Assad, A.A., 2005, *An Annotated Timeline of Operations Research: An informal history*, Springer/Kluwer Academic Publishers, New York.

Goldratt, E.M., 1997, *Critical Chain: A business novel*, The North River Press Publishing Corporation, Great Barrington, MA.

George, Jr., C.S., 1968, *The History of Management Thought*, Prentice-Hall, Englewood Cliffs, NJ.

Humphreys, G.C., 2002, *Project Management Using Earned Value*, Humphreys and Associates, Inc., Orange, CA.

Heizer, J., and Render, B., 2008, *Operations Management*, 9th edition, Pearson/Prentice Hall, Upper Saddle River, NJ.

Kelley, Jr., J.E., and Walker, M.R., 1959, "Critical-path planning and scheduling," *Proceedings of the Eastern Joint Computer Conference*, Boston, 160–173.

Kemps, R.R., 2007, *Fundamentals of Project Performance Management*, 5th edition, Humphreys & Associates, Inc., Orange, CA.

Kerzner, H., 2009, *Project Management: A systems approach to planning, scheduling, and controlling*, 10th edition, Wiley, New York.

Kim, E.H., Wells, Jr., W.G., and Duffey, M.R., 2003, "A model for effective implementation of earned value management methodology," *International Journal of Project Management*, **21**, 375–382.

Kwak, Y.H., and Anbari, F.T., 2006, "Benefits, obstacles, and future of Six Sigma approach," *Technovation: The International Journal of Technological Innovation, Entrepreneurship and Technology Management*, **26**(5–6), 708–715.

——, 2008, *Impact on Project Management of Allied Disciplines*, Project Management Institute, Newtown Square, PA.

Leach, L.P., 2004, "Critical chain project management," in Morris, P.W.G., and Pinto, J.F. (eds), *The Wiley Guide to Managing Projects*, Wiley, Hoboken, NJ.

Lipke, W., Zwikael, O., Henderson, K., and Anbari, F.T., 2009, "Prediction of project outcome: The application of statistical methods to earned value management and earned schedule performance indexes," *International Journal of Project Management*, **27**, 400–407.

Pritsker, A.A.B., 1966, *GERT: Graphical Evaluation and Review Technique*, The Rand Corporation. Retrieved on January 12, 2010 from http://ntrs.nasa.gov/archive/nasa/casi.ntrs.nasa.gov/19670022025_1967022025.pdf

Project Management Institute, 2005, *Practice Standard for Earned Value Management*, Project Management Institute, Newton Square, PA.

——, 2008, *A Guide to the Project Management Body of Knowledge (PMBOK® Guide)*, 4th edition, Project Management Institute, Newtown Square, PA.

Roy, B., 1959, "Contribution de la théorie des graphes a l'études de certains problèmes linéaires," *Comptes Rendus des Séances de l'Académie des Sciences*, **248**, 2437–2439.

Simon, H.A., 1955, "A behavioral model of rational choice," *Quarterly Journal of Economics*, **69**, 99–118.

Slack, N., Chambers, S., and Johnston, R., 2006, *Operations Management*, Financial Times/Prentice Hall, London.

Turner, J.R., 2009, *The Handbook of Project-Based Management*, 3rd edition, McGraw-Hill, New York.

Williams, T., 2002, *Modelling Complex Projects*, Wiley, Chichester.

3 Modeling

The project as a mirror

With contributions by Terry Williams

3.1 Modeling rather than optimization

Terry Williams (2002) suggested that, "it is generally held that the complexity of projects is also increasing." He proposed that the compounding causes of complexity in projects included the increasing complexity of products being developed and tightening of timescales. Descartes' reductionism approach divides a complex problem into its parts, solving each part, and then integrating back to solve the entire problem. In project management, decomposition methods such as work breakdown structures (WBS), critical path method (CPM), and so on, cannot cope with the uncertainty caused by complexity. These methods are linear and deterministic, regard the project as the sum of its parts, and treat it as a mechanical machine, where things will behave in predictable ways. More sophisticated modeling is required to deal with what project managers actually experience in real life (Cicmil *et al.*, 2006).

Thus the Optimization School evolved into the Modeling School, in which project management is not broken into its main elements for study and understanding, but rather looked at as an integrated whole to obtain a full view of the total system. Projects are complex entities, and it is difficult to understand their behavior intuitively without models. The aim of the Modeling School is to build models of projects to explain why they behave the way they do, and help understand what would happen if we were to manage them differently by taking various actions within projects.

This also enables a larger number of variables to be analyzed and some of which may be optimized, including time, cost, performance of the output, quality, and risk. Frank Anbari (1985) discussed elements of the project management system and their interactions, and postulated the quadruple objectives of project management: scope, time, cost, and quality (Figure 3.1). Rodney Turner (2009, first published in 1993) independently developed the five objectives of scope, time, cost, quality and project organization, which he represented as a tetrahedron (Figure 3.2) with organization at the center, and all five influencing each other. More recently, Anbari *et al.* (2008) have suggested two sets of constraints: the primary triple constraints (scope, time, and cost) and the secondary triple constraints (meeting customer expectations, final quality, and mitigation of risks).

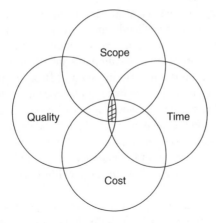

Figure 3.1 Frank Anbari's four objectives of project management

The techniques used in modeling the "hard" parameters of a project came from the same stable as the Optimization School, resulting in what we call "hard systems modeling." But "hard" effects do not explain all of the behaviors of projects, and sometimes the most crucial effects that have the most impact on project behavior are "soft." Work by various authors – particularly the team from Strathclyde University (Eden *et al.*, 2000), and the team from PA consulting (Cooper *et al.*, 2002), working as expert witnesses to create models of failed projects – developed

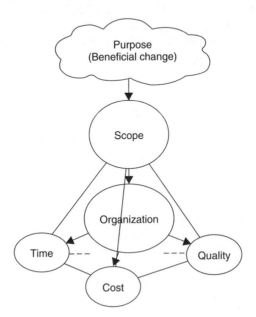

Figure 3.2 Rodney Turner's five functions of project management

a more comprehensive approach to building models to understand the behavior of complex projects. They showed that projects can contain complex causal chains of effects (which will often combine "hard" and "soft" effects, emphasizing the need to consider both), and that these chains can, crucially, form reinforcing feedback loops. Even worse, sometimes the application of standard project management theory can exacerbate these loops. This is reminiscent of Brooks's law (Brooks, 1995): "Adding resource to a software project that is going late makes it later still." Adding resource, which CPM would predict would speed the project up, can exacerbate the problems that are causing the delay and create further delays. More sophisticated modeling tools are needed (Williams, 2005). Techniques have to be developed to include softer effects and bring an integrated view to modeling the actuality of projects. Modeling is useful throughout the project life-cycle:

- before the project starts, in estimating and risk analysis;
- at the start of the project, at both the organizational and tactical level, for exploring possible options for implementation, analysis of success factors and their inter-relationships, establishing feasibility, and identifying and understanding project-control metrics;
- during the project, in decision-making and supporting project monitoring and re-planning;
- after the project, in supporting post-project reviews and feeding resulting information into post-project claims and on-going organizational learning.

Work in the Modeling School is now extending to the challenge of modeling ever more complex projects (Cooke-Davies *et al.*, 2007). This is a significant current area of research in project management.

In this chapter we describe the Modeling School. We describe hard and soft systems modeling, systems dynamics and the current work into modeling complex projects.

3.2   The cause of project overruns

The expert-witness work introduced above was carried out by two teams who derived similar results:

1   the team from PA consulting consisting of Kenneth Cooper, James Lyneis, Benjamin Bryant and Sharon Els (Cooper, 1980, 1993; Cooper *et al.*, 2002), with support from MIT (Graham, 2000);
2   the team from Strathclyde University (near Glasgow) consisting of Colin Eden, Terry Williams, Fran Ackerman and Susan Howick (Eden *et al.*, 2000).

Both teams were involved in postmortem analysis of a range of projects. The disruption-and-delay model developed on the first Strathclyde claim, arising on the Channel Tunnel (the "Shuttle Wagons"), is described in Ackermann *et al.* (1997), and successive claims have been characterized by the use of this technique. While this was not a particularly large project, "the value of the final claim was above 2 billion French Francs ($300 million), of which about 45 per cent was accounted for by the outcome of the disruption-and-delay model" (Ackermann *et al.*, 1997). Colin Eden and Fran Ackermann had already developed cognitive/causal mapping techniques, appropriate for studying structures of causality. When applied to project postmortems, they revealed significant structures of positive feedback loops. This technique not only provides a structuring mechanism for apparently "messy" problems, it also provides a logical structural interface with the System Dynamics technique for producing quantitative results (Williams *et al.*, 2003).

The elements used in these models are the same as those used in the Optimization School: developing mathematical models of elements of the project and looking to see how they combine. The same ideas are used in Earned Value Management (EVM), for example. However, there are four clear differences in this work: the first, the existence of reinforcing feedback loops, falls within the concept of hard systems, the latter three we will discuss under soft systems.

The technique used in this work is known as System Dynamics, or "SD" for short. SD was developed in the late 1950s by Jay Forrester of the Sloan School of Management at the Massachusetts Institute of Technology (Forrester, 1961), and since then the method has been applied to a wide variety of situations, and a whole body of knowledge has built up around it (see, for example, Sterman, 2000). While fundamentally being a similar method to Discrete Event Simulation, the modeling approach focuses on an understanding of feedback and feed-forward relationships.

It is these feedback relationships, particularly positive feedback loops, that can often be most significant in determining how projects behave. A positive feedback loop is not necessarily one with a beneficial outcome; it is one where effects are magnified around the loop. Each event in a loop can either increase or decrease the effect of the next event on the loop. These are positive and negative impacts respectively. A loop with an even number of positive impacts (including none) is a positive feedback loop; a variance in one event will tend to reinforce itself through the impact on itself around the loop. A reinforcing negative variance is called a "vicious cycle." But there can be positive feedback loops with beneficial results. If there are an odd number of negative impacts, then a variance will tend to nullify itself and it is called a negative feedback loop.

There are several such loops in Figure 3.3. For instance there is one in the center:

- increased activity durations, which lead to
- increased delays, which lead to
- increased running of activities in parallel, which leads to
- increased cross-relation between activities, which leads to
- increased activity duration.

This positive feedback loop can be triggered by tight timescales, rework, lack of qualified resources, or more work to do. It also illustrates that standard project management theory based on CPM suggests the wrong action. CPM would suggest that if there is a delay or if there are tight timescales, activities should be run in parallel

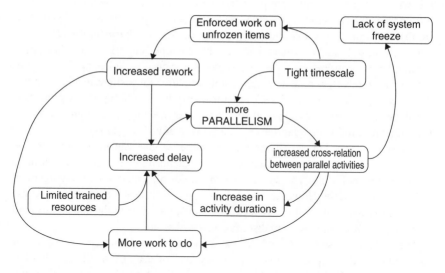

Figure 3.3 Key feedback loops (adapted from Williams *et al.*, 1995b)

to recover the plan. But that is a key event in the loop causing the problem to be magnified. Another possible response suggested by CPM is to throw resources at the problem. But, as suggested by Brooks's Law above, if the resources are unqualified, which they are likely to be initially, that triggers the problem. The loop at the center is fairly obvious. The one that goes via lack of systems freeze is more insidious.

This work provides explanations for project behavior deriving from systemic interrelated sets of causal factors rather than tracing effects to single causes. Williams *et al.* (1995a), for example, show how positive feedback loops in one project, the Shuttle Wagons project, some of which are shown in Figure 3.3 (from Williams *et al.*, 1995b), cause a behavior which is much more than the sum of the parts. This explains "the difficulty in determining the true causes of project performance" (Cooper *et al.*, 2002). This work shows how the "systemicity" involved produces a totality of effects beyond the sum of the results that would be expected from individual causes. In particular, key results derive from dynamics set up by these effects turning into positive feedback loops, or "vicious cycles," producing "run-away" projects with huge (or "catastrophic") over-runs. Cooper *et al.* (2002) discuss feedback structures as the root of the complexity, pointing to three particular structures that they say generally underlie project dynamics. The main one is the rework cycle, Figure 3.4 (including discovery of unexpected rework; see also Friedrich *et al.*, 1987), which they suggest truly reflects work flows on projects, and not the linear, deterministic models suggested by CPM and EVM. The other two feedback cycles are effects on productivity and work quality, and knock-on effects from upstream phases to downstream phases (Cooper, 1993; Lyneis *et al.*, 2001). The work of the team from Strathclyde University looks for positive feedback

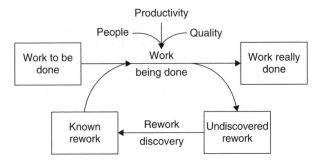

Figure 3.4 Rework cycle (after Cooper *et al.*, 2002)

generally in projects, but it is still this positive feedback which causes the unexpected over-runs. Eden *et al.* (2004), for example, describe in more detail four typical projects post-hoc (and one mid-project); two of the projects overspent by "over 40%" (aerospace) and one "58% above estimate" (construction); the other two (rolling-stock) were actually around 100 percent overspent; they describe reasons for these overspends, but the quantification, using Systems Dynamics methods (Williams *et al.*, 1995a, 1995b) is based on the positive feedback modeling.

3.3 Hard systems modeling

So on projects with:

- multiple variables that need modeling;
- branching;
- feedback loops, particularly positive or reinforcing ones;

or on projects that are just plain complex, with complex interactions between people or technology or both, more sophisticated modeling may be required than that offered by the simple project management tools such as CPM, PERT or EVM, and more sophisticated project management methodologies may be required than suggested by the basic bodies of knowledge. This is the focus of the Modeling School. Mike Pidd (2004) defines a model as: "a representation of a part of reality as seen by people who wish to use it to understand, change, manage and control that part of reality." A model is a mirror on the world where we try to understand it by creating a simplified version which we can analyze. You try to strip the complexity out of a situation to create a model which you can actually analyze to make predictions about the future performance of the system you are modeling. Having done that successfully, you try to overlay layers of complexity, making the model more sophisticated and hopefully getting more accurate results, until the model becomes too complex to analyze. However, this also illustrates that we have a compromise, between having a model that is simple enough to analyze but is of little use because it does not adequately represent reality (as is often the case with CPM and PERT), or having a model that is sophisticated but is also of little use because it is so complicated and too difficult to use. But that is a positive side of modeling, you can start simple, and then try to add complexity back, and see how that changes your predictions. A related issue is labeled Ockham's Razor. William of Ockham was a fourteenth-century philosopher who suggested that if there are two possible explanations for something, a simple one and a complicated one, the simple one is more likely to be correct. We should remember that when modeling projects.

Mike Pidd's definition suggests that there are several possible reasons for developing a model of our project:

- to better understand it;
- to make decisions about it;
- to control it;
- to optimize its performance or otherwise improve on it.

Modeling hard systems

A hard systems model is effectively a mathematical model of our project. You can develop a model with a pencil and a piece of paper. But if the project is complicated or complex enough to require modeling, it is probably complicated or complex enough to justify using a computer program. As we suggested above, CPM and PERT are simple modeling techniques, but they suffer from the shortcomings outlined above. However, you can develop more sophisticated models using other computer packages. We find it sad that project managers are so wedded to their traditional tools, such as CPM and PERT, that they just don't think of using these other, more sophisticated modeling approaches which can produce much more accurate representations of their projects, modeling the feedback loops as suggested above.

If thinking of using a computer-based model for your project, you need to recognize it may take some considerable effort to develop the model. You should only do it if that effort is going to be repaid, for instance if:

- the project is particularly complex;
- your organization does a large number of similar projects;
- you need a rigorous way of analyzing a complex environment; or
- you need an aid to decision making to select among complex alternatives.

The steps for developing a computer-based model of your project are:

1   Find yourself a problem.
2   Find an appropriate piece of software.
3   Isolate the factors that interact to cause the identified phenomena.
4   Trace cause and effect relationships, branching and feedback loops.
5   Develop the model.
6   Test the model and accept it if it can predict known phenomena.

The first two steps are not as flippant as they sound, because the software will influence the way you can analyze the problem, and so you need software that suits the problem, but also you need to know the functionality of the software before you begin to deconstruct the problem and construct the model.

Having constructed the model you can use it to try to predict the response of control interventions on projects. Also, as we said, you can try to identify further cause and effect relationships, and slowly add them to increase the sophistication of the model. But remember that there is a balance between the model being so simple that it is of little use (because it does not adequately represent reality), versus it being so complicated it is of little use (because it is too difficult to use).

3.4 Soft systems modeling

In Section 3.2, we said that there were four clear differences between the Modeling School and the Optimization School. The first, the concentration on feedback, we have dealt with. The other three differences come under the heading of "soft systems."

The first difference comes from the observation that, when models are built of how projects actually behave, we find that the important factors within the feedback loops are not only hard "concrete" factors, but also "soft" variables that are often important links in the chains of causality and are thus critical in determining the project behavior. Such variables can include morale, schedule pressure, clients changing their mind and so on. In Figure 3.3, two of the triggers of the feedback loops are lack of qualified resources and a perception of tight timescales. If we ignore these elements, we do not see the complete feedback loop, and so we do not explain the behavior of the project. Work in common "bodies of knowledge," and generally in the Optimization School, looks only at what can be counted, or what can be directly measured. Albert Einstein suggested that "not all that can be counted counts, and not all that counts can be counted."

The second feature is management response to perturbations. Having identified the systemic interaction between effects and positive feedback as key explanations for project behavior, we often find that the effects are exacerbated by the way managers respond. The effect of such actions can sometimes be counter intuitive (such as Brooks's law, and as we saw in Figure 3.3), magnifying small effects (Williams *et al.*, 1995a; Eden *et al.*, 2000). This is particularly the case in time-constrained projects. Where there is a small change to the project as planned, a project manager may respond by taking decisions to try to retain planned delivery and planned quality; that is, he or she will try to accelerate the project, by increasing parallelism or by throwing resources at the problem. Eden *et al.* (2000) show that the consequence of such actions can be to increase the power of the vicious cycle, because these actions are also disruptions that, in turn, must be contained within a shorter time scale. By taking actions that are implied or suggested by commonly accepted wisdom to try to deal with late-running projects, managers themselves are exacerbating the feedback and making the over-runs worse (Brooks's law). Bodies of knowledge do recognize the importance of this aspect of projects, but rather than recognizing the potential for feedback, the Pathways document (Stevens, 2002), for example, in talking about the "time-constrained project" says that

> time is a constraint in all projects. The project management approach, there-fore, has been developed overtime to cope specifically with the time constraint element of projects, and it is clear that the project management process or framework should be used in all circumstances.

The effects described in Section 3.2, however, would suggest the exact opposite approach.

Finally, there is a third, more philosophical difference from the Optimization School. The underlying paradigm of the Optimization School, and indeed that of widely accepted bodies of knowledge, is effectively positivist:

- reality is "out there" and the "facts" of the situation can be observed;
- the observer is independent of what is being observed and can stand back and observe the "real" world objectively;
- the observer, in observing, does not influence or change the thing being observed.

For example, in EVM, activities are assessed periodically to see how far they have progressed, and this is deemed to be a concrete reality that can be measured. Our inclusion of "soft" factors already challenges this view. But we can also challenge this view when we recognize that our models need to incorporate not only "real" data but management perceptions of data and the impact of the measurement itself on project performance and data. It was noted above that conventionally it is assumed that, in using (say) EVM, each activity is assessed to see how far it has pro-gressed: but this is not necessarily a concrete reality which can simply be measured but an individual's (or a team's) interpretation of the state of the activity, particu-larly when we are looking at (for example) a systems engineering project. Models are managed and analyzed by people who do not have a magical access to some underlying truth, but have to observe and judge to gain data to populate their mod-els. Further, their approach to how they go about making the measurement can influence the numbers recorded. This would be the case, for instance, with the rework in Figure 3.4. The systemic models that we discuss in this chapter try to bring in some consideration of the causes of attitudes and biases, and thus start to capture the socially constructed nature of "reality" in a project (Bredillet, 2004). Often projects are not clear paths but have to start with the use of problem-structuring methods such as Soft System Methodology (Checkland, 1981; Winter, 2006), and continue by trying to make sense of the project (Cicmil *et al.*, 2006) rather than following a plan. We will return to this in Chapter 9. By including soft systems, the Modeling School aims to address organizational, behavioral, political and other issues affecting projects and the complex environments within which they operate. Whereas the focus of hard systems is optimization, the focus of soft systems is clarification and making sense of the project and its environment.

The soft systems methodology (SSM) was first proposed by Peter Checkland (1972) to resolve unstructured management, planning and public policy problems that often have unclear or contradictory multi-objectives. Thus, SSM extends the ideas of optimization to modeling of what Peter Checkland called "real-world" messy problems. SSM does not assume a systemic view of such problems but uses ideas of systems analysis to help form the process of inquiry (Checkland, 1972, 1981; Gass and Assad, 2005). Mark Winter and Peter Checkland (2003) examined the main differences between hard systems and soft systems thinking through a comparison of their different perspectives on the practice of project management. Lynn Crawford and Julian Pollack (2004) identified dimensions of hardness and softness of projects based on differences in the philosophical basis of that dichotomy. Mark Winter (2006) highlighted the importance of problem structuring during the front-end of projects and the potential role that soft systems methodology can play. We will return to this in Chapter 9. Julian Pollack (2007) indicated there is a growing acceptance of the soft paradigm, and suggested that a paradigmatic expansion to include soft systems thinking could provide increased opportunities for researchers and practitioners.

Modeling soft systems

Soft systems modeling is offered as a purposeful activity where we create a model as an intellectual device to help structure exploration of the problem being addressed. The resulting model is not necessarily a model of the real situation, as in the hard models above, but just a model to help structure our thinking and debate. Thus soft systems models are social constructs rather than true representations of reality.

The principle behind soft systems modeling is to recognize that what creates complexity is relationships between people. A social system can be said to be complex if all the people in the system cannot communicate directly with each other, and we want some way of exploring the relationships in the social system. We do this by creating models of purposeful activity that try to create a mirror on the world. These are world views which we use to try to stimulate, feed and structure debate, rather than strict representations of reality. Through the model we try to identify important questions that will help us understand the situation or problem we wish to address, so we can formulate actions to address the situation and find accommodations between people. The idea is to find a result the interested parties can all live with. The process can in theory be never ending, and is best conducted with a wide range of interested parties.

There are two components of soft systems modeling:

1 the development of a rich picture;
2 the development of an understanding of the purposeful activity being modeled.

Rich picture

The rich picture is a representation of the situation you are in. It is a map of the real world the way you see it. But that means it is *your* world view, not necessarily a true representation of reality. It should help structure your thinking, not constrain it. While developing the rich picture, don't seek consensus, just allow everybody's ideas to be included. The rich picture can consist of drawings, words and phrases, links, relationships, arrows – anything that will help you understand your situation.

Purposeful activity

From the rich picture you can formulate a definition of the purposeful activity you wish to undertake. This is some form of transformation process to address the problem or situation you have. The purposeful activity can be described by what is called the CATWOE:

Customers: These are the people impacted by the transformation process. You need to think about what they have now, what they will have after the change, and who will be the winners and losers.

Actors: These are the people who will carry out the transformation process. You need to think about what will be the impact on them and how they will react.

Transformation process: This is the solution to the problem. Think about what inputs are required and what the desired outputs are, and the activities that need to be done in between. Think also about why the change is being done (to solve the problem and create some benefit), what will be produced (the desired outputs) and how it will be done (the activities).

World view: Think about the situation that is creating the problem, what the actual problem is, and the wider impact of any solution.

Owner: Try to identify the owner of the proposed transformation, what they can do to help or hinder you, how they might give you support, or how they might block you.

Environment: Finally, try to identify the constraints imposed by the environment, the legal implications, financial constraints, and ethical issues. Consider how these might constrain or otherwise influence your solution. Consider how you can overcome any barriers.

The project as a mirror

Figure 3.5 shows how soft system modeling works. We have a project situation which we find difficult to interpret and therefore cannot see our way forward. So we draw a rich picture. This is a reflection of reality, and inevitably a simplification of it. But based on our rich picture we can see our way forward more easily, so we develop a planned response in our reflective space. We can then interpret that into practical tasks. Of course at each step there is a simplification, and the situation becomes slightly more detached from reality, but people do find that this approach helps them see their way through difficult situations, to identify practical steps to deal with the real situation and implement their project.

We have used the metaphor of the project as a mirror to describe all project modeling, because in fact hard systems modeling is doing the same thing, but using a mathematical model of the project. The mathematical model is a reflection and

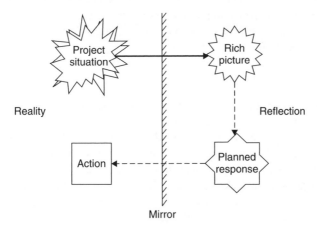

Figure 3.5 The project as a mirror

simplification of reality. But it helps us understand the real situation, plan responses and take action. So at first sight the hard and soft systems modeling may seem quite different – the former creating a mathematical model as close as possible to reality, to enable us to optimize the system, the latter creating a rich picture to enable us to comprehend relationships between people. But in fact they are both very similar; they are both about creating a mirror on the world to enable us to understand a situation, make decisions about it, control it and otherwise improve on it. Hard systems, including simulation, provide a way of reflecting how a system evolves according to the influence and level of the initial conditions of its parameters. As such, hard systems are about sense-making as well. Thus, the Modeling Perspective is about sense-making, understanding and acting; a mirror to reflect the project and shape our understanding of it.

3.5 Modeling propositions

Another form of soft-systems modeling is the modeling of propositional knowledge. There are several types of knowledge. The two we are most familiar with are:

Acquaintance knowledge, or knowledge we have of a person, place or thing:

- I know the nine body of knowledge areas in the PMI PMBoK;
- I have been to Paris;
- I have read Rodney Turner's books.

Procedural knowledge, or knowledge of how something works, or a procedure or methodology for doing something:

- I know how to conduct critical path analysis;
- I am PRINCE2™ certificated;
- I know how to get from New York to Washington.

With propositional knowledge we have propositions about things. A proposition consists of a sentence with a subject and a predicate. The subject is an item we have an interest in and the predicate is information about that item which may or may not be useful. For example:

The dog is hairy.

This may not be a useful proposition, but if we were about to put the dog in the car, then it tells us we may need to take precautions.

Figure 3.6 shows a knowledge cycle which we will develop to model propositional knowledge. We have data which in its raw form is not useful. But we collate the data into information, and by analysis of the information generate knowledge. The knowledge helps us make better decisions, so we can take action and produce results. The results generate new data. Notice again the mirror. The left-hand side is reality; the right hand side is a model of reality.

Figure 3.7 illustrates the application of the knowledge cycle to propositional knowledge. We have a large number of propositions about our project (the data), but they are scattered and of little use. The next step is to group the propositions into related sets. In Figure 3.7 we have two ways of grouping the items in the data set. There are circles, hexagons, diamonds and stars. Or there are items with solid, dashed and dotted boundaries. In the event we chose to group them as circles, hexagons, diamonds and stars. Further we decided the items with dotted boundaries were of little use so discarded those bits of data. Having grouped the items we need to develop a single proposition to reflect the whole group. The grouping of the items together with the header proposition is known as an affinity diagram. Table 3.1 is an affinity diagram for the nine perspectives of project management.

To gain useful knowledge we need to know how the groups of items interact. We draw a model, known as an interrelationship digraph, that shows the interactions. If

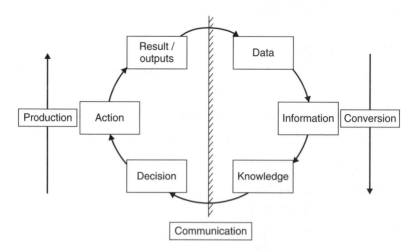

Figure 3.6 The knowledge cycle

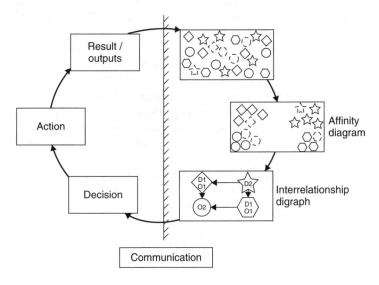

Figure 3.7 Propositional modeling

two groups interact we draw a line linking the two groups. Having identified a link, we need to decide which of those two drives the other, and which is the outcome of the other. In reality, the influence is often both ways, but the key thing is to decide

Table 3.1 Affinity diagram for the nine perspectives of project management

Code	Perspective	Proposition
OPT	Optimization	The three components of the triple constraint should be balanced to provide the optimum outcome for the project
MOD	Modeling	Project modeling provides us with a mirror to analyze complex situations to identify the optimum solution for the project
SUC	Success	The identification of the success criteria of a project can help us choose the best methodology for implementing the project
GOV	Governance	The governance of project management provides a clear link between corporate strategy and project strategy
BEH	Behavior	Projects are implemented by people and so they are complex social systems which require careful management
MAR	Marketing	Project stakeholders should be made aware of the benefits delivered by the project so that they will provide appropriate support.
PRO	Process	The project process is an algorithm which helps us convert vision into reality
DEC	Decision	End-of-stage reviews provide a clear audit trail of decisions throughout the project life-cycle, both to ensure the project progresses in the optimum way towards the best outcome, and to be able to review the reason behind decisions at any point in the future
CON	Contingency	All projects are different and so each requires a project methodology tailored to the particular needs of that project

which is the primary driver of the other; that is to make a firm decision. In the completed digraph we can assign each group a D and O score. The D score is the number of arrows coming out of that group; that is the number of other groups it is Driving. The O score is the number of arrows coming into that group; that is the number of groups driving it or the number of other groups of which it is the outcome. Groups where the D score is much larger than the O score are driving the system. Groups where the O score is much larger than the D score are being driven by the system. This provides us with knowledge about where we should put our effort to influence the system. We may be able to identify small wins; that is things that we can do that will have a positive effect on groups with a high D score that will have an overall positive effect on the system.

Figure 3.8 is the interrelationship digraph for the nine perspectives on project management. The Optimization Perspective has an O score of 4 and a D score of zero. That is, it is the outcome of all the other perspectives. It is where we should be aiming, not where we start. The contingency perspective is the only other one where the O score is bigger than the D score, and so it is a consequence of most of the rest. No perspective has an O score of zero, but the Success School has the biggest difference (D minus O). So it is the primary driver of the system. We should start by identifying the success criteria of the project, but the success criteria will be driven by the governance of the project.

We can also look for loops, that is, three groups where the first drives the second drives the third which in turn drives the fist. This is an area where if we can make a

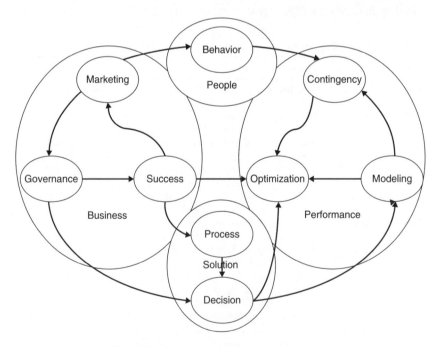

Figure 3.8 An interrelationship digraph for the nine perspectives

positive impact on one we can make a positive impact on all three. In an interrelationship digraph we tend to limit ourselves to loops of just three as being things where we can have a focused positive impact. Larger loops may exist, but trying to make improvements will be less focused. In Figure 3.8 there is just one loop, Success–Marketing–Governance. By clearly identifying the project success criteria and showing the project to be beneficial, we can win the support of key stakeholders, particularly senior executives, who will then be committed to the project and improve its governance, and so increase the chance of achieving the success criteria.

Thus the interrelationship digraph provides us with knowledge to help us to make better decisions about what actions will lead to better results. If we take such actions, the actual results will provide further data about what works and doesn't work.

3.6 Here comes the philosophy

The key idea of the Modeling Perspective is to integrate hard- and soft-systems theory to model the project. This perspective combines Parmenides' emphasis on a permanent and unchanging reality (being) and Heraclitus' view of a changing and emerging world (becoming). Being is dependent on acquaintance knowledge, and becoming on procedural knowledge (Section 3.5). This perspective integrates objectivism (reality exists independently of consciousness – there is an objective reality "out there") with constructivism ("truth" and meaning are created by the subject's interaction with the world), and subjectivism (meaning is imposed on the object by the subject; subjects construct meaning from within collective unconsciousness). This approach allows us to integrate positivist views (scientific observation, empirical inquiries, and dealing with facts), interpretivist views (symbolic interaction, social constructivism), critical inquiry (discarding of false consciousness to develop new ways of understanding as a guide for effective action), and postmodernism (emphasis on multiplicity, ambiguity, ambivalence, and fragmentation).

Work in the "hard systems" approach enables us to explain the complexity of projects. Herbert Simon (1982) suggests that a complex system is one in which the behavior of the whole is difficult to deduce from understanding the individual parts; so, when we look at a complex project, while we might know the effects that impacted the project and the project outcome, it can be difficult to understand intuitively how the latter resulted from the former. The systemic models do go beyond the decomposition models of the Optimization School and explain the behavior of complex interrelated systems. This echoes developments in complexity theory, as it explains aspects such as the "butterfly" effect, emergence, and the behavior of complex adaptive systems (which are self-organizing systems that learn and adapt). Concepts of complexity theory were initiated by Jack Edmunds (1965) and extended by several others. Some of these thoughts have been used to enhance our understanding of projects and to interpret some project management practices (Cicmil *et al.*, 2009). Projects are carried out by groups with political power-structures sense-making together within this complexity. Hard approaches cannot explain sufficiently, and soft approaches do not give us the decision-support we need, so we need an integrated, combined, or multi-methodology approach. Projects are not made up only of inter-linking mechanisms, but also of people, and much of what we see in projects results from complex, responsive relationships between human beings, communicating and negotiating status and power relationships. This is a large area, initiated by Stacey (2001), and is promising to explain more about how projects behave in actuality. Cooke-Davies *et al.* (2007) started to use these ideas. Bringing in models of the interactions among people and their relationships, communications, and power relationships, could add even much more power to the tools of the Modeling School (Williams, 2008). Some of these thoughts are being used to clarify and suggest enhancements to collaborative academic and practitioner research in project management (Walker *et al.*, 2008a, b).

George Box, the pioneer in the design of experiments, time series analysis, and statistical model building, proclaimed that "all models are wrong but some are useful" (Box, 1979). This statement is often quoted and debated. It is similar to Dwight Eisenhower's remark that: "In preparing for battle I have always found that plans are useless, but planning is indispensable." Box pointed out that it would be indeed remarkable if any system in the real world could be exactly represented by any simple model. However, carefully chosen parsimonious models often do provide remarkably useful approximations. We hope that the Modeling School is advancing to a level where it provides useful approximations of the reality of projects.

3.7 Are we modeling the right things?

There is an assumption at the heart of the Optimization School that what we have to optimize is the time, cost and quality performance of projects, and this is now being questioned. The assumption pretty much carries on into the Modeling School, although as we said in the introduction, Anbari and Turner have suggested a wider set of parameters. Williams (2003) pointed out that researchers have recently begun to build dynamic models that explain behaviors of projects that conventional decomposition models do not explain. The two schools then bring a range of tools to bear on modeling and optimizing the project. But at no time have we really questioned whether these are the right tools. It is just an underlying assumption that they are.

In the early 1980s, people began to do work on project success factors, trying to identify the tools which would help us achieve more successful projects. But in that early work, success was still judged by achievement against the triple constraint. John Wateridge (1995) was the first to say that we could not know what the right tools were until we knew how we were going to judge our projects to be successful. He suggested that we should define how we will judge success, then identify success factors that would help us achieve these criteria, and then choose tools to match the success factors. It is also becoming apparent, for instance through the work of Aaron Shenhar and Dov Dvir (2007), that the triple constraint is almost completely irrelevant to project success. What is more important is the achievement of business objectives and the satisfaction of key stakeholders. Before leaping into applying optimization and modeling tools, we really ought to think about what we mean by project success.

References

Ackermann, F., Eden, C., and Williams, T., 1997, "Modelling for litigation: Mixing qualitative and quantitative approaches," *Interfaces*, **27**, 48–65.

Anbari, F.T., 1985, "A systems approach to project evaluation," *Project Management Journal*, **16**(3), 21–26.

Anbari, F.T., Carayannis, E.G., and Voetsch, R.J., 2008, "Post project reviews as a key project management competence," *Technovation: The International Journal of Technological Innovation, Entrepreneurship and Technology Management*, **28**(10), 633–643.

Box, G.E.P., 1979, "Robustness in the strategy of scientific model building," in Launer, R.L. and Wilkinson, G.N. (eds), *Robustness in Statistics*, Academic Press, New York.

Bredillet, C.N., 2004, "Understanding the very nature of project management: A praxiological approach," in Slevin, D.P., Cleland, D.I., and Pinto, J.K. (eds), *Innovations: Project Management Research 2004*, Project Management Institute, Newtown Square, PA.

Brooks, F.P., 1995, *The Mythical Man-Month*, 20th anniversary edition, Addison Wesley, Boston, MA.

Checkland, P., 1972, "Towards a systems-based methodology for real-world problem solving," *Journal of Systems Engineering*, **3**(2), 87–116.

———, 1981, *Systems Thinking, Systems Practice*, Wiley, Chichester, UK.

Cicmil, S., Cooke-Davies, T., Crawford, L., and Richardson, K., 2009, *Impact of Complexity Theory on Project Management: Mapping the field of complexity theory, and using one concept of complexity as an interpretive framework in studying projects and project management practice*, Project Management Institute, Newtown Square, PA.

Cicmil, S., Williams, T., Thomas, J., and Hodgson, D., 2006, "Rethinking project management: Researching the actuality of projects," *International Journal of Project Management*, **24**, 675–686.

Cooke-Davies, T., Cicmil, S., Crawford, L., and Richardson, K., 2007, "We're not in Kansas anymore, Toto: Mapping the strange landscape of complexity theory, and its relationship to project management," *Project Management Journal*, **38**(2), 50–61.

Cooper, K., 1980, "Naval ship production: A claim settled and a framework built," *Interfaces*, **10**, 20–36.

———, 1993, "The rework cycle: Benchmarks for the project manager," *Project Management Journal*, **20**, 17–21.

Cooper, K., Lyneis, J.M., and Bryant, B.J., 2002, "Learning to learn, from past to future," *International Journal of Project Management*, **20**(3), 213–219.

Crawford, L., and Pollack, J., 2004, "Hard and soft projects: A framework for analysis," *International Journal of Project Management*, **22**, 645–653.

Eden, C., Williams, T., Ackermann, F., and Howick, S., 2000, "On the nature of disruption and delay (D&D) in major projects," *Journal of the Operational Research Society*, **51**, 291–300.

Eden, C., Ackerman, F., and Williams, T., 2005, "The amoebic growth of project costs," *Project Management Journal*, **36**(2), 15–27.

Edmunds, J., 1965, "Paths, trees, and flowers," *Canadian Journal of Mathematics*, **17**, 449–467.

Forrester, J.W., 1961, *Industrial Dynamics*, MIT Press, Cambridge, MA.

Friedrich, D.R., Daly, J.P., and Dick, W.G. 1987, "Revisions, repairs and rework on large projects," *Journal of Engineering Construction Management*, 113, 488–500.

Gass, S.I., and Assad, A.A., 2005, *An Annotated Timeline of Operations Research: An informal history*, Springer/Kluwer Academic Publishers, New York.

Graham, A.K., 2000, "Beyond PM 101: Lessons for managing large development programs," *Project Management Journal*, 31, 7–18.

Lyneis, J.M., Cooper, K.G., and Els, S.A., 2001, "Strategic management of complex projects: A case study using system dynamics," *Systems Dynamics Review*, 17, 237–260.

Pidd, M., 2004, *Systems Modelling: Theory and practice*, Wiley, Chichester.

Pollack, J., 2007, "The changing paradigms of project management," *International Journal of Project Management*, 25, 266–274.

Shenhar, A.J. and Dvir, D., 2007, *Reinventing Project Management: The diamond approach to successful growth and innovation*, Harvard Business School Press, Boston.

Simon, H.A., 1982, *Sciences of the Artificial*, 2nd edition, MIT Press, Cambridge, MA.

Stacey, R., 2001, *Complex Responsive Processes in Organisations: Learning and knowledge creation*, Routledge, London.

Sterman, J.D., 2000, *Business Dynamics: Systems thinking and modeling for a complex world*, Irwin McGraw-Hill, New York.

Stevens, M., 2002, "Project context," in *Project Management Pathways*, Association for Project Management, High Wycombe, UK.

Turner, J.R., 2009, *The Handbook of Project-Based Management*, 3rd edition, McGraw-Hill, New York.

Walker, D.H.T., Cicmil, S., Thomas, J., Anbari, F.T., and Bredillet, C., 2008a, "Collaborative academic/practitioner research in project management: Theory and models," *International Journal of Managing Projects in Business*, 1(1), 17–32.

Walker, D.H.T., Anbari, F.T., Bredillet, C., Söderlund, J., Cicmil, S., and Thomas, J., 2008b, "Collaborative academic/practitioner research in project management: Examples and applications," *International Journal of Managing Projects in Business*, 1(2), 168–192.

Wateridge, J.H., 1995, "IT projects: A basis for success," *International Journal of Project Management*, 13, 169–172.

Williams, T., 2002, *Modelling Complex Projects*, Wiley, Chichester, UK.

——, 2003, "The contribution of mathematical modelling to the practice of project management," *IMA Journal of Management Mathematics*, 14, 3–30.

——, 2005, "Assessing and moving on from the dominant project management discourse in the light of project overruns," *IEEE Transactions on Engineering Management*, 52, 497–508.

Williams, T.M., 2008, "Project modelling," in Turner, J.R. (ed.), *The Gower Handbook of Project Management*, 4th edition, 587–599, Gower, Aldershot, UK.

Williams, T.M., Eden, C.L., Ackermann, F.R., and Tait, A., 1995a, "Vicious circles of parallelism," *International Journal of Project Management*, 13, 151–155.

——, 1995b, "The effects of design changes and delays on project costs," *Journal of the Operational Research Society*, 46(7), 809–818.

Williams, T.M., Ackermann, F.R., and Eden, C.L., 2003, "Structuring a disruption and delay claim," *European Journal of the Operational Research*, 148, 192–204.

Winter, M., 2006, "Problem structuring in project management: An application of soft systems methodology," *Journal of the Operational Research Society*, 57, 802–812.

Winter, M., and Checkland, P., 2003, "Soft systems – a fresh perspective for project management," *Proceedings of the Institution of Civil Engineers: Civil Engineering*, 156(4), 187–192.

4 Success

The project as an objective

4.1 Modeling success

John Wateridge (1995) suggested that before you leap into adopting the optimization tools to optimize the time, cost and quality performance of your projects, you should consider what you understand by project success. There are two main elements of project success, success factors and success criteria, which unfortunately many people confuse:

- success criteria are the dependent variables by which we are going to judge the successful outcome of our project;
- success factors are the independent variables of things we can influence to increase the likelihood of achieving a successful outcome.

Lynn Crawford (2003) has said that people writing about project success fall into three camps:

1   those who write about success criteria;
2   those who write about success factors;
3   those who don't understand the difference.

You see people writing about "success factors" who slip seamlessly between talking about success factors and success criteria, or produce lists that contain both. John Wateridge suggested that you should start by identifying the success criteria for your project; decide what your project is trying to achieve and how you are going to judge it to be successful. Once you understand what you are trying to achieve you can identify those elements of the project that will help you achieve your objectives, the success factors. Then and only then do you try to identify appropriate tools for planning and managing your project.

In this chapter we describe project success. We start where the management of a project should start, thinking about how the project will be judged to be successful. From that we can choose success factors that will help us achieve those success criteria, and then choose tools and techniques to help us manage the project, which may or may not include CPM and the other memes of project management. As we shall see, the early work into success factors studiously ignored the project manager. A chimpanzee with the right tools, with the right software package, could manage a project. That is not correct and we describe the influence of the project manager on project success.

4.2 Judging success: Success criteria

The proper place to start when considering the success of our project is to identify success criteria: how are we going to judge our project to be successful? In identifying how people judge project success, John Wateridge identified a necessary condition for success: "To have a successful outcome for your project it is necessary to agree the success criteria with all the stakeholders before you start." It is probably impossible to identify all the stakeholders, let alone get complete agreement, but you need to make a good effort. There is no point trying to agree the success criteria at the end; it is too late. Quite small differences in understanding at the start can lead to quite large divergences at the end. Just giving different emphasis to time, cost or quality can lead to quite widely different outcomes. There is a story of a British shipbuilding company that had traditionally made submarines. They bid to build a new frigate for the Royal Navy. They had never built surface vessels before so they bid a low price, with the strategy of winning the work and then delivering to quality and on time to prove they could make such a boat for future orders. Unfortunately nobody told the project manager, so he tried to reduce costs to make a profit, and time and quality suffered.

John Wateridge investigated the success of IT projects. He conducted a questionnaire where he asked people to think of their last two projects, to say what their role was (sponsor, user, designer or project manager), whether each project was a success or failure and how they made that judgment. On successful projects he found:

- the sponsors thought it was a success because it provided them with value;
- the users thought it was a success because it provided the sponsor with value;
- the designers thought it was a success because it provided the sponsor with value;
- the project managers thought it was a success because it provided the sponsor with value.

On unsuccessful projects he found:

- the sponsor thought it was a failure because it didn't provide them with value.

But don't be fooled:

- the users thought it was a failure because it didn't provide the functionality they wanted;
- the designers thought it was a failure because it was a poor design;
- the managers thought it was a failure because it was late and overspent.

What a surprise! When all the stakeholders are focusing on the same success criterion, and balancing their needs against all the other stakeholders, the project is a success. When the stakeholders each separately focuses on their own little requirement the project is a failure. But what is sad is the things people are focusing on in the second list are important for achieving success. To provide value the project must have good functionality, be well designed and finish at or near time and budget. But there is a way of putting all of those things into the basket and coming up with an overall best solution, and another way in which each stakeholder focuses just on their requirement and pulls the team apart.

When Rodney Turner has described this, project managers have said they hear what he says. But in their annual appraisal, they are judged on how many of their projects finished on cost and time. That is what determines their annual bonus, not on the value they provided for their sponsors. So they ask, what should they focus on, finishing on cost and time or providing value for the sponsor? Rodney says they should focus on changing their appraisal system, and their annual objectives, to reflect good project management.

Judging project success

That is just four stakeholders. In reality projects have many more. It is now increasingly common to recognize that projects have a wide range of stakeholders, who assess the success of projects in different ways, and over different timescales. We will now review the widening view of how project success is measured.

The triple constraint

The basic view of how project success is measured is that the project is finished on time, within budget and to quality. It is sad how people thoughtlessly trot this out as the measure of project success. It is often called the "triple constraint," in North America "the iron triangle" and in Europe "the golden triangle." We might take this to mean that Europeans think project success is golden, whereas Americans think it is made of base metals, but Americans have other reasons for not calling it the golden triangle. However, there is a serious point. Iron is rigid, so that metaphor might lead us to believe that once set the measures of success are rigidly cast in iron, whereas they are meant to be malleable, optimized against each other, and so gold as a malleable metal is a better metaphor.

An immediate problem is what we mean by "quality." People will trot out time, cost and quality as the three success criteria, and then variously say quality means finish, meets specification, functionality, performance, and so on. In the discussion above, both good design (finish) and functionality (performance) were important measures of success to different stakeholders.

This view of project success is very limited. Aaron Shenhar and Dov Dvir (2007) have now shown it to be almost irrelevant on many projects, with it making very little contribution to the overall assessment of project success.

Introducing different stakeholders

John Wateridge's research showed that the success of the project can be judged by
different stakeholders in different ways. The project excellence model (Figure 4.1),
developed by Eddy Westerveld (2003), views project success as the appreciation
by different stakeholders: the client; the project team; the users; the contractors;
and other interested parties. It doesn't say how each stakeholder will judge success
but shows that different stakeholders may have different views. Rodney Turner and
Ralf Müller (2006), in conducting their research into the leadership styles of
successful project managers, initially used this as their measure of project
success. However, during the early stages of their research they found this list to be
inadequate, and so for the main phase of their research they extended the list of
success criteria to include some measures of performance, including the triple
constraint:

- meeting project's overall performance (functionality, budget and timing);
- meeting user requirements;
- meeting the project's purpose;
- client satisfaction with the project results;
- recurring business with the client;
- end-user satisfaction with the project's product or service;
- suppliers' satisfaction;
- project team's satisfaction;
- other stakeholders' satisfaction.

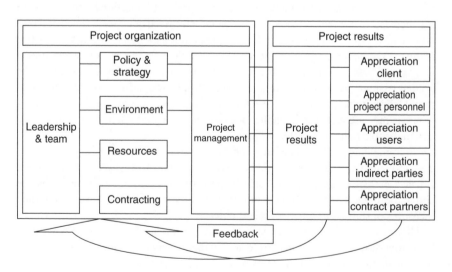

Figure 4.1 The project excellence model

Introducing different timescales and different project results

Based on the work of Peter Morris and Gordon Hough (1987), Rodney Turner (2009, first edition 1993) identified that success is judged by different stakeholders, against different criteria, over different timescales (Table 4.1). The bottom three criteria relate to the work of the project and the new asset produced (the project's output, Figure 1.3). They incorporate the triple constraint. But they also include appreciation by the project team and contractors. The middle four criteria relate to whether or not the asset performs as desired, it achieves the desired outcomes (Figure 1.3). These judgments reflect appreciation by the users and consumers, and are made in the months after the asset is commissioned. We differentiate between the users, people who operate the asset, and consumers, people who buy the product produced by the asset. Finally, the top three reflect whether or not the project makes a profit, and the asset achieves its long-term goals, or has the desired impact (Figure 1.3). These judgments are made by the project's investors, and are made years after the asset is commissioned.

We started this chapter by saying that a necessary condition of project success is to get the agreement of all the stakeholders. It is necessary before the start to achieve a compromise between all stakeholders and their requirements for success. Focusing on just a few will lead the other stakeholders to perceive the project as a failure. This is quite a common syndrome, where some stakeholders think the project is a success and some a failure.

Table 4.1 shows that the stakeholders make their judgments over different time frames; some as the project finishes, some over the following months and some over the following years. The things judged at the end of the project relate to the project's outputs; those judged over the following months relate to the outcomes; and those judged over the following years to the impact (Figure 1.3). So how should the project manager be judged and rewarded? It is quite easy to build first year's performance and immediate appreciation by the owners, users and consumers into

Table 4.1 Different stakeholders' perspectives of project success (after Turner, 2009)

Success Criteria	Interested Stakeholders	Timescale
Increases shareholder value	Shareholders, sponsor	End + years
Makes a profit for the owner	Owner	End + years
Satisfies owner and sponsor	Sponsor, owner	End + years
Satisfies consumers	Consumers	End + months
Satisfies users and champion	Users, champion	End + months
Achieves purpose	Users, champion, owner	End + months
Meets specification	Users, champion, team	End + weeks
• Functionality		
• Flexibility, Reliability, Availability, Maintainability, Elasticity, Security		
Time, cost, quality	Project team, users	End
Satisfies project team	Project team	End
Makes a profit for the contractor	Project team	End

the project manager's annual objectives. So the project manager can be judged by the results measured at the end of the project and over the coming months. But it is very difficult to build in assessments against the impact of the project made over years following the project.

Five categories of project success

Aaron Shenhar and Dov Dvir (2007) identify five categories of project success (Table 4.2). Against each category there are a number of different criteria of project success with assessments being made by different stakeholders. In this model the users, consumers and investor are in one sense swept into a single stakeholder, called the customer. However, business success and preparing for the future are of interest to the investor rather than the other two. Aaron Shenhar and Dov Dvir (like Rodney Turner, 2009) suggest that the criteria to the left are judged at the end of the project, those in the middle in the months following the project, and those to the right years later.

An integrated model

Rodney Turner, Roxanne Zolin and Kaye Remington (2009) have combined these ideas into a single integrated model (Table 4.3). They say that assessments of project success will be made against all three levels of project results: output, outcome and impact (Figure 1.3), and that these assessments will be made at the end of the project, in the months, and the years following, respectively. They also suggest that the different stakeholders will make assessments against all three levels of results over all three timescales using different criteria.

The investor or owner: This is the person or group who pays for the project. They buy the project's output (new asset), pay for its operation after the project and obtain the benefit to repay their investment. Their interest in the outcome is that the

Table 4.2 Model of project success (after Shenhar and Dvir, 2007)

Efficiency	Impact on team	Impact on customer	Business success	Preparation for the future
Meeting schedule	Team satisfaction	Meeting requirements	Sales	New technology
Meeting cost	Team morale	Meeting specification	Profits	New market
Yield, performance, functionality	Skill	Benefit to the customer	Market share	New product line
Other defined efficiencies	Team member growth	Extent of use	ROI, ROE	New core competency
	Team member retention	Customer satisfaction	Cash flow	New organizational capability
	No burnout	Customer loyalty	Service quality	
		Brand name recognition	Cycle time	
			Organizational measures	
			Regulatory approval	

Table 4.3 A new model of project success

Results	Project output	Project outcome	Impact
Timescale	End of project	plus months	plus years
Stakeholder			
Investor or owner	Time	Performance	Whole life value
	Cost	Profit	New technology
	Features	Reputation	New capability
	Performance	Consumer loyalty	New competence
			New class
Consumers	Time	Benefit	Competitive advantage
	Price of benefit	Price of product	Price of product
	Features	Features	Features
		Developments	Developments
Operators/users	Features	Usability	New technology
	Performance	Convenience	New capability
	Documentation	Availability	New competence
	Training	Reliability	New class
		Maintainability	
Project executive	Features	Performance	Future projects
or project sponsor	Performance	Benefits	New technology
	Time and cost	Reputation	New capability
		Relationships	New class
		Investor loyalty	
Senior supplier	Completed work	Performance	Future business
(design and/or	Time and cost	Reputation	New technology
management)	Performance	Relationships	New competence
	Profit from work	Repeat business	
	Safety record		
	Risk record		
	Client appreciation		
Project manager	Time	Reputation	Job security
and project team	Cost	Relationships	Future projects
	Performance	Repeat business	New technology
	Learning		New competence
	Camaraderie		
	Retention		
	Well-being		
Other suppliers	Time	Reputation	Future business
(goods, materials,	Profit	Relationships	New technology
works or services)	Client appreciation	Repeat business	New competence
Public	Environmental	Environmental impact	Whole life social
	impact	Social costs	cost–benefit ratio
		Social benefits	

asset continues to perform, and the operating costs and revenue are such that they can make a profit. They will also be interested in customer loyalty so they continue to receive their revenue stream. Their interest in revenue, operating costs and profit will extend over the years to the whole life value the new asset provides. Aaron Shenhar and Dov Dvir (2007) also suggest that their interest in the impact covers the new technology, competence and capability the asset provides.

The consumers: These are the people or group who buy the product the new asset produces. They obtain the benefit from the project's outcomes, which they pay for, and provide the investor with their revenue stream. Their interest in the project's output is the time that they begin to receive the product or benefit, and the price they pay for it. The price reflects the cost of the project and of operating the new asset. They buy the features the new asset gives. This interest will continue throughout the life of the asset.

The operators or users: These are the people or group who operate the asset on behalf of the investor. Their interest, on project completion, will be in the performance of the asset, and in the documentation and training they are given. During early operation, their interest will be in the usability of the asset, and its availability, reliability and maintainability (ARM). Over the years they will be interested in the new technology, capability, and competence.

The project sponsor or project executive: These are senior managers from the owner or user organization, who prior to the project identify the need for the new asset, and the potential benefit it will bring. They will persuade the investor to provide the finance and during the project will continue to sponsor and support it to win financial and political support. On project completion, they are concerned that the new asset should have the desired features and perform to solve the problem or exploit the opportunity identified. Their concern with time and cost will be that the asset should provide the investor with a profit. Their concern over the coming months will be that the new asset is performing to provide the predicted benefits, so that the support they have given the project is justified, and that they are maintaining their reputation and relationship with the investor.

The senior supplier: This group is senior management in the lead contractor. They may be from within the engineering or information systems department of the owner organization, they may be the consultant in the traditional (FIDIC, remeasurement) contract, or they may be a managing or prime contractor (Turner, 1995, 2003). At the end of the project they are concerned that it is completed to time and cost and that they make a profit from the work. They are also interested in the safety record and risk record for the project. During operation they are concerned that the asset performs as expected, to maintain their reputation as a prime contractor, and so maintain client loyalty.

The project manager and project team: At the end of the project they are of course concerned by the triple constraint. However, they are also interested in what they have learned from the project and the camaraderie they have gained by working on it, their future career moves and their personal well-being. In the months following the project, they are concerned about the reputation of their work, the maintenance of relationships, and whether they get repeat business.

Other suppliers: These are people or groups who provide goods, materials, works or services. Immediately after the project they are concerned by whether the project finished on time so that they get paid promptly, and whether they made a profit. Over the coming months their interest will be in their reputation and repeat business.

The public: The last stakeholder we consider is the public. Their concern throughout the life of the asset will be with environmental and social impacts. If the project is publicly funded they may also be concerned about whether it is representing value for money, so that they know that their taxes have been well spent.

Key performance indicators

Key performance indicators (KPIs) are measures of the success criteria that can be judged throughout the project, to ensure that the project is progressing towards the successful achievement of the success criteria. It is no good waiting until the end of the project to ask, "How did we do?" and finding that the project has failed. The project team need to track progress throughout the project against measures of the success criteria, and take action early on to counter any shortfall.

Now we come to another frequently made mistake by project managers. The success criteria as defined are good functionality, good quality, remaining within budget, or making a profit for the owner, but the project progress reports track time only, because that is all that Microsoft Project tracks. The project team must choose their control methods (methodology) and their key performance indicators to reflect the success criteria. That is if the success criteria are to:

1   *make a profit for the owner:* the team need to track net present value throughout the project, as calculated on the first day of the project, and from this point forward;
2   *make a profit for the contractor:* they need to perform earned value analysis to calculate the forecast cost to completion, and compare that to the price to be paid for the project;
3   *deliver appropriate functionality:* configuration management needs to be used;
4   *deliver the facility within the defined timescale:* then the schedule needs to be tracked using bar charts, milestone tracker charts or critical path networks.

The project team may need to track a number of these key performance indicators, but they need to agree in advance what their relative importance is when faced with a critical decision during the project: do you give priority to net present value, functionality, cost or time? (Remember the frigate discussed above.) Rodney Turner (2009) has shown that to maximize value for the owner, functionality should almost always take precedence. The relative importance of time and cost will depend on the circumstance. However, there are some projects where if they are not done by a certain date they have no value, the Olympic games for instance.

As the project progresses you want a way of tracking the key performance indicators. People have suggested the use of a project dashboard as a way of having all the key performance indicators of a project on one page. Figure 4.2 shows a simplified project dashboard, tracking time, cost and first year production. The triangle under the bar shows the target for the KPI. The cross shows the current prediction. Figure 4.3 shows a dashboard for the construction of a large process plant. The key performance indicators are:

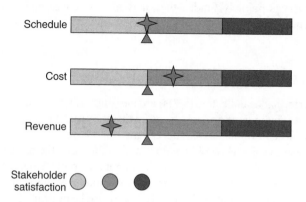

Figure 4.2 Simplified project dashboard

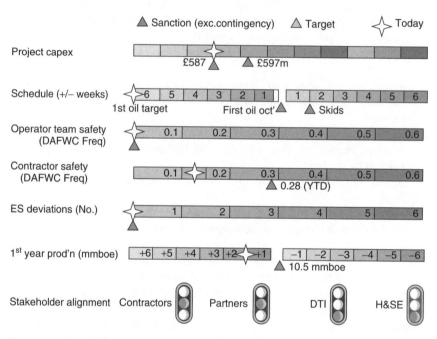

Figure 4.3 Project dashboard for the construction of a large process plant

- time (schedule);
- cost (capex – capital expenditure);
- own labor safety;
- contractor labor safety;
- deviations from plan;
- first year production.

Here the project manager's bonus is dependent on value to the sponsor (as measured by first year production). The dashboards use a color scheme due to the

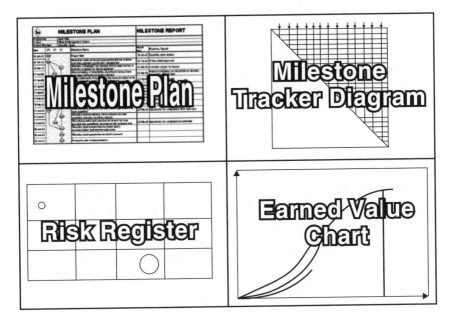

Figure 4.4 Key performance indicators represented on a single page

Lockheed Aircraft Corporation. Green (light gray) means on or ahead of target; yellow (medium gray) means just behind target, but controllable; red (dark gray) is well behind target. Figure 4.4 is another way of presenting the key performance indicators for a project on a single page. Here the four KPIs are progress against the milestones, time, cost and risk. Figure 4.5 is a traffic-light report, showing progress

Project name	Budget	Cost	Time	Risk	Benefit	Status
Project 1	100	◯	●	3	◯	◯
Project 2	200	◯	◯	3	●	●
Project 3	300	◯	●	4	◯	◯
Project 4	900	●	●	1	◯	●
Project 5	450	◯	◯	3	◯	◯
Project 6	600	●	◯	2	●	●
Project 7	750	◯	●	4	◯	◯
Project 8	800	◯	◯	3	◯	◯

◯ As planned   ● Problems   ● Crisis

Figure 4.5 Project traffic light reports giving KPIs for the projects of a portfolio

on the key performance indicators for all the projects in a portfolio. This enables senior management to keep track of all the projects simply and easily.

One last thing about key performance indicators. If they are "key," you will have six maximum. Rodney Turner spoke to a consultant once working with the National Health Service in the UK. He said the hospital he was working with had 125 "key" performance indicators. In that case at least 119 of them could not be really "key."

Hartman's three questions

Francis Hartman (2000) has suggested three questions to help identify the success criteria and stakeholders on a project. If the team members (or attendees at the start-up workshop) are asked to complete these questions separately, then it can help identify differences of opinion within the team. The three questions to ask the team are:

Q1: On the last day of the project, what will the project team hand over to operations?

Q2: How will success of the project be judged?

Q3: Who has an opinion on questions 1 and 2?

Question 1 defines the facility or asset to be delivered by the project; question 2 helps identify the success criteria; and question 3 the stakeholders. It is important to get the team to complete the questions on their own initially to tease out differences of opinion. Francis Hartman gives examples of teams whose members are all working to the same end date giving answers to question 1 ranging from completion of acceptance testing to successful operation for a year:

1   The first project was the construction of a petrochemical complex in Alberta. There were two project managers, one for design and the other for construction. In response to question 1, one said the project was over at mechanical and electrical completion and the other when the plant delivered 60 percent of its design plate capacity, two dates at least three months apart, and yet both gave the same completion date.

2   The other team were replacing the accounting software for their organization. About thirty people attended the workshop, and responses to the first question ranged from:

- beta test successfully completed;
- the system has run for 12 months without fault;
- 30 people have been made redundant.

The first two of these were now at least 15 months apart. The third was unfortunate because some of the people in the room were those to be made redundant and this was the first they had heard of it. The teams probably blamed failure of their projects on circumstances beyond their control, saying "We were unlucky."

4.3 Achieving success: Success factors

Identifying success factors

There have been two periods of intense research into project success factors:

The 1980s and 1990s

One of the first lists was produced by Kristoffer Grude while Managing Director of a software company in the early 1980s. They were having a problem with failing projects, so conducted post-completion reviews on all projects and identified a list of pitfalls. These are reported by Rodney Turner (2009), and Andersen *et al.* (2009). Kristoffer Grude identified pitfalls in the way the project is established, planned, organized and controlled. They are presented as success factors in Table 4.4. Peter Morris (1988) identified both success factors and failure factors, again with different factors identified at successive stages of the project management life-cycle (Table 4.5). Jeffrey Pinto and Dennis Slevin (1988) in a now classic piece of work identified ten project success factors (Table 4.6). This is now one of the most widely quoted lists. In Tables 4.5 and 4.6, the factors are presented in order of decreasing impact.

Most of the lists of success factors produced did not consider how they might change through the project life-cycle. The lists in Table 4.4 and 4.5 are unusual in this regard. Also lists of factors produced have also tended to studiously ignore the impact of the project manager. The lists in Tables 4.4 and 4.5 are also unusual in this regard. Peter Morris (Table 4.5) mentions leadership as a factor, and Kristoffer Grude (Table 4.4) mentions the project manager's competence.

Table 4.4 Kristoffer Grude's list of success factors

Project stage	Success factors
Foundation	Align the project with the business
	Gain commitment of involved managers
	Create a shared vision
Planning	Use multiple levels
	Use simple friendly tools
	Encourage creativity
	Estimate realistically
Implementation	Negotiate resource availability
	Agree cooperation
	Define management responsibility
	Gain commitment of resource providers
	Define channels of communication
	Project manager as manager not chief technologist
Control	Integrate plans and progress reports
	Formalize the review process through
	• defined intervals
	• defined criteria
	• controlled attendance
	Use sources of authority

Table 4.5 Peter Morris's (1988) list of project success factors

Stage	Success factors	Barriers
Formation	Personal ambition	Unmotivated team
	Top management support	Poor leadership
	Team motivation	Technical limitations
	Clear objectives	Money
	Technological advantage	
Build-up	Team motivation	Unmotivated team
	Personal motivation	Conflict in objectives
	Top management support	Poor leadership
	Technological expertise	Poor top management support
		Technical problems
Execution	Team motivation	Unmotivated team
	Personal motivation	Poor top management support
	Client support	Deficient procedures
	Top management support	
Close-out	Personal motivation	Poor control
	Team motivation	Poor financial support
	Top management support	Ill-defined objectives
	Financial support	Poor leadership

Table 4.6 Pinto and Slevin's (1988) list of project success factors

Success factor	Description
1. Project mission	Clearly defined goals and direction
2. Top management support	Resources, authority and power for implementation
3. Schedule and plans	Detailed specification of implementation process
4. Client consultation	Communication with and consultation of all stakeholders
5. Personnel	Recruitment, selection and training of competent personnel
6. Technical tasks	Ability of the required technology and expertise
7. Client acceptance	Selling of the final product to the end users
8. Monitoring and feedback	Timely and comprehensive control
9. Communication	Provision of timely data to key players
10. Trouble-shooting	Ability to handle unexpected problems

The 2000s

There has recently been a revival of interest in project success factors. The two most interesting pieces of work have been produced by Terry Cooke-Davies (2002) and Jim Johnson (2006). Terry Cooke-Davies identified four sets of factors (Table 4.7):

1   project management success factors contributing to successful time completion;
2   project management success factors contributing to successful cost completion;
3   project success factors contributing to successful benefits realization;
4   factors in the way the parent organization supports the project.

Table 4.7 Terry Cooke-Davies' (2001) list of project success factors

Project management success factors contributing to time completion:
F1   Adequacy of company-wide education on risk management
F2   Maturity of organization's processes for assigning ownership of risk
F3   Adequacy with which a visible risk register is maintained
F4   Adequacy of an up-to-date risk management plan
F5   Adequacy of documentation of organizational responsibilities on the project
F6   Project or stage duration as far below three years as possible, preferably below one year

Project management success factors contributing to budget completion:
F7   Changes to scope only made through a mature scope change control process
F8   Integrity of the performance measurement base-line

Project success factors contributing to successful benefits realization:
F9   Existence of an effective benefits delivery and management process that involves the mutual cooperation of project management and line management functions

Project success factors contributing to successful achieving corporate strategy:
F10   Portfolio and program management practices that allow the enterprise to resource fully a suite of projects that are thoughtfully and dynamically matched to the corporate strategy and business objectives
F11   A site of project, program and portfolio management metrics that provide "direct line of sight" feedback on current project performance and anticipated future success, so that project, program, portfolio and corporate decisions can be aligned
F12   An effective means of learning from experience on projects that combines explicit knowledge with tacit knowledge to encourages people to learn and to embed that learning into continuous improvement of project management processes and practices

His list was obtained from benchmarking project performance in several benchmarking networks he manages, so is based on subjective assessment of actual project performance.

From his work as CEO of the Standish Group, and its regular report on success rates of information systems projects, Jim Johnson developed a list of 100 success factors, grouped into ten categories: he calls them ten lessons. Table 4.8 shows the ten categories.

Table 4.8 Ten lessons of project success (after Johnson, 2006)

Ten lessons of project success

Involve the users
Identify your sponsor
Identify clear business objectives
Control scope
Adopt agile processes
Use professional project management
Forecast return on investment realistically and honestly; adopt a realistic business plan
Use sufficient skilled and competent workers to complete the task
Use formal project management methodologies, best supported by a project office
Collaborate with your stakeholders

Matching success criteria and factors

As we said in the introduction, John Wateridge (1995) suggested that you should choose appropriate success factors for the identified success criteria. Table 4.9 shows his suggestions. The success criteria are not identical to those in Table 4.1, but they are similar.

Models of success factors

Over the years, several models of project success factors have been produced.

The seven forces of project management

The idea of the seven forces (Figure 4.6) was developed by Rodney Turner (2009), based on the work of Peter Morris (Morris and Hough, 1987). It shows seven forces influencing the project, three internal and four external. The internal forces drive the project and are:

- the planning and control systems;
- the people;
- the project organization.

Of the four forces external to the project, two are internal to the parent organization and two external to the parent organization; two are driving the project and two resisting it:

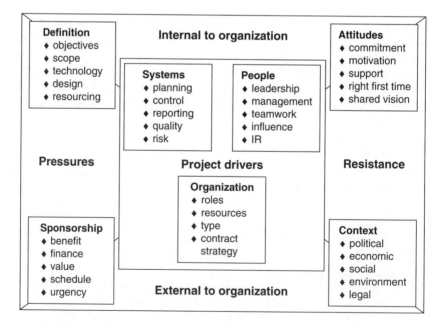

Figure 4.6 The seven forces model

Table 4.9 John Wateridge's suggestions for success criteria and associated success factors

	Success criteria								
Success factors	Commercial success	Meets user requirements	Meets budget	Happy users	Achieves purpose	Meets timescales	Happy sponsor	Meets quality	Happy team
Leadership				Secondary			Secondary		Primary
Motivation				Secondary					Primary
Planning	Primary	Secondary	Primary	Secondary	Secondary	Primary	Secondary	Secondary	Secondary
Monitoring	Primary		Primary			Primary			Secondary
Development method	Primary	Secondary						Primary	
Management method									Primary
Delegation				Secondary					Primary
Communication	Secondary	Primary		Primary			Primary		
Clear goals	Secondary	Primary			Primary		Primary	Secondary	
User involvement		Primary		Primary	Primary		Primary	Primary	
Top management	Primary		Primary			Primary			

- internal-driver: project definition;
- external-driver: sponsorship;
- internal-resistor: attitudes;
- external-resistor: context.

We describe this more fully in Section 9.2.

The project excellence model

Several people have produced project excellence models combining success factors and success criteria. These are often based on the EFQM model of organization excellence and quality. Figure 4.1 shows one produced by Eddie Westerveld (Westerveld and Gaya-Walters, 2001). The left-hand side shows success factors as project organization, and the right-hand side success criteria as the appreciation of various stakeholders. A similar model was produced independently by Otto Zieglemeyer for the International Project Management Association, and is used in their international project excellence award.

Five necessary conditions for project success

Through the work of two of his doctoral students, Rodney Turner (2009) has identified five necessary conditions for project success. They are necessary conditions, so if they are not fulfilled your project will fail. Unfortunately they are not sufficient conditions; doing them doesn't guarantee success. Other things can cause failure. The five necessary conditions are:

1 Agree the success criteria with all the stakeholders before you start.
2 Continue to agree the success criteria with all the stakeholders at configuration review points throughout the project.
3 View the project as a partnership, especially between the sponsor and manager and between the client and contractors.
4 Maintain medium levels of structure. Don't impose rigid control allowing no flexibility to deal with risk, or no control which will lead to anarchy.
5 The client should take an interest in progress.

4.4 The project manager as a success factor

There are two strongly held beliefs pervading the project management community.

1 The first is held by omission. There is a belief that the project manager, and his or her competency and leadership style, make no contribution to success. The project success literature studiously ignores the project manager as a success factor on projects. It talks about the tools used, but it does not mention the project manager. You might say that the project manager's competence is implied. If it is said that good planning, good risk management, or good communication

are success factors, then by implication the project manager must be competent in those things. But the project manager is ignored, and you might be forgiven for thinking that as long as you use good, appropriate tools, the project will be successful regardless of the project manager's competence. As long as you have the right tools, the project can be managed by the proverbial chimpanzee. Perhaps this is one reason why project managers are so undervalued in some quarters.

2   The other is a tenet of project management: once you have learned how to use the tools, you can manage any project, regardless of technology and industry. This is the issue of domain knowledge, and people hold strong views. Some say that to manage an IT project you need to be an information systems professional, and to manage the construction of a nuclear power station you need previous experience of the nuclear industry. Others say, no, the tools of project management are generic, and once you have learned them they can be applied to any project. The interesting thing is these discussions are always in terms of the technology. Can you apply your project management skills to managing an information systems project, even if you know nothing about computers? Can you apply your project management skills to the construction of a nuclear power plant even if you know nothing about welding a reactor together? The discussions are never in terms of temperament. Do you have the temperament to manage a team of computer programmers? Do you have the temperament to stand on top of a nuclear reactor at two o'clock in the morning as the pressure test is conducted?

These two beliefs at first sight appear different; the first saying the project manager does not make any difference, while the second focuses on the project manager. But they are two sides of the same coin. The first says it is only planning and control tools that make a difference, not the project manager and his or her competence, while the second is saying that once somebody has learned how to apply the tools and techniques, they can apply them to any project, regardless of their domain knowledge and temperament. There was an advertisement recently for a software product in a project management magazines. It said, "If you can use a mouse, you can manage a project." So if you have the right project management tool, in this case our software, you can manage a project regardless of your personal competence. So with our software the proverbial chimpanzee could manage a project. There is another saying: "A fool with a tool is still a fool." We all understand that an incompetent fool may have access to the best woodworking tools; they are not going to turn him or her into a master craftsman. Why is it that with project management we think any idiot can manage a project as long as they use the right tools and have access to the best software? In a general management context it has been shown that the manager's leadership style influences success, and different leadership styles are appropriate in different contexts. Particularly the most recent schools, the Emotional Intelligence and Competence Schools, suggest that it is the manager's personality and leadership style which make the most significant contribution to success (see Section 6.4). We all have access to the tools, but it is how we use them, and how we manage and lead our subordinates that makes the greatest contribution to success. It is emotional intelligence and leadership that differentiates the truly effective manager, not the tools they use. We return to this issue in Section 6.4.

Competence and success

Significant work on correlating the project manager's competence to success was done by Lynn Crawford (2003). She defines competence as the knowledge skills and personal traits (including behaviors) that enable an individual to achieve the performance required to do the job according to defined standards. Her measure of success was not the success of the project, but the assessment by project manager's supervisor, so it was a subjective assessment by the line manager, and was an assessment of their overall performance, not on a specific project. She found that once a project manager has achieved an entry level of knowledge, more knowledge does not make them more competent. This is in line with the Emotional Intelligence School of leadership (Section 6.4). You need a basic level of intellect and skills at using the tools to be competent, but once you have achieved those levels, more does not make you more competent. What makes you more competent is having the appropriate behaviors, traits and leadership qualities to achieve superior performance. This means that project management certification, by PMI®, IPMA or PRINCE2, is an essential entry-level requirement to being an effective project manager. But it is only an entry-level requirement. Appropriate traits, behaviors and leadership qualities are essential to be an effective manager. You *do* need to be able to do more than use a mouse, or have access to the best tools and techniques.

Management style through the life-cycle

David Frame (2003) suggested that different leadership styles are appropriate at different stages of the project life-cycle. He defines four leadership styles – laissez-faire, democratic, autocratic, and bureaucratic – depending on how much the project leader involves the team in making or formulating decisions, the amount he or she involves the team in taking decisions, and how flexible they are (Table 4.9). Formulating decisions is defining the problem, identifying possible solutions and evaluating the solutions. Taking decisions is choosing which option to implement. They then show that these four styles are each appropriate at different stages of the project life-cycle, and with different types of project team (Table 4.10).

Laissez-faire style: This style is appropriate at the research or feasibility stage of project. On a research project the project team members will be leading experts in their field. The project manager can only guide, suggest and lead. He or she cannot instruct. Also, when a contracting company is bidding for work, the bid manager will often be junior in strict hierarchical terms to some of the other team members, who may include the contracts manager, engineering manager and potential project manager. Again, the bid manager can only guide and not instruct. The other team members respect his or her expertise in preparing the bid, and take guidance, but

Table 4.10 Four styles of project leadership

Parameter	Laissez-faire	Democratic	Autocratic	Bureaucratic
Team decision-making	High	High	Low	Low
Team decision-taking	High	Low	Low	Low
Flexibility	High	High	High	Low

Table 4.11 Project leadership styles, project team types and the project life-cycle

Leadership style	Stage	Team type	Team nature
Laissez-faire	Feasibility	Egoless	Experts with shared responsibility
Democratic	Design	Matrix	Mixed discipline working on several tasks
Autocratic	Execution	Task	Single discipline working on separate tasks
Bureaucratic	Close-out	Surgical	Mixed working on a single task

won't accept orders. The team type is called "ego-less," it is not a forum for the project manager to express his or her ego, nor anybody else, as *the* boss.

Democratic: In the design stage, the team comprises professional engineers, experts in their field, but junior to the design manager. Also, several different professionals may each contribute to the design of different parts of the asset. Their relationship with the design of the asset is as a matrix, each team member contributing to the design of several parts. The team members are the experts. They formulate the decisions. However, since several different professionals are contributing to each part of the new asset, the manager has to set the overall strategy, and take the final decisions about how the various elements of design will fit together. The manager listens to what the team members have to say, but then rules on the final decision.

Autocratic: During the construction phase, the project team members may now be artisan labor. The will be formed into task forces, each task force delivering a different part of the new asset. The manager needs to be autocratic. All the time for discussion is over. The asset is being built and it must be built as designed. Changes cost money, and so the team members must just do as they are told. The manager is autocratic.

Bureaucratic: During the close-out stage of the project, the team will form into a single task force to tidy up all the loose ends. The project manager will be like a surgeon, leading a team working on the patient. The manager must now be bureaucratic. There are many check-lists to be completed, work to be finished off, inspections and tests to be done. The manager must make sure that ticks are put in all the right boxes, and closely follow the procedures to make sure that happens according to the rule book.

Rodney Turner (2009) considers how different cultural styles are appropriate at different stages of the life-cycle. Using Hofstede's (1991) four cultural parameters – power distance, uncertainty avoidance, individuality and masculinity – he shows different combinations of the four parameters were appropriate at different stages of the life-cycle.

1   During start and finish you must have high power distance, team members must respect the boss and his or her wishes. But during the design and execution stages power distance must be low, the team members must work with the project manager as a close-knit team.
2   During the early stages of a project individualism must be high. People must express their views about the best way of doing the project during the brainstorming and problem solving stages. This changes to medium during design and execution, and to low at project completion. During the completion stages people must follow the plan.
3   During the start-up stages uncertainty avoidance must be low, this is when you need to take risks. This changes to medium during design and execution and low during close-out. During close-out you must not take risks.
4   The masculinity–femininity dimension is unimportant on projects.

Multi-cultural projects

This leads us into multi-cultural projects. Many authors have written about the leadership styles appropriate on multi-cultural projects (see, for instance, Rees, 2007). Projects are now becoming so culturally diverse, with people from many backgrounds working on just one project, that it is now becoming recognized that it is almost impossible to be knowledgeable in the cultural traits of everybody working on the project team. Four personality traits are becoming important for the managers of multi-cultural projects:

*   sensitivity;
*   agreeableness;
*   people-orientation;
*   relationship-orientation.

You cannot be knowledgeable in the cultural traits of all members of the project team, but you must be sensitive to the fact that people may be different than you, and be cautious in the way you approach situations. Agreeableness makes project managers better able to respond to situations. This is a significant personality trait for managers of multi-cultural projects. People orientation and relationship orientation also make the manager better able to approach situations in a sensitive manner.

Summary

The project manager's competence, including his or her leadership style, does have an impact on project success. People who use the tools well can be good transactional managers. They will not be transformational leaders unless they develop and use appropriate traits, behaviors and leadership styles. And yes, the same tools and techniques are appropriate for all projects – there is only one body of knowledge in project management. But they are used in different ways on different projects (see

Chapter 10). Furthermore, different traits, behaviors and leadership styles are appropriate on different types of project. So it is not domain-specific knowledge you need to manage different types of projects, it is domain-specific traits, behaviors and leadership styles. You are more likely to know what makes IT techies tick if you come from that industry, and more likely to know what makes welders, fitters and riggers in the nuclear power industry tick if you come from that industry.

4.5 But who is in charge?

So we have defined the objectives of our project, identified the success criteria and appropriate success factors, and chosen the tools to manage our project. But do they deliver what the business actually wants? Are senior management committed to the project, and do they support us? Are adequate resources being made available to the project in terms of money, materials and people, and under what contractual conditions are the people working for the project? The project is a temporary organization, and owes its existence to the support of one or more parent organizations, which create it for the express purpose of achieving some business objective. The project's objectives must be clearly linked to the business objectives of the parent organization(s), and then it must be governed in such a way so as to achieve those business objectives. In the next chapter we look at the governance of projects and project management.

References

Andersen, E.S., Grude, K.V., and Haug, T., 2009, *Goal Directed Project Management*, Kogan Page, London.

Cooke-Davies, T., 2002, "The 'real' project success factors," *International Journal of Project Management*, **20**(3), 185–190.

Crawford, L.H., 2003, "Assessing and developing the project management competence of individuals," in Turner, J.R. (ed.), *People in Project Management*, Gower, Aldershot, UK.

Frame, J.D., 2003, *Managing Projects in Organizations*, 3rd edition, Jossey Bass, San Francisco.

Hartman, F.T., 2000, *Don't Park Your Brain Outside: A practical guide to improving shareholder value with SMART management*, Project Management Institute, Newtown Square, PA.

Hofstede, G., 1991, *Cultures and Organizations: Software of the mind*, McGraw-Hill, London.

Johnson, J., 2006, *My Life is Failure*, Standish Group, West Yarmouith, MA.

Morris, P.W.G., 1988, "Managing project interfaces," in Cleland, D.I., and King, W.R. (eds), *Project Management Handbook*, 2nd edition, Van Nostrand Reinhold, New York.

Morris, P.W.G., and Hough, G., 1987, *The Anatomy of Major Projects: A study of the reality of project management*, Wiley, Chichester.

Pinto, J.K., and Slevin, D.P., 1988, "Critical success factors in effective project implementation," in Cleland, D.I., and King, W.R. (eds), *Project Management Handbook*, 2nd edition, Van Nostrand Reinhold, New York.

Rees, D., 2007, "Managing culture," in Turner, J.R. (ed.), *The Gower Handbook of Project Management*, 4th edition, Gower, Aldershot, UK.

Shenhar, A.J., and Dvir, D., 2007, *Reinventing Project Management: The diamond approach to successful growth and innovation*, Harvard Business School Press, Boston.

Turner, J.R. (ed.), 1995, *The Commercial Project Manager*, McGraw-Hill, London.

——, 2003, *Contracting for Project Management*, Gower, Aldershot, UK.

Turner, J.R., 2009, *The Handbook of Project-Based Management*, 3rd edition, McGraw-Hill, New York.

Turner, J.R., and Müller, R., 2006, *Choosing Appropriate Project Managers: Matching their leadership style to the type of project*, Project Management Institute, Newtown Square.

Turner, J.R., Zolin, R., and Remington, K., 2009, "Modelling success on complex projects: Multiple perspectives over multiple time frames," in *Proceedings of IRNOP IX: The Ninth Conference of the International Research Network for Organizing by Projects, Berlin, October*, ed. Gemünden, H.-G., Technical University of Berlin.

Wateridge, J.H., 1995, "IT projects: A basis for success," *International Journal of Project Management*, 13(3), 169–172.

Westerveld, E., 2003, "The project excellence model: lining success criteria and critical success factors," *International Journal of Project Management*, 21, 411–418.

Westerveld, E., and Gaya-Walters, D., 2001, *Het Verbeteren van uw Projectorganisatie: Het Project Excellence Model in de Praktijk*, Kluwer, Dementen, The Netherlands.

5   Governance

The project as a legal entity

5.1 Governing success

A project is not an island existing in isolation; a project exists because some other person or organization (a natural or a legal person) creates it to achieve a desired outcome (Figure 1.3). In Chapter 1 we defined a project as "a temporary organization to which resources are assigned to bring about beneficial change." Somebody (whether that is a natural person or a legal person) has a vision of a future state, where things are better than they are now. The improvements offered by that future state have value to that person, so he, she or it is willing to spend money and devote other resources to achieve it. The person creates the project as the vehicle through which the money and resources will be channelled to do the work to deliver the desired outcomes. The project therefore exists as a child of that person. The person may be a natural person, an individual human being, or a legal person, a company or other organization, or it may be a consortium of people or organizations. We assume the parent organization can be considered to be permanent over the timescale during which the project exists.

It was traditional to view a project as a temporary endeavor, a large complex activity, or in the field of project contract management as an interface over which the client and contractor interact. Our view of the project as a temporary organization brings a different perspective to the management of projects. Some things that we might previously have thought of as projects because they fell within the definition of a project as a temporary endeavor, we would now categorize as temporary tasks given to the routine organization. Thus we would not use project management to manage them. Also we recognize that the project as a temporary organization needs governing, and as a child of the parent organization needs to fall within the governance structures of that organization. Third, rather than fighting over the interface, the client and contractor should work together in partnership within the temporary organization to the benefit of the project and thus to their mutual benefit.

In this chapter we start by considering the nature of the project as a temporary organization. We show how this view of the project leads to the concepts of principal–agency theory. We then consider the governance of project management. Governance exists on at least three levels:

- at the level of the parent organization;
- at the level linking the objectives of the parent organization to the project;
- at the level of the project.

We consider governance at all three levels. Finally, most organizations do not have access to all the resources they need to do their projects. The project exists to create a new state, and that implies that it is something that the parent organization has not done before and may not do again in the near future, and so it is not sensible for the parent organization to employ permanent staff to do that work. He, she or it seeks external contract staff to do the work, and so part of the governance structure is the contracts by which those temporary staff are employed. We consider project contracts and the move towards more cooperative working relationships between clients and their contractors. We saw in the last chapter that a necessary condition of project success is that the client and contractor should view the project as a partnership within which they work towards mutually beneficial objectives. Project contract management should support that cooperative working relationship.

5.2 The project as a temporary organization

It has been traditional to think of the project as a temporary endeavor, a large complex activity. Over the years, the following definitions of projects have been suggested:

> [A] complex effort to create a specific objective, within a schedule and budget target, which typically cuts across organizational lines, is unique and is usually not repeated within the organization.
>
> (Cleland and King, 1983)

> [A] unique endeavour in which human, financial and material resources are organized in a novel way to undertake a unique scope of work, of given specification, within constraints of cost and time, so as to achieve beneficial change defined by quantitative and qualitative objectives.
>
> (Turner, 2009, 2)

> [A] temporary endeavour undertaken to create a unique product, service or result.
>
> (Project Management Institute, 2008, 5)

These definitions all emphasize several things:

- the project as an endeavor;
- its temporariness;
- the uniqueness of the work and the novelty of the work processes;
- the mixed resources from across the organization working on the project;
- the mixed objectives.

However, by defining the project as an endeavor, or complex set of activities, the definitions fail to differentiate between projects and temporary tasks given to the routine organization. You can look at a range of types of activity, and ask whether they are projects or not:

1   the construction of the Three Gorges Dam in China, lasting several decades – this was a program of projects;
2   the construction of a submarine, lasting five to seven years – this is a major project;
3   the construction of a coal-fired power station, lasting several years – this is a large project;
4   the repair of a ship, lasting six months – this is a medium-sized project;
5   the shut-down, turnaround maintenance of a petrochemical plant, lasting a month – this is a medium-sized, but actually quite complex project;
6   an unplanned outage of a process plant, lasting ten days, in which maintenance jobs are done to repair non-fatal faults (which won't cause the plant to fail, but are making it inefficient) which cannot be repaired on-line – this is a small, but quite complex project;
7   the repair of my motor car after an accident – this is a temporary, and admittedly unique, task given to the routine organization, and so is not a project;
8   routine, on-line maintenance of a manufacturing plant, conducted daily – this is a temporary, but not at all unique, task performed repetitively by the routine organization;
9   the making of a cup of tea – this is also a temporary, but not so unique task, given to the routine organization.

These are all temporary, which would fit within the above definitions. But the further you go down the list the less like projects they are. Numbers 4 to 8 are all maintenance jobs, deliberately chosen to illustrate that some maintenance jobs definitely are projects, but some may not be. So there is a sense that there must be more to the definition of what a project is than suggested by the ones above.

However, before moving on we would like to say that we do not want to say rigidly one thing is a project and another is not, and that somebody is "wrong" to consider what they are doing as a project. If somebody gets value from looking upon what they are doing as a project, and wants to use some project management tools to help manage it, we would encourage them to do so. There is a spectrum of endeavors from the totally routine to the totally unique. At some point in the middle of that scale, people working on an endeavor may want to look upon part of it as a project and use project management tools, and part as a routine operation and use operations management tools. That is really the point – which perspective gives people value to help them manage what they are doing better.

The project as a temporary organization

The alternative view, which emerged in Sweden in the mid-1990s (Lundin and Söderholm, 1995) is to view the project as a temporary organization. The project is not the task, or endeavor, rather, the group of people and other resources assembled for a limited period of time to do it. The project is an organization we create with the purpose of bringing about beneficial change and when we have achieved the change it is disbanded. This was the basis of Premise 1 in Section 1.4 (Figure 1.3). Viewing the project as a temporary organization means quite clearly that endeavors 1 to 6 in the list above are projects, and 7 to 9 are temporary tasks given to the routine organization.

The critical theorists (Hodgson and Cicmil, 2006) suggest people "reify" projects; that is, they create a construct out of something that does not really exist in its own right. Those who view a project as an endeavor are open to this charge, because it can be difficult to delineate. But if you view a project as a temporary organization, then that organization does exist, and it is much easier to identify the boundary. However, as we said above, whoever wants to construct their work as a project, whether as an endeavor or temporary organization, because they find value from doing so, we would support them. At its most elemental, a project is a social construct, whether you view it as an endeavor or a temporary organization, and once you have constructed your work as a project, it is real, at least for you.

There are several features of the project as a temporary organization, including the following:

An agency of the parent organization

As a temporary organization, the project is an agency established by the parent organization to achieve desired objectives. The sponsor in the parent organization becomes the principal for the project, and needs to appoint a project manager, an agent, to manage the project on his, her or its behalf. We discuss the principal–agency relationship that results below. The sponsor needs to construct communication channels to monitor the manager's decisions and ensure they are aligned with the parent organization's objectives.

An agency for assigning resources

An organization is a collection of people with common purpose. Thus by viewing a project as a temporary organization, we focus on the people we need to assign to the project. This raises the need for human resource management practices to manage the assignment of people to projects, and manage their dispersal once the project is over (see Chapter 6).

Glenn Carroll (1995) says the success of an organizational form depends on its ability to attract resources. Clearly project management is a successful organizational form; it is widely used to achieve change objectives. But Glenn Carroll also says that the longevity of an organization form depends on its efficiency. We see below, when we talk about the principal agency relationship and associated agency costs, that project management is actually an inefficient organizational form. We adopt it because it is an effective way of achieving change, but abandon it when we have achieved the change and return to routine working.

An agency for change

Project management is a successful organizational form, because it has proved effective as a means of bringing about change. The routine organization can be very inflexible and slow to change. Routine organizations create projects to achieve change objectives they are not able to achieve through the routine organization. There are several reasons for this:

1   Functional organizations have high inertia to change. Projects can provide impetus to overcome the inertia. The parent organization establishes a project as a temporary organization that has little or no inertia and can build up the momentum of change. One tactic can be to establish the project off-site to prototype the desired change, adapt it as necessary, and then retrofit it back into the parent organization once it has proved successful (or adapt it or drop it if it's not successful). This tactic was adopted by the UK insurance company, Norwich Union, in a significant change project (Briner *et al.*, 1996).
2   Projects as temporary organizations are more flexible and better able to respond to uncertainties in the change process and change objectives.
3   The functional organization is designed for managing the routine and so is not well suited for managing change.

The principal–agency relationship

A consequence of viewing the project as a temporary organization is the recognition that the client and contractor, or sponsor and project manager, are in a principal–agency relationship. Michael Jensen (2000) says a principal–agency relationship exists when one party, the principal, relies on another, the agent, to perform a task on his or her behalf. Principal–agency theory developed to explain the relationship between the owners (shareholders) of a company and the board of directors. But it also applies to the relationship between the owner of a project (the sponsor) and the manager. Principal–agency theory identifies two problems in the relationship:

1   *The adverse selection problem*: In selecting the agent (project manager) the principal (client) cannot be completely sure that they are competent to do the job, and having once selected the project manager, cannot be certain why he or she takes the decisions they do.
2   *The moral hazard problem*: The agent (project manager) as a rational person will act to maximize his, her or its economic outcome from the project, and not the client's. They will only optimize the client's outcomes if their objectives happen to be aligned. The manager may even behave opportunistically to make significant profits at the client's expense. The contractor is in business to optimize profits for its shareholders, not the client's; the contractor is required by law to work in its shareholders' best interests.

Michael Jensen identifies a number of costs associated with establishing and managing the relationship between the two parties, which he calls *agency costs*:

1   The cost of setting up and maintaining the contractual relationship between the two.
2   The cost of setting up and maintaining communication mechanisms between the two. The principal has to make sure the agent truly understands what is required, and then wants to be kept informed of what the project manager is doing (to minimize the adverse selection and moral hazard problems).
3   Bonding costs by the agent to ensure the principal does trust him, her or it. This explains why professionalism is so important to project managers; it is a sign both of their competence, but also that they will adhere to the code of conduct of the professional association to which they belong. Project managers adhering to a code of conduct should not behave opportunistically.
4   Residual loss, which occurs because the product of the project as delivered does not perform exactly as the client would like.

There are several reasons why residual loss can happen:

•   The first is because the project manager works to maximize his or her profit from the project and not the client's. Sometimes project managers behave opportunistically, but usually they try to deliver what the client requires. Part of their assessment of their "profit" from the project is a desire to continue working for the client and so they are keen to do what the client wants. But the project manager has to make a profit to stay in business and so their actions will always be influenced by that. Indeed under modern compliance regimes the primary responsibility of the directors of the contracting company is to make a profit for their shareholders and not the shareholders of their client organization. They are duty bound to put their shareholders' interests first. Don't forget that.
•   The second reason is what is called bounded rationality. The project manager would like to fulfill the client's requirements but because of human frailty cannot do so perfectly. There are three elements of human frailty that cause bounded rationality. First, the project manager cannot get access to all the information required to completely understand the client's requirements. Thus they never have a perfect picture of what the client wants. Second, that information they do have they cannot process fully. Thus the project manager tends to "satisfice," aiming for an adequate solution rather than a perfect one. Indeed if you believe that "the perfect is the enemy of the good," it is better to satisfice than work vainly towards the perfect solution. Finally, the project manager cannot foretell the future, so they cannot predict all the risks. Unexpected things will happen which will cause the project outcomes to be less than perfect. But also, in responding to forecast risks, the project manager may adopt an adequate solution that is guaranteed to be successful rather than a perfect one which may fail.

Rodney Turner and Stephen Simister (2001) suggest that appropriately motivating the contractor to minimize residual loss is the main criterion for choosing contract type.

Because of these agency costs project management is inefficient. But often it is the only way to overcome organizational inertia to achieve change objectives. Project management is successful at attracting resources because it is a fast, flexible way of managing change, but as soon as the change is achieved you must disband the project and return to the routine to manage the new state (Carroll, 1995). So the project is necessarily a temporary organization.

5.3 The governance of project management

The Organization for Economic and Cooperative Development (OECD, at www.oecd.org) in defining the governance of a company, a legal entity, says (Clarke, 2004):

> Corporate governance involves a set of relationships between a company's management, its board (or management team), its shareholders and other stakeholders. Corporate governance provides the structure through which the objectives of the company are set, and the means of attaining those objectives and monitoring performance are determined.

There are two essential elements to this definition. The second part of the definition says what governance does. For an organization governance defines:

1   its objectives;
2   the means of obtaining the objectives;
3   the means of monitoring progress.

These three steps need to be done not just for the parent organization of which the project is a part, but also the project itself as a temporary organization. The first part of the definition says for whom governance is done. It is done for the shareholders and other stakeholders. In the field of corporate governance there are two schools of thought, the shareholder view and the stakeholder view (Clarke, 2004). The shareholder view says that the board of directors' sole responsibility is to maximize returns to shareholders. In the extreme this view leads to abuses such as Enron and WorldCom. The stakeholder view says, by contrast, that the directors have a responsibility to maximize returns to a much wider set of stakeholders, including the shareholders, but also including employees, customers and the wider community. As we saw in the last chapter, this can also be applied at the level of the project, with project success being viewed as just satisfying the client, or a wider set of stakeholders including the user, the suppliers and the project team. At the level of the project it is more obvious that you should adopt the wider view.

This definition of governance applies not just at the level of the company, but in a cascade down organizational units within the company, including elements of the routine organization, and to temporary organizations (projects and programs). Thus within a project-oriented organization, the governance of projects takes place on at least three levels:

1   At the level of corporate governance, where corporate governance defines the objectives of the company, and initiates project, program and portfolio management as the means of obtaining corporate objectives and monitoring progress.
2   Between corporate governance and the individual project, where appropriate portfolio and program governance structures (including the project office) link project objectives to corporate objectives and ensure they are achieved, and where organizational capabilities and competencies are developed to enable projects, programs and portfolios to thrive.
3   At the level of the individual project, where governance mechanisms are required to ensure the right projects are undertaken in the right way to deliver the right products, and to ensure the products will deliver the desired business benefits.

We describe governance at the level of corporate governance first. Then we describe the level of the individual project because we introduce ideas we draw on at the program and portfolio level.

At the level of corporate governance

The UK's Association for Project Management (APM) has a Special Interest Group (SIG) looking at the governance of project management (GoPM), for which they have produced a guide (Association for Project Management, 2004). They mainly focus on the governance of project management at the corporate level, where the board of directors takes an interest in projects being undertaken by the organization. APM's guide says that good GoPM can result in:

*   a clear link between corporate strategy and project strategy;
*   clear ownership of projects by senior management;
*   engagement with key stakeholders;
*   the development of organizational capability;
*   contact with key suppliers at a senior level;
*   a clear definition of the value of projects to the organization;
*   the dividing of project management into manageable parts.

APM suggests that there are four aims of GoPM:

1   portfolio direction;
2   project sponsorship;
3   project management;
4   disclosure and reporting;

and sets out 11 principles for the achievement of these aims:

1   the board has overall responsibility for GoPM;
2   roles, responsibility and performance criteria of GoPM are clearly defined;
3   disciplined governance arrangements are applied throughout the project life-cycle;
4   there is a coherent relationship between business strategy and the project portfolio;
5   all projects have authorization points at which the business case is approved, and the results of those authorization points are clearly communicated;
6   members of delegated authorization bodies have sufficient representation, competence, authority and resources to take empowered decisions;
7   the project business case is supported by accurate and relevant information;
8   the board or its delegated agents are able to identify when external scrutiny of projects is required and will act accordingly;
9   there are clearly defined criteria for reporting project status and escalating risks and issues;
10   the organization fosters a culture of improvement and frank disclosure of project status;
11   project stakeholders are engaged at a level that reflects their importance to the organizations and in a way which fosters trust.

End-of-stage reviews

Principle 5 suggests that there should be an audit trail of points at which the business case is approved, with the basis of the approval clearly documented. Principle 3 also suggests that there should be clear governance arrangements throughout the project life-cycle. The adoption of end-of-stage reviews helps fulfil these principles. End-of-stage reviews are variously called stage-gate reviews, toll-gate reviews or gateway reviews. In PRINCE2 they are an essential part of the process, Managing Stage Boundaries (Office of Government Commerce, 2009a). End-of-stage reviews provide disciplined governance arrangements, building into the project process key points at which current progress is reviewed, and adherence to the business case is checked. In that way they provide a clear audit trail where decisions to proceed with the project, and the basis of those decisions, can be checked both during and after the project.

End-of-stage reviews fulfil another important function. The governance structure on the project must be aligned with the project, not with the functional hierarchy. That requires the project manager to be empowered to take decisions without constant reference back to the line hierarchy. Line managers can be uncomfortable with releasing control in this way. However, the adoption of end-of-stage reviews means that line managers only need to release authority to the next review. The project manager is empowered between reviews, but at the reviews line managers, particularly the sponsor and the project board, take back control, and based on a clear, auditable decisions process then approve progression of the project to the next review.

Audits

Principle 8 says the board of directors must decide when independent scrutiny of the project is required. This means that they will commission an audit of the project. There are two reasons why the board of directors may require an audit of a project currently in progress. A significant project may be failing and it is important to recover progress. The audit will attempt to identify why the project is failing and what can be done to recover it, and then help the project team implement the recovery plans. But also there may be a key strategic project which absolutely must not fail. The board of directors may then commission an audit even if there is no indication of any problems. The role of the auditors will be to check that the project has been properly established and it is on a path to a successful outcome. The auditors are there to confirm that the project is on target. They may also identify potential risks and issues, and give the project team guidance on how to avoid them. We describe how to conduct audits in Section 5.5.

Sufficient representation

Principle 6 requires that the project manager should have sufficient representation, competence, authority and resources to take empowered decisions. This requires that the project manager should have appropriate status within the organization. Rodney Turner worked with a company once, making defense equipment, which was trying to move from a functional focus to a project focus. He told the man he was discussing this with that the reward structure could sometimes work against a project focus, and he said, "Funny you should say that." He went on to tell Rodney that salaries in the company were determined by the number of subordinates a manager had. So the manager of the Engineering Department with 1,000 subordinates was very senior. The manager of a project worth £5 million, with a forecast profit of £0.5 million, and critical to the defense of the UK, might only have one or two direct subordinates, and so would be very junior. So junior in fact that he or she might not have the procurement authority to order coffee for a client meeting. That does not foster appropriate governance of projects.

At the individual project level

The project itself is a temporary organization and so needs governing, and that is what we consider next. Premises 3 and 4 in Section 1.4, based on the OECD definition of corporate governance, define what we mean by governance of the project. As at the corporate level, the roles of governance are to define the objectives of the project, define the means of obtaining those objectives and define the means of monitoring progress. Figure 1.6 illustrates what that means for a project, using the results-based model from Figure 1.3, and shows that it implies four governance roles.

We illustrate by discussing a project undertaken by the Chinese government to build a bridge across the Yangtze River near its mouth to the north of Shanghai. The desired performance improvement (the client need) was to achieve economic development on the north side of the river. The area around Shanghai is the most economically developed part of mainland China, but the area on the north side of the river used to be substantially less developed. So the top-level objective, to achieve the client need and desired performance improvement, was here economic development on the north side of the river. Next we identify the project's desired outcomes. This is the new competencies the parent organization needs to achieve the desired performance improvement. What was stopping economic development was poor traffic flows across the river. The only way across was by slow ferry, so people were not building their factories on the north side of the river. The outcomes are the means to obtaining the desired performance improvement, but they then become the next level of objective (Figure 1.5). Having defined the desired outcomes, we identify the project's output, the new asset the project will deliver. The output is the means to obtaining the outcomes, but then becomes the objective at the next level of the project. In order to achieve faster traffic flows there were several possible solutions, including better ferries, a tunnel or a bridge. The chosen solution was a bridge.

Having identified the objectives at the three levels of results, we identify the means to delivering the project's output, that is the planned project process and the resources required to implement it. We then need to monitor progress. We monitor the doing of the work of the project, that is project control. As the new asset is delivered we check that it is as required. We then monitor that the desired outcome is achieved and ultimately that the client's requirement and desired performance improvement is achieved. These last two steps are known as benefits delivery, and the benefits map (Figure 1.4) can be used in that process. In the case of the bridge across the Yangtze River, the faster traffic flows and economic development did not happen right away. People were not aware that they could get their products across the river more quickly. So the Chinese government put effort into raising people's awareness, and offering inducements to people to build their factories on the north side of the river, and with time they achieved the desired performance improvement.

Figure 1.6 shows that there are four roles associated with the governance of the project:

1   *The sponsor*: This is somebody from the business who identifies the potential for performance improvement and that some change can be undertaken to achieve it. So the sponsor defines the client's requirement, begins to identify the project's outcomes and out puts, and begins to draw the benefits map (Figure 1.4). Some people say that the sponsor has the resources to do the project, but that is not necessarily the case. The sponsor may need to seek monetary support from a financier and technical resources from the technical department. But the sponsor does have an ambassadorial role to sell the project's benefit to the organization, and thereby win support for the project in terms of money, materials and people. That ambassadorial role continues throughout the project. In the case of the bridge across the Yangtze River, the sponsor might have been an official from Jiangsu Province or from a central government department responsible for economic development.

2   *The steward*: The sponsor will not be a technical expert and so will need to seek technical advice to finalize the definition of the desired outcomes and output, and to finalize the benefits map. He or she will turn to a senior technical manager, whom we call the steward. The steward will also begin to design the possible project process and identify the necessary resources for its implementation. In the case of the bridge, the steward will be a senior manager from the Ministry of Works.

3   *The project manager*: This is the person responsible for managing the implementation of the project, and monitoring and controlling the work to deliver the desired output at a time and a cost to make a profit for the parent organization. For the bridge, the project manager will be supplied by the construction contractor.

4   *The owner*: This is the person or organization who will own and operate the project's output during its life, and obtain the benefits to repay the investment in the project. This is an entirely post-project role. For the bridge, the owner may be the transport department of Jiangsu Province.

We have identified four roles. PRINCE2 (Office of Government Commerce, 2009a) calls them the project executive, the senior supplier, the project manager and the senior user, respectively. There may only in fact be two people – the sponsor and the owner may be the same person, and the steward and the project manager may be the same person. But as we saw above, the sponsor of the bridge was a department responsible for economic development, but the operator of the bridge is the transport department, and the steward is somebody from the Ministry of Works, but the project manager works for a contractor. There must be at least two people. The sponsor and owner come from the business, while the steward and project manager come from the technical department. Their focus is essentially different. The sponsor must also be an optimist, and shoot for the moon; whereas the steward must be a pessimist, and bring him or her back down to earth. That tension between the two leads to better solutions. If you only have an optimistic sponsor, you will aim for the impossible; if you only have a pessimistic steward, you will have nothing to fear except fear itself. The tension is good for business, leading to the best results.

We see there are four governance roles, whereas traditionally people have focused on one, the project manager. Although people first identified the need for the sponsor role over 20 years ago (Frame, 2003, first edition 1987; Turner, 2009, first edition 1993), it is only recently that it has become widely recognized. The sponsor is responsible for identifying the strategic objectives that the project should deliver for the organization; the project manager is responsible for focusing on the delivery of the project. Rodney Turner used to get frustrated with project managers who just wanted to get on with implementing the project, and not be involved with strategic decisions. Rodney would say, "No! No! No!" – the project manager should be involved in all those decisions. But having studied project governance he has changed his mind. Project management can be difficult and the project manager needs to be focused on the task at hand, leaving it to other people fulfilling other governance roles to:

- identify the business objectives;
- identify the required project outputs;
- identify the appropriate process to deliver these;
- identify the competencies required;
- assemble a team with those competencies.

The project manager's governance roles are:

- ensuring the project team are motivated to achieve the outcomes;
- ensuring risks and uncertainties are dealt with flexibly to achieve the outcomes;
- monitoring performance on the project and communicating progress to the client.

However, the sponsor and steward also have governance roles to ensure the project manager is suitably empowered to achieve those roles. The project manager should be aware of what the business need is, and what the desired project outcomes are and why they are appropriate. But he or she does not need to be involved in defining them, or agreeing changes to them.

At the organizational context level

The middle level of GoPM is at the organizational context level, which links the governance of the project to corporate governance. There are two key issues:

1 Defining the objectives of projects: by linking them to the objectives of the organization, through portfolio and program management, and through leadership and communication.
2 Defining the means of delivering projects: by developing enterprise-wide project management capability, which includes organizational learning and knowledge management and the development of individual competence.

Portfolio and program management

Peter Morris and Ashley Jamieson (2004) identify the key role of portfolios and programs in cascading corporate strategy down to project strategy and thereby linking project objectives to corporate objectives. They adopt the model developed by Rodney Turner (2009), shown in Figure 1.5. Although the concepts of program and portfolio management are not new (Turner and Speiser, 1993; Turner, 2009), it is only recently that their key role in linking project strategy to corporate strategy has been identified (Office of Government Commerce, 2007, 2009b; Project Management Institute, 2006a, b).

We like to keep our definitions simple and focus just on the key point. So we define a program as follows (Turner, 2009):

A program is a group of projects that contribute to a common objective.

Often, to achieve the desired outcome from a change requires several project outputs. Rodney Turner (2009) uses the example of the Malaysian Government developing a palm nut oil industry, which required them to develop several plantations, road and rail networks to get nuts from plantations to factories, factories to convert nuts to oil, and logistics networks to get oil to customers. In Figure 1.5, the corporate objective was to increase economic activity, and the portfolio objective was to develop a number of new industries. The program objective was to develop the palm nut oil industry, with several projects to deliver different components as just described. In Figure 1.3, the top level goal was increased economic activity, and the desired program outcome was the ability to make and sell palm nut oil. That required several project outputs including plantations and factories, and road, rail and logistics networks.

We can define a portfolio as follows (Turner, 2009):

A portfolio is a group of projects sharing common resources.

The common resources can be money, materials, people, data, technology, and so on. Portfolios can exist at several levels. Figure 5.1 shows a firm's investment portfolio, which is the sum total of all its investment activity. The investment portfolio can consist of large projects and programs, but also miscellaneous portfolios of small and medium-sized projects. When we discuss the sharing of money between projects in the investment portfolio below, small and medium-sized projects cannot compete alongside the large projects and programs. We define medium-sized projects as being one-tenth the size of large ones and small projects one-tenth the size of medium. The estimating error in estimating projects is 5 percent to 10 percent and so medium-sized projects are the same size as the estimating error in large projects and so cannot be seen in the noise of the large projects. They have to be treated separately, and similarly small projects need to be treated separately again because they cannot be seen in the noise of the medium-sized projects.

Are programs a special case of portfolios? Some people say they are; a program is a portfolio that happens to have a common objective. However, they have very different key features: a program has common outputs; a portfolio has common inputs. Sometimes the projects in a program also have common inputs; for instance

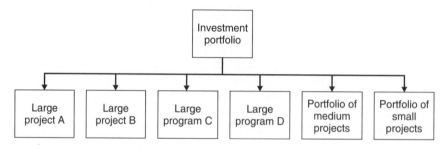

Figure 5.1 The investment portfolio

if you are developing a shopping center. But the projects in the palm nut oil industry have different inputs.

Governing the investment portfolio

There are five essential steps in governing the investment portfolio:

Step 1: Maintain a list of all projects, programs and portfolios in a project database.
Step 2: Monitor progress on all projects, programs and portfolios.
Step 3: Prioritize all projects, programs and portfolios and assign resources appropriately.
Step 4: Plan the resource needs of all projects and programs in the portfolio and coordinate the assignment of resources between them.
Step 5: Evaluate business benefits post implementation, to continuously improve selection and management procedures.

We call these "steps" which implies that one follows the other. But if you are doing portfolio management you do all five in parallel all of the time. However, if you are not doing portfolio management you tend to start at step 1 and work through in order.

In 1988 Rodney Turner worked with a famous food manufacturing company at their factory in the north-east of London. In the early 1980s the company had had more than 50 percent of market share for canned food in the UK. In 1988, their market share had fallen below 50 percent but they still had the largest market share. However, projecting a few years ahead, they were going to lose that. The company was trying to implement a new production line that was going to halve their cost per can leaving the factory. This had been planned for two and a half years. In 1988 it had been going four and a half and had at least six months to run. The company was losing market share and their key strategic project was 100 percent behind schedule. Rodney's client was the manager of a project to implement a material monitoring computer system to further improve the cost base. He kept trying to arrange meetings with the factory managers to discuss user needs, and they would cancel at the last minute because of a "production crisis." He couldn't get to meet with the users and so his project was going the same way as the new production line. First Rodney worked out the resource needs of those two large projects, and a third, the implementation of TQM. Those three projects required on average each week a day and a half of all factory managers' time for the next six months. So if they were working Monday to Friday on production, they were working Saturday and Sunday morning on their project activities. Next Rodney drew up an inventory of all the projects in the factory: there were 100. The three largest required a day and a half of factory managers' time each week, and there were 100 projects. This company had neither the means for doing their projects nor the means for monitoring progress.

Project inventory and progress

Steps 1 and 2 require the maintenance of an inventory of all projects, programs and portfolios, with progress shown on all projects. A traffic-light report (Figure 4.5) is a useful tool for listing the projects in a portfolio and showing their progress against identified key performance indicators. Figures 4.2 to 4.4 are useful tools for showing progress on individual projects from which the traffic light report can be compiled.

Prioritizing projects

To avoid the problems encountered by the food company it is necessary to prioritize projects and only admit to the portfolio projects for which there are enough resources to do them. This will be the responsibility of a project portfolio committee. At the level of the investment portfolio they typically meet every three months. At their meeting they are presented with a list of proposed projects, in rank order of prioritization. They admit projects to the portfolio up to the limit of money and other resources available to do them. Once they have reached the initial limit, they may look at the next two or three projects and ask if they are higher priority than projects already under way. If the answer is "yes," these current projects may be cancelled and the new projects admitted to the portfolio. Many of the projects not admitted to the portfolio will be discarded. However, for some it may be the decision this time around was borderline, or it may be there is reason to believe the priority will change in the future, and so some of the projects will be reconsidered at future meetings. The two main criteria for prioritizing projects will be benefit and risk (Figure 5.2). But other criteria may include:

- stakeholder commitment;
- process effectiveness;
- learning opportunity;
- type of project.

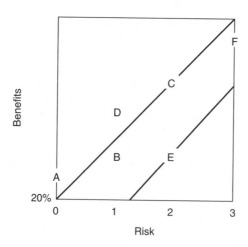

Figure 5.2 The benefits–risk plot

Paul Dinsmore (1999) also suggests you create portfolios for different types of investment projects:

- product and market development projects;
- capital expansion projects;
- operational improvements;
- strategic projects.

You can use a weighted average (or balanced score card) to prioritize projects. Weighted average assigns a weight (often on a scale of 1 to 3) to each criterion. Each project is then scored against each criterion (again often on a scale of 1 to 3), and the overall score calculated. In a balanced score card, the weights are fractional numbers and sum to 100 percent.

Table 5.1 shows an example of a company that has six projects or programs proposed, each costing 30 units. The company also has proposals for 60 projects of 3 units and 600 of 0.3 units. The total funds available are 300, against a totals demand of 540. The portfolio committee first has to decide how many of the large projects and programs to do. If it does three, there will be 210 units left over for the medium and small project portfolios; if it does four there will be 180 left over; and if it does five, there will be 150 left over. The company increases the hurdle rate of internal rate of return (IRR) by 3 percent for each unit of risk. So the six large projects and programs are plotted in Figure 5.2. We can see that projects A, D and C fall in the area where projects definitely are done. Since there are three, we can do all of them. Project E falls in the area where projects definitely are not done and so is discarded. We may also be able to afford one of B or F, but which one? They are on the same parallel; line and so are equally acceptable. Do we do the low risk operational improvement project or the high risk strategic project? That will depend on what view you take, but the other one can be reconsidered in three months' time.

Sharing resources between projects

The means of sharing resources between projects in a portfolio is now well understood. Up to about ten years ago, the approach people adopted was to maintain a gigantic plan of all their projects in one database. Each project was planned in detail, with their resource requirements, and the plans merged into a single

Table 5.1 Proposed projects in a portfolio

Project	Cost	IRR	Risk	Project type
Program A	$30 m	21%	0	Operational improvement
Program B	$30 m	22%	1	Operational improvement
Program C	$30 m	26%	2	Capital expansion
Project D	$30 m	24%	1	New product
Project E	$30 m	22%	2	New product
Project F	$30 m	28%	3	Strategic repositioning

meta-project plan. The computer was then asked to schedule all the project activities subject to the resource constraints. The problem was, you had to give the computer some rule for prioritizing one activity over another when a clash occurred. These rules are called heuristics. Having given the computer a rule, computers are dumb things; it will apply the rule absolutely, without question. That led to silly outcomes.

A different approach has been suggested for the past ten years, based on work done by Rodney Turner and Aaron Speiser (1992). There is a four-step process:

1   Each project is planned individually, and its resource requirements calculated.
2   Instead of merging all the project plans into a gigantic meta-plan, a rough-cut capacity plan is maintained. This is called the Master Project Schedule. In that plan, each project appears as a single activity, with a simplified resource requirement. That provides a very rough view (a rough-cut) of the resource requirement.
3   Projects are then moved, extended or deleted in the Master Project Schedule, to smooth out the resource requirements within the resource constraints. This will be done manually, with management control. This produces a rough resource balance, accurate enough for the purpose of deciding which projects can be done, and when they can start and finish. That gives each project a window of when it can start and finish, and what its resource availability is.
4   Each project is then managed within its start and finish date and resource availability. As long as the project manager can keep to those constraints, there is no need to refer back to the Master Project Schedule. If some disturbance occurs, the project is delayed, or another project requires additional resources, the response can be planned in the Master Project Schedule.

This is not easy, but if you are doing it you have some semblance of control. If you are not doing it, you are out of control, and have no way of responding to disturbances.

There are three roles involved in this process (Figure 5.3). New projects and programs are given to the portfolio director. He or she asks the project managers to plan the projects and calculate resource requirements. The portfolio director receives predictions of resource availability for resource managers and balances the projects in the rough-cut capacity plan. They should balance because only the right number of resources should have been admitted to the portfolio. The project managers are then given projects to manage within the time and resource windows they are given, and make requests for resources to the resource managers.

Post-project evaluation

The last step in the portfolio management process is to evaluate projects post-implementation. This is a key process in PRINCE2 (Office of Government Commerce, 2009a). The reason this is necessary is that without it people are

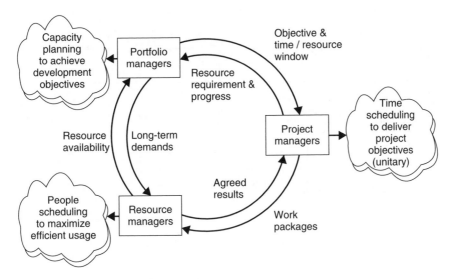

Figure 5.3 Sharing resources in a portfolio

encouraged to "lie" at step 3, to over-inflate the benefits of their projects and under-inflate the costs and risks. A post-project evaluation must be held on all projects, and people held accountable if their projects have failed to deliver the benefits, within the envelope of risk. This last phrase means project F above should deliver an internal rate of return of 20 percent, not 28 percent. Once the project is over there is no risk, so post-project it only needs to deliver the basic hurdle rate, not the higher rate used for project appraisal. This is an essential step in the means of monitoring progress to ensure the organization's objectives are achieved.

Types of program

There are three types of programs:

1   Once-through programs;
2   Cyclic programs;
3   Hybrid programs.

The once-through programs are very similar to large projects. All the project outputs need to be commissioned together because they are all needed to obtain the outcomes of the program. An example is Terminal 5 at Heathrow Airport. Outputs consisted of the main terminal building, the B pier, the baggage handling system, car parks, road access. In the terminal building there were shopping and other facilities that were treated as separate projects to the terminal itself. Most of the projects needed to be finished for the terminal to be commissioned. Some of the terminal facilities could be left for later, and in fact the C pier is being left for years later.

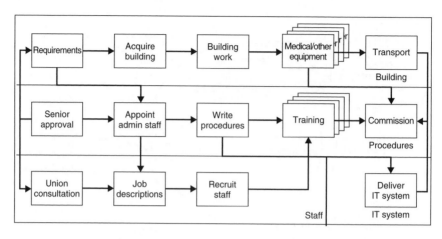

Figure 5.4 A map of projects in a program

With a once-through program it can be useful to draw a map of all the projects that make up the program. Figure 5.4 is such a map.

With a cyclic program, the projects are done in several cycles. For instance, with the palm nut oil industry, the plan may be to develop five plantations and six factories in three cycles. Two factories will be built in each cycle. Two plantations will be developed in the first two cycles and one in the third. Appropriate road and rail networks will be developed in each cycle. There are at least two advantages of the cyclic approach:

1   You get early benefits from the early cycles which can be used to pay for the later cycles, increasing the profitability of the program. In a project or once-through program, you have to spend all the money before commissioning the output and getting any returns. But in the cyclic program, you only spend part of the money before getting returns, improving your cash flow.
2   At the end of each cycle, you can revisit the definition of later cycles, and decide whether to do more or less than originally envisaged. For instance, at the end of the second cycle in the palm nut oil project you might decide it is going so well that you will develop a sixth plantation, or perhaps you will decide four is enough. Projects and once-through programs have what are said to be SMART objectives, Specific, Measurable, Achievable, Realistic and Time-lined. Cyclic programs have sMARt objectives. At the end of each cycle you can decide to do more or less, and move the end date forward or back. Cyclic sMARt programs are made up of SMART projects, so you can deliver very specific outputs while continuously revisiting the objectives of the program, and the end date.

Hybrid programs are a mixture of the two. Rodney Turner works at the University of the Basque Country in Bilbao. Next door is the Bilbao football stadium which is going to be rebuilt on a new site across the road. The site of the old stadium and surrounding area will then be redeveloped. The building of the new stadium is a once-through program, the redevelopment of the old site and surrounding area is a cyclic program.

Program life-cycle

All types of program follow a similar program life-cycle (Figure 5.5) (Office of Government Commerce, 2007), with four stages:

1   identify;
2   define;
3   govern;
4   dissolve.

However, during the *govern* stage cyclic programs also follow a three-stage embedded cycle:

1   plan;
2   deliver;
3   renew or dissolve.

Interestingly, the govern stage clearly shows the two governance roles:

•   the project and program managers responsible for delivering the project outputs and new capabilities (project outcomes);

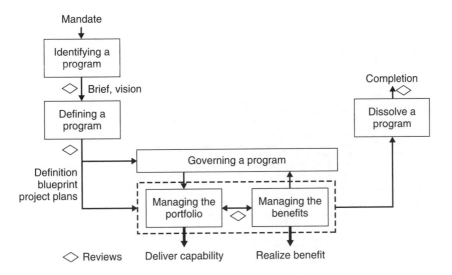

Figure 5.5 The program life-cycle

- the business change managers, working for the program owner, responsible for taking the outcomes and using them to achieve the desired benefit: this is significant in the cyclic programs because the benefits will be used to pay for the later stages.

Program governance roles

Figure 5.6 illustrates the program governance roles. These reflect the project governance roles in Figure 1.6. Figure 5.7 shows the roles in three columns. The middle column contains the program and project management roles, people responsible for designing and delivering the project outputs to achieve the desired outcomes. These reflect the roles in the bottom of Figure 1.6. The right-hand column shows the business roles, the people responsible for identifying the desired performance improvement and business goals, and acting as ambassadors to obtain the resources. They are also responsible for embedding the change as the project outputs are delivered. These roles reflect the top roles in Figure 1.6. The left-hand column is not reflected in Figure 1.6. This is the program office, responsible for establishing and enacting the monitoring and control mechanisms.

The project, program and portfolio management office (PMO)

The PMO is another area of project management with a long history (Turner, 2009, first edition 1993), but which has only recently entered the mainstream consciousness (Duggal, 2007; Office of Government Commerce, 2009c). Figure 5.7 shows

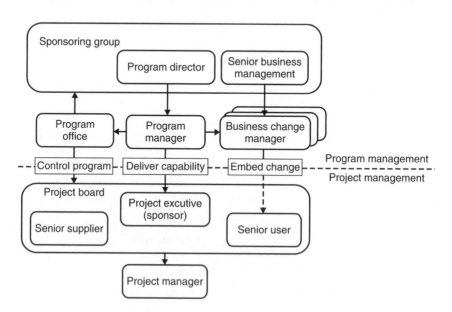

Figure 5.6 Program governance roles

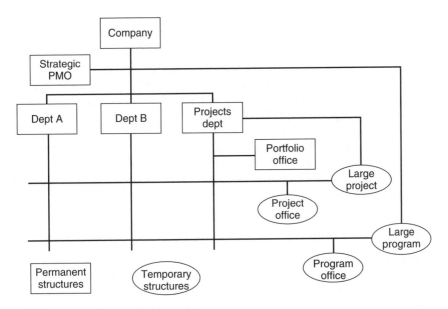

Figure 5.7 The project, program or portfolio office

that there are a number of different forms of PMO, some permanent structures in the organization and some temporary structures. The strategic project office is a permanent structure responding directly to the board, responsible for:

- setting policies and standards for project management in the organization;
- supporting project managers, and providing training and consultancy;
- aligning projects with corporate strategy;
- auditing projects and programs where necessary.

The portfolio office is also a permanent structure, perhaps in the projects department. It is responsible for:

- implementing the standards in a business unit;
- prioritizing projects and linking them to corporate strategy;
- prioritizing resources across projects within the portfolio;
- tracking progress of projects and programs in the portfolio.

The project and program office are temporary structures supporting a large project or program for as long as it exists. It is responsible for:

- supporting large complex projects or programs;
- implementing standards on the project or program;
- planning the project or program and managing progress;

- managing interfaces with clients and suppliers;
- managing materials;
- managing risk and issues.

The PMO, especially the permanent structures, should be implemented as a project, with a business plan, and a sponsor. A major reason why PMOs fail is they are implemented as a knee-jerk reaction to a problem, or worse, a temporary structure on a project or program morphs into the permanent structure when the organization finds it needs it as the project or program comes to an end. As with auditors, the personnel of the project office must not act as policemen or control freaks. They are there to support project and program managers, to take problems away from them, and provide them with administrative support. They must not overlay them with bureaucracy; that will cause the PMO to fail.

5.4 Developing project management capability

Organizational capability exists at several levels.

The organizational level: The organization needs to know how to manage projects in general. It needs to have a defined methodology of managing projects and to be able to train its project managers in the use of that methodology. (An organization may in fact have several methodologies, for different types of projects.) The organization's methodology needs to define several things:

1   *The project life-cycle*: The organization needs to have an understanding of the stages its projects go though from conception to completion. A standard life-cycle is concept, feasibility, design, execution and close-out, but the organization should develop a definition of the life-cycle appropriate to its types of projects. Organizations may also need to define a program life-cycle as above.
2   *The management life-cycle*: The organization needs to understand the management processes applied at each stage of the project life-cycle to deliver those stages. A typical project management life-cycle is:

 - plan the work;
 - organize the resources required to undertake the work;
 - implement by assigning work to people;
 - control the progress of the work.

3   *The project management functions*: The organization needs to know how to manage the functions of project management. These may be the six functions suggested by Rodney Turner (2009): scope, organization, quality, cost, time, and risk. Or they may be the nine body of knowledge areas defined by PMI® in its PMBoK (Project Management Institute, 2008): scope, integration, quality, cost, time, risk, HR, communication and procurement.

We describe the life-cycle and functional processes further in Sections 8.2 and 8.3.

The project level: The second level at which organizations need to be competent is at the project level. They need to be able to establish and manage individual projects to successfully deliver the objectives for that project, to achieve the business needs of the organization.

The technological level: The third level is the technological level. The organization needs to be able to use its technology to do the work of the project in the most efficient way possible.

Building and maintaining organizational competence

So how do organizations build and maintain organizational competence? We suggest four themes:

Procedures: These are the explicit statement of how the organization manages projects; they are the codification of its knowledge and competence. Through its procedures the organization defines how it manages projects. An organization may in fact need several sets of procedures for different types of projects. Also, the procedures should be treated like flexible guidelines not rigid rules. Every project is different. So an organization should have its project management procedures, which are a statement of good practice. However, at the start of every project, the manager should develop the project-specific version to say how this project will be managed, and that will become part of the quality plan for the project. Rodney Turner is a consultant in one engineering construction company that makes its apprentice project managers follow the procedures to the letter, but will not let someone manage a project on their own until they know how to adapt the procedures appropriately to meet the needs of individual projects. Procedures are described further in Section 8.4.

Project reviews: It is through project reviews that an organization learns how it is doing on individual projects, but also learns how to improve its project management procedures and processes. There are several types of review:

- audits: these are reviews conducted by people external to the project team;
- health-checks: these are reviews conducted by the project team on themselves;
- project control reviews: these are reviews conducted as part of the normal control cycle of the project, including end-of-stage reviews.

Benchmarking: It is important for the organization to know how it is performing compared to other people undertaking similar projects. This is the purpose of benchmarking. The organization gathers data about its project performance and compares it to organizations doing similar projects. It is relatively easy to compare project data with other people in the same parent company. It is more difficult to compare data with other companies, especially competitors.

Project management community: Through the project management community the organization develops its implicit or tacit knowledge. The project management community is an important part of the organization's learning processes, where apprentice project managers are trained and mentored. An effective community will also arrange events where project managers can meet and share experiences. Typically a meeting is arranged once every three months. There are perhaps one or two lectures lasting 90 minutes, followed by socializing. Project managers meet. Perhaps at some future time if a project manager has a problem, he or she will remember discussing a similar problem with a colleague, and can contact the colleague to discuss it further.

Organizational project management maturity

An organization's ability to deliver its projects successfully to achieve business benefit is often defined as its project management maturity. Many models of organizational project management maturity have been developed (see, for instance, Gareis and Huemann, 2007; Project Management Institute, 2003). Many models are based on the Capability Maturity Model developed by the Carnegie-Mellon Institute in the United States for information systems development (Paulk *et al.*, 1995). This model defines five levels of maturity:

Level 1 – Initial: The organization has no defined process for project management. It uses ad-hoc processes with no consistency.

Level 2 – Repeatable: The organization starts to develop individual processes for how it manages the project management functions. It may define how it manages scope, quality, cost, time, or risk for instance. It begins to develop the project management community and give project managers guidance on how to apply the embryonic processes.

Level 3 – Defined: The individual processes become combined into a set of procedures for project management, defining holistically how the organization manages projects. The project management community is developed to provide project managers with group support.

Level 4 – Managed: Through the review process, lessons are learnt and metrics gathered. These are fed back into the procedures to continuously improve them. As further metrics are gathered project performance can be benchmarked against other organizations.

Level 5 – Optimized: The procedures are continuously improved and defects patched. Nirvana is achieved.

You will notice the four themes defined above are at play here, with procedures and the project management community dominating at levels 2 and 3, and reviews and benchmarking dominating at levels 4 and 5.

The value of increasing maturity

It costs money to achieve increasing organizational project management maturity. Is it worthwhile? Work done at the University of California in Berkeley (Ibbs and Reginato, 2002) show that increasing project management maturity can lead to substantial improvement in cost and schedule performance. (Cost performance index, CPI, and schedule performance index, SPI, are defined in Chapter 2.). In more mature organizations on average projects cost less, and deliver their expected benefits earlier, leading to performance improvement. Performance improvement of 30 percent or more can be achieved from increasing maturity, but it comes at a cost. You can define a project management return on investment (PM ROI) where:

PM ROI = (Annual spend on projects * Efficiency gain from increasing maturity) / Cost of achieving that gain

One problem is that increasing maturity is a learning curve. The efficiency gain of going from maturity level N to N + 1 is half that of going from N – 1 to N, while the cost of achieving the increased maturity is double. So the PM ROI of going from level N to N + 1 is one quarter that of going from N – 1 to N. For many organizations with moderate annual spend on projects it is just not worthwhile going beyond maturity level 3. It is only large project-based organizations with substantial project spend for whom it is worthwhile achieving maturity levels 4 and 5.

Bill Ibbs and Justin Reginato (2002) also discovered that with increasing maturity the cost of project management at first rises and then falls.

- For organizations with maturity level 1 the cost of project management was between 2 percent and 4 percent of the cost of the project. They are not doing very much of it and they are not doing it very well.
- For organizations with maturity level 3 the cost of project management was between 2 percent and 10 percent of the cost of the project. They are doing much more project management. They are doing it well and it is delivering benefit, but it is taking a lot of effort to get it right.
- For organizations with maturity level 5 the cost of project management was back to between 2 percent and 4 percent of the cost of the project. They are still doing it well, but are becoming very clever at it.

This is an apparent competency trap, as organizations on low maturity find that increasing maturity requires more project management effort, and they think that cost is not worthwhile. However, it is worthwhile as that increased project management effort repays dividends in the form of better performance (Thomas and Mullaly, 2008). Further, having achieved a maturity level 3, an organization can work on trying to reduce its cost of project management, to become more slick at project management, trying to ensure the cost of project management is closer to the 2 percent than the 10 percent. If increasing maturity is not worthwhile, reducing the cost of project management becomes the focus of improved project performance.

Achieving capability improvement

We suggest a four-step process for achieving capability improvement:

1 *Variation:* New ideas are created, sometimes by deliberate problem solving and purposeful creativity, sometimes by random occurrences and fortuitous happenstance.

2   *Selection:* Through a review process, good, successful new ideas are chosen for reuse.
3   *Retention:* Those ideas chosen for reuse are stored in the organization's memory where they can be used by people in the organization.
4   *Distribution:* Ideas are distributed from the organization's memory to people working on projects, who may be working at some distance from the center.

The first three steps in this process were originally suggested in the evolution literature to explain the evolution of species. New features (genes) in species occur by random variation. Successful features (genes) are selected by survival of the fittest, and are then stored in the memory (the gene pool). The three-step process was later adopted by the management learning literature to explain learning in organizations. New ideas arise in organizations, sometimes by chance, but sometimes purposefully with people deliberately trying new ideas. Good ideas are selected for retention, and those ideas selected for reuse are stored in the organization's memory.

In a functional organization it ends there. Knowledge is stored in the function for reuse by people working in the function. People's careers are limited to one function, climbing the ladder up the functional silo. As their career develops in the function, they are exposed to the retained knowledge in the function, where it is available for them to draw on locally. It is different in project-based organizations. New ideas occur on projects which come to an end; so they must be captured and transferred to the function to be stored. People also work on projects away from the functional center sometimes geographically quite distant. In order for the good new ideas to be used, they must be distributed somehow from the functional memory banks to people working on projects as new projects start. Thus distribution of the knowledge is an important fourth step in knowledge management process in a project-based organization, which is not necessary in a functional organization.

Top management support

We cannot stress enough the importance of top management support in improving maturity and enterprise-wide project management capability through innovation and learning. Without senior management support junior people will either fear making changes or not take the initiative. A manager in IBM told Rodney Turner that junior people may avoid making honest reports in project reviews for fear of upsetting middle managers. Particularly they fear that if they make an honest report it may put their boss in a poor light. Organizations must learn not to shoot the messenger, and the support of senior management will help junior people to make honest reports.

Some people may not make changes because they have done something a certain way for a long time, and they just don't want to try new things. They are locked into a competency trap. They may fear that if they try something new and it goes wrong they will lose their job. Senior management need to make it clear that it is the other way around, if they *don't* try something new they will lose their job. If they aren't occasionally making mistakes people will be asking why they aren't trying new things. Top management need to make it clear that they want to see new innovative ways of working.

5.5 Reviews, health checks, audits, and benchmarking

In the discussion we have seen the importance of reviews, health checks, audits and benchmarking. Reviews and health checks are checks made by the project team on themselves. An audit is a check made by an external group. Benchmarking is a comparison with the performance of external projects.

Reviews

A review is a normal check of project progress or project performance conducted according to a predetermined schedule. Reviews may be calendar-driven or event-driven.

Calendar-driven reviews: These are conducted as part of the normal control cycle (Turner, 2009). Current project performance data is gathered, analyzed and converted into reports, for the project manager and project team to control progress and for senior management, particularly the sponsor.

Event driven reviews: These are normally held at the achievement of a project milestone, or at the end of a stage. End-of-stage reviews are described further in Section 9.3.

Health-checks

Health-checks are ad-hoc reviews, conducted by the project team, to do a once-off assessment of the health of their project or of the project context. Rodney Turner (2009) suggests you may conduct two types of health-check: project management capability health-checks, and project performance health-checks.

Project management capability health-checks

These are an assessment of the project management capability of the organization. Rodney Turner (2009) calls them "projectivity health checks," through which an organization tries to assess whether its project management procedures meet best practice. Through a series of questions which force the organization to assess its procedures, it will assess whether they meet its needs for project effectiveness. Organizations should be competent in three things:

1   their application of the project life-cycle, including go/no-go/go-back decisions at end-of-stage reviews;
2   their application of the project management life-cycle;
3   their management of the project management functions or knowledge areas.

So to assess its project management capability, the organization should develop a set of questions (Turner, 2009), which ask:

PROJECT LIFE-CYCLE

- How well do we initiate projects?
- How well do we make the decision to proceed to feasibility?
- How well do we conduct feasibility studies?
- How well do we make the decision to proceed to design?
- How well do we plan and design projects?
- How well do we conduct investment appraisal and decide to proceed to execution?
- How well do we plan, execute and control projects?
- How well do we take the decision to proceed to closure?
- How well do we finish the work, commission the asset and achieve the benefit?
- How well do we conduct post-completion reviews?

PROJECT MANAGEMENT LIFE-CYCLE

- How well do we plan projects?
- How well do we assign roles and responsibilities for undertaking projects?
- How well do we assign resources to projects?
- How well do we control progress on projects?

TOOLS AND TECHNIQUES

- Do we use appropriate tools and techniques on our projects?
- Do we tailor our procedures appropriately to the size and type of projects?
- How well do we manage scope?
- How well do we manage project organization?
- How well do we manage cost?
- How well do we manage time?
- How well do we manage quality?
- How well do we manage risk?
- How well do we manage communication?
- How well do we manage project procurement?
- How well do we manage human resources?
- How well do we manage anything else that is important?

What we suggest is that you ask people from different departments to complete the questionnaires and look for areas where:

- they agree you are weak;
- they have differences of opinion about whether you are weak or strong.

Project performance health-check

This is a check of the performance of a project. The team step back from the project coal face for half a day or so to check that it has been properly set up, and that all the relevant controls are in place and are being properly used, so that the project is progressing to a likely successful outcome. It is very easy, once you are in the thick of a project, to miss simple problems. You are so busy working on the project that you can't think about whether it is being done properly. You might even think that you don't have time to step back from the coal face for even a short time to consider how you are doing. But it is better to spend the time to discover a mistake that might cost weeks or months, than to rush headlong only to discover the mistake when it is too late. Health checks should be conducted about a quarter of the way into the design and execution stages, to check that they have been properly established and that they are progressing to a likely successful conclusion. To conduct a health-check on an individual project, we suggest you develop a questionnaire to help you investigate key points (Turner, 2009). The questionnaires may cover issues like:

- Are the project objectives understood and accepted by all?
- Are the success criteria and key performance indicators understood and accepted by all?
- Are the success factors understood and accepted by all?
- Have appropriate tools and techniques been adopted to achieve the success factors and success criteria?
- Has the project been well planned?
- Are the tools and techniques being properly applied?
- Is the project being well controlled, with the right progress data being gathered and analyzed in the right way, and useful reports produced to control progress?

Again the questionnaire should be completed by all project team members, and other people including the users and other stakeholders. You should focus on:

- where team members disagree about the answers;
- where they all agree the project is not being well managed.

Audits

Audits are essentially the same as health-checks, except they are conducted by external, independent auditors. It is useful for the project team to step back and consider how they are doing, but because they are close to the problem, they can still miss a serious mistake. If a project is highly critical to an organization, of high strategic value and a significant commitment of (financial) resources, the parent organization may want to ensure it has been properly set up and so will invite independent auditors to take a look. However, it is essential that the approach of the auditors is that they are there to help the project team achieve a successful outcome, not that they are there to check up on the project team. If they adopt the latter approach, they can meet considerable resistance from the project team, and a reluctance to help. If however, they adopt the former approach, and work with the project team in a spirit of partnership to help the project team achieve a successful outcome, then the audit process can be highly valuable.

Some post-completion audits are conducted to find out why a failed project failed so catastrophically. In that case the auditors are there to check up on the project team, and may only meet with resistance. But if the project team failed so badly, they may be feeling guilty and so may offer little resistance. We have conducted post-completion audits where members of the project team were trying to blame each other, or senior management, so collaborated with the auditor in trying to blame each other. Often they were unaware of their own contribution to the failure, so in doing that condemned themselves as well.

Conducting a project management audit

Rodney Turner (2009) suggests a seven-step process for conducting an audit:

1   Conduct interviews.
2   Analyze data.
3   Sample management reports.
4   Compare against standards of best practice.
5   Repeat steps 1 to 4 as necessary.
6   Identify strengths and weaknesses.
7   Define opportunities for improvement.

Martina Huemann (2004), based on more recent experience, also suggests a seven-step process:

1   Analyze the situation.
2   Plan the audit.
3   Prepare for the audit.
4   Conduct the audit.
5   Generate the report.
6   Present the results to the project owner.
7   Terminate the audit.

She suggests that Step 4, the audit itself, consists of four sub-processes:

4.1 Analyze documentation, including control data and control reports.
4.2 Conduct interviews with the project team as necessary.
4.3 Observe the project team in action.
4.4 Ask the project team to assess their own performance, perhaps against a health-check.

Benchmarking

Benchmarking is essentially different from reviews, audits and health-checks. The emphasis of those is to determine how the project is being managed in comparison to the organization's standards of best practice, whether it is financially viable, and to learn from successes and failures to improve the organization's standards. The emphasis of benchmarking is to compare the organization's standards and its project performance to industry current best practice. (We say industry "current best practice." Hopefully there is always a better practice, which we can learn and improve. But we also want to know how we are doing against the people who are currently achieving the highest standards of performance.) Benchmarking may be quantitative or qualitative.

Qualitative: In qualitative benchmarking, the organization compares its standard procedures against industry standards. This is closely linked to project management maturity. Maturity models effectively provide questionnaires for qualitative benchmarking.

Quantitative: In quantitative benchmarking, an organization compares its project performance against other projects from the industry. It doesn't compare against individual projects, but against the mean and standard deviation of a collection of projects.

Qualitative benchmarking

In benchmarking you are trying to assess your performance against industry best-practice. Martina Huemann (2004) suggests there are four steps in benchmarking:

1   Understand the detail of your own processes.
2   Analyze the processes of others.
3   Compare your performance with that of the others.
4   Close any gaps identified.

As we have said, project management maturity models provide a ready-made set of questions to help you both analyze your own processes and that of others. However, many benchmarking communities also exist.

In comparing your performance it is common to prepare a spider-web diagram (Figure 5.8). First you plot your own performance, against parameters that you consider important on a scale, say 1 to 6. Then you plot the performance of others, the datum. The gaps will be obvious. The datum may also represent the standard you need to achieve to achieve the next level of maturity. One slight problem with comparing with the standards of maturity is the maturity models require you to achieve a defined standard against all the parameters, regardless of your own needs as an organization. Against one or two parameters you may not need to achieve the standard defined, and against one or two others you may feel you need to achieve a higher standard. So conducting your own benchmarking exercise enables you to tailor the standards to your own needs. Against that, the maturity models provide a ready-made set of questions.

Quantitative benchmarking

It is sometimes possible to benchmark project performance against industry databases. For instance, the European Construction Institute and the Construction

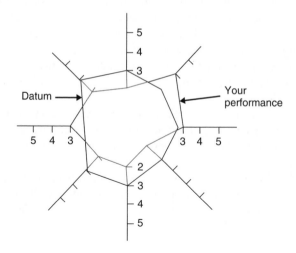

Figure 5.8 Spider web diagrams

Industry Institute maintain a benchmarking database. Members can enter project performance data for individual projects and compare their performance to all the projects currently in the database.

   This does not give members direct comparison of their projects to their competitors, but they are able to see how they are performing in comparison to industry norms. Members are then able to improve their performance in areas where they are weak.

5.6 Project contract management

Theories of contract procurement, contract management and contract law are much older than the science of project management. However, as project management developed during the mid-twentieth century it was realized that good project contract management could make a significant contribution to improved project performance, and so project contract management became an area for focus in research in project management. Nigel Smith (2003) says that effective project contract management can lead to an 8 percent improvement in project performance, an amount greater than the profit margin of many companies in the construction industry. Sir Michael Latham (1994) in a report for the British government suggested that the effective combination of project procurement and project planning and control can lead to a 30 percent improvement in project performance. For a developing country, or for a firm, a 30 percent improvement in project performance means it can increase economic growth or annual turnover by one third.

   In this section we look at the development of project contract procurement over the last 25 years. But we would like to start with four quotations. The first is by Harold Coase, a Nobel laureate in economics. He was asked by the US government to look into appropriate forms of contract for US government contracts and in his final report said: "The relevant comparisons are with feasible alternatives, all of which are flawed." That is, in any situation there is no perfect solution for choosing a form of contract, and there is definitely no form of contract that works in all circumstance. When choosing a form of contract you need to recognize the strengths and weaknesses of different forms and try to achieve the best match to your project. Having chosen a form of contract you need to recognize its weaknesses and try to minimize their impact on your project. But if you have chosen the correct form, the strengths will far outweigh the weaknesses.

> The problem of organizing [is] seen as one of transforming a conflict (political) system into a cooperative (rational) one. A conflict system is one in which individuals have objectives that are not jointly consistent. It organizes through exchanges between strategic actors. A cooperative system is one in which individuals act rationally in the name of a common objective.
>
> (Levitt and March quoted in Turner, 2003, p. 35)

The aim of organizing anything should be getting the parties to work together in cooperation, working towards a common objective. In a project, there is no such thing as a win–lose game; it is either win–win or lose–lose. If one party tries to win at the other's expense, all that will happen is both will lose, one will just lose more than the other. The project contract is the governance structure through which we organize our project if we wish to involve external parties. The aim of the contract should be to get jointly consistent objectives between the client and the contractor, and have them work together in cooperation. Unfortunately, so often parties to project contracts think it is smart to win at the other party's expense. If you think about it for five seconds you will realize that is stupid. The project is a coupled system: what is good for the project is good for all parties to the contract. What is seemingly good for one party and bad for another is bad for the project and therefore bad for everybody.

The last two quotations contain a related idea and are commonly attributed to the nineteenth-century British left-wing economist and philosopher, John Ruskin:

> It is unwise to pay too much for a contract, but it is worse to pay too little. When you pay too little, you sometimes lose everything, because the thing you bought was incapable of doing the thing it was bought to do. The common law of business balance prohibits paying a little and getting a lot. It can't be done. If you deal with the lowest bidder, it is well to add something for the risk you run, and if you do that you will have enough to pay for something better.

> There is scarcely anything in the world that some man cannot make a little worse, and sell a little more cheaply. The person who buys on price alone is this man's lawful prey.

Don't work with the contractor that gives you the cheapest price, work with the contractor that gives you best value for money. In the public sector and in the water, energy, transport and telecommunication (WETT) industries, European law actually demands the client chooses the contractor that gives the best value for money and *not* the cheapest. We find it sad that these two quotations are about 150 years old and we don't seem to have moved on.

The traditional form of contract

Figure 5.9 illustrates the traditional form of contract used in Europe for hundreds of years. This is the basis of the UK's Institution of Civil Engineers Standard Form of Contract (Institution of Civil Engineers, 1995), and also that of FIDIC. Under this form of contract, it is assumed the client is naïve, they are not able to design or manage the construction of the asset for themselves. They are an operating company skilled in operating the asset, but with no knowledge of its design or construction. So they use an engineer or consultant to give them expert advice. It is assumed the engineer first designs the asset, and then manages its construction. It is also assumed that the engineer does not have the ability to do the actual construction work. So it is necessary to employ a construction contractor (and sub-contractors) to do the actual construction work. The engineer does the procurement to appoint the contractor, and manages their work on site. So the engineer switches from being designer to project and contract manager.

Under this form of contract, the construction contractor is rewarded on a remeasurement basis; that is they are paid according to the amount of work they do using a pre-agreed schedule of rates to work out the value of the work. In the worst cases, the engineer is paid a fee that is a percentage of the out-turn cost of the project. In better cases they are paid according to the amount of work they do on a remeasurement basis, or they are paid a fee that is a percentage of the original estimate, with a bonus if the project is finished early or under-spent. This form of contract works very well for reasonably low risk projects, where:

*   the design can be completed before construction starts;
*   there is likely to be little change in the design during construction work.

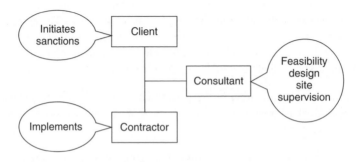

Figure 5.9 The traditional form of contract

If the design can be completed before construction starts the engineer's role can change quite clearly from being designer to project manager. But if design and construction overlap, then the engineer's roles overlap, and there may be a conflict of interest. In their role as project manager, it is their interest to hide their mistakes as designer. Also, as you will gather above, we do not like a payment mechanism whereby their fee is a percentage of out-turn cost. Then, the person responsible for controlling cost is motivated to spend as much as possible. We much prefer payment mechanisms based on a percentage of the target cost with a bonus.

Three dimensions

The traditional form works well on simple projects where the design is unlikely to change, but does not work well on more complex projects where changes are more likely. To that end various other forms of contract have been developed. The Institution of Civil Engineers has captured some of these in an alternative standard form of contract, the Engineering and Construction Contract, sometimes called the New Engineering Contract (Institution of Civil Engineers, 1995). The alternative forms of contract tend to be based on three dimensions:

1   the scope of supply;
2   management responsibility;
3   the pricing mechanism.

Scope of supply

This usually relates to how much of the project life-cycle the contractor is responsible for. Recognizing the conflict of interest above where the design and construction may overlap, or the design may change during construction, the next simplest form of contract is design and build. One contractor is responsible for both the design of the asset and its construction. In its simplest form it is assumed the one contractor will do the design and most of the construction, using only a limited number of sub-contractors, so little procurement is necessary. This form tends to be used in the building industry. A somewhat more extensive form is Engineering–Procurement–Construction (EPC), which tends to be used on the process plant industry. The engineer is responsible for design, procurement and managing work on site, but with a pricing mechanism that now makes them responsible for the performance of the contractors on site, so removing the conflict of interest mentioned above. A specific form of this contract is the so-called lump sum turn key contract. The EPC contractor is paid a fixed price for the delivery of the asset, and the contractor takes total responsibility so at the end of the project figuratively hands the client a key, so they can open the door, turn on the ignition and drive the new asset away. Under concession arrangements, the contractor is responsible for the project from feasibility through to operation. A concession will typically last 30 years, after which the asset is decommissioned or handed over to the client for further operation. A concession has the added advantage of encouraging the contractor to deliver lowest life-cycle cost, not lowest capital cost, giving the owner better value for money.

Management structure

Management contracts define the project management responsibility of the contractor. The contractor may just be responsible for managing the construction work on site, or may be responsible for managing the design and construction process. The management contractor is usually responsible for procurement. Three main forms are described:

1   *Construction management:* Under this form the contractor is responsible for appointing the main construction contractor and sub-contractors, and managing their work on site. However, under construction management, the site contractors and sub-contractors contract with the client for their work. So the construction management contractor is responsible for managing work on site, but is not responsible for performance of the site contractors and sub-contractors. The latter are usually paid by the owner on remeasurement basis, and the construction management contractor is paid a percentage fee with a bonus.

2   *Management contracting:* This is similar to construction management, except the site contractors and sub-contractors now contract with the management contractors, and so the management contractor is responsible for their performance. This work will usually be done on a fixed price basis, but may be done on a remeasurement basis. If it is done on a remeasurement basis, the management contractor will be paid according to the amount of work performed and they will be responsible for paying the site contractors and sub-contractors.

3   *Design and management:* This is the same as management contracting, except the management contractor is also responsible for managing the design contractor.

An important principle in these forms of contract is the party responsible for appointing a contractor or sub-contractor should be responsible for their performance. So under management contracting, the client should not insist that the construction management contractor use a certain sub-contractor and then make the management contractors responsible for their performance. Likewise, under construction management, the construction management contractor should not insist that a certain sub-contractor be used and then make the client responsible for their performance. The contractor will do the procurement but the client must approve the appointment of all sub-contractors and sub-contractors.

Terms of payment

There are three fundamental terms of payment:

1   *Fixed price:* Here the contractor is paid an amount for doing the work fixed by agreement before work starts. The work can be defined in one of three basic ways:

- by cardinal points: that is the functionality the asset is required to deliver;
- by a schematic design;
- by a detail design.

The latter two can lead to uncertainties in the scope of work, leading to claims and variations, and making the contract virtually remeasurement.

2   *Remeasurement:* The contractor is rewarded according to the amount of work done, but the work is priced according to a pre-agreed schedule of rates. Thus the client takes on the risk of the amount of work, but the contractor takes on the risk of the productivity of their workforce and the rate of use of materials. If the design can be done very accurately before works start, this contract becomes virtually fixed price, and that is the assumption behind the traditional form of contract. If the design is very uncertain the contract becomes virtually cost plus.

3   *Cost plus:* The contractor is paid what they spend plus a profit margin. Thus the client takes the risk of both the amount of work and the productivity of the work-force. The profit margin can be calculated either as a percentage of the out-turn cost or as a percentage of the target cost. The latter can be combined with an incentive. You will gather from the above that we do not like the profit margin calculated as a percentage of out-turn. Many years ago Rodney Turner worked with a large company who said that their building maintenance jobs were managed by architects working for cost plus percentage fee. Rodney asked if they ever felt their architects were ripping them off. They said all the time. So he then asked what sanction they had. They said they put the architects on a black-list of banned architects. Rodney asked if they were running out of architects to use. They said they took them off the black-list after two years.

Figure 5.10 shows the classic view of risk sharing on projects, with the pricing mechanism varying from remeasurement to fixed price. (This ignores cost plus.) As you move from remeasurement to fixed price you transfer risk from the client to

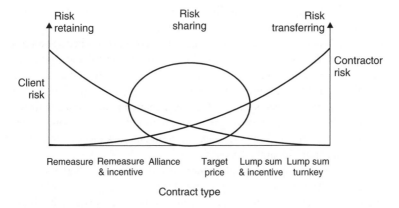

Figure 5.10 Risk sharing with different forms of contract

the contractor. In the middle, this picture shows two further pricing mechanisms, target price and alliance. We discuss alliances briefly below.

Contract strategy

You need to choose a form of contract that suits the needs of your project. Choosing a contract type based on the three dimensions above is the process of contract strategy and selection. Many different authors suggest different ways of developing your contract strategy. Rodney Turner (2003) developed a model based on who controls the risk. There are three possibilities:

1   *Client controls the risk*: If the client controls the risk, it probably lies in the definition or design of the asset. Then some form of remeasurement is best. If the project is relatively simple, the traditional form of contract works well. If it is more complex, then construction management is best.
2   *Contractor controls the risk*: If the contractor controls the risk, then it lies in the method of doing the work, and some form of fixed price is best. For simple projects, design and build is best. For more complex projects then you require management contracting, EPC or lump sum turnkey.
3   *Both control the risk*: If both control the risk, then it lies in both the design and definition of the product and in the method of doing the work. For simpler projects then target price or prime contracting are suggested. For more complex projects, alliancing is required.

Partnering and alliancing

From the 1970s to the present day, there has been a shift in attitude to risk sharing on project contracts.

*   In the 1970s the attitude was to dump risk down the contract chain, from client, to contractor to sub-contractor. The problem is you may take a risk the client can do something about controlling and give it to a contractor who can only allow a contingency, and charge it back to the client.
*   In the 1980s people started saying you should assign risk where it can be controlled. Give risk the client can control to the client, and risk the contractor can control to the contractor. On a fixed price contract the client may retain some risk, and on a remeasurement the contractor may retain some. The problem is that projects are coupled systems; making a change in one area can impact on another. The client may be trying to reduce their risk and increasing contractor A's, and contractor A trying to reduce theirs and increasing contractor B's, and so on. You cannot separate the risks.
*   So in the 1990s, people adopted partnering and alliancing where risk is shared on projects. As we said above, if the risk is all the client's you can use remeasurement, if it is all the contractor's you can use fixed price, but where it is shared you need to use partnering and alliancing (Scott, 2001).

Under partnering and alliancing the client and main contractors form a partnership, and work together to achieve the best outcome for the project as a whole, not just for their part of it. So although a particular risk may be under the control of the client or one of the contractors, in selecting a risk response strategy they need to do what is best for the project as a whole. That might require contractor B to take an increase in their risk, to achieve a bigger reduction in the client's and contractor A's risk. All the parties work together in partnership to do what is best for the project as a whole, that is, they work together rationally to achieve mutually consistent goals. The client and contractors share any savings made from the risk reduction according to previously agreed rules so they are all compensated for working together in this way.

That takes us back to where we started. On all contracts the client and contractors must work together to achieve mutually consistent objectives. However the precise way of doing that will depend where control of the risk lies:

- if the risk is on the design of the product, the client controls the risk and they take responsibility for it;
- if the risk lies in the method of doing the work, the contractor controls the risk and they take responsibility for it;
- if the risk lies in both the design of the product and the method of doing the work, the partnership can be formalized in an alliance.

But always the client and contractor should work together to achieve mutually consistent results.

5.7 But where is the green parrot?

When Rodney Turner's son Edward was a young child, they had a book called *Where is the Green Parrot?* This book had quite detailed pictures on each recto page, and on the facing page was text describing the picture. Hidden in each picture was a green parrot, and the last line of the text on each page was the question, "But where is the green parrot?" That really is a metaphor for projects. A consequence of the Optimization School and its systems focus is the project is treated like a machine operated by androids. As long as you adopt the right tools and apply them in the right way, the project is supposed to work perfectly, just like a well oiled machine. The people are not important. You wonder where they are. Where is the green parrot? We have seen the people. In Section 4.4 we showed that a consequence of this systems focus is that the project manager's contribution to project success is often overlooked. But we showed how the project manager is a significant success factor on projects. And in this chapter we discussed the need for contracts to motivate the contractors to achieve the client's objectives. But often organizations are governed for the benefit of the managers, or even just the shareholders, and not of the people working in the organization. However, we saw in the last chapter that the satisfaction of the project team is both a success criterion and a success factor, and so managing the satisfaction of the people working on projects is an important part of project success. We need to find the green parrot and make sure it is happy.

References

Association for Project Management, 2004, *Directing Change: A guide to governance of project management*, Association for Project Management (APM), High Wycombe, UK. Retrieved on June 15, 2007 from http://www.apm.org.uk/Governance2.asp

Briner, W., Grundy, A., Tyrell, F., and Turner, J,R., 1996, "Case studies from the insurance service industry," in Turner, J.R., Grude, K.V., and Thurloway, L. (eds), *The Project Manager as Change Agent*, McGraw-Hill, London.

Carroll, G.R., 1995, "On the organization ecology of Chester I. Barnard," in Williamson, O.E. (ed.), *Organization Theory: From Chester Barnard to the present and beyond*, Oxford University Press, New York.

Clarke, T., 2004, "The stakeholder corporation: A business philosophy for the information age," in Clarke, T. (ed.), *Theories of Corporate Governance: The philosophical foundations of corporate governance*, Routledge, London.

Cleland, D.I., and King, W.R., 1983, *Systems Analysis and Project Management*, 3rd edition, McGraw-Hill, New York.

Dinsmore, P., 1999, *Winning in Business with Enterprise Project Management*, AMACOM, New York.

Duggal, J.S., 2007, "The project, programme or portfolio office," in Turner, J.R. (ed.), *The Gower Handbook of Project Management*, 4th edition, Gower, Aldershot.

Frame, J.D., 2003, *Managing Projects in Organizations*, 3rd edition, Jossey Bass, San Francisco.

Gareis, R., and Huemann, M., 2007, "Project management competences in the project-oriented organization," in J.R. Turner (ed), *The Gower Handbook of Project Management*, 4th edition, Gower, Aldershot.

Hodgson, D., and Cicmil, S., 2006, "Are projects real? The PMBoK and the legitimation of project management knowledge," in Hodgson, D., and Cicmil, S. (eds), *Making Projects Critical*, Palgrave Macmillan, Basingstoke, 29–50.

Huemann, M., "Improving quality in projects and programmes," in Morris, P.W.G. and Pinto, J.K. (eds), *The Wiley Guide to Managing Projects*, Wiley, New York.

Ibbs, C.W., and Reginator, J., 2002, *Quantifying the Value of Project Management*, Project Management Institute, Newtown Square, PA.

Institution of Civil Engineers, 1995, *The Engineering and Construction Contract*, 2nd edition, Thomas Telford, London.

Jensen, M.C., 2000, *The Theory of the Firm: Governance, residual claims, and organizational forms*, Harvard University Press, Cambridge, MA.

Latham, M., 1994, *Constructing the Team: Final report of the government/industry review of procurement and contractual arrangements in the UK construction industry*, The Stationery Office, London.

Lundin, R.A., and Söderholm, A., 1995, "A theory of the temporary organization," *Scandinavian Journal of Management*, **11**(4), 437–455.

Morris, P., and Jamieson, A., 2004, *Translating Corporate Strategy into Project Strategy: Achieving corporate strategy through project management*, Project Management Institute, Newtown Square, PA.

Office of Government Commerce, 2007, *Managing Successful Programs*, 2nd edition, The Stationery Office, London.

——, 2009a, *Managing Successful Projects with PRINCE 2*, 5th edition, The Stationery Office, London.

——, 2009b, *Portfolio Management Guide,* final public consultation draft, Cabinet Office, London.

——, 2009c, *P3O: Portfolio, Programme and Project Office*, The Stationery Office, London.

Paulk, M.C., Weber, C.V., Curtis, B., and Chrissis, M.B., 1995, *The Capability Maturity Model: Guidelines for improving the software process*, Addison-Wesley Longman, Boston.

Project Management Institute, 2003, *Organizational Project Management Maturity Model (OPM3®)*, Project Management Institute, Newtown Square, PA.

——, 2006a, *Standard for Portfolio Management*, Project Management Institute, Newtown Square, PA.

——, 2006b, *Standard for Program Management*, Project Management Institute, Newtown Square, PA.

——, 2008, *A Guide to the Project Management Body of Knowledge (PMBOK® Guide)*, 4th edition, Project Management Institute, Newtown Square, PA.

Scott, R. (ed.), 2001, *Partnering in Europe: Incentive-based Alliancing for Projects*, Thomas Telford, London.

Smith, N.J., 2003, "Roles and responsibilities in project contract management," in Turner, J.R. (ed.), *Contracting for Project Management*, Gower, Aldershot.

Thomas, J., and Mullaly, M., 2008, *Researching the Value of Project Management*, Project Management Institute, Newtown Square, PA.

Turner, J.R., 2003, "Farsighted project contract management," in Turner, J.R. (ed.), *Contracting for Project Management*, Gower, Aldershot.

——, 2009, *The Handbook of Project-Based Management*, 3rd edition, McGraw-Hill, New York.

Turner, J.R., and Simister, S.J., 2001, "Project contract management and a theory of organization," *International Journal of Project Management*, **19**(8), 457–464.

Turner, J.R., and Speiser, A., 1992, "Meeting the information systems needs of program management," *International Journal of Project Management*, 10(4), 196–206.

6 Behavior

The project as a social system

6.1 Governing people

In August 2003, Rodney Turner spoke on Thursday afternoon of a week-long project management seminar. After the seminar one of the delegates told him that he was the first person all week to mention people. You might have been forgiven for thinking from the first three and a half days of the seminar that projects are machines operated by androids. This is a consequence of the Optimization Perspective, and the associated (hard) systems focus, that project management is just about using the right tools. It also leads to the downplaying of the project manager's role, as discussed in the introduction to Section 4.4. (The project as a machine is the metaphor we used for the Optimization Perspective.) But projects, as temporary organizations, are workplaces for people. Hence we need to define their roles and responsibilities, how they will interact, and how they will be managed and cared for, and that is the focus of the behavior perspective. So here we use the metaphor of the project as a social system, in the sense that people and interactions between people are important on projects. (In Chapter 9 we introduce Niklas Luhmann's (2006) view of the project as a social system which consists of and constitutes itself by decisions.)

People have been writing about the people side of project management since the 1970s, so it has not been totally ignored. Writers have considered project organization, people working in project teams and their motivation. However, the Optimization Perspective and the associated memes of project management have been so strong that even 30 years later it takes three and a half days of a project seminar before the people issues and project organization are mentioned. Projects are temporary organizations, and so designing an appropriate project organization, staffing the project and managing the individuals and the project team are essential elements of project management. This perspective is influenced by ideas from the fields of organizational behavior (OB) and human resource management (HRM).

In this chapter we discuss elements of OB and HRM on projects. We start by discussing project organization. We explore the roles people adopt on projects and suggest ways of designing project organizations. Next we consider project teams, their formation and maintenance. We consider diversity in teams, and show how it can represent potential rather than a threat. We look at the leadership of the project manager. We consider six schools of leadership and how they apply in a project context. In particular we look at the Emotional Intelligence and Competence Schools and what they tell us about emotionally competent leadership for project managers. Finally we discuss human resource management on projects and in the project-based organization. Team members' performance on projects needs to be appraised, both for their motivation and future development, and people need to be developed to meet the needs of the current project, to meet the future resource requirements of the organization, and for their own career advancement. We suggest how human resource management should be applied within the project-oriented organization, identifying new practices that need to be applied on projects and how practices in the line need to be adapted to interface with and support project-based working.

6.2 Project organization

A project is a temporary organization, and so we need to define its nature. We need to define where the members of the organization will come from, their working relationships, and their roles and responsibilities, including their leadership roles. David Cleland and Bill King (1983) made it two of their premises that the people working on a project would come from across the organization and that the organization structure adopted would usually be a matrix. The first of those features is the consequence of our premise that the project is a temporary organization, and we will show that the matrix is just one of many forms of organization that can be adopted, and one that is in fact not used much any more.

Roland Gareis (2005) has shown that the use of effective project organizational models can bring competitive advantage. The design of an effective project organization will include the design of an organization structure, the definition of project roles and responsibilities, as well as the creation of a project culture. Project managers often say that they cannot influence the design of their project organization; it has to be taken as a given. We challenge this, and encourage project managers to try to influence the design of the project organization along with the team, and to treat these as more important than schedule, cost, scope, or quality.

Project organizational forms

The traditional form of project organization is the matrix (Cleland and King, 1983), in which the project team members come from a functional department to work on the project, and the project and functional line managers share responsibility for their management. In a classic piece of work, David Gobeli and Erik Larson (1989) identified five structures (Figure 6.1):

- functional line;
- coordinated matrix;
- balanced matrix;
- secondment matrix;
- project line.

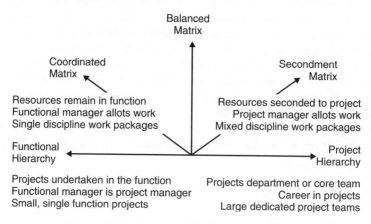

Figure 6.1 Five project organizational forms

Rodney Turner (2009) suggests that the middle of these, the balanced matrix, and the traditional matrix structure cannot work; project team members cannot simultaneously receive instruction from both the project manager and line manager, it doesn't work. It must be clear whether project team members are receiving instruction from the line or project manager. We therefore define just four forms of project organization, two line and two matrix forms:

Functional line: If the project is small enough it will draw on people from just one function within the hierarchical line organization. Then all the project team members including the project manager come just from that one function and report to the departmental manager.

Project line: At the other extreme, if the parent organization does many large projects, it can create a project hierarchy. This will be a permanent structure within the organization (Figure 5.8), and project team members will be drawn from the projects department and report ultimately to the projects department manager. The parent organization may be a construction company, or a software house, or consulting organization. Or it may be an organization whose business is just projects, such as NASA.

In between are the two matrix forms.

Secondment matrix: Project team members are seconded onto the project team for the duration of their involvement with the project. While seconded onto the project they receive instruction from the project manager as to what work they will do day-to-day. They may only be seconded part time and they may only be seconded temporarily, but while seconded they receive instruction from the project manager. You have to do this if the work requires people from two or more functional departments to work together.

Coordinated matrix: The functional manager takes responsibility for the assigning of people to project tasks. The project manager passes responsibility for the completion of a package of work to the functional manager, and the functional manager assigns people from within his or her function to the work. Thus project team members receive instruction from the functional manager. This only works if the work package requires the input from just one resource type. It is useful if the people from the department are working on several projects simultaneously and also have functional duties. The functional manager can then balance their work loads, while meeting the delivery dates for the project work packages.

In the secondment matrix people receive instruction for the project manager; in the coordinated matrix they receive instruction from the line manager. It is clear.

You can combine the organization forms. The organization may have a project hierarchy, which forms the core project team, and then people are seconded onto the project from the functions for the duration of their input. This is how the NASA Space Flight Center works. You may also identify packages of work with just one resource type and delegate those to the functional manager, combining three forms on one project. Similarly you may be operating a functional line but second somebody from another department onto the project, or identify an element of work which you ask another department to do.

Empowered and integrated organization

Roland Gareis and Martina Huemann (2008) suggest an alternative way of representing the project organization (Figure 6.2), which emphasizes the empowerment of the project team members and graphically represents their relationships and

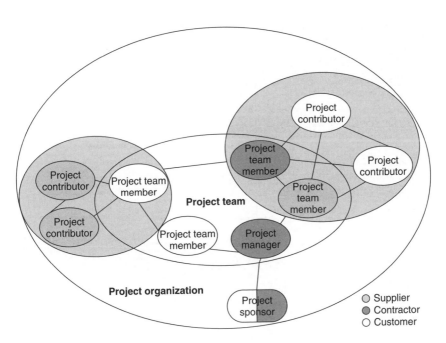

Figure 6.2 Project organization chart of an empowered and integrated project organization

level and type of involvement with the project. This model moves away from the traditional forms and their focus on hierarchy and matrix, and emphasizes team structures, team work and shared commitment between organizational units and companies.

Project roles

Individuals contribute to the project through different roles, such as the project manager, sponsor (or owner), a technical expert, or project worker. The project is their workplace and they fulfill expectations which are aligned to their particular role in the project. The expectations towards the particular role depend on the project organizational form and the project management understanding of the company. People's roles and responsibilities on projects need to be carefully defined, and there are several ways of doing that:

Responsibility chart

The classic way of defining people's roles and responsibilities on projects is the responsibility chart (Andersen *et al.*, 2009; Turner, 2009), or responsibility assignment matrix (Project Management Institute, 2008). Figure 6.3 is an example as suggested by Rodney Turner (2009). In this chart, the rows represent deliverables (products) at a given level of breakdown, and the columns organizational units. The

TriMagi PROJECT RESPONSIBILITY CHART — PROJECT SCHEDULE

Project: Intranet Phase: 1
Project Champion: Martin Pacific
Project Manager: Frances Seeker
Period: | Week ending | Target end: 30-Jun-02

Legend:
- X — eXecutes the work
- D — takes Decisions solely / ultimately
- d — takes decisions jointly
- P — manages Progress
- T — on the job Training
- I — must be Informed
- C — must be Consulted
- A — may Advise

Week-ending (weeks 1–15): 22-Aug, 29-Aug, 05-Sep, 12-Sep, 19-Sep, 26-Sep, 03-Oct, 10-Oct, 17-Oct, 24-Oct, 31-Oct, 07-Nov, 14-Nov, 21-Nov, 28-Nov

No	Milestone Name	Managing Director	Board	Personnel Manager	Personnel Department	Marketing Manager	Marketing Department	IS Manager	IS Department	Users	Contractors	Project Manager	Project Team	Consultant	Procurement	Duration	End Date
M0	Ready to start	D	d		I		I		I			d					18 Aug
M1	Overall context and style agreed	D	d	C	d	C	d	C	C			X	X	T		7	26 Aug
H1	Hardware and data inventory							P	X							9	28 Aug
M2	Home and news pages agreed	D		C	d	C	d	X				X		T		5	02 Sep
M3	Document processing pages agreed	D		C				d	X			X		T		5	02 Sep
M4	Personal information pages agreed	D		C				d	X			X		T		5	02 Sep
P1	Procedures rewritten			P	X											5	03 Sep
M5	Ready to design	D	d		d				d			d				5	09 Sep
H2	Hardware defined							P	X							12	15 Sep
P2	New jobs designed			P	X											8	15 Sep
H3	Hardware designed								PD	X					Xd	5	22 Sep
D1	Home and news pages developed			d	C	d	C	Pd	X	C	X			A	Xd	12	25 Sep
D2	Document processing pages developed			d	C	d	C	Pd	X	C	X			A	Xd	12	25 Sep
D3	Personnel information pages developed			d	C	d	C	Pd	X	C	X			A	Xd	12	25 Sep
P3	New procedures piloted			I	C						C			X		10	25 Sep
D4	Site assembled								PD	X	X			X		8	29 Sep
D4	Procedures optimized			P	X											5	07 Oct
D5	Site signed off	I	I	I				D	X			d	X			3	14 Oct
P5	Ready to deploy	D	d	X	d			d	X			d	X			3	17 Oct
H4	Hardware installed								Pd		X					17	17 Oct
H5	Data entered and migrated			C	C				PD		X					17	11 Nov
P6	Site goes live	I	I	I				D	X			d	X			1	11 Nov
M6	Ready to proceed to Phase 2	D	d	X	d			d	X			d	X			1	14 Nov

© 2003 Goal Directed Project Management Systems Ltd.

Figure 6.3 Responsibility chart

Table 6.1 Use of symbols in the responsibility chart

Letter	Responsibility
X	eXecutes the work
D	takes **D**ecision solely or ultimately
d	takes **d**ecision jointly or partly
P	controls **P**rogress
T	provides **T**uition on the job
C	must be **C**onsulted
A	available to **A**dvise
I	must be **I**nformed

chart in Figure 6.3 corresponds to the first level of breakdown for a medium-sized project, and so the products are packages of work (or milestones) and organizational units, functions or departments in the parent organization, or external companies. At the next level of breakdown the products would be activities making up work packages and the organizational units named people or skills. The symbols in the matrix represent the roles and responsibilities of the organizational units. Different authors suggest different types of symbol. The chart in Figure 6.3 uses eight (Table 6.1).

Role descriptions

In projects where the project participants are not familiar with project work or when they come from different organizations it is worthwhile to develop role descriptions to have a common understanding of what is expected from whom. Table 6.2 shows a role description of a project manager, and Table 6.3 for a project team, based on a process-oriented project management approach (Gareis and Huemann, 2008).

Project culture

When designing a project organization it is important to develop a project culture. Roland Gareis (2005) suggests the following elements for designing a project organization and developing a project culture:

- empowerment;
- integration;
- partnering;
- virtuality.

Empowerment

Empowerment means increasing the autonomy and self-reliance of the project team members. To make it work in projects, empowerment must consider not just individual team members, but also the project team as a social system and the

Table 6.2 Role description of a project manager (after Gareis and Huemann, 2008)

Objectives
Contribution to the realization of project objectives and to optimization of the business case
Leading the project team and the project contributors
Representation of the project towards relevant environments

Organizational position
Member of the project team
Reports to the project owner team

Tasks

In the project start process
Know-how transfer from the pre-project phase into the project
Development of adequate project plans
Design of an adequate project organization
Performance of risk management
Design of project-context-relations
etc.

In the project controlling process
Determination of the project status
Redefinition of project objectives
Development of project progress reports
etc.

In the resolution of a project discontinuity
Analysis of the situation and definition of ad-hoc measures
Development of project scenarios
Definition of strategies and further measures
Communication of the project discontinuity to relevant project environments
etc.

In the project close-down process
Coordination of the final contents work
Transfer of know-how into the base organization
Dissolution of project environment relations
etc.

project itself. The prerequisite is the empowerment of the project. The project should be made autonomous so it can establish itself with its own identity. To empower the project, it is necessary to make an explicit project assignment, with measurable project objectives, and to establish the role of the project sponsor. The project assignment provides the framework for the project, within which the project manager and the team members can act. It is their contract. The project sponsor takes on an explicit governance function and represents the project related interests of the company. The sponsor steers an essential relationship between the temporary project and the permanent line organization. In the empowered project organization, the project team members also take on responsibility. They are responsible to choose the appropriate work processes and for the quality of their work package results. In addition, the project team is explicitly considered and takes on a specific group role (Table 6.3). The project management responsibility is shared and all

Table 6.3 Role description of the project team (after Gareis and Huemann, 2008)

Objectives
Develop a common "Big Project Picture"
Ensure synergies and commitment in the project performance
Solve conflicts
Organize learning in the project

Organizational position
Part of the project organization
Assigned by the project owner team

Tasks

In the project start process
Exchange information between the project team members
Jointly decide on the design of the project organization and about project planning
Agree on project rules
etc.

In the project controlling process
Jointly determine the project status
Jointly agree on adaptations of project objectives, schedule, costs, etc.
Jointly agree on adaptations of the project organization and the project context relationships
etc.

In the resolution of a project discontinuity
Jointly suggest the definition of a project discontinuity
Jointly design the process for resolving the project discontinuity
Jointly develop immediate measures
etc.

In the project close-down process
Jointly design the project close-down process
Jointly transfer know-how into the permanent organizations
etc.

project team members have a shared leadership understanding. Figure 6.2 visualizes an empowered project organization.

Empowerment needs to be applied appropriately. It is probably essential on projects or project stages where the project team members are knowledge workers. But on the execution phase of a construction project, where the project manager needs to be much more authoritarian (Table 4.11), and the project team members are unskilled laborers, empowerment may not work and the team members may not want it.

Integration of partners and partnering

An integrated project organization has members from different companies or company units. Representatives of the customer and suppliers work together in a common project organization to optimize an holistic project view, instead of having competing parallel project organizations with project hierarchies. Partnering or alliancing (Section 5.6) is based on the concept of integration but goes beyond it.

Partnering is based on common contractual arrangements between the project partners such as an alliance contract or consortium agreement. A common incentive system for the project partners supports the achievement of common project objective.

Virtuality

Projects can be set up as virtual organizations due to the cooperation of several organizations or due to the members working in different locations. Work in virtual projects is characterized by team members in different locations (and time zones) without a common work space, a lack of personal contact and lack of informal contact between the project team members and a lack of common history among the team members (Gareis, 2005). A common communication infrastructure is essential for virtual project organizations. Figure 6.4 suggests a structure.

6.3 Project teams

Teams are central to projects. The common understanding is that a project is a project team, (or on larger projects several teams within the project organization). Jon Katzenbach and Douglas Smith (1993) define a team as: "a small number of people with complementary skills who are committed to a common purpose, set of performance goals and approach for which they hold themselves mutually accountable." The two authors clearly differentiate between a team and a working group

Time		
	Same	**Different**
Same	**Face-to-face communication** Workshops Meetings Informal contracts	**Separate communication** Fax, e-mail Documentation management Discussion forum Notice board
Different	**Communications at a distance** Fax, e-mail Telephone conference Video conference	**Separate communication** Fax, e-mail Documentation management Discussion forum Notice board

Figure 6.4 Communication forms in projects

Table 6.4 Work groups versus teams (after Katzenbach and Smith, 2005)

Work groups	Teams
Strong, clearly focused leader	Shared leadership roles
Individual accountability	Individual and mutual accountability
Purpose same as the broader organization mission	Specific team purpose that the team itself delivers
Individual work products	Collective work products
Runs efficient meetings	Encourages open-ended discussion and active problem-solving meetings
Measures effectiveness indirectly by influence on others (e.g. financial performance of the business)	Measures performance directly by assessing collective work products
Discusses, decides, and delegates	Discusses, decides, and does real work together

(Table 6.4). The project team has a central role in the project, and as we saw above (Table 6.3), its functions can be described in role descriptions (Gareis and Huemann, 2008).

Team formation and maintenance

Bruce Tuckman (1965) suggested that there are several team stages of team formation and maintenance, which he calls: forming, storming, norming, and performing. Later he added a closing stage, adjourning.

Forming

The team members assemble. They are keen that they have been chosen for this key project. But they have uncertainties about how this project will work, and how they will work together, which limits their effectiveness. The second worst case scenario is that they stay on this level of second-rate effectiveness for the entire duration of the project.

Storming

But what normally happens is the uncertainties spill over into disagreement. The team members disagree about the desired impact of the project, its outcomes and outputs; the work they have to do to deliver the output, and who is responsible for what; and how the project will be managed. The worst case scenario is that they never recover from these arguments.

Norming

But usually the team find they can get agreement about the impact, outcomes and outputs, and then about the work of the project, the project organization structure, and who is responsible for what, and about how the project will be managed. The norming stage is key. We can draw a relation between project management and the team development and emphasize that norming is done in the project start-up process (Gareis, 2007; Turner, 2009), where common rules and culture, shared commitment in the project team, a Big Project Picture and shared goals and a shared approach are created. To gain common agreement on project plans is a strong feature for the norming stage. Also during this stage the project team members must come to identify with this project and not the projects they have just left. That requires the development of common goals, values and language. Reflecting and renorming take place in project controlling and supports the further development of the project team (Gareis, 2005).

Performing

So throughout the delivery stages of the project the project team can perform at peak effectiveness. The project manager needs to focus on continuing to motivate the project team and communicating with the stakeholders (Section 7.2).

Adjourning

The project team disbands. The project manager needs to debrief the project team as part of the organizational learning process (Section 5.4), and to ensure the performance of the project team is properly recognized and rewarded. If you don't reward the project team for good performance on this project, they may not want to work for you on the next. An end of project party coupled with a debriefing meeting can achieve both those ends. But also, as part of their HRM roles (Section 6.6), the project manager may need to do end-of-project appraisals on the team members and ensure that these are included in their annual appraisals in the line.

While Bruce Tuckman describes the team stages, other writers see the possibility for managing the team explicitly and influencing the team phases as the team has to be actively established and developed (Katzenbach and Smith, 2005). Table 6.5 extends the traditional team phases perspective and relates it to project starting, project controlling and project closing down. In the project start we combine forming and norming to try to bypass storming, and quickly make the team productive. Norming is done by agreeing common structures, values and rules. In project controlling, the team could reflect how they are performing and if new structures and norms are required. In the project close-down we reflect how well the team has worked together and organize for a common farewell.

Table 6.5 Team phases and their relationship to project management

Project management	Tasks
Project start-up	Forming and norming (to minimize storming)
Project controlling	Reflecting and renorming
Project closing down	Reflecting and adjourning

Project start-up

The adoption of structured project start-up process (Gareis, 2007; Turner, 2009) can be very useful for leading the team through the first three stages. By using a structured start-up process you can take people quickly through the forming and storming stages, and minimize the level of disagreement. You can then concentrate on the norming process, and that is what we will mainly discuss here. The objectives of the project start-up are:

- to agree the project's impact, outcomes and output;
- to agree the project plans and roles and responsibilities;
- to design the project management process and project organization;
- to brief project team members joining the team;
- to obtain psychological attachment of the project team.

Methods of project start-up include: holding workshops; producing reports to brief the team; using external consultants to advise on how similar projects have been done in the past or to manage the team development process. Workshops, using an external facilitator to manage team development , are the most effective for developing the project team and obtaining psychological attachment. A possible agenda for a workshop is:

1 Review the current project definition – the purpose, scope and outputs of the project.
2 Define the objectives of the current stage.
3 Determine the success criteria of the project and the current stage – set a project mission
4 Prepare a Milestone Plan for the current stage.
5 Prepare a Responsibility Chart against the plan.
6 Estimate work content and durations for the work-packages.
7 Schedule the work-packages.
8 Define the quality objectives of the current stage.
9 Assess risk and develop reduction strategies.
10 Prepare initial activity plans.
11 Prepare a management and control plan.

This mainly focuses on the project definition, planning and control elements, but by holding the workshop off-site, with a facilitator in attendance and also building in social elements, will help achieve team development and build psychological attachment.

Psychological attachment

Charles Handy (1987) defines a team as "a group of people working together with a common objective and psychological attachment." The concept of psychological attachment is important. All the people in a restaurant one evening are working together with a common objective: enjoy the food in this restaurant and socialize with their friends or do business. But they are not a team. The people at different tables have no psychological attachment; they don't even know who the others are. We said above that you want the project team members to feel closer attachment to this project than the one they have just come from, and building psychological attachment is the way to achieve that. Methods for achieving psychological attachment include the following:

Sharing photographs

Rodney Turner's former sister-in-law is an air hostess with Qantas. She told Rodney about something which she as a German finds uncomfortable. When the air crew gets on a plane 30 minutes before the passengers, they may never have previously met. She found that they started showing her photographs, of their husband, their house, their children, their dog, the last party they went to (which in Sydney may be a party where you were limited to one piece of clothing). She was expected to reciprocate. But this is important. These people who five minutes ago were total strangers have to work together as a team for the next ten hours on the flight to Bangkok. To help build the team it is useful to know whether or not people have a husband, children, dog, house, and what they look like in their party clothes.

Project web page

A project web page is a way to continue to share project management documents or even the photographs with the other project team members throughout the project. It is a marketing tool, but equally important is that such a project web page can serve as a home for the project, something the project team members feel aligned to, especially when the project team is geographically dispersed.

Project name and logo

All NASA projects, including every space shuttle mission, has a name and a logo. They are important for giving a sense of identity to the team. The project name is especially important as otherwise the team members cannot even say for which project they are working. Often for external projects, the name is equivalent to the name of the customer, but hopefully the relationship with the customer is longer than one project, or there are several projects with the customer, and that can lead to misunderstandings. If a project has no clear and unique name, how can a project team member feel committed to it? Another extreme are fancy names – but nomen is omen – What do you think happened to the ambitious internal IT project "Atlantis"? Yes, it sank!

Social events

Mostly people want to socialize in projects. People are interested in knowing who they are working with. Appraising each other to gain trust and commitment is important. One way to organize this is by allowing for informal time together, for instance during the project start-up workshop. Social events can also include team events such as milestone parties or excursions, attending a project management conference, and a weekend skiing trip.

Project charter

The agreements can be captured in a project charter. Obviously the project charter should include elements covering items 1 to 4 of the objectives of start-up, as captured in the project definition report (Turner, 2009) or the project brief (Office of Government Commerce, 2009). But it should also include items covering objective 5:

- project name and logo;
- team values;
- agreements on how to work together;
- agreements on how to resolve inter-team conflicts;
- how to assess team effectiveness;
- key performance goals.

Competence of the project team

Project managers often find that they have to accept the project team members they are given. In the next section we describe how to use the diversity of project team members as an opportunity on projects. But the project manager should also assess how the competence of the project team meets the needs of the project. Using a tool like IPMA's self-assessment document of certification (International Project Management Association, 2006), you can assess the levels of competence demanded by the project and the levels of competence of individual team members. Figure 6.5 shows the needs of one project compared to two team members. Clearly there is one area where team member 1 can aid the learning of team member 2, and vice versa. There is one area where they have greater competence than the project needs, but another area where neither team member meets the needs of the project. The project manager would need to overcome this by either providing the team members with on-the-project training, or by seeking an additional team member with that strength.

Motivation

During the performing stage of the team development cycle, the project manager needs to continue to motivate the project team. Rodney Turner (2009) suggests there are five things that can help motivate the project team members:

Purpose: creating the visions for the project and having the project team members buy into that vision. We see below that Aristotle and Confucius identified the importance of this two and a half millennia ago.

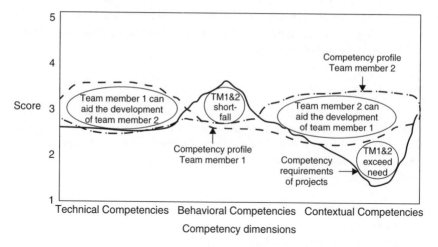

Figure 6.5 Comparing the competence needs of the project with the competence of team members

Proactivity: helping the project team members to feel they have control over their work. We discussed this under empowerment, above.

Profit sharing: let the team share in the fruits of their labor, perhaps through project bonuses. Rodney Turner (Turner *et al.*, 2008a) interviewed a company that set aside money in the project budget to pay rewards to the project team members.

Progression: the project team members must see the project as an important step in their career development.

Professional recognition: team members must receive recognition for their contribution.

These things can be powerful motivators in the opening stages of the project and in the closing stages if the project has gone well. They are powerful de-motivators in the closing stages if the project has gone badly. However, in the middle of the project, focus on them can be lost, and the project manager must remain vigilant to continue to use them to help motivate the project team.

6.4 Diversity in projects

The individuals working together in a project differ in personality, gender, age, disciplines, management status, work experience, seniority, cultural or organizational backgrounds, etc. In any social system such as a project, diversity is inherent and cannot be prevented. The model developed by Lee Gardenswartz and Anita Rowe (1994) can help us understand what diversity means. They propose a four layer model of diversity (Figure 6.6). The dimensions of diversity include:

- personality, which is not immediately visible to others;
- internal dimensions, which are partially visible, such as age, gender, etc.;

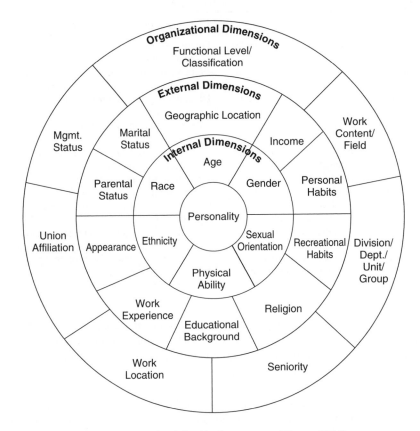

Figure 6.6 Dimensions of diversity (after Gardenswartz and Rowe, 1994)

- external dimensions, such as work experience, geographical location, parental status, educational background, work experience, etc.;
- organizational dimensions within the organizations, such as functional level, work content field, management status, seniority, etc.

These dimensions of diversity can be questioned. For instance, do we consider gender as a biological fact or as socially constructed? In different contexts further criteria could be added and some might be less important than others. However the model does provide guidance on the criteria we can consider, when we discuss or analyze diversity in projects.

Individuals are diverse in the sense that the different dimensions have different meanings and different parameters emerging from individual biographies as well as cultural backgrounds influencing those aspects. In some criteria two individuals may have commonalities and in other criteria they may have differences. Diversity comprises two sides, differences and commonalities. That implies that diversity is inherent in any group, team, project or project-oriented organization.

Table 6.6 Diversity as deficit versus potential in projects

Diversity in projects as deficit	Diversity in projects as potential
Diversity is perceived only as differences	Diversity is perceived as differences and commonalities
Being different is perceived as deficit in comparison to the norm	Being different is perceived as a potential which allows for different contributions
Diversity brings conflicts in projects thus diversity should be ignored	Diversity in projects must be analyzed and managed
Diversity in projects is a threat to effectiveness	Diversity in projects brings business benefits
Values and norms of the organization are not to be questioned	Values and norms of the organization are subjects to be questioned
Equal treatment means treating people equally	Equal treatment means providing equal opportunities considering diversity
Project manager and team members need social competences to deal with diversity They must change, not the organizational structures	Organizational structures must support diversity management; not only social competences required by project owners, project managers and project team members
Diversity management is an extra in projects, considered as a nice-to-have	Diversity management is an integral part of project management

If we accept that on any project diversity is inherent, it becomes clear it is not an extra the project manager can choose whether he or she wants to deal with, but a must. Diversity in the project causes complexity and thus ensures requisite variety to be able to achieve the desired results. Diversity increases the potential for different perceptions, communications and ideas. Cognitive conflicts improve the quality of decisions, because the synthesis emerging from different perceptions is generally higher than the individual perspective (Chelly and Boisard-Castelluccia, 2007). Diverse teams have the potential to be more creative and innovative, but the diversity has to be actively managed (Hanappi-Egger *et al.*, 2007). Table 6.6 provides a summary of the two perceptions on diversity. Martina Huemann (2006) suggests that diversity can be perceived as deficit (in comparison with the norm) or as a potential for a project.

Diversity management comprises planning and implementing organizational systems and practices to manage people so that the potential advantages of diversity are maximized while the potential disadvantages are minimized. For projects that means diversity management comprises planning for diversity, designing project organizations which allow for diversity and considering diversity as one object of consideration in project management. Diversity management in projects allows an increase in complexity of the project to better deal with the different relevant environments and relate to those in appropriate ways.

6.5   Emotionally competent project leadership

A key OB issue on projects is the leadership style of the project manager. In a recent study, Rodney Turner and Ralf Müller (2006) showed that one of the most significant contributors to project success is the emotional intelligence of the project manager. During the twentieth century, six schools of leadership developed (Table 6.7) which have been reflected in project management writings. Table 6.7 also shows three historical schools.

The historical schools

Confucius writing 2,500 years ago identified four virtues (*de*) that leaders should possess:

- relationships (*jen*, love);
- values (*xiao*, piety);
- process (*li*, proper conduct);
- moderation (*zhang rong*, the doctrine of the mean).

The first three are a recurring theme throughout the following two and a half millennia. But subsequently managers have forgotten about the need for moderation, the doctrine of the mean, sometimes called the Goldilocks principle. Leaders should take a balanced approach, whereas the tendency of modern managers is to do things in extremes.

Two hundred years later, Aristotle identified the first three as important, saying that the leader should obtain the commitment of their team in three steps:

- build relationships (*pathos*);
- sell their values or vision (*ethos*);
- persuade with logic (*logos*).

Unfortunately modern managers tend to leap in at the third step, trying to persuade with logic. That is a difference between a manager and a leader. The manager knows what has to be done and how and why. But the leader knows that first he or she must build relationships with their team, and sell their values and vision to be able to lead the team rather than just push them. Looking at politicians is informative. The American president, Ronald Reagan, and British Prime Minister, Margaret Thatcher, were good at the first two steps, and were great leaders. Mrs Thatcher also showed the leader does not need to be liked, just respected. Mrs Thatcher's successor, John Major, focused on the logic and was perceived as the gray man.

Chester Barnard (1938) identified two types of chief executive, those that manage by process and those that lead through relationships. Between Confucius and Chester Barnard we hadn't come very far. Now look at the six modern schools.

Trait School

The Trait School suggests that leaders exhibit certain traits they are born with. Shelley Kirkpatrick and Edwin Locke (1991) suggested effective leaders exhibit the following traits:

Table 6.7 The schools of leadership and their interpretation in a project context

School	Period	Main idea	Example authors	What the project management literature has said	References
Confucius	500BC	Relationships, values, process, moderation			
Aristotle	300BC	Relationships, values, process			
Barnard	1938	Relationships versus process			
Trait	1930s–1940s	Effective leaders show common traits Leaders born not made	Kirkpatrick and Locke, 1992	Traits of effective project managers: problem solving; results orientation; self-confidence; perspective; communication; negotiation; energy	Turner, 2009
Behavior or style	1940s–1950s	Effective leaders adopt certain styles or behaviors Leadership skills can be developed	Blake and Mouton, 1978	Four leadership styles: guiding; democratic; autocratic; bureaucratic	Turner, 2009 Frame, 1987
Contingency	1960s–1970s	What makes an effective leader depends on the situation	Fiedler, 1967 House, 1971	Different leadership styles at different stages of the life-cycle: feasibility-guiding; design-democratic; execution-autocratic; close-bureaucratic	Turner, 2009 Frame, 1987
Visionary or charismatic	1980s–1990s	Two styles Transformational concern for relationships Transactional concern for process	Bass, 1990	Transactional styles on simple projects Transformational styles on complex projects	Keegan and den Hartog, 2004
Emotional intelligence	1990s–2000s	Emotional intelligence has a greater impact on performance than intellect	Goleman et al., 2002	The project manager's perception of success can have a significant impact on project performance.	Lee-Kelly and Leong, 2004
Competency	2000s	Effective leaders exhibit certain competencies, including traits, behaviors and styles, emotions, intellect, process Certain profiles of competence better in different situations	Dulewicz and Higgs, 2003		Crawford, 2003, 2005 Turner et al., 2003 Dainty et al., 2005 Turner and Müller, 2006

- drive and ambition;
- the desire to lead and influence others;
- honesty and integrity;
- self-confidence;
- intelligence;
- technical knowledge.

Rodney Turner (2009) identified seven traits of effective project management:

- problem solving;
- results orientation;
- self-confidence;
- perspective;
- communication;
- negotiating ability;
- energy and initiative.

Behavior School

The Behavior School assumes effective leaders display certain behaviors or styles, which can be developed. Most theories from this school characterize leaders by how much they exhibit styles based on one or more of the following parameters:

- concern for people or relationships (*jen, pathos*);
- concern for production or process (*li, logos*);
- use of authority (*xiao, ethos*);
- involvement of the team in decision-making (formulating decisions);
- involvement of the team in decision-taking (choosing options);
- flexibility versus the application of rules.

Blake and Mouton (1978) developed a grid based on the first two parameters. They graded each on a scale of 1 to 9 and identified five leadership styles, which they said were appropriate in different circumstances:

- impoverished (1,1);
- authority obedience (1,9);
- country club (9,1);
- compromise (5,5);
- team leader (9,9).

David Frame (2003) identified four styles of project leaders (Table 4.10), depending on the amount they involve the team in making decisions (formulating options), the amount they involve the team in taking decisions (choosing options), and how flexible they are.

Contingency School

Most authors from the Behavior School assume different behaviors or styles are appropriate in different circumstances, but this was formalized by the Contingency School. Contingency theories tend to follow the same pattern:

1   Assess the characteristics of the leader.
2   Evaluate the situation in terms of key contingency variables.
3   Seek a match between the leader and the situation.

One theory that has proved popular is path-goal theory (House, 1971). The idea is the leader must help the team find the path to their goals. It identifies four leadership behaviors:

*   directive leaders;
*   supportive leaders;
*   participative leaders;
*   achievement-oriented leaders.

David Frame (2003) suggested that the four styles in Table 4.10 are each appropriate at different stages of the project life-cycle (Table 4.11), and with different types of project team. That was discussed in Section 4.4.

Visionary School

The Visionary School identifies two types of leaders: those who focus on relationships and communicate their values, and those who focus on process, called transformational and transactional leaders respectively (Bass, 1990). This is reminiscent of Chester Barnard (1938).

Anne Keegan and Deanne den Hartog (2004) attempted to show that project managers need a transformational leadership style. In the event they found a slight preference for transformational leadership, but not a strong preference. We think the reason for this is that complex projects need a transformational style, but simple projects need a conscientious, structured (transactional) style. This has been borne out by the research by Rodney Turner and Ralf Müller (2006) described below.

Emotional Intelligence School

This school assumes all managers have a reasonable level of intelligence. Therefore what differentiates leaders is not their intelligence, but their emotional response to situations. Daniel Goleman, Richard Boyatzis and Annie McKee (2002) identify nineteen emotional competencies grouped into four dimensions (Figure 6.7). This suggests that the leader starts by being self-aware. They can then manage their own emotional responses to situations and become socially aware. Based on those two things they can manage relationships.

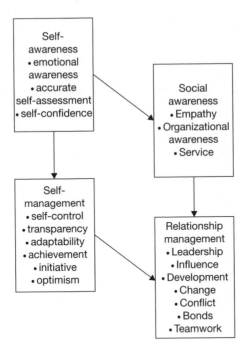

Figure 6.7 Competencies of emotional intelligence

The authors identify six management styles: visionary; coaching; affiliative; democratic; pacesetting; and commanding, and identify situations in which these different styles are appropriate. The first four are best in certain situations, but all four are adequate in most situations, medium to long term. They classify the last two styles as toxic. They say they work well in turn-around or recovery situations, but if applied medium to long term they can poison a situation, and demotivate subordinates. You find many project managers adopt one of these two styles, but many projects are short term.

In a project context, Liz Lee-Kelley (2003) has shown that a project manager's perception of success improves with experience. Jason Dolfi and Edwin Andrews (2007) have also shown that a project manager's optimism improves with experience.

Competence School

This school says effective leaders exhibit certain competencies. It encompasses all the other schools because traits and behaviors are competencies, certain competency profiles are appropriate in different situations, it can define competency profile of transformational and transactional leaders, and some of the competencies encompass emotional intelligence. Vic Dulewicz and Malcolm Higgs (2005) identified fifteen competencies which influence leadership performance (Table 6.8). They group them into three types, intellectual (IQ), managerial (MQ) and

Table 6.8 Fifteen leadership competencies (after Dulewicz and Higgs, 2003)

Group	Competency	Goal	Involving	Engaging
Intellectual	1. critical analysis and judgment	High	Medium	Medium
(IQ)	2. vision and imagination	High	High	Medium
	3. strategic perspective	High	Medium	Medium
Managerial	4. engaging communication	Medium	Medium	High
(MQ)	5. managing resources	High	Medium	Low
	6. empowering	Low	Medium	High
	7. developing	Medium	Medium	High
	8. achieving	High	Medium	Medium
Emotional	9. self-awareness	Medium	High	High
(EQ)	10. emotional resilience	High	High	High
	11. motivation	High	High	High
	12. sensitivity	Medium	Medium	High
	13. influence	Medium	High	High
	14. intuitiveness	Medium	Medium	High
	15. conscientiousness	High	High	High

emotional (EQ). They also identified three leadership styles, which they called Goal-Oriented, Involving and Engaging (Table 6.8), and showed that goal-oriented leaders are best on low complexity projects, involving leaders best on medium complexity projects and engaging leaders best on high complexity projects. Thus, Vic Dulewicz and Malcolm Higgs showed that on organizational change projects certain leadership styles lead to better results than others: transactional leadership is better on simple projects and transformational leadership better on more complex projects.

There have been several studies to try to identify the competence profiles of project leaders, (Crawford, 2005, 2007; Turner *et al.*, 2003; Dainty *et al.*, 2005). Rodney Turner and Ralf Müller (2006) identified the competence profiles of the managers of different types of projects using the competency dimension of Table 6.8. We describe their results below. But first we wish to differentiate between the schools of leadership and theories of team behavior.

Personality versus leadership style

Several personality profiles have been developed to explain performance in teams, for instance the Myers-Briggs Type Indicator (Briggs-Myers, 1992), the 16PF (personality factor) profile (Cattell *et al.*, 1970), and profiles by Meredith Belbin (1986) and Margerison and McCann (1990). These suggest a team leader should aim to balance personality types across a team. Some people (incorrectly) put the team behavior profiles forward as an indicator of success as a leader. They are not intended for that. Vic Dulewicz and Malcolm Higgs (2005) have shown there is no correlation between Belbin's personality profile and performance as a leader, and only weak correlation between the 16PF factors and performance as a leader.

Competency profiles of the effective project leaders

Using the competency profiles in Table 6.8, Rodney Turner and Ralf Müller (2006) showed the project manager's leadership style is a success factor on projects, and different leadership styles are appropriate for different types of project. Emotional intelligence is positively correlated with project success on almost every type of project. The exception was projects where cost is important where managerial competencies dominated. They also found that different dimensions were more or less important on different types of project (Table 6.9).

6.6 Human resource management

Up to this point we have focused on OB issues on projects and in the project-oriented organization. Now we want to consider how the project-oriented organization manages and cares for its human resources. We draw on work done recently by Rodney Turner and Martina Huemann with Anne Keegan (2008a). They identified that in order to align its HRM practices with the decision to be project-oriented, and in order to support project-based working within the organization, the project-oriented organization needs to adopt new and different HRM practices not seen in the traditional permanent organization. It needs to adopt HRM practices on the project, implemented by the project manager, and adapt the practices in the routine, line organization so that the practices in the line, and the practices on the project are mutually consistent and supportive. Both project managers and line managers have responsibility for ensuring that what they do supports the other.

Challenges

The project-oriented company is confronted with specific human resource management challenges (Huemann *et al.*, 2007):

* *Temporariness*: Projects and programs are temporary organizations. Thus every time a new project or program is started, the human resource configuration of the organization must change.
* *More dynamic*: Project-oriented companies have dynamic boundaries and contexts. The number and the sizes of the projects performed are constantly changing, permanent and temporary resources are employed, and cooperations with clients, partners and suppliers are organized in teams, some of them

Table 6.9 Importance of competencies in different project types

Project type	Competencies which are important
Engineering projects	Conscientiousness, motivation and sensitivity
Organizational change	Motivation and communication
IT projects	Self-awareness, communication and developing
Highly complex projects	Emotional intelligence, especially sensitivity
Medium complex projects	Emotional resilience and communication
Fixed price contracts	Sensitivity and communication

are virtual. Thus projects and programs entail greater uncertainty, creating a more dynamic environment with more discontinuity.

- *Project-portfolio*: At any given time a project-oriented organization holds a project portfolio of different internal and external project types. A person can have multiple roles. A person can work in different projects at the same time, maybe even in different project roles. In one project he or she is a project manager, in another project a project team member. Or a person can carry a role in a project and at the same time carry another role in the permanent organization, for example in the PM office. Consequences are challenges in the multi-resource allocation.
- *Specific project management culture and management paradigm*: The ideal project-oriented company has a specific project management culture expressed in the empowerment of employees, process-orientation and team-work, continuous and discontinuous organizational change, customer-orientation, and networking with clients and suppliers. Therefore specific competences and skills are needed by the project management personnel to successfully work together in projects.

A process-oriented HRM model

Thus HRM needs to be designed to meet the needs of the project-oriented organization. Rodney Turner, Martina Huemann and Anne Keegan (2008a) showed that:

- novel HRM processes need to be adopted within the project as a temporary organization (on-project HRM practices);
- different HRM processes need to be adapted in the line so that they are consistent with and supportive of project-oriented ways of working (in-line HRM practices).

Figure 6.8 shows a process-oriented HRM model for the project-oriented company, which visualizes on-project HRM and in-line HRM.

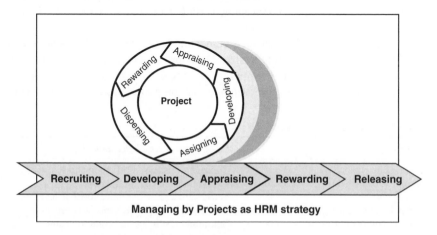

Figure 6.8 Process-orientated HRM model for the project-orientated company

On-project HRM

Certain HRM practices need to be enacted on the project.

Assigning to projects

Processes are required to identify people to work on projects and to transfer them to projects. These processes are usually initiated in the permanent organization but terminate on the project. There are differences between firms undertaking small to medium and large projects. In organizations undertaking large projects, typically lasting more than a year, project assignment is linked to the annual budgeting cycle. Organizations undertaking smaller projects need much more specific practices for identifying future resource demands of known and forecast projects, prioritizing projects in the portfolio, and then sharing resources between the projects undertaken.

Assessing performance on projects

Formal (annual, bi-annual, quarterly) appraisal of employees' performance is almost always conducted in the line, as the time horizon for decisions made is longer than the duration of individual projects. The main exception is on large projects lasting more than a year. Then people may be transferred to the project so the project director becomes their line manager. For the sake of motivation of project team members, and cohesion of the project team (Graham, 1989), appraisal information should be gathered on projects, and so project managers have a role in appraisal. Some organizations conduct formal project appraisals, and the information is given to the line manager. Others conduct 360-degree appraisals; so many people from the project are necessarily involved. Some rely on the line manager to informally seek information from the project manager, but this is not recommended. In some organizations, line managers do not seek the project manager's opinion, and some positively avoid it.

Rewarding on projects

Again reward is primarily determined in the line. However, often rewards are given linked to project performance, particularly the achievement of major milestones. These may be financial, but are more likely to be in kind, or festivals linked to the achievement of milestones.

Developing on projects

The need for development is also usually determined at the appraisal in the line and funded by the line. However, sometimes development is required on the project. For instance, a project team member may need to learn a new competency to work on the project. Some firms still insist it is paid for by the line, but most pay for it out of the project budget. However, we identified a major development need on many projects: team members joining the project need to be briefed about the current status of the project, both in the progress of the work and the development of the technology. This can be a major constraint to the rate at which people can join the project team. There may also be a need to train project team members in the use of new technology being developed by the project.

Dispersing from projects

At the end of a project, project team members need to be assigned to a new project, or returned to the line. If they are being returned to the line the parent organization needs to determine how to utilize them. Will they be returned to functional duties, or held in abeyance in some way (sitting on the bench) awaiting their next project? For some personnel, the organization needs to determine whether it is better to immediately assign them to a project, or hold them for a project starting at some point in the future where their competence will be of more value. During the dispersement process, project team members need to be debriefed as part of the organization's knowledge management processes.

Adapted in-line HRM

The HRM practices in the line and on the project need to be consistent and mutually supportive. Thus practices in the line need to be adapted from traditional HRM to be supportive of project-based working.

Selecting and recruiting

Project-oriented organizations tend to adopt organic recruitment processes (Keegan and Turner, 2003) and they tend to use a high ratio of peripheral workers who need to be recruited into the organization as part of the project assignment process. It is also often necessary to recruit peripheral workers quickly to meet the needs of project mobilization. Companies with a long history of project-based working maintain a network of peripheral workers who can be brought on board quickly. But companies with more traditional HRM practices can find the recruitment process takes months.

Appraising in the line

As we have seen, appraisal in the line needs to incorporate information from projects requiring both for the project manager to be consulted and for project appraisals to be conducted.

Developing

Many organizations have career paths for project managers, with defined levels and competency profiles. The development of project personnel needs to be linked to the career paths, and project opportunities found to offer suitable experiences. These needs will be identified at the appraisal in the line. This often requires dedicated training and development programs. Some organizations have identified that they need training programs specifically designed for project professionals. They may have standard programs suitable for a range of functional managers but require specific programs for project professionals.

Releasing from the organization

Capturing knowledge from peripheral workers leaving the end of a project is a significant issue. Many organizations find they lose knowledge with the departure of peripheral workers. Some organizations may use only contract staff to undertake a project, and all knowledge about the project is lost as they leave, meaning the organization can never develop. Some organizations also put substantial effort into maintaining contact with their peripheral workers. It is cheaper to reuse someone than recruit a new person.

Well-being

Employee well-being is an issue, particularly in organizations doing small to medium-sized projects. In organizations doing projects lasting longer than a year it is much easier to manage the employee work-load, and plan for project peaks. Also usually people are working on just one project, so peaks in that one project can be managed. The main problem on large projects can be if they entail long periods working away from home. Achieving a work–life balance is much more problematic in organizations doing smaller projects, because (Turner *et al.*, 2008b):

- future project workloads can be less easy to predict, many are not known about at the time of drawing up the annual budgets;
- the individual may be working on more than one project at once and workloads can peak together;
- there is more uncertainty about future assignments, future colleagues and work location.

Profit and responding to client demands takes precedence over employee well-being. Organizations need to adopt practices to manage employee workloads better, but clients also need to be aware of the consequences of the demands they make on employee well-being and work–life balance. However, we also found that people working on projects seem to enjoy the work and the life. But, it does also tend to be self-selecting. People who enjoy it stay, and those who don't leave.

Consequences for project managers and project owners

HRM roles are more and more shifting to project managers for the project team members and to project owners for taking on HRM responsibility for project managers. We believe that for the sake of motivation of project team members and cohesiveness of the project team, the project manager should be formally involved in appraisal, reward and development. Team members must all feel that hard work on the project is being recognized and rewarded, and they are all being appraised and rewarded in the same way, against the same standards.

6.7 Are the people hearing?

Over the last three chapters, we have discussed the importance of gaining people's commitment to our projects. In Chapter 4 we saw that a necessary condition for project success was to gain the commitment of the stakeholders to the success criteria before we start, and repeatedly at project review points throughout the project. In Chapter 5 we saw that we needed to seek top management backing so that they would support and fund the project. We needed to ensure that the project is aligned with corporate objectives and convince senior management that it will deliver beneficial change for them. Then in this chapter we saw the need to win the support of the project team so that they work diligently towards the project's objectives. Project managers must be effective communicators to communicate with all three groups of stakeholders, to communicate up to top management, outwards to the other stakeholders and down to the project team.

Phrasing the right communication and delivering it in the right way is a marketing function. Project managers have to segment the market for their communication, and deliver each piece of communication in a way that will appeal to the relevant segment of the market, and at a time and a place and in a way that they will listen to and hear it. They need to promote their project, help the various stakeholders appreciate its benefit to them, and be willing to give (and pay for) their support. This is the classic "four Ps" of marketing: the product (the project), the price (the cost of support), the promotion (the message that needs communicating), and the place of sale. So the Marketing School is the last of this initial sequence of schools with a business focus.

References

Andersen, E.S., Grude, K.V., and Haug, T., 2009, *Goal Directed Project Management*, 4th edition, Kogan Page, London.

Barnard, C.I., 1938, *The Functions of the Executive*, Harvard University Press, Boston.

Bass, B.M., 1990, "From transactional to transformational leadership: Learning to share the vision," *Organisational Dynamics*, **18**(3), 19–31.

Belbin, R.M., 1986, *Management Teams*, Heinemann, London.

Blake, R.R., and Mouton, S.J., 1978, *The New Managerial Grid*, Gulf, Houston.

Briggs-Myers, I., 1992, *Gifts Differing*, Consulting Psychologists Press, Palo-Alto.

Cattell, R.B., Eber, H.W., and Tatsuoka, M.M., 1970, *Handbook for the 16PF*, IPAT, Champaign, IL.

Chelly, A., and Boisard-Castelluccia, S., 2007, "Is managing the intra-entrepreneurial teams' conflicts a source of creativity?," *Journal of Academy of Business and Economics*, **7**(2), 38–49.

Cleland, D.I., and King, W.R., 1983, *Systems Analysis and Project Management*, 3rd edition, McGraw-Hill, New York.

Crawford, L.H., 2005, "Senior management perceptions of project management competence," *International Journal of Project Management*, **23**(1), 7–16.

——, 2007, "Assessing and developing the project management competence of individuals," in Turner, J.R. (ed.), *The Gower Handbook of Project Management*, 4th edition, Gower, Aldershot.

Dainty, A.R.J., Cjeng, M., and Moore, D.R., 2005, "Competency-based model for predicting construction project managers' performance," *Journal of Management in Engineering*, **January**, 2–9.

Dolfi, J., and Andrews, E.J., 2007, The subliminal characteristics of project managers: An exploratory study of optimism overcoming challenges in the project management work environment," *International Journal of Project Management*, **25**(7), 674–682.

Dulewicz, V., and Higgs, M.J., 2005, "Assessing leadership styles and organizational context," *Journal of Managerial Psychology*, **20**, 105–123.

Frame, J.D., 2003, *Managing Projects in Organizations: How to make the best use of time, techniques and people*, 3rd edition, Jossey-Bass, San Francisco.

Gardenswartz, L., and Rowe, A., 1994, *Diverse Teams at Work: Capitalizing on the power of diversity*, Irwin Professional Publishing, Chicago.

Gareis, R., 2005, *Happy Projects!*, Manz, Vienna.

——, 2007, "Managing project start," in Turner, J.R. (ed.), *The Gower Handbook of Project Management*, 4th edition, Gower, Aldershot.

Gareis, R., and Huemann, M., 2008, "Maturity models for the project-oriented company," in Turner, J.R. (ed.), *The Gower Handbook of Project Management*, 4th edition, Gower, Aldershot.

Gobeli, D., and Larson, E., 1989, "Relative effectiveness of different project structures," *Project Management Journal*, **18**, 81–85.

Goleman, D., Boyatzis, R.E., and McKee, A., 2002, *The New Leaders*, Harvard Business School Press, Boston.

Graham, R.G., 1989, *Project Management as if People Mattered*, Primavera Press, Bala Cynwyd, PA.

Hanappi-Egger, E., Köllen, T., and Mensi-Klarbach, H., 2007, "Diversity management: Economically reasonable or 'only' ethically mandatory?," *The International Journal of Diversity in Organisations, Communities and Nations*, **7**, 1–17.

Handy, C.B., 1987, *Understanding Organizations*, Penguin, London.

House, R.J., 1971, "A path-goal theory of leader effectiveness," *Administrative Science Quarterly*, **September**, 321–338.

Huemann, M., 2006, "Managing project management personnel and their competencies in the project-oriented company," in Cleland, D.I. and Gareis, R. (eds), *Global Project Management Handbook*, McGraw-Hill, New York.

Huemann, M., Keegan, A.E., and Turner, J.R., 2007, "Human resource management in the project oriented company: A critical review," *International Journal of Project Management*, **25**(3), 315–323.

International Project Management Association, 2006, *International Competence Baseline: The eye of competence*, 3rd edition, International Project Management Association, Zurich.

Katzenbach, J.R., and Smith, D.K., 1993, "The discipline of teams," *Harvard Business Review*, **71**(2), 111–120; reprinted July–August 2005, 162–171.

Keegan, A.E., and Den Hartog, D.N., 2004, "Transformational leadership in a project-based environment: A comparative study of the leadership styles of project managers and line managers," *International Journal of Project Management*, **22**(8), 609–618.

Keegan, A.E., and Turner, J.R., 2003, "Managing human resources in the project-based organization," in Turner, J.R. (ed.), *People in Project Management*, Gower, Aldershot.

Lee-Kelley, L., 2003, "Turner's five functions of project-based management and situational leadership in IT services projects," *International Journal of Project Management*, **21**(8), 583–591.

Luhmann, N., 2006, *Organisation und Entscheidung*, 2nd edition, VS Verlag für Sozialwissenschaften, Wiesbaden.

Margerison, M., and McCann, D., 1990, *Team Management*, Mercury Press, New York.

Office of Government Commerce, 2009, *Managing Successful Projects with PRINCE2*, 5th edition, The Stationery Office, London.

Project Management Institute, 2008, *A Guide to the Project Management Body of Knowledge (PMBOK® Guide)*, 4th edition, Project Management Institute, Newtown Square, PA.

Tuckman, B., 1965, "Developmental sequence in small groups," *Psychological Bulletin*, **63**, 384–399; reprinted in *Group Facilitation: A Research and Applications Journal*, **3**, Spring 2001.

Turner, J.R., 2009, *The Handbook of Project-Based Management*, 3rd edition, McGraw-Hill, New York.

Turner, J.R., Huemann, M., and Keegan, A.E., 2008a, *Human Resource Management in the Project-Oriented Organization*, Project Management Institute, Newtown Square, PA.

Turner, J.R., Huemann, M., and Keegan, A.E., 2008b, "Human Resource Management in the project-oriented organization: Employee well being and ethical treatment," *International Journal of Project Management*, **26**(5), 577–585.

Turner, J.R., Keegan, A.E., and Crawford, L.H., 2003, "Delivering improved project management maturity through experiential learning," in Turner, J.R. (ed.), *People in Project Management*, Gower, Aldershot.

Turner, J.R., and Müller, R., 2006, *Choosing Appropriate Project Managers: Matching their leadership style to the type of project*, Project Management Institute, Newtown Square, PA.

7 Marketing

The project as a billboard

7.1 Communicating with people

The project is a temporary organization to which resources are assigned to deliver beneficial change (Figure 1.3). For the project to start and to run smoothly, and for the end product to be accepted, the project manager must win the support of many people who have to commit substantial resources including time, effort, money, emotion and political will. Figure 7.1 shows the project managers and project sponsor sitting at the center of an array of people. To win the support of these people they must communicate upwards, outwards and downwards:

- upwards to win the support of top management including the owner and financier;
- outwards to win the support of professional colleagues, the users and operators of the project's output, and managers who will provide resources to the project;

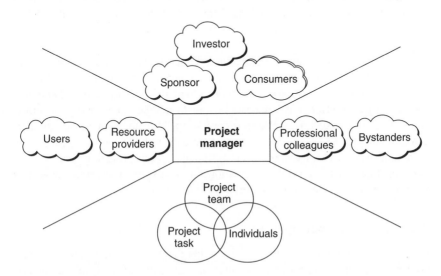

Figure 7.1 The project manager at the center of a web of influence

- downwards to win the support of the project team members who have to make considerable personal commitment to undertaking the project.

It is also necessary to win the support of the consumers who will buy the product or service produced by the project's output. All of these people are generically called stakeholders, but the nature of the communication in the three directions can be different. We dealt with downwards communication in the last chapter; here we deal with that outwards and upwards.

This communication has the nature of classical marketing. In designing the communication the project manager and project sponsor need to:

1 Sell the benefit of the project so people can see the value to themselves and the organization. This is marketing the product of the project. (According to classical marketing theory people buy benefits and not products (Kotler and Keller, 2005).)
2 Then people will be willing to make commitments to the project in terms of the resources they can personally provide. With different people the commitment will take different forms. With some people it will be time and effort, others money, others political will, emotional support, and so on. This is the price of the project to these people individually, and with different people the project has a different price.
3 The communication itself is the promotion of the project, but it has to be designed differently for different people. They will appreciate the project differently depending on what value they attach to it and what contribution they have to make. You need to segment the market for the communication.
4 Finally you need to decide when and how to make the communication for the different stakeholders. There are different modes of communication which will be more effective in reaching different stakeholders. You need to design the place of sale differently for different stakeholders.

In this chapter we describe the marketing of the project. In the next section we describe generic stakeholder management. We then describe internal marketing of the project, and how to design a communication plan for the different stakeholders, and the project sponsor. We then describe how to sell the project and project management to senior executives. We consider how to obtain top management support, and how the project manager should communicate with the sponsor. Much of the communication has to be done by the project manager and project sponsor working together; they exist in a symbiotic relationship, and so the project manager must keep the sponsor feeling comfortable about the project.

7.2 Stakeholder management

In effect, everybody we would want to market the project to is a potential stakeholder, but when talking about stakeholder management we usually take a narrower view than that. We look upon a stakeholder as anybody who is directly affected by the project or its results (Figure 1.3). Stakeholders may be affected by the work of the project, by the project's output, the new asset produced, by the project's outcome, the operation of the asset, or even by the long term impact. Table 4.3 illustrated the views of different stakeholders to different levels of project results. Figure 7.2 suggests a stakeholder management process, which we describe next. It can be useful to capture the results of the analysis in a stakeholder register (Table 7.1). It is our belief that over half the value of this register comes from filling it in, as that helps you understand the stakeholders and how you are going to respond to them. The register is of course also a valuable control tool.

Table 7.1 Stakeholder register for the development of a data network

TriMagi Stakeholder register					
Stakeholder	*Objectives*	*For/ Against*	*Influence*	*Informed*	*Communication strategy*
Board	Expand operations; improved customer service; improved profitability	For	Hi	Must be	Regular briefing Explain solution and benefits
Operations managers	Improved customer service; excellent support	For	Med	Must be	Regular briefing Explain solution and benefits
Maintenance managers	Operation that works; maintain position and influence	For	Hi	Yes	Seek opinions Regular consultation Confirm solution with them
Maintenance staff	Ease of operation; maintain jobs	For	Med	Not at start	Briefings/ company newspaper Consultation Explain solution
Operations staff	Support their work; minimum disruption	Ambivalent	Low	Not at start	Briefings/ company newspaper Explain solution
Technology manager	Influence technical solution; develop power base	For	Med	Must be	Regular consultation Seek opinions Explain solution
Suppliers	Make profit; ongoing business with company	For	Med	Not at start	Open channels Regular consultation
Customers	Good service	For	Low	Not at start	Customer newsletters
Local community	Minimum disruption to environment	Ambivalent	Low	Low	Local newspaper advertisements

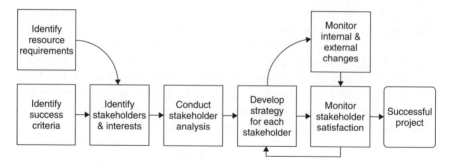

Figure 7.2 The stakeholder management process

Identify the stakeholders and their objectives

Identify stakeholders

You can identify your stakeholders by identifying your resource requirements. The obvious resource requirement is the people who will do work for you, either during the project in the delivery of the asset, but also after the project during operation of the asset. But many other types of people will provide support of different types, financial, political, and emotional support, and acceptance of the project and its results. All those types of support are resources and the providers are all stakeholders. Table 4.3 suggests a number of different stakeholders.

Identify project success criteria

Another approach is to work from the different views of project success criteria, as shown in Tables 4.1 and 4.3. There we identified that project success comprises a variety of criteria, and different stakeholders are interested in different criteria. We said at the time that the project manager should aim to get agreement by the different stakeholders to a balanced portfolio of the criteria, and aim to maintain that agreement at configuration review points through the project. So the process of defining project success helps identify various stakeholders and their different interests.

Analyze the stakeholders

To analyze the stakeholders, we ask three questions about each stakeholder:

1   Do they support or oppose the project? If their objectives are aligned with the project then presumably they will support it, if they are misaligned presumably they will oppose it. There can be some stakeholders who don't care. Some contractors, for instance, may not care if the project is a success or a failure as long as they get paid.

2   Can they influence the outcome? The people who support us and can influence the outcome are our friends; those who oppose us and can influence the outcome our enemies.

A SWOT analysis of each stakeholder will help answer these first two questions. We ask ourselves what the strengths and weaknesses of each stakeholder are (can they influence the outcome or not?), and whether they view the project as an opportunity or a threat (are they for or against?). There is a moral issue. If we identify that somebody is supporting the project but an element of the project is a threat to them, do we tell them? If the project is mainly positive for them but there is a small element that is a threat, it is best to discuss it with them and try to solve the problem. They will respect you for it. If you try to hide it, then when they find out, and they will find out, they may turn against you. But if they have got the project totally wrong and it is entirely a threat to them, then you may try to keep it secret for as long as possible – that is the moral problem, whether withholding information is a lie.

3   Have they adopted their position with full knowledge of the project or are they ignorant? In answering this question you want to think both about where people are starting and where you want them to be. If you think people may be ignorant of the project but they should support it, you want to tell them sooner rather than later. You want people to start with positive attitudes about the project. We believe if people hear about the project on the grapevine, as a rumor, they will be against it from the start. If they hear about the project as a rumor, they will assume management is trying to keep it secret, and if management are trying to keep it secret it must be bad. Psychologists have shown that if people form a wrong opinion based on incomplete or incorrect information, they find it very hard to change their opinion when they get correct complete information. Make sure they hear about the project from you first and that they hear positive messages.

Develop an influence strategy

You next develop an influence strategy for communicating with each stakeholder. There are models that suggest different strategies for different types of stakeholders.

Attitude–Knowledge

The first model is based on the answers to the last two questions (Table 7.2): do the stakeholders support or oppose the project; and are they knowledgeable or ignorant about it?

1   *Knowledgeable–Support:* These people must not be taken for granted. Make sure you continue to communicate with them, and work with them to maintain their support.

2   *Ignorant–Support:* Most people who are ignorant will not start here. Try to identify those people who are likely to be ignorant about the project but should be in favor of it and try to be the first to tell them about the project. Sell them

Table 7.2 Stakeholders' influence based on knowledge-support

		Support for the project	
		Support	*Against*
Knowledge of the project	*Knowledgeable*	Work with them to maintain their support	Change the project to win over or isolate
	Ignorant	Be the first to inform them to sell positive messages	Try not to let anyone start here

positive messages about the project, and show them how it will be beneficial to them to win their support before they receive negative information about the project from its opponents.

3   *Ignorant–Against:* If people start off with a negative view of the project for the wrong reason it will be very hard to change their views. Psychologists have shown that if people form a wrong opinion based on wrong information they find it very difficult to change their view when they get correct information. In the modern world, people are much less respectful of people in authority than they were 50 years ago. They almost assume that "the-powers-that-be" are trying to mislead them. They form opinions based on misinformation they have read in the tabloid press and are totally convinced they are correct and that the authorities are wrong. Once people have got a wrong opinion about the project it is almost impossible to change their minds. Also, when communicating with stakeholders you must express things in terms they understand, in layman's language. There was a case of a British company that was developing a uranium mine in Canada. At the public inquiry an engineer was mischievously asked by a lawyer representing the environmental lobby what the radiation level would be of waste water leaving the site. He gave a precise technical answer, so many becquerels, to six decimal places. The next day the local newspapers were full of it; the waste water leaving the site would be radioactive. Everybody would die of cancer, children would be born with two heads. The correct answer was "half the level of rainwater" – the waste water was to be twice as pure as rain water. The company tried to correct the misinformation. But it was too late, nobody was listening anymore, the genie was out of the bottle, Pandora's Box was opened, there was no closing them again, the damage was done.

4   *Knowledgeable–Against:* These people are almost easier to deal with than the ones just above. They are against for good reason. The project is damaging to them. You can have a rational discussion with them. In the process it might be possible to change the project to win them over. If not you have to find ways of reducing their influence.

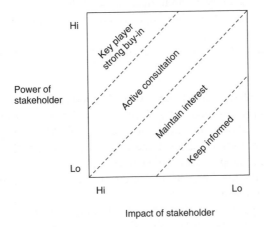

Figure 7.3 The power–influence map

Power–Influence

The second influence strategy considers:
1   What is the power of the stakeholder in the parent organization?
2   What is the impact of the stakeholder on the project?

This leads to four influence strategies as shown in Figure 7.3. This is sometimes drawn as the dreaded two-by-two matrix, but we prefer the four bands.

Commitment–Acceptance

The third influence strategy asks (Figure 7.4):

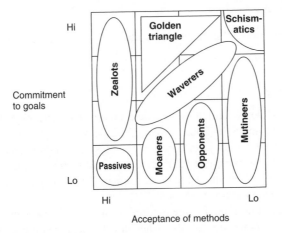

Figure 7.4 The commitment–acceptance map
With acknowledgment to Mr Olivier D'Herbemont, Mr Bruno César, Mr Pascal Etcheber and Mr Tom Curtin, *Managing Sensitive Projects*, published 1998, Palgrave Macmillan, reproduced with permission.

1   What is the stakeholder's commitment to the goals?
2   What is their acceptance of the proposed methods to achieve the goals?

From this we can identify several different types of stakeholder (D'Herbemont *et al.*, 1998):

- The Passives: They often represent about 40 to 60 percent of the stakeholders, and the way they feel about the project is usually influenced by the Waverers.
- The Waverers: They in turn are influenced by the Golden Triangle.
- The Zealots: You might think that the zealots are your best allies, but they just give unthinking support, which often does not help very much.
- The Golden Triangle: These people, on the other hand, by questioning the project help to improve it.
- The Schismatics: They can be very difficult. In essence they support the project, but they are constantly carping about how it is being done. The former managing director of the company often sits here.
- The Moaners, Opponents and Mutineers: From the last three groups we see decreasing support and increasing opposition. The mutineers are the opposite of the zealots, exhibiting unthinking opposition.

Monitor progress through the project

As the project progresses, you need to monitor the stakeholders' reactions, and whether you are getting the desired response, and take action accordingly – like all other project control. The stakeholder register (Table 7.1) can be used as a project control tool.

7.3 Marketing the project

The second component of this school is the marketing of the project to the organization.

Internal marketing

Susan Foreman (1996) wrote an early article on internal marketing of projects. More recently Cova and Sale (2005) investigated the marketing of projects. Their focus was on marketing of projects to customers; they quoted Pinto and Rouhainen (2001) to say the focus of project management should shift from managing time, cost and quality to emphasizing value for customers. They compared project management and project marketing (see Table 7.3).

A standard marketing model is the marketing mix, or 4Ps (Kotler and Keller, 2005). The marketing mix suggests that when developing a marketing strategy for your product you should consider the balance between the product, price, promotion and place of sale. To this list some people add three more Ps, the people, process and physical environment.

Table 7.3 A comparison of project management and project marketing

Issue	Project management	Project marketing
The project	Temporary organization	Transaction
Focus	The project	Relationships
Project origin	Given	Constructed
Project start	Request for proposal	Concept, project opportunity
Performance measures	Time, cost, quality	Value to the customer
Stakeholders	People with a direct positive or negative impact on the project	People in the business milieu in which the project is imbedded

Product

Classic marketing says that you are not selling a physical product, you are selling a benefit. People buy your product because it gives them some benefit. It is the same with projects. You need to market the project's outputs, outcomes and impact, but in selling those you need to sell their benefit to the organization and the people involved in the project. People will buy into the benefit of the project. That is the fifth line in Table 7.3. Don't talk about the triple constraint; sell the value of the project to the customers.

Price

As we have just said, the stakeholders have to buy into the project. What it costs them is often not money, but other commitments. There are several different types of commitment people make to a project, including money, their own time, the time of their subordinates, political support, emotional commitment, and so on. You need to understand the different types of commitment people will make and tailor your communication to them accordingly.

Promotion

You will promote the project to the various stakeholders by developing a communication strategy to influence their behavior. In the last section we introduced three different models for categorizing the stakeholders and suggested different stakeholders would require different communication strategies. You need to segment the market of stakeholders and tailor your communication accordingly.

Place of sale

The project is being delivered within the parent organization, and so you must gain the acceptance of the stakeholders to the project in that context. But you also need to think about where and how you are going to communicate with the different stakeholders. Not only must you tailor the message for different stakeholders, you must tailor the media for communication with them and the method of delivery.

People

Both this chapter and the last chapter have been about people. Projects involve people; projects don't exist without them. Internal marketing is about trying to influence the behavior of people throughout the organization, including the project team, to support the project.

Process

We consider the project process in the next chapter. It is essential not just to get people's support of the projects output, outcome and impact and the benefit they provide to the organization, but also to get their support for the method of delivering the project. They must support not just the goals but also the method of achieving the goals (Turner and Cochrane, 1993). We show below that in making the sponsor feel comfortable you must convince them not just about the project goals but also the adopted process.

Physical environment

With some stakeholders, the impact is not that they have to give time or effort, but that it changes the physical environment within which they work or live. You must understand who those stakeholders are and win their support. There have been several road construction projects in the UK where protests by the environmental lobby have added significantly to the cost of the project. Being seen to conduct an environmental impact assessment, and tailoring the design of the project's product accordingly, can be one way to win the support of these stakeholders.

Communicating with stakeholders

Internal marketing means promoting the project and building relationships with the people involved. A key component of that is communicating with the stakeholders. The following questions can help you develop a communication plan for your project:

Who is the target audience?

You need to understand the target audience. Research the client organization. Understand its objectives, and align the project objectives with the client objectives. Segment the market for the communication. We have seen that you need to communicate with different groups of people, and they have different needs in terms of the messages they want to hear, and the best media for getting those messages to them. The British grocery company Tesco felt they weren't communicating well with the employees, so they employed consultants to help. The consultants identified that whereas Tesco carefully segmented their customers, they treated their employees as one amorphous mass. The consultants identified six different segments of employees, and suggested Tesco communicate different messages to them in different ways. You need to do the same with your project stakeholders. With the stakeholders in Table 7.1, you will need to tailor the messages and the methods of reaching them in different ways.

What are the objectives of each communication?

Next you need to think about the objectives of your communication. Objectives can include:

- to raise awareness of the organization of the project and the benefit it will provide;
- to gain commitment of the people in the organization to the project – they must make a commitment to the project which will cost them something and so must understand what benefit it will be to them in return;
- to keep business areas informed so that they can understand how the project impacts them, what contribution they have to make and what they can expect in return;
- to promote key messages so that people truly understand what the project is about and what it entails, and to avoid rumor and misinformation;
- to show that senior management are committed to the project, and what it will do for the organization;
- to make communication two way, seeking feedback about the project, and responding to people's concerns;
- to maximize benefits by ensuring that people understand what the project's output will do and how it should be used.

What are the key messages?

You need to design the messages to be communicated to achieve the objectives. Different messages are needed for each segment of the target audience. The communication needs identified in the stakeholder register will help in the design of the messages.

What information will be communicated and by whom?

You need to choose the information that should actually be communicated to get the key messages across. Different messages are best sent by different people. The project manager will tell stakeholders about the scope of the project, and when certain things will be done. But information about the desired performance improvement and the benefit to the organization is better coming from the project sponsor, or even more senior managers so they can show their commitment, and the importance of the project to the organization.

When will the information be given?

Timing is critical. The sponsor and senior managers should show their commitment early on. The project manager can take responsibility for the later communication.

Also, as we said above, you want key stakeholders to hear about the project from the project manager or the sponsor first, and not as a rumor, so they gain positive views about the project from the start.

How will feedback be encouraged?

It is essential that communication is two way, so that you talk with people not talk at them. If you want people committed to the project and the change it will introduce, they must feel involved, and that they have some influence over the design. (It is important that they *feel* they have some influence, whether or not they actually do is not so important.) But for this reason it is important that you are seen to be looking for and listening to feedback. You must show through your body language that you are listening to the feedback, and respond to the questions asked, if not right away, then at the next meeting. Also, you perhaps need to make some change to the design of the project and its product so that you are seen to be responding to people's concerns. Perhaps you will try to keep the changes cosmetic so that the overall thrust of the project does not change, but by making some changes no matter how small you show you are responding to people's concerns.

What media will be used?

As we have said, different media will be used for different stakeholders, different market segments. Possible media include:

- seminars and workshops;
- press and the media;
- bulletins, briefings, press-releases, web pages, project newsletter;
- site exhibitions;
- video and CD.

Communication between the project manager and the sponsor

The communication just described ought to be planned by the project manager and sponsor working together, to show a united front, and support by senior management for the project. However, one very special relationship is between the project manager and sponsor. In order to maintain the sponsor's commitment, the project manager needs to maintain the sponsor's comfort levels about performance on the project and his or her own competence and professionalism, and that is best achieved through effective communication. So how should the project manager communicate with the sponsor to maintain their comfort levels? To answer that question we need to ask ourselves which questions the client wants answering and what the mode and frequency of communication should be.

Questions the client wants answering

Bob Graham (2007) says that when thinking about communication we often ask ourselves what data people want. He says it is better to think about what questions the client wants answering. To improve their comfort and trust clients want several questions answering:

1 Will the end deliverable meet their functional requirements?
2 Is the right project process being followed to successfully deliver the required end deliverables in the optimum way?
3 Will the project meet the required quality, budget and schedule requirements?
4 Is the project manager behaving in a professional and trustworthy manner?
5 Are appropriate control mechanisms in place to achieve all the above?

These can be summarized as questions of product and process, project performance and surprise avoidance.

Questions of product and process

The client wants to know that the asset as designed will operate to achieve the desired project outcomes and that those will help achieve the desired impact with time. This requires communication at the start of the project. The project manager needs to explain the design to the client, and show how the asset will perform. This is best done in a face-to-face meeting. At the same time the project manager will need to explain the project plan to the client, and demonstrate that it will deliver the asset in the agreed time. This will require the project manager to show that the work is feasible in the time, and that adequate resources have been assigned. Constructibility may also be an issue. That is, the project objectives must be realistic; they must be technically feasible. But they must also be achievable; it must actually be possible to build them. In explaining the design and the project plan, the project manager may also need to explain how the work will be done and demonstrate that it is achievable.

Questions of performance

Answering questions of performance is best done in written reports. The project manager needs to show that the work is being done in the desired time. Time and cost reports, such as tracked bar charts, milestone tracker diagrams and earned value reports (Chapters 2 and 4) will be useful tools here. The client will continue to want to know that adequate resources are being applied. The earned value report will help with that, but resource histograms will also be useful.

Performance reports can be event driven or calendar driven. That is you can make them on the achievement of project milestones or at regular intervals. Project managers often prefer to make event driven reports, but Rodney Turner and Ralf Müller (2004) have shown that calendar-driven reports are best. Rodney used to say that reports could be made one a month or even once every six weeks. But our work in 2004 showed that reports made once every two weeks are best. It is a balance between the client taking an interest in project progress and the cost of making reports. Clients would like reports daily, but the cost would be prohibitive. Project managers would like to make reports about once every two months, but then the client will feel very uncomfortable. Reports once every two weeks provide the best balance.

One of the necessary conditions for project success we introduced in Section 4.3 was that "the client or sponsor must take an interest in project performance" (Turner and Müller, 2004). We suggested that on high-performing projects, the client takes an interest in project progress. On those projects the client has a pessimistic view of performance; it is usually doing better than they think. On low-performing projects, the client does not take an interest in progress. On those projects the client has an optimistic view of progress; it is usually doing less well than they think. This is a bit sad for project managers. You want your client to take an interest in progress to achieve a successful outcome, but then they probably won't give you full credit for how well the project is doing. But for best performance on projects the client should insist on receiving the written reports, and to keep the client happy the project manager should submit them once every two weeks.

Questions of surprise avoidance

Rodney Turner and Ralf Müller (2004) found that clients are somewhat schizophrenic. They trust the written reports to give them a true picture on performance, but they don't trust them to give them a true view of project issues. There may be risks lurking in the undergrowth which the project manager knows about, but there is no need to volunteer information about them in the progress reports. Thus, to answer questions of surprise avoidance the client also wants face-to-face meetings with the project manager, and wants those meetings about once a week. At that meeting the client can ask the project manager about risks and issues on the project. But the client can also ask questions related to the adverse selection and moral hazard problems (Chapter 5). Why is the project manager making the decisions they are? Are they actually behaving competently and in a professional, trustworthy way?

Mode of communication

Thus there are two main modes of communication: written and verbal.

The project manager makes written reports once every two weeks to answer questions of performance, and makes verbal reports weekly to answer questions of surprise avoidance.

7.4 Selling project management to senior executives

Up to now we have looked at marketing the project to the organization. We now turn our attention to selling project management itself to top management. We saw above the importance of convincing the stakeholders that the correct process has been adopted. It is also important to convince senior management of the value of adopting project management as the technique for implementing strategic change within the organization. In this section we consider top management support as a success factor on projects and the nature of the support senior management should provide. We then consider the need to speak the language of senior management to win their support. We end with a report of the value of project management based on the results of a recent research project. Understanding the value of project management may help you convince senior management and win their support.

Top management support as a success factor

It has long been recognized that top management support is a success factor on projects. Tables 4.2, 4.3 and 4.4 give lists of success factors on projects and all three mention the importance of senior management support. As part of their support for projects, top management must understand their commitment to projects. This requires several things:

Showing an interest

Senior management must understand and support the projects taking place in the organization. In order for the project manager and project team members to be motivated to deliver the best for the project, they must believe that senior management care about what happens. In the past this has not been the case. Senior management were concerned about maintaining the routine business and projects were something that took place in the "skunk works," out the back in temporary accommodation on waste ground. Project team members worked away unnoticed and unrewarded to produce new businesses. Top management took an interest when the new business was transferred to the routine. The best people did not want to work on projects because it was a path to oblivion, to a place where top management would not notice you or promote you. That is not good for projects. The project sponsor, of course has the ambassadorial role to ensure that top management take an interest, but top management as well need to recognize that their taking an interest is a necessary condition for project success.

Fulfilling their governance roles

A significant way in which senior management must take an interest is in fulfilling their governance roles. In Section 5.3, we identified three roles: the sponsor, the owner and the steward. The board of directors must take responsibility for ensuring that appropriate governance structures are in place, that people in the organization fulfill their roles above, and that APM's 11 principles of the governance of projects (Section 5.3) are enacted. The board must ensure that people have appropriate responsibility, authority and competence to fulfill their roles, that appropriate monitoring and control procedures, including end-of-stage reviews, are in place, and that audits are conducted where necessary.

In order for all of these things to happen, senior managers and the board of directors must be convinced that project management is the appropriate vehicle for managing strategic change within the organization, that it can help the organization achieve its strategic objectives and provide value to the organization. We discuss this further below.

Understanding risk exposure

Top management should also take an interest in understanding the risk exposure of projects. In understanding future cash flows for the business, it is important that directors understand the risk to the cost of projects and the risk to potential revenues. Having understood the risk, they must then make available support to help project, program and portfolio managers overcome the risk. Projects must be treated as a partnership between the client and project manager, whether the client is internal or external to the project manager's organizations. The client and project manager must work together in partnership to make whatever adaptations are necessary to reduce the exposure to risk and to deal with the risks that actually occur.

In Section 5.2 we met the concept of "bounded rationality." The project manager would like to to deliver a perfect solution for the client, but because of human frailty cannot do so perfectly. The project manager's ability to work perfectly and rationally is bounded by:

- they cannot gather all the necessary data to make perfect forecasts about the project;
- they cannot perfectly process all the data they do have, and so tend to satisfice – do what is adequate rather than perfect;
- they cannot foretell the future – now there is a shortcoming.

When the project starts, the manager cannot perfectly forecast how it will progress through to completion. Changes will be necessary; risks will need to be dealt with. Top management need to understand that, and work with the project manager to achieve appropriate adaptations so that the project delivers the best solution for the business.

Monitoring data

Top management also has a commitment to monitor performance on projects, programs and portfolios in the business. They are now required to do this by law to be able to forecast future cash flows in the business. We said above that a necessary condition for project success is that the client takes an interest in progress. Now we are not advocating micro management, where top management become involved and interfere in the day to day running of the project. We are talking more about management by exception. Managers of large projects, programs and portfolios produce a single-page report to summarize performance once a month, highlighting potential problems. Figures 4.2 to 4.5 suggested a number of reports for this purpose.

Consistently supporting project management

Top management must consistently support project management within their organization. We have seen that this requires the development of enterprise-wide project management capability (Section 5.4). But in order to do this, top management must:

- ensure project management is valued as an essential corporate delivery capability, a key competence;
- initiatives to improve project management are consistently funded, supporting (financially) knowledge management and the project management community;
- consistently show support for project management.

Top management must also:

- make sure the contribution of project managers is appreciated in the organization;
- project management is not assigned to the skunk works, but takes place as a central and core part of the operation of the business;
- there is a career track for project managers, leading to senior positions in the organization.

Selling project management to senior executives

For top management to provide the necessary support to projects within the organization, they must be convinced of the efficacy of project management for delivering the organization's strategic objectives. Table 7.4 shows a value continuum based on the work of Janice Thomas and her co-workers (2002). Many project managers are at the tactical end of this spectrum, especially those wedded to the Optimization Perspective and the systems approach. They talk about achieving the triple constraint of time cost and quality, and using the critical path method, the earned value method and Gantt charts to help them do this. Senior managers are in the middle of this spectrum, concerned about developing new products, new markets and new competencies to grow and develop the business. Boards of directors are at the competitive end, trying to achieve competitive advantage for their business, to meet the objectives of their shareholders and other stakeholders.

The problem is, as illustrated in Table 7.5, when project managers talk about the triple constraint, Gantt charts and CPM, senior managers cannot see how it is relevant to developing new competencies for the business, let alone boards of directors seeing how it is relevant to providing shareholder value. When talking to senior

Table 7.4 The value continuum (after Thomas et al., 2002)

Nature	Tactical selling		Strategic selling		Competitive selling
What is sold	Products		Solutions		Relationships
Values	Foundation values		Innovation values		
Aims	Efficiency Improvement	Effectiveness	Market expansion		Advantage creation
Objectives	Profit Reduce costs Quality Timely finish	Customer service Collaboration Knowledge Effectiveness	New products New markets New competencies		Competitive advantage Strategic change

managers and boards of directors, project managers have to change their selling mode. When talking to senior managers, project managers have to talk about the project's outcomes, the new competencies it will develop for the business, and how the use of project management will help achieve those outcomes. The triple constraint is almost irrelevant. All that is important is that the new competencies are obtained at a time, cost and level of performance that will enable the business to effectively utilize the new competencies. In order to sell to boards of directors, project managers and project sponsors together need to switch into competitive selling and focus on the project impacts, the improvement in competitive advantage and performance improvement that the project will provide the organization with over the medium to long term.

Table 7.5 Selling project management

		Buyers		
		Tactical	Strategic	Competitive
Sellers	Tactical	Tools, techniques, methodologies Efficiency values Superficial relationship	No buyer interest	No buyer interest
	Strategic	Services, people, methodologies Efficiency/effectiveness One-off relationship	Project outcomes New competencies Effectiveness values Stable relationship	Value of project management Efficacy Treadmill relationship
	Competitive	No seller interest	No seller interest	Project impacts Performance Competitive advantage Growing relationship

Tactical sellers cannot make a sale to strategic and competitive buyers because they are just not talking the right language. The sellers are talking about low-level efficiency improvements which the buyers are not interested in. The strategic and competitive buyers say they are not interested in how the project is delivered; they want to know what results will be achieved. Strategic sellers can sell to tactical buyers, selling people or methodologies that will help them do their projects more efficiently. But this tends to be a once-off sale, because once the buyer has bought the new methodology, he or she has it to use. The strategic seller can sell the value of project management to the competitive buyer, showing how the use of project management can improve performance and lead to competitive advantage. We describe this as a treadmill relationship based on the work of Janice Thomas and Mark Mullaly (2008). They show that appreciation of performance improvement from the use of project management only lasts a short time. The new state becomes the norm and so no longer valued. To maintain this relationship you need to go on delivering ever more performance improvement.

The value of project management

In research sponsored by the Project Management Institute, Janice Thomas and Mark Mullaly (2008) demonstrated quite clearly that the adoption of project management delivers value to organizations. You need to demonstrate that value to senior management so that they make the necessary commitment to develop enterprise-wide project management capability and the investment to improve project management maturity in the organization.

7.5 How do we get there?

There is a scene in Lewis Carroll's book, *Alice in Wonderland*, where Alice, who is lost in the forest, is talking to the Cheshire Cat. Alice asks the cat which road she should take from here, and the cat says that all depends where she wants to get to. Alice is lost so she says she doesn't care much where, so the cat says it doesn't matter which road she takes. The six perspectives up to now have been about deciding where we want to get to, and winning support from the various stakeholders to that vision of the project. Now we need to convert that vision into reality. We need to follow a road, a process, which takes us to our goals.

Hopefully it is reasonably obvious where the road we need to take starts. There are some yellow bricks to begin to follow. But the nature of projects and project management is that there will be no clear road map. This is not a well-trodden path we are about to follow. We won't be handed a map. Depending on the uniqueness of the project the road will be clearer in some cases than others. In Section 1.5, we introduced is a categorization of projects: runners, repeaters, strangers, and aliens (Turner, 2008). For runners and repeaters, the current project will be very similar to things we have done in the past and so we will have a reasonably clear map. There will just be slight variations along the way, of which we must be aware. With aliens, we will be exploring uncharted territory, and we must pick our way along, and learn enough about where we are to make it to the next intermediate goal. Strangers will be in between. For some parts of the project there will be a reasonably clear map. But we will need to explore our way from where one map finishes to where the next one starts, and we will need to work out how to put the pieces of map together. We now consider the process perspective.

References

Cova, B., and Sale, R., 2005, "Six points to merge project marketing into project management", *International Journal of Project Management*, **23**(5), 354–359.

D'Herbemont, O., Cesar, B., Etcheber, P., and Curtin, T., 1998, *Managing Sensitive Projects: Lateral approach*, revised edition, Palgrave Macmillan, London.

Foreman, S., 1996, "Internal marketing," in Turner, J.R., Grude, K.V., and Thurloway, L. (eds), *The Project Manager as Change Agent*, McGraw-Hill, London.

Graham, R., 2007, "Managing conflict, persuasion and negotiation," in Turner, J.R. (ed.), *The Gower Handbook of Project Management*, 4th edition, Gower, Aldershot.

Kotler, P., and Keller, K.L., 2005, *Marketing Management,* 12th edition, Prentice Hall, New York.

Pinto, J.K., and Rouhainen, P.J., 2001, *Customer-based Project Organization*, Wiley, New York.

Thomas, J., Delisle, C., and Jugdev, K., 2002, *Selling Project Management to Senior Executives: Framing the moves that matter*, Project Management Institute, Newtown Square, PA.

Thomas, J., and Mullaly, M., 2008, *Researching the Value of Project Management*, Project Management Institute, Newtown Square, PA.

Turner, J.R., 2008, *The Handbook of Project-Based Management*, McGraw-Hill, New York.

Turner, J.R., and Cochrane, R.A., 1993, "The goals and methods matrix: Coping with projects for which the goals and/or methods of achieving them are ill-defined," *International Journal of Project Management*, **11**(2), 93–101.

Turner, J.R., and Müller, R., 2004, "Communication and cooperation on projects between the project owner as principal and the project manager as agent," *The European Management Journal*, **22**(3), 327–336.

8 Process

The project as an algorithm

8.1 Converting vision into reality

Project management can be perceived as a process of converting vision into reality. We start with a vision of some future state we would like to achieve, a change that will provide us with benefit. However, when we start the project there may be some uncertainty about the precise nature of that future state (the goals we are going to achieve), and how we are going to get there (the methods of achieving the goals) (Figure 1.7). So to achieve our vision, to make it a reality, we need to follow a structured process, which will lead us to that end state.

In this chapter we describe the process perception on projects. We describe project processes and describe different forms of life-cycle, including the product, project and management life-cycle models. We liken the process to an algorithm. An algorithm is a process that defines rules that tell us how to take the next step towards our solution, and that is how we view the project process. The nature of the project processes will differ for different types of projects, in particular in which quadrant of Figure 1.7 the project sits. For projects in the bottom left quadrant (well-defined goals, well-defined methods, traditional engineering projects), the process will be very deterministic. We will slip quickly into activity-based planning. This is of course traditional project management for which the tools of the Optimization Perspective were designed. For projects in the top-right (poorly defined goals, poorly defined objectives, such as organizational change projects), the process will help us solve the problem of identifying the methods and identifying the ways of achieving our objectives. Now we have only a hazy idea of what our solution looks like and where it lies. But the process (algorithm) helps us identify the first step to take towards the solution. Having taken the step, we have a clearer idea of what the solution looks like, and where it lies, but also of what the next step should be. And so on until we reach the solution (or abandon the project because the process has shown us it is not feasible – either the solution is not realistic, or not achievable, or both). This is very much what the project processes are like, using guidelines to take steps closer to the solution and improving your understanding of it.

We start by describing the various life-cycles, including product, portfolio, program and project life-cycles. We call these project processes. We will then focus on project management processes. Project management as a process may be perceived in different ways:

- processes for delivering individual project management functions such as scope management, quality management and risk management;
- processes based on the control cycle, or plan;
- a business process, consisting of project start, project controlling and project close down.

Finally we describe the adoption of procedures manuals to capture the knowledge of the project processes or project management processes in a given organization.

8.2 Project processes

We start by considering project processes. These occur on several levels:

The product life-cycle

At the highest level is the life-cycle of the product delivered by the project. But there are in fact several interpretations of that. There is the project's output, the new plant produced by the project; and there is the project's outcome, the product made by that plant.

One of the earliest models was developed by Stephen Wearne (1973) (Figure 8.1), showing the life-cycle of a heavy engineering plant. This is a life-cycle for the project's output. Many people would now add decommissioning as yet another step at the end. Projects can occur at each one of the steps of this process, or as we shall see shortly, the project life-cycle can encompass several steps, for instance, from evaluation to commissioning. The World Bank (Table 8.1) and the European

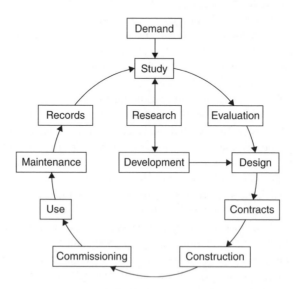

Figure 8.1 Life-cycle for industrial plant (after Stephen Wearne, 1973)

Table 8.1 Project life-cycle used by the World Bank

Stage
Identification of project concepts
Preparation of data
Appraisal of data and selection of project solution
Negotiation and mobilization of project organization
Implementation including detail, design, and construction
Operation
Post-project review

Table 8.2 Life-cycle proposed by the European Construction Institute

Stage
Concept
Feasibility
Front-end design
Project plan
Specification
Tender and evaluation
Manufacturing
Construction
Commission
Operation and maintenance
Decommission
Disposal

Construction Institute (Table 8.2) have produced similar life-cycles. The World Bank's cycle reflects the fact that other people actually design and build the new asset. So the cycle focuses on those areas of concern to the bank, the decision to invest in the asset, and the post-project review. The European Construction Institute's cycle is very similar to Stephen Wearne's but does indeed have decommissioning and disposal of the asset as the final steps. These three life-cycles are sometimes called investment life-cycles (Gareis, 2005).

Figure 8.2 shows a classical marketing view of the product produced by the new asset. This is a life-cycle for the project's outcome. Again the project can cover several steps of this process, or there may be projects at each step. Rodney Turner (2009) also introduces the life-cycle shown in Figure 8.3, covering the new product development stages of Figure 8.2.

The cycles so far are from the private sector. Figure 8.4 shows a life-cycle for government policy, developed by the Office of Government Commerce (2004) in the UK. This has three levels. At the top is a four-step process for government policy: policy design, policy implementation, policy maintenance, and policy review. Nested within this is a program life-cycle for programs of government policy, and within that project life-cycles. The diamonds are end-of-stage reviews, which are discussed further in the next chapter.

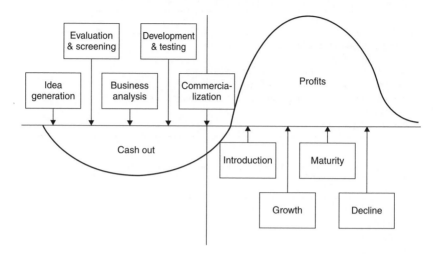

Figure 8.2 Classical marketing view of the life-cycle of the product

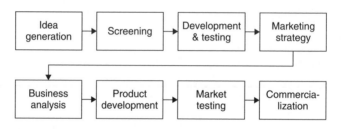

Figure 8.3 New product planning process (project life-cycle)

Parts of Figure 8.2 are outside the control of the sponsoring organization, and are a life-cycle of the market within which the organization operates, whereas all the elements of Figures 8.1, 8.3 and 8.4 are within the scope of the sponsoring organization. The next two life-cycles occur at the middle level of governance discussed in Section 5.3.

The portfolio life-cycle

Figures 8.1 to 8.3 and Tables 8.1 and 8.2 follow a single product. But an organization will have a portfolio of products, and so needs processes for the management of its product portfolio and project portfolio. Management of the product portfolio will be linked to organizational strategy and will use tools such as Ansoff's Matrix or the Boston Consulting Matrix (Johnson *et al.*, 2008). The management of the project portfolio takes place at the middle level of governance (Section 5.3), and follows the process suggested in that section:

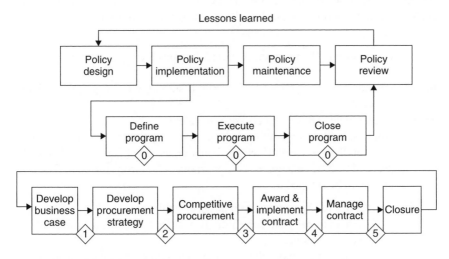

Figure 8.4 Life-cycle for government policy

Step 1: Maintain a list of all projects, programs and portfolios in a project data-base.

Step 2: Monitor progress on all projects, programs and portfolios.

Step 3: Prioritize all projects, programs and portfolios and assign resources appro-priately.

Step 4: Plan the resource needs of all projects and programs in the portfolio and coordinate the assignment of resources between them.

Step 5: Evaluate business benefits post-implementation, to continuously improve selection and management procedures.

The top level of Figure 8.4 is a portfolio management process for the public sector, but is a product portfolio process rather than a project portfolio, elements of gov-ernment policy being governmental products. The UK government is currently developing its portfolio management standard (Office of Government Commerce, 2009a).

The program life-cycle

Nested within the product and portfolio processes is the program life-cycle, as illus-trated by Figure 8.4 for government policy. The program life-cycle is aimed more at strategic change within organizations. Strategic change often requires several smaller unrelated projects to be undertaken to achieve the higher-order strategic objectives. These smaller projects may by undertaken over several cycles. The change may be to develop new business areas including new products, and so may be linked to Figures 8.2 and 8.3. But it may be to introduce new technology, new organizational structures or cultural change. In Section 5.3 we introduced a five-stage program life-cycle representing the cyclic nature of programs:

Step 1: Formulation: The program is started. Options are considered and choices made.
Step 2: Organization: A cycle of the program is started. Projects are planned and selected.
Step 3: Deployment: Those projects are undertaken.
Step 4: Appraisal: At the end of the cycle, progress is assessed. Progress towards the overall objective and business benefit is assessed. It is decided either to proceed with another cycle of the program, or to stop the program. The program will be stopped if:

- the desired business benefit has been achieved;
- the benefit has been substantially achieved and further work will not be cost effective;
- circumstances have changed and the original objectives are no longer worthwhile.

Step 5: Dissolution: If it is decided to stop the program, the team is disbanded.

Figure 5.5 is another version of the program life-cycle from the Office of Government Commerce (2007). This shows a four-step life-cycle very similar to the project life-cycle which follows. Step 1 above covers the first two stages in this life-cycle: identifying and defining the program. Steps 2, 3 and 4 then cover the middle stage: governing the program, and the left-hand sub-stage, managing the portfolio. The life-cycle above does not directly address the issue of benefits realization although one of the main advantages claimed for undertaking the program in cycles is that you can obtain early benefits realization. Step 5 covers the last stage: dissolution of the program. Figure 5.5 also shows that different people are responsible for undertaking the portfolio of projects that comprises the program and for delivering benefit. The program and project managers are responsible for undertaking the projects and delivering new capability or competence to the organization. They are responsible for delivering the project outputs, and commissioning those outputs to show that they are capable of achieving the outcomes. The business change managers are responsible for using the projects' outcomes, the new capabilities given to the organization, to realize the benefits from the projects and the program.

Smaller projects are nested within Figure 5.5, and occur at the Step 3 deployment above or at the step called Governance of the Program within Figure 5.5. Almost all smaller projects will be part of a program or a portfolio or both, and so will be nested in either the program life-cycle, Figure 5.5 or the portfolio process above. Those smaller projects will then usually not have their own life-cycle, but will be managed using the management processes presented below. Thus the standalone project life-cycle will only apply to larger projects.

The project life-cycle

In parallel with the program life-cycle is the project life-cycle which applies to standalone, larger projects of similar sizes to programs. Figure 8.1 can be offered as a comprehensive project life-cycle, but is of course primarily the life-cycle of the asset produced by the project, an investment life-cycle. It is now common to suggest a standard five-stage process (Figure 8.5 and Table 8.3).

This life-cycle illustrates the process as an algorithm. We start in the concept stage with an unclear picture of the project, perhaps with estimates accurate to ±50 percent. By illustration, consider a project which in the germination stage we estimate will cost $100 and generate $50 per year revenue. That is two years' payback, a wonderful return in most industries. But at germination the $100 might be as high as $150 and as low as $50, and the $50 might be as high as $75 and as low as $25. Best and best, spend $50 to get $75 per year revenue, eight months' pay back is wonderful, what are we waiting for? However, worst and worst, spend $150 to get $25 per year revenue, six years' payback, is awful in some industries. But we know roughly where the solution is, where to look for it, and what it looks like. Based on the mid-range estimates we can commit a small amount of money, 0.25 percent of the project cost, to conduct a feasibility study. A full design will cost 5 percent of the cost of the project. We cannot afford that while there is still a chance that the project may have six years' payback. But we can afford to spend 0.25 percent to improve our understanding. As a result of the feasibility study we improve our estimates. We are now predicting that the project will cost $120 with $40 per year revenue, three years' payback. That is still good business. The accuracy is now ±20 percent, so the cost may be as high as $140 and as low as $100, and the revenue as high as $50 and as low as $30. So the best and best case ($100, $50) gives a payback of two years, very good, and the worst and worst ($140, $30) gives a payback of almost five years, not good. The mid-range is still good, but the range of accuracy is still worrying. But we feel confident to commit more money, now 1 percent of the

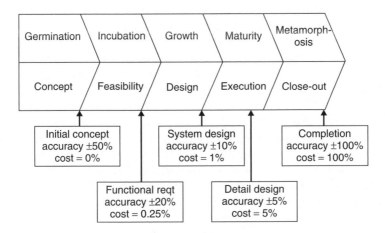

Figure 8.5 Standard five-stage project life-cycle

Table 8.3 The basic project management life-cycle

Stage	Name	Process	Outputs	Cost as % of project
Germination	Concept	Identify opportunity for performance improvement Diagnose problem	Initial options Benefits map Commit resources to feasibility Estimates ±50%	0.05%
Incubation	Feasibility	Develop proposals Gather information Conduct feasibility Estimate design	Functional design Commit resources to design Estimates ±20%	0.25%
Growth	Design	Develop design Estimate costs and returns Assess viability Obtain funding	Systems design Money and resources for implementation Estimates ±10%	1%
Maturity	Execution	Do detail design Baseline estimates Do work Control progress	Effective completion Facility ready for commissioning Estimates ±5%	Detail design 5%
Metamorphosis	Close-out	Finish work Commission facility Obtain benefit Disband team Review achievement	Facility delivering benefit Satisfied team Data for future projects	

cost of the project to conduct a design study. Before I continue, I want to point out that the first estimates were not *wrong*. You should not say that the original estimate was a cost of $100 and revenue of $50, and now we are saying $120 and $40. The original estimate was somewhere between $50 and $150 for the cost and now we are saying somewhere between $100 and $140. The new range lies wholly within the old range. Similarly with the revenue. So the original estimate was correct, just not accurate enough. As a result of the design study we confirm that the cost will be $120 and the revenue $40, but the accuracy is now ±10 percent. So the mid-range payback is still three years, best and best ($110, $45) is about two and a half years, and worst and worst ($130, $35) is about three and a half years. That is accurate enough for us to commit to detail design (which will cost us 5 percent of the project) and implementation. So we have worked through an algorithm, working closer and closer to our solution. But most importantly, we have not committed ourselves to the full cost of the project against very inaccurate estimates. We have followed the algorithm to improve our understanding before committing ourselves to the last step, where 99 percent of the money is spent.

It is unusual for the five stages to be encompassed within one project. The strict application of PRINCE2 will result in that. Gareis (2005) suggests that each stage of the life-cycle could be a project in its own right. On Engineering Procurement and Construction (EPC) and Design and Build contracts, concept and feasibility are one project, and design, execution and commissioning another. The latest edition of the PMI PMBoK (Project Management Institute, 2008) downplays the whole concept of project life-cycle, and talks instead about one- and multiple-phase projects.

Milestone planning

Figure 8.6 illustrates a milestone plan, where each milestone represents a deliverable in the course of the project. This planning method can be extremely helpful in complex and dynamic projects, where the processes are not (so) well known, then the project team can focus on the deliverables and do detailed planning on a rolling-wave basis, as more information is available.

The process of milestone planning was developed by Andersen *et al.* (2009, first English edition 1987, first Norwegian edition 1984) and is recommended by Turner (2009). It can be used to plan individual projects, either sub-projects covering individual stages in any of Figures 8.1 to 8.6 or Tables 8.1 to 8.3, or smaller projects in the portfolio or program (Figure 5.5). The milestone plan is a process flow diagram for the individual project or sub-project, and so defines the algorithm for how the project will be solved. The technique applies best for all projects in Figure 1.7, except those in the bottom left-hand quadrant. For those in this quadrant activity-based planning is best, that is, traditional project management using the tools of the Optimization Perspective. But in the other three quadrants milestone planning can be a powerful way of using a process approach to plan the project.

Type 2 Projects – goals well-defined, methods poorly defined: Here the milestones in the milestone plan will represent intermediate products delivered through the project. The goals and intermediate goals are well defined; what needs to be identified as we work through the project is the work methods. The milestones represent known intermediate deliverables, and the activities are planned on a rolling-wave basis, milestone by milestone as we generate information in doing the work of earlier milestones on how best to achieve the later ones.

Type 3 Projects – goals poorly defined, methods well-defined: Now we know the work methods we are going to use, but the goals to be delivered by those work methods are poorly defined. The milestones in the plan will now represent known process steps, perhaps life-cycle stages, end-of-stage reviews, or other work processes. As we work through those work processes we try to improve our understanding of the goals.

Type 4 Projects – both goals and methods poorly defined: Now we recommend you use something like soft-systems methodology (Section 3.4) to help define the goals and then plan the project as if it is a Type 2 Project. A Type 2 project is more than twice as likely to be successful as a Type 3 Project (60 percent as opposed to 30 percent).

The plan in Figure 8.6 in fact combines both Type 2 and Type 3 elements. Columns M and P are working through defined stages trying to clarify objectives,

	TriMagi MILESTONE PLAN						
Project:	Intranet Phase I						
Project Champion:	Martin Pacific						
Project Manager:	Frances Seeker						

Date	P	M	D	H	Milestone Name	Short Name	End Date
18 Aug		M0			When the managing director and manager approve that the project is ready to start	Ready to start	18 Aug
26 Aug		M1			When the overall context and style of the web space has been agreed	Overall context and style agreed	26 Aug
28 Aug				H1	When the context inventory of hardware and data has been identified	Hardware and data inventory	28 Aug
02 Sep		M2			When the context of the home and news pages has been agreed	Home and news pages agreed	02 Sep
02 Sep		M3			When the context of the document processing pages has been agreed	Document processing pages agreed	02 Sep
02 Sep	P1	M4			When the context of the personnel information pages has been agreed	Personnel information pages agreed	02 Sep
03 Sep		M5			When existing procedures have been reviewed and revised procedures written and the software development tools have been agreed	Procedures rewritten	03 Sep
09 Sep	P2			H2	When the overall context has been agreed ready for design	Ready to design	09 Sep
15 Sep				H3	When the hardware requirements have been defined	Hardware defined	15 Sep
22 Sep			D1		When new jobs required by the revised procedures have been designed	New jobs designed	22 Sep
25 Sep			D2		When the home and news pages have been designed and developed	Home and news pages developed	25 Sep
25 Sep			D3		When the document processing pages have been designed and developed	Document processing pages developed	25 Sep
25 Sep	P3				When the personnel information pages have been designed and developed	Personnel information pages developed	25 Sep
29 Sep			D4		When the new procedures have been piloted and adjustment approved and developed	New procedures piloted	29 Sep
07 Oct	P4				When the site has been assembled	Site assembled	07 Oct
14 Oct			D5		When the procedures have been optimized and adjustments made to the web site	Procedures optimized	14 Oct
17 Oct	P5				When the site has been signed off and is ready to be deployed	Ready to deployed	17 Oct
11 Nov				H4	When the new hardware has been installed	Hardware installed	11 Nov
11 Nov				H5	When the data for personnel information has been entered or migrated	Data entered and migrated	11 Nov
12 Nov	P6				When the site goes live	Site goes live	12 Nov
14 Nov		M6			When the success of Phase 1 has been reviewed, a report produced and Phase 2 can begin	Ready to proceed to Phase 2	14 Nov

Figure 8.6 The milestone plan

whereas columns D and H assume the objectives are known, they just need to be designed. Also, Milestones M0, M5, P5 and M6 are end-of-stage reviews.

The milestone plan is the defined process for the individual project or project stage, and so begins to define the management process for the project, which leads us into the next section.

8.3 Project management processes

There are other versions of the project life-cycle. One is the problem solving cycle (Figure 8.7). This leads to a ten-step management process (Table 8.4). This process is of course very closely linked to the life-cycle as an algorithm, but is in fact more a process for managing the project, than a life-cycle for the project. To manage the project, processes for project management are required. These can be at the level of the overall project, the individual project management functions, or the control process.

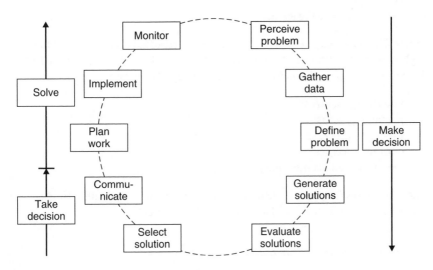

Figure 8.7 Ten-step problem solving cycle

Table 8.4 Management process derived from the ten-step problem solving cycle

Step	Management Process
Perceive the problem	Identify an opportunity for providing benefit to the organization
Gather data	Collect information relating to the opportunity
Define the problem	Determine the value of the opportunity and its potential benefits
Generate solutions	Identify ways of delivering the opportunity and associated benefits
Evaluate solutions	Identify the cost of each solution, the risk and expected benefit
Select a solution	Chose the solution that gives best value for money
Communicate	Tell all parties involved of the chosen solution
Plan implementation	Complete a detail design of the solution and plan implementation
Implement the solution	Authorize work, assign tasks to people, undertake the work and control progress
Monitor performance	Monitor results to ensure the problem has been solved and the benefits obtained

Project management processes

These are the management processes that are applied to plan the work, assign it to people and manage progress. There are different versions of this. Rodney Turner (2009) suggests the four-step process (Figure 8.8) based on the work of Henri Fayol (1949). He suggests it is necessary to:

- plan the work;
- organize the resources to do the work;
- implement by assigning work to people;
- control progress;
- manage and lead the team.

Figure 8.9 shows that these processes need to be repeated at each stage of the project life-cycle. The Project Management Institute (2008), in the *Guide to the Project Management Body of Knowledge* (PMBoK), suggests five processes:

- initiating processes;
- planning process;
- executing processes;
- closing processes;
- monitoring and controlling processes.

They then show how this cycle may be applied just once on smaller, single-phase projects, or multiple times on larger, multi-phase projects.

Project management as functional processes

Nested within the project life-cycle are processes to manage individual project management functions. The most well developed of these is the risk management process.

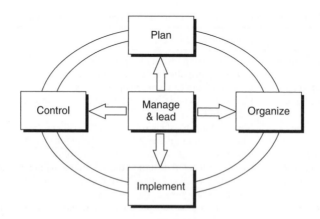

Figure 8.8 The management process (after Turner, 2009)

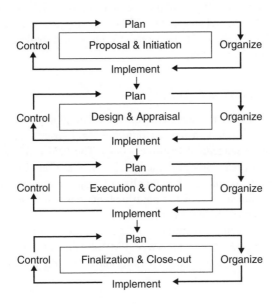

Figure 8.9 The management processes repeated at each stage of a project

Risk management

Almost every recommendation for risk management follows a structured process. Chris Chapman and Stephen Ward (2003, 2007) argue the case strongly for a risk management process and outline a nine-step process, which forms the basis for the process in the Association for Project Management's (2004) *PRAM Guide*. Table 8.5

Table 8.5 Generic risk management process

Generic Process	APM PRAM (2004)	PMI PMBoK (2004)	PRINCE2™ (OGC, 2005)	Chapman and Ward (2003, 2008)
Focus on risk	Initiate			Focus
Identify risk	Identify	Identify	Identify	Identify Structure Assign ownership
Assess (qualitatively)	Assess	Assess	Evaluate	Estimate Evaluate
Prioritize				
Analyze (quantitatively)		Analyze		(Evaluate)
Reduce	Plan response Implement response	Mitigate	Identify response Select response	Harness
Control	Manage response	Manage	Plan & resource Monitor & report	Manage

presents a generic risk management process, and compares it to the processes of the Association for Project Management (2004), the Project Management Institute (2008), PRINCE2™ (Office of Government Commerce, 2009b) and Chris Chapman and Stephen Ward (2003, 2008).

Other project management functions

There are those project management functions commonly known as "Body of Knowledge Areas," although that terminology only strictly applies to the PMI PMBoK (Project Management Institute, 2008). The PMI PMBoK suggests nine body of knowledge areas. However, the PMI PMBoK is offered as the minimum set required on all projects, and much longer lists of project management functions can be defined. Table 8.6 shows a list of possible functions and several books or international procedures where they are described.

The Project Management Institute (2008), in the latest edition of its *Guide to the Project Management Body of Knowledge* (PMBoK), in fact shows what is done on each of the nine body of knowledge areas at each of the four stages of the management process.

Project management as control cycle

The control cycle says to manage the project you should follow a standard four-step process, derived from classical control theory:

- plan the desired results;
- monitor the results achieved;

Table 8.6 Project management functions and their coverage in international standards

Function	Turner (2008)	Turner (2007)	PMI (2008)	OGC (2009b)	IPMA (2006)
Managing integration			PMI		
Managing requirements/business case		T7		P2	Eye
Managing scope	T8	T7	PMI		Eye
Managing benefits		T7			
Managing project organization	T8	T7		P2	Eye
Managing quality	T8	T7	PMI	P2	Eye
Managing configuration	T8	T7		P2	
Managing cost	T8	T7	PMI		Eye
Managing time	T8	T7	PMI		Eye
Managing risk	T8	T7	PMI	P2	Eye
Managing communication	T8	T7	PMI		Eye
Managing stakeholders	T8	T7			Eye
Managing people	T8	T7	PMI		Eye
Managing procurement			PMI		Eye
Managing health and safety		T7			Eye
Managing environment		T7			Eye
Plans, controls, changes				P2	Eye

- calculate differences between desired results and achieved results;
- take action to eliminate differences.

This can be applied to most of the functions of project management, including most in Table 8.6. Focusing on the control process changes the emphasis from many of the traditional approaches to project management. They emphasize the tools: work breakdown, responsibility assignment matrices, critical path analysis, bar (Gantt) charts, and earned value analysis. It is not that either approach is wrong. However, following the control cycle focuses attention on what is required, to achieve planned results, and highlights that the tools are the means to the end, and not the end in themselves. The control cycle also focuses attention on problem solving, using the control cycle as an algorithm, finding the best route to the end objectives by working out how far we are away, and what needs to be done to bring us closer.

The PRINCE2™ methodology: A process-oriented management approach

The PRINCE2 methodology, developed by the UK government (Office of Government Commerce, 2009b) is a process-based approach to project management. It includes three elements:

The first element is the PRINCE2 processes (Figure 8.10). The PRINCE2 processes encompass the life-cycle, and more. The PRINCE2 life-cycle is closer to the PMI management processes than it is to the classic life-cycle of Figure 8.5 and Table 8.3. Each process is supported by a number of sub-processes. The PRINCE2 processes are:

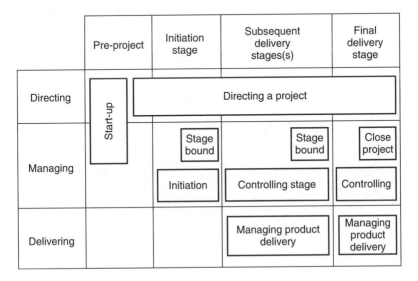

Figure 8.10 The PRINCE2™ processes

- directing the project;
- starting-up the project;
- initiating the project;
- managing stage boundaries;
- controlling a stage;
- managing product delivery;
- closing the project.

The second element is the PRINCE2 themes (Figure 8.11):

- business case;
- plans;
- organization;
- quality;
- progress;
- change;
- risk.

There are seven themes, three exactly equivalent to three of the body of knowledge areas from the PMI PMBoK, but the other five representing things considered important by PRINCE2. Indeed two, the Business Case and Organization, might be said to be omissions from the PMI PMBoK. The other three are not what we would call primary functions of project management, but supporting functions. These are Plans, Controls, and Change. We have included them as one line at the bottom of Table 8.6 to illustrate their supporting nature.

The third element of PRINCE2 is called principles. There are seven principles:

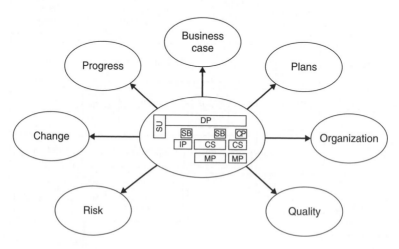

Figure 8.11 The PRINCE2™ themes

- continued business justification;
- learn from experience;
- defined roles and responsibilities;
- manage by stages;
- manage by exception;
- focus on products;
- tailor to suit the project environment.

Project management as business process

Roland Gareis (2005) defines projects as a temporary organization for the performance of a relatively unique, short- to medium-term strategic business process of medium or large scope. He differentiates the project management processes and content-related processes and develops a generic ideal description of a project management process applicable in any project type. Project management is explicitly considered as a business process, consisting of several sub-processes:

- project starting (made consistent with the figure);
- project coordinating;
- project controlling;
- project closing down.

In cases of a project crisis or a phase transfer the process resolving of a project discontinuity is required, which is shown in a dotted box in Figure 8.12. For describing the project management process business process management is applied. The

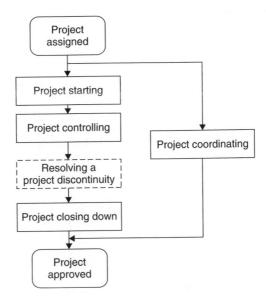

Figure 8.12 Project management as a business process (after Gareis, 2005)

Table 8.7 Boundaries of the project management process (after Gareis and Stummer, 2008)

Process: Project management

Start:	Project assigned	End:	Project approved
Objectives	• Assuring the realization of the project objectives • Efficient performance of the project starting, project controlling, project closing down and project coordinating • Management of the social-, time- and content-related project boundaries • Management of the relationships of the project to the project context • Building up and reducing of project complexity • Management of the project dynamics • Possibly: Efficient resolution of a project discontinuity		
Non-objectives	• Realization of conten- related processes (i.e. this is a project objective and not a project management objective)		

boundaries of the project management process are provided in Table 8.7. The project starts with a project assignment and ends with the project approval of the project owner (sponsor).

Project start-up as process

Roland Gareis describes the project start-up as a very central process that sets the structures for the project (Gareis, 2007). Table 8.8, provides a description of the process boundaries of the project starting process. Table 8.9 visualizes a description of the project start-up process showing tasks, responsibilities and documentations in the project start-up process. Similar process descriptions can be applied for the other sub-processes.

Table 8.8 Boundaries of the project starting process (after Gareis and Stummer, 2008)

Process: Project start-up

Start:	Project assigned	End:	Project start documentation filed
Objectives	• Information transfer from the pre-project phase into the project • Definition of expectations regarding the post-project phase • Development of adequate project plans for managing the project objectives, scope, schedule, resources, costs, income and risks • Design of the project organization, integration into the permanent organizations • Development of the project culture • Establishment of communication relationships, initial project marketing • Communicating the "big project picture" to members of the project organization • Planning of measures for discontinuity management • Definition of the structures for the following project management sub-processes • Developing the project start documentation • Efficient design of the project start process		

Designing the project management process

The benefits of such process descriptions lie in a clearer understanding of what project management is and which tasks should be performed. Such or similar process description can be used in project management procedure manuals, which will be further described in the next section. How the project start or any other sub-process is then planned and performed for a particular project in detail depends on the requirements of the project. Project management as process needs to be explicitly designed. Elements for designing the project management process include the application of appropriate project management methods, selection of standard project plans and project management checklists, and the selection and the design of appropriate project communication structures (Gareis, 2005). This includes, for instance, decisions about which form project-start communications should take place (workshop, presentations, single meetings, or combinations of such); how much time is appropriate to invest into the project starting, project controlling, and project closing; and who should be invited to take part. For designing the project management process, social competence and experience of the project manager and the project team is required.

8.4 Procedures manuals

The CMM Maturity Model, developed by the Software Engineering Institute of Carnegie-Mellon University (Paulk *et al.*, 1991), has as a requirement for level 3 (of 5) maturity that the organization has integrated procedures. At level 1 maturity it is assumed the organization has ad-hoc procedures. At level 2, the organization has begun to define individual procedures – how to manage the life-cycle, the management process, or some of the functions in Table 8.6 – but to obtain level 3 maturity it must have integrated these into a holistic set of procedures. A set of procedures manuals embodies the organization's project management capability (Section 5.3). Once captured, the procedures manual is the document that can be used to train and develop apprentice project managers.

Purpose of the procedures manual

There are several reasons why organizations need procedures manuals. They can provide:

- a guide to the management processes;
- a consistent approach and common vocabulary;
- a basis for company resource planning;
- training of new staff, especially apprentice project managers;
- demonstration of procedures to clients, perhaps as part of contractual conditions;
- the basis for quality accreditation.

Table 8.9 Process description of the project starting process (after Gareis and Stummer, 2008)

Responsibilities / Tasks	Project owner team	Project manager	Project team	Project team members	Project management consultant	Expert Pool manager	Representatives of relevant project enviroments	Documents
Planning the project start								
• Checking the project assignment and the results of the pre-project phase		P						
• Selecting start communication form		P						
• Selecting project team members (and a PM consultant)		C				P		
• Selecting PM methods and PM templates to be used		P						
• Agreeing with project owner	C	P						1)
Preparing the project start communications								
• Hiring of a project coach (possible)		P			(C)			
• Preparing start communications I, II, etc.		P			(C)			
• Inviting participants		P				C		
• Documenting the results of the pre-project phase		P		C	(C)	C	C	2)

Activity							Documents
• Developing drafts for planning, organizing and marketing the project		P	C	(C)		C	
• Developing information material for start communication		P	C	(C)		C	3)
Performing the project start communications							
• Distributing information material to participants	C	P				C	
• Performing start communication I, II, etc	C		P	(C)		C	
• Developing draft of PM documentation "Project start"		P		(C)		C	
Follow-up to the project start communications							
• Completing draft of PM documentation "Project start"	C	P		(C)			
• Agreeing with project sponsor	C	P		(C)		C	4)
• Project marketing: Initial information	C					C	
• Distributing and filing PM documentation "Project start"		P			I	P	
Performing first work packages (parallel)		P				P	

Key:
P . . . Performance
C . . . . Contribution
I . . . Information

Documents:
1) List of project management methods to be used
2) Invitation of participants to the project start workshop
3) Information material for the project start workshop
4) Project Management documentation "Project start"

Table 8.10 Contents page for a procedures manual (after Turner, 2009)

TriMagi
Project success

CONTENTS

	INTRODUCTION
PM	PROGRAM MANAGEMENT
P0	INFORMATION SYSTEMS PROJECT MANAGEMENT
P1	PROPOSAL AND INITIATION
P2	DEFINITION AND APPRAISAL
P21	Develop work breakdown
P213	Develop milestone plan
P214	Work-package scope statements
P215	Activity plans
P216	Develop project networks
P22	Define specification and configuration
P23	Schedule resources and work
P233	Estimate resource and material requirement
P234	Update project network
P235	Schedule project network
P236	Produce resource and material schedules
P24	Schedule cost and expenditure
P25	Assess risks
P256	Define controls
P26	Appraise project viability and authorize
P3	CONTRACT AND PROCUREMENT
P31	Develop contract and procurement plan
P36	Make payments
P4	EXECUTION AND CONTROL
P41	Finalize project model
P42	Execute and monitor progress
P43	Control duration
P44	Control resources and materials
P45	Control changes
P46	Update project model
P5	FINALIZATION AND CLOSE-OUT

APPENDICES

A	Project planning and control forms
B	Supporting electronic databases
C	Sample reports
D	Staff abbreviations (OBS)
E	Resource and material codes (CBS)
F	Management codes (WBS)

Structure of the procedures manual

An organization's project management procedures manual could follow a similar approach to PRINCE2, with a definition of the main project and/or program process or life-cycle, and of the primary, secondary and even tertiary project management functions. A procedures manual could have the following parts:

Part 1 – Introduction: This explains the structure and purpose of the procedures manual.

Part 2 – Project strategy: This describes the approach to project management to be adopted by the organization, and the basic philosophy on which it is based, as explained above.

Part 3 – Management processes: This describes the procedures to be followed at each stage of the life-cycle. The inputs, outputs and their components are listed, and the management processes required to convert the former to the latter are listed sequentially. Table 8.10 is the contents page of a manual for an information systems project, which shows that in some areas the breakdown was taken to between one and three levels below the project stage. Figures 8.13 and 8.14 are pictorial representations for two of the processes in Table 8.10. Where there is a lower level of definition, the process is shown as a light box. Where the process is the lowest level, it is shown as a bold box. Against each bold box were listed the inputs, outputs and steps required to achieve it.

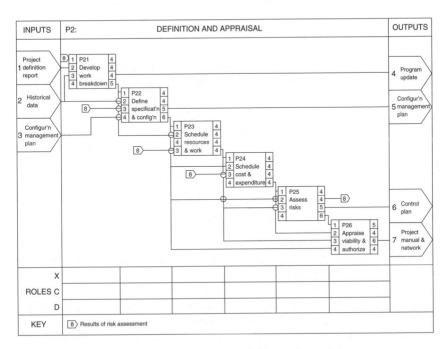

Figure 8.13 Representation of the process P2: Definition and appraisal

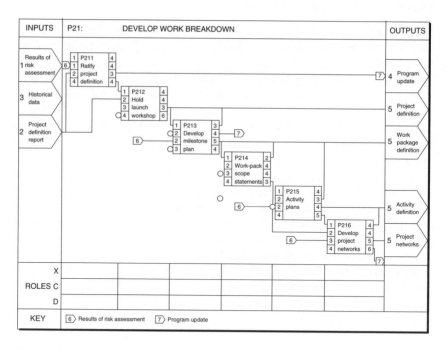

Figure 8.14 Representation of the process P2.1: Develop work breakdown

Part 4 – Supporting functions: This part explains the supporting functions used throughout the project. It may describe the method of managing the primary project management functions as shown in Table 8.10 or it may explain some administrative procedures, such as program and portfolio management, configuration management, or conducting audits and health checks, or methods of data collection (including time sheets), or the role of the project support office. Only those important in the particular environment will be necessary.

Appendices: These may contain blank forms and samples.

8.5 Are we going in the right direction?

As we work through the project process, especially if there is some uncertainty at the start about the goals or methods, and the process is an algorithm, we are taking decisions all the time about what path to follow. Above we focused on the project process, but we must not forget about the decision making process. As we work through the project we gather information which we must process to help make the decisions. Graham Winch (2010) describes the project as a computer. We gather and process information and thereby convert desire to memory. In the next chapter we consider the Decision School.

References

Andersen, E.S., Grude, K.V., and Haug, T., 2009, *Goal Directed Project Management*, 4th edition, Kogan Page, London.

Association for Project Management, 2004, *Project Risk Analysis and Management Guide*, 2nd edition, Association for Project Management, High Wycombe, UK.

Chapman, C.B., and Ward, S.C., 2003, *Project Risk Management: Processes, techniques and insights*, 2nd edition, Wiley, Chichester.

——, 2007, "Managing risk," in Turner, J.R. (ed.), *The Gower Handbook of Project Management*, 4th edition, Gower, Aldershot.

Fayol, H., 1949, *General and Industrial Management*, Pitman, London.

Gareis, R., 2005, *Happy Projects!*, Manz, Vienna.

——, 2007, "Project start process," in Turner, J.R. (ed.), *The Gower Handbook of Project Management*, 4th edition, Gower, Aldershot.

Gareis, R., and Stummer, M., 2008, *Projects and Processes*, Manz, Vienna.

International Project Management Association, 2006, *ICB: The International Competence Baseline: The eye of competence*, 3rd edition, International Project Management Association, Zurich.

Johnson, G., Scholes, K., and Whittington, R., 2008, *Exploring Corporate Strategy*, 8th edition, Financial Times/Prentice Hall, London.

Office of Government Commerce, 2007, *Managing Successful Programs*, 2nd edition, The Stationery Office, London.

——, 2004, *The OGC Gateway™ Process: Gateway to Success, OGC Best Practice Guide*, Office of Government Commerce. Retrieved January 15, 2010 from http://www.ogc.gov.uk/documents/cp0002-Gateway_Gateway_to_Success.pdf

——, 2009a, *Portfolio Management Guide*, final public consultation draft, Cabinet Office, London.

——, 2009b, *Managing Successful Projects with PRINCE 2*, 5th edition, The Stationery Office, London.

Paulk, M.C., Curtis, B., and Chrissis, M.B., 1991, *Capability Maturity Models for Software*, Carnegie Mellon University, Pittsburg.

Project Management Institute, 2008, *A Guide to the Project Management Body of Knowledge*, 4th edition, Project Management Institute, Newtown Square, PA.

Turner, J.R., 2007, *The Gower Handbook of Project Management*, 4th edition, Gower, Aldershot.

——, 2009, *The Handbook of Project-Based Management*, 3rd edition, McGraw-Hill, New York.

Wearne, S.H., 1973, *Principles of Engineering Organization*, Edward Arnold, London.

Winch, G.M., 2010, *Managing Construction Projects: An information processing approach*, 2nd edition, Wiley-Blackwell, Chichester.

9   Decision

The project as a computer

9.1 Converting desire into memory

Not only is the project an algorithm, a process that guides us towards the solution for the project, helping us to identify the goals of the project and the method of achieving them, it is also a computer that helps us gather and process the data to solve the algorithm. As we work through the project process, we gather information which we process to help us reach our goals and define the method of achieving them. The information we gather and decisions we take tell us which road to take, and at points along that road which fork to take. They tell us whether we are on target and if not what action to take to bring us back on target. As we start the project we start with a vision, a desire to reach our goals, but we don't fully know what that goal actually looks like, nor how to get there. When we complete our project we know what we achieved and how we did it. The project has helped us convert desire to memory.

In looking at decision making in project management we focus on three areas. The first is during the start-up stages, and particularly on feasibility and design. The catalog of failed projects is legion. But often the mistake wasn't made during the project delivery. It was made back in the early stages, when over-optimistic assumptions were made about the project. This over-optimism can result from bias in the decision making process, people just assuming that they are able to do much better than they really can. Or it can result from political pressure pushing people to declare that they are able to do better than they honestly know that they can. In the next section we consider the nature of decision making in the start-up processes, and the need for a project strategy for the execution stage.

The second area of focus is decision taking during project delivery. As we work though the project process we improve our understanding of what the project is about, and at the transition from one stage to the next we decide whether to proceed with the project, abandon it, or go back and gather more information. Graham Winch (2004) views the project organization as a vehicle for processing information, as a computer. When we discussed the APM's governance model in Section 5.3, we identified end-of-stage reviews as a key element in the governance process. It is particularly at end-of-stage reviews that we review progress on the project and decide whether to proceed, abandon it, or go back to gather more information. We also said in Chapter 5 that it is essential that between end-of-stage reviews project managers are empowered to take necessary decisions to progress the project. The governance of the project must be aligned with the project process. But at end-of-stage reviews senior management can take governance responsibility back, to assess the project against the business plan, and decide whether to allow it to proceed to the next review. Throughout the project, people aim to take the optimum decisions. However, through human frailty, they often do not. This is known as bounded rationality, the inability to take perfect decisions through the inability to perfectly gather and process the necessary information. That can result in a less than optimum outcome for the project, meaning it does not perform as well as we would like.

The third area of focus is on the development of a project strategy. Having a project strategy helps define the goals of the project, linking them to the strategy of the parent organization, and helps define how we will achieve the strategy, setting out basic principles for how we will enact the project. But it also lays down rules for processing the algorithm, providing guidance as to how decisions should be formulated and taken, and setting parameters that will guide decision, for instance in setting the relative importance of the functionality of the end product, and the time and cost at which it is achieved.

9.2 Deciding where to go

The Decision Perspective first focuses our attention on the front-end of the project; helping us, as well as we can, to define its end objectives and the methods of getting there. It is often during the feasibility and design stage that the project's outcome is determined. All you can do during project execution is implement what has been determined during feasibility and design. Methods of monitoring cost and time, CPA and earned value (Section 2.2), are so well developed that during execution you know how long the project will take and how much it will cost, and you can find yourself managing your way towards known failure that you have no influence over. The project must be set up correctly to be delivered correctly.

During the early stages we are taking critical decisions with the minimum of information, whereas during execution we have much more information, but the outcome has now been set in stone. This is a critical paradox on projects, we don't have the information when we need it, and we do have it when we don't. There is also a well-known human failing, that if people make a wrong decision based on incorrect or incomplete information, they find it very difficult to change their minds when they get correct or complete information. This has been well documented by psychologists, but a classic case of where it happened was 30 years ago at a nuclear power station in the eastern United States, called Three Mile Island. It came within a hair's breadth of meltdown. There was a faulty instrument that should have been ringing to tell the plant operators that the plant was going off spec, but it wasn't because it was faulty. A second instrument started ringing. The operators formed a correct diagnosis of the problem given the information they had – instrument two ringing, instrument one not – but it was a wrong diagnosis because they had incorrect information.

They reacted to their diagnosis, and instrument three ringing should have told them, "Wrong diagnosis." But they continued reacting to their diagnosis even when the whole plant was shouting at them, "Wrong diagnosis." Fortunately the emergency team diagnosed the correct problem, and pulled the plant back from the edge of disaster. The very nature of projects is that we are making the early critical decisions when we have incomplete or even incorrect information, and so we risk making wrong decisions, which we fail to correct later when we have correct complete information, and which can have a lasting serious impact on the project.

We begin by defining our vision for the project, what the solution may look like and what road we may take to get there. We want to know at least the first step of our algorithm to begin to find our way to the solution. On some engineering projects, projects in the bottom left of Figure 1.7, from a very early stage we can clearly define the objectives of the project and the method of delivering them. On the other hand, on some organizational change projects, in the top right-hand corner of Figure 1.7, all we will have at the start is an understanding of the impact we would like to achieve, and early progress will be like walking through a fog, with just clues as to where the next milestone is.

The anatomy of projects

Very early work on the definition of the front end of the project was done by Peter Morris and George Hough (1987) in a now classic piece of work. They surveyed the performance of eight major projects in the UK from the 1960s, 1970s and 1980s, and identified factors that contributed to their success or failure. From that they

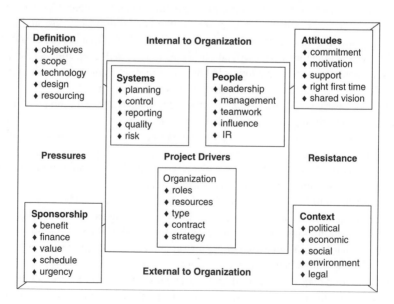

Figure 9.1 The seven forces model of project strategy

developed a model for developing a project strategy, which Rodney Turner (2009) adapted into the Seven-Forces Model (Figure 9.1). This model identifies seven forces influencing a project's success or failure, and it suggests that the project manager and project sponsor must develop a strategy for how to manage these seven forces during the early stages of the project. Four forces are external to the project – two external to the parent organization and two internal, two driving the project and two resisting it. The other three forces are internal to the project, acting as the engine of the project. The four external forces are:

- the context;
- the business case;
- the attitudes of stakeholders;
- the project's requirements and design.

The three internal forces are:

- the plan;
- the project organization;
- the people.

The context

External influences can be a primary cause of many issues on projects. Figure 9.2 shows the classic PESTLE analysis, illustrating the external forces impacting on the project. We might ask how much management can influence these factors. But often it is possible to exert some influence, if only to provide protective action or contingency. Many projects raise political issues, and hence require political

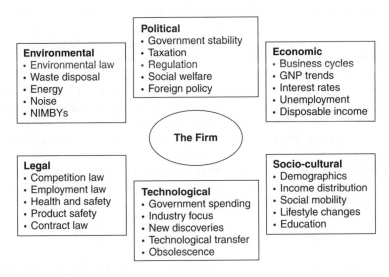

Figure 9.2 PESTLE analysis

support. We discussed that in Chapter 7. Political support has to be sought from the outset. Project managers must be attuned to political issues and be ready to manage them. They must learn to manage upwards and outwards, as well as downwards and inwards (Figure 7.1). They must court the politicians and influential managers, helping allies by providing information needed to champion their program. Adversaries should be co-opted, not ignored. Stakeholders, especially the local community, are also an important external influence.

The business case

Projects must have finance to begin, and that will only be forthcoming if the owner believes the project will provide adequate returns (Figure 1.3). Corporate strategy will help define the expected benefit (at least for deliberate projects, Section 9.4), and the desired benefit and available finance should be reflected in the business plan for the project. A key parameter in a project's viability can be the completion date, with even a small slippage leading to a significant loss of revenue and increased financing charges. Determining the timing of a project can be crucial in formulating the project strategy. How much time is available for each stage, together with the amount and difficulty of the work to be accomplished, influences the nature of the task to be managed. Therefore, in specifying the project, the manager should ensure the right amount of time is spent within the overall duration. A degree of urgency should be built into a project, but can itself lead to problems. However, be aware that it is better to spend a bit longer on the feasibility and design stages and be sure that the design is correct before starting execution. There is a rule of thumb that in a given industry for every \$1 it costs to correct a mistake in feasibility, it costs \$n in design, $\$n^2$ in execution and $\$n^3$ in close-out. In ship-building there is empirical evidence that shows the numbers are 1:3:9:27. In ICT people say the numbers are 1:10:100:1000. It is expensive to correct mistakes in execution, and it causes extensive delays as well. A student of Rodney Turner's worked on an ICT project which the local government wanted completed in 18 months, so they only allowed two weeks for feasibility. In the event, it took five years with all the changes required during execution. Better to allow two months for feasibility and get the end product in 20 months. You should also try to avoid beginning implementation before technology development and testing are complete. This situation is known as *concurrency*. There are different forms of overlap. Concurrent engineering is where technical development of different components is run in parallel, but construction doesn't start until development is finished. Then fast build, fast track and concurrency lead to increasing amounts of overlap between design and build. If faced with one of these, be under no illusion as to the risk. Analyze the risk rigorously, work element by work element, milestone by milestone.

Attitudes

This is probably the most important force. The chances of success are substantially diminished unless:

- there is a major commitment to making the project a success;
- the motivation of everyone working on the project is high;
- attitudes are supportive and positive.

To achieve positive attitudes it is vital to develop a clear vision or mission, by linking the project's plans to corporate strategy (Section 9.4), and by functional and task managers being seen to cooperate to achieve the same objectives. It is particularly important for top management to show visible commitment and support (Section 5.3); without this the project is probably doomed. However, while commitment is important, it must be towards viable goals. Great leaders can become great dictators. If sensible projects are to be initiated, they must not be insulated from criticism (Figure 7.4). Critique the project at the feasibility stage, and ensure it continues to receive frank reviews throughout.

Project definition

A clear definition of the project is vital to its success, and this should be developed starting in the feasibility stage. It should include statements on the project's purpose, ownership, technology, cost, schedule, duration, financing, sales and marketing, and resource requirements. Without it, key issues essential to the project may be left out or not given adequate attention. Key elements of project definition include:

Setting objectives: Little can be done until clear, unambiguous objectives have been set for the project. This should be done by defining the desired impact of the project from corporate strategy, and then working down through the results in Figure 1.3. We discuss the linking of the project objectives to corporate strategy further in Section 9.4.

Defining the scope: Scope definition is intimately related to cost, time and performance criteria. If unrealistic expectations are set, they may not be met, and the project will be perceived to have failed. You should also develop a comprehensive strategic plan for attaining the project's objectives from the start. If the project's objectives change, the scope definition and investment criteria must be reconsidered.

Setting functional strategies: The setting of functional strategies must be handled with care, and requires the setting of the design, the technology to be used, the method of its implementation and eventual operation. The design standards selected will affect the difficulty of construction and eventual operation of the plant. You should give particular attention to technical risk. Technical problems can have a huge impact on the success of the project.

Managing the design process: The design is never complete; technology is always improving. A key challenge is to achieve a balance between meeting the schedule and making the design that bit better. But the design really needs to be frozen before execution starts (see above). A core idea of modern project management is configuration management, by which the design and its technical basis are taken through an orderly sequence of review stages. At each stage, the level of detail is refined, with strict control of technical interfaces and changes. As we described above, changes can result in extensive rework, as people on other parts of the project will have based their assumptions on the agreed design. You should aim for a progressive design freeze. This is feasible in traditional engineering projects, but an early design freeze may conflict with meeting the customer's requirements, especially in organizational development, high technology and information systems projects. In setting up projects, care should be taken to appraise technical risk, prove new technologies, and validate the project design, before freezing the design and moving into implementation.

Identifying resources: It is no good defining what to achieve if you do not have the right number of good, committed people, sufficient money, adequate infrastructure, etc. Getting adequate resources, managing them well and ensuring that the context is supportive are at the heart of successful strategic management.

Planning and control systems

This of course has traditionally been the main, and often the only, focus of project management. It is the only focus of the Optimization Perspective and the memes of project management. It is nevertheless important. You need to put in place systems to plan and control all the functions, including scope, quality, cost, time, risk (Turner, 2009). The plan should progress through the same sequence of orderly reviews as the design, starting at a broad, systems level with detail being provided on a rolling-wave basis. Changes of course should be carefully controlled. Implementation of systems and procedures should be planned carefully so all those working on the project understand them. Start-up meetings should develop the systems procedures in outline, and begin substantive planning while simultaneously "building" the project team.

Project organization

There are three organization issues to be considered:

Management structure: We described project organization structures in Section 6.2.

Client involvement: You need to consider to what extent the client continues to be involved, even after hiring contractors to undertake the work. We said in Section 7.3 that you should keep the client informed of progress to keep them happy, and indeed projects where the client takes an interest in progress are more likely to be successful. However, on certain types of project, particularly fixed price contracts, the client should not be involved in the day-to-day running of the project. However, they may feel they have a legal or moral responsibility to ensure it is done to a certain standard, or may just want to ensure it is for their own comfort. The dilemma is between not being involved at all, versus constantly tinkering with the design, both frustrating the contractor and adding expense. A solution is to schedule milestone review points and limit owner involvement to those reviews.

Use of contractors: No organization has all the resources needed to undertake all its projects, and therefore it will need to buy in goods and services. At an early stage of project definition it is necessary to determine the contract and procurement strategy. We discussed this in Section 5.6 and used the organization map (Figure 6.2) to illustrate the involvement of contractors in the project.

People issues

People issues are the focus of Chapter 6. Projects demand extraordinary effort from people (often with the prospect of working yourself out of a job). This puts enormous demands on the quality of the project team, from senior management through the professional teams to artisans. The initial stages of a project may require considerable leadership and championing to get started. Beware though of unchecked champions and leaders, and of the hype and optimism which too often surrounds projects in their early stages. We should recognize the importance of team working, of handling the conflicts which arise on projects positively, and of good communications. Consideration should be given to formal start-up sessions (mixing planning with team building). The composition of the team should be looked at from a social angle as well as the technical: people play social roles on teams, and these will be required to vary as the project evolves.

Results-based management

The seven-forces model identifies the importance of clear project definition from the start. In Figures 1.3 and 1.4 we introduced three levels of results in the project deliverables:

1   *The outputs:* the new asset delivered by the project;
2   *The outcomes:* the new competencies or capabilities the owner or the parent organization gets from operation of the asset, and the revenue generated from the benefits arising;
3   *The impact:* the higher order strategic objectives that will be achieved from the long term exploitation of the new competencies.

All of these must be clearly identified during the initiation stages of the project, and more importantly, governance roles identified at the three levels, as illustrated in Figure 5.1. There is a tendency just to design the new asset and then the project manager takes responsibility for delivering that to time and cost and quality, and loses sight of what is really required. Monitoring and control mechanisms must be put in place from the start to identify the desired outcomes and impact and monitor progress towards their achievement, and people must be identified to fulfill the higher-level governance roles, and be given responsibility and authority to undertake them effectively, as required by APM's principles of governance (Section 5.3).

In China, 800 water treatment plants were built. The desired outcome was to be able to treat waste water and the desired impact to improve public health. Some time after they were built a survey was done on 500 of them to see how well they were operating. Of those 500, 200 (40 percent) were not operating at all, because no pipes had been put in place to connect the plant to the homes with waste water. The project managers had been given responsibility of building the plants to time and cost and quality, and that is what they had done. It was not their responsibility to build the sewerage collection facility. Perhaps they should have raised the sponsors' awareness that no sewerage collection facility was being built and therefore the plant would not operate, but it is quite likely that no sponsor had been appointed. This also raises the point of the difference between the project and the program. There should have been a program to create a water treatment facility, consisting of at least three projects: a sewerage collection facility, a water treatment plant, and a discharge facility to discharge treated water back into the river. The program director has overall responsibility for improving public health. The program manager (and business change manager, Figure 5.2) has responsibility for delivering the water treatment facility and ensuring it works to take waste water from homes and delivers pure water back to the river, with individual project managers responsible for delivering components of the program. These different levels of objectives and program roles must be defined as part of the early stages of the program (Figure 8.5) in fact before any of the projects start.

Estimating bias

Bent Flyvberg (2006) and his co-workers have investigated bias that occurs during project estimating. Projects, especially large infrastructure projects, are notoriously late and overspent. For instance, data collected by Bent Flyvberg shows that road projects are on average 20 percent overspent, bridges and tunnels 33 percent and rail projects almost 50 percent overspent. These are similar to the figures compiled by the Standish Group for large information systems projects (Johnson, 2006). Flyvberg *et al.* (2004) have investigated whether these overruns are due to technical, psychological or political-economic reasons. Technical reasons would include mistakes made in estimating or project delivery. They suggest that if the cause was technical, the distributions of project out-turns would have a normal distribution. This is not the case and so they suggest that the causes are psychological and political-economic. Psychological reasons they call optimism bias, and occur because people have a tendency to judge future events in a more positive light than is warranted by past experience. Political-economic reasons they call strategic misrepresentation, and occur because people deliberately underestimate the costs of their project and over-estimate the benefit so that their projects and not the competition will win approval for funding. Both types of bias involve deception, but whereas the latter involves deliberate misrepresentation (lying) the former only involves self-deception. The two tend to complement each other, so where political and organizational pressures are low optimism bias is high, and where political and organizational pressures are high, strategic misrepresentation is high, resulting in similar total bias. There is also an element of self-delusion. Often people are aware of the bias, but ignore it. Rodney Turner and Christophe Bredillet know a member of the French committee that evaluated the Channel Tunnel in the 1980s. He says they knew that out-turn costs were likely to be twice the estimates and the revenues half the estimates, but the political pressure was to approve the project, because everyone wanted it.

Bent Flyvberg (2006) suggests the use of a technique called Reference Class Forecasting to overcome these biases. The technique was first developed by Daniel Kahneman and Amos Tversky (1979), for which Daniel Kahneman won the Nobel Prize in Economics in 2002. The idea is to gather data about a class of projects and measure the distribution of the ratio of out-turn cost to the original estimate. That then indicates by how much the estimate for a project should be uplifted to give a certain probability of success. There are essentially three steps to Reference Class Forecasting:

1   Identify a relevant reference class of similar past projects. The class must be broad enough to gather statistically significant data but narrow enough to provide a true comparison.
2   For that reference class determine the probability distribution of the ratio of out-turn cost to estimate. This requires access to a set of credible, empirical data of a sufficient number of projects to provide statistically significant conclusions.
3   Compare the project at hand to the reference class to determine a probability distribution for the likely out-turn for the project.

Using his own database for large infrastructure projects, Bent Flyvberg suggests that for road projects you need to uplift the estimate by 15 percent to have a 50 percent chance of success and by 32 percent to have an 80 percent chance of success. The figures for rail projects are 40 and 57 percent, and for bridges and tunnels, 23 and 55 percent. He does not have data for other types of project, but says that data produced by Mott Macdonald (2002) for the UK treasury suggests building projects are between 4 to 51 percent overspent, IT projects between 10 to 200 percent overspent, standard civil engineering projects between 3 and 44 percent overspent and non-standard civil engineering projects 6 to 66 percent. It might be possible to derive the 50 and 80 percent figures for IT projects from the data gathered biennially by the Standish Group (Johnson, 2006). Bent Flyvberg goes on to suggest that organizations doing a portfolio of projects should use the 50 percent percentile figures as their estimates for project sanction because overspend on one project can be balanced by underspend on another, but organizations doing one project only should use the 80 percent percentile figure.

9.3 Deciding which fork to take

Having headed out along the road towards our project objectives, we need to continuously check we are on the right path. But we may also be continuously faced with options and alternatives, and have to decide what the best route to take is. If the process is an algorithm, at the end of each step, and the start of the next, we must decide in which direction the next step should be. Thus we need to continuously gather and process information to determine where we are, whether that is where we want to be, and which way we should go from here. The project becomes like a computer, which enables us to gather and store the data, and to process it to give us the required information.

The project as vehicle for processing information

Graham Winch (2004) views the project organization as a vehicle for processing information. He takes as his starting point the work of J.R. Galbraith (1977) which sees organizations as essentially information processing systems. To function, they must monitor their environment, make decisions, communicate their intentions and manage progress to ensure they achieve what they want to achieve. Service organizations just need to control the flow of information, whereas in manufacturing companies the information also generates and controls the flow of materials. Information management is at the heart of business processes in all organizations, and this is as true for temporary organizations as much as permanent organizations.

The fundamental problem for management is lack of information to make the optimum decision at a given point of time, and that creates uncertainty. Uncertainty is the difference between the information to make a decision and the information available. It is by this definition immeasurable because you don't know how much information you are lacking. Graham Winch says that uncertainty has two sources:

*   *complexity:* where the information is in principle available, but too costly or too time-consuming to collect or analyze – this arises from bounded rationality (Chapter 5);
*   *unpredictability*: where the past is not a reliable guide to the future.

As we have seen in the last chapter and this, at the start of the project the uncertainty is high. There is uncertainty both about the nature of the asset to be delivered and the method of achieving it (Figure 1.7). Thus the aim of the project is to gather information as the project progresses, to reduce uncertainty and to make better decisions about the nature of the end product and the method of delivering it. The aim is to convert the desire to achieve the vision we have into the memory of how we achieved it.

End-of-stage reviews

We saw in Section 5.3 that end-of-stage reviews are an essential part of the project governance process. The project manager must be empowered to take decisions to progress the project between reviews, but end-of-stage reviews offer senior management the opportunity to take control back before authorizing the project manger to progress to the next review. This is how the PRINCE2 process works (Office of Government Commerce, 2009). The project manager is authorized to undertake the current stage of the project, and as long as the performance targets (time, cost, quality, risk) remain within the tolerance set for that stage, then the project manager can progress to the next end-of-stage review, called Managing Stage Boundaries. At the end-of-stage review the project's steering committee check that the project is still on target to achieve its business plan, and if so authorize the project manager for the next stage. If the project goes outside the tolerances set for the whole project, then the project steering committee must refer to higher management still.

Graham Winch describes end-of-stage reviews as points of catharsis; they contribute to a process of sense making, helping to convert desire to memory. Table 9.1 shows the focus of attention of end-of-stage reviews at the end of the concept, feasibility and design stages of a project. You can see in particular how our understanding of cost improves from order of magnitude, to ± 30 to ± 10 percent accuracy at each of the three stages.

PRINCE2 is designed for medium-sized projects. The UK Government (Office of Government Commerce, 2004) has also developed a gateway review processes for larger projects. There are six gateway reviews:

0   Strategic assessment.
1   Business justification.
2   Procurement strategy.
3   Investment decision.
4   Readiness to service.
5   Benefits realization.

Table 9.1 End-of-stage reviews

Item for review	End of stage		
	Concept	Feasibility	Design
Management	Need for performance improvement Change identified Appoint sponsor First draft of benefits map	Business plan Outputs and desired outcomes defined Appoint project manager Risks identified	Finalize business plan Appoint team
Design	High level options	Identify and assess options Select preferred option	Complete design
Planning	High level scheme	Milestone plan	Activity plans
Cost	Order of magnitude	$\pm 30\%$	$\pm 10\%$ Risk analysis Review benefits
Procurement	Options considered	Contract strategy Invitation to tender (ITT) prepared	Issue ITT
Users	Early consultation	Review user requirements	Finalize user requirements
Compliance	Health, safety and environmental (HSE) issues identified	HSE plan	Implement HSE plan

The first takes place at the program level, which is why it is labeled 0. Whereas for PRINCE2 it is assumed the project will be managed internally, for larger projects it is assumed they will be contracted out, and so the focus of this gateway review process is on tracking the contracting process.

Bounded rationality

Throughout the process, we would like to take the optimum decisions, but human frailty is such that this is usually not the case. We take less than optimum decisions, contributing to the residual loss identified in Section 5.2. Herbert Simon (1957) labeled this bounded rationality; we would like to make rational decisions, but our ability to do so is bounded by human frailty. Three elements of human frailty contribute to bounded rationality:

1   *Our inability to gather all the necessary data relevant to the decision.* The project is a computer, but it is not an electronic computer, it is a social system, and so it is not always possible to get all the data necessary to fully formulate the decision. We end up making and taking the decision with incomplete data

2   *Our inability to fully process all the data we do have.* Sometimes we have too much data; sometimes we just don't have the analytical or mathematical tools to comprehend the data and convert it to information and knowledge.

These two frailties cause us to satisfice. We cannot take perfect decisions, so we do the best we can with the information we have. Indeed, there is a saying in English, that "the perfect is the enemy of the good." We strive for perfection and in the process we fail to achieve anything, even something that is adequate. We need to accept that we are taking decisions with incomplete or imperfect information and do the best we can. But we need to try very hard to avoid the element of human frailty we described earlier, the inability to change our minds as new data and new information becomes available. We must make and take the best decisions we can, so that we can make progress on the project, but we must be willing to recognize that we made the decisions on incomplete and imperfect data and be willing to change our decisions as new information becomes available. That must be part of the project review process.

The third element of human frailty leading to bounded rationality is:

3   *Our inability to foretell the future.* We can't foretell the future. We don't know which risks will occur, or what the impact of those issues that do occur will be. We have to live with that uncertainty and manage it. We make a decision assuming that an event of 80 percent likelihood will occur, but then the event of 20 percent likelihood occurs. This is almost like playing the prisoners' dilemma with fate. If we plan for the 80 percent event, but the 20 percent one occurs it will cost us more than if we had planned for the 20 percent event. But it works the other way, if we plan for the 20 percent event and the 80 percent event occurs, it will cost us more than if we had planned for the 80 percent

event. And planning for the 20 percent event will cost more than planning for the 80 percent event. So risk analysis says we have to plan for the 80 percent event, but if the 20 percent event occurs it will then cost us even more. If only we had a crystal ball!

Crystal balls and social systems

Niklas Luhmann's (2006) social systems theory even goes one step further: It is not the limited availability of information which makes us wish for a crystal ball, but it is the very nature of social systems, which are dynamic and unpredictable so there are no linear deterministic relationships (see Table 9.2).

A social system such as a project consists of and constitutes itself by decisions (Luhmann, 2006). Martina Huemann (2002) and Roland Gareis (2005) have shown that social systems theory is of relevance for projects and project managers.

- Social systems such as projects are constituted by decisions. They are socially constructed (Gareis, 2005). What is and is not included in the project is negotiated with the project owner and the relevant stakeholders. Project managers can make it clear what the project objectives are by explicitly listing the project non-objectives.
- If projects are considered as social systems, the context in which they are organized becomes relevant to understanding the project itself. Decisions taken in the pre-project phase influence the project itself, and expectations about the post project phase. In Chapter 4 we told the story of the company that had traditionally made submarines but wanted to enter the surface vessel market. So they made a bid for the construction of a frigate, bidding a low price (effectively at no profit), so that they could win the work to demonstrate that they could build frigates to time and quality. Unfortunately nobody told the project manager, so he tried to save money, sacrificing time and quality. We see how the strategic decision made before the project should have influenced what happened on the project, for the sake of project marketing and the building of long-term relationships after the project.
- From a systemic perspective managing the task of managing is about building up and reducing complexity. For instance, building up complexity is done by creating more complex project organizations which allow suppliers and contractors work together cooperatively in one project, rather than parallel project

Table 9.2 Trivial versus social system

Trivial system	Social system
Predictable	Not predictable
Not depending on the context	Depending on the context
Possible to influence directly	Not possible to influence directly
Results of influence clear	Results of influence unclear
Application of standards	Allowance of contradictions

organizations where claims management then becomes a central method to manage the project.

9.4 Setting project strategy

Every organization should identify how its strategic choices are converted into projects. This is a two-step process. First we need to look at how corporate strategy is converted into project strategy, and secondly we need to look at how to develop a project strategy.

From corporate strategy to project strategy

Figure 1.5 shows a cascade from corporate strategy, though portfolios and programs to projects and project strategy. Figure 1.5 suggests that projects contribute to the deliberate strategy of organizations (Mintzberg *et al.*, 2005). Peter Morris and Ashley Jamieson (2004) suggest that all projects should be deliberate. The definition of programs can be emergent, but all projects should be deliberate. Peter Morris and Ashley Jamieson (2004) from a survey of four project-based organizations identified a number of key issues in linking project strategy to corporate strategy.

Role of project management in formulating and implementing strategy

What should be the role of projects in formulating and implementing strategy? Some people believe that project managers should not be involved in formulating strategy (Crawford, 2005). The work done by Rodney Turner and Ralf Müller (2006) suggested that project managers should concentrate on doing the work of the project and not be diverted by the bright lights of strategy. That should be left to other governance roles such as the project sponsor. Of course it will depend on the size of project. The manager of a €100 million project will be fairly senior and so will be involved in strategy formulation, whereas the manager of a €100,000 project will be more junior and won't. There is now a growing view that business and organizational change are best managed through program management (Office of Government Commerce, 2007; Project Management Institute, 2006b), rather than by project management.

Business models

Peter Morris and Ashley Jamieson (2004) suggest that organizations should properly understand their business management model and the position of project, program and portfolio management within it. People should understand how project management sits alongside, and is perceived by, the business management functions. One of the reasons new product innovation projects fail is because they lack wider organizational support. Project managers may think their function is central to the success of a company, but it will have little meaning if it is not clearly established and embedded within the enterprise's structure and business models and processes. If senior management are to have control over expenditure and intended action, the involvement of other disciplines in the management of projects and strategy implementation should be defined, and senior management involvement is required if project management is to be successful in strategy implementation. We dealt with the importance of top management support in Section 7.4. Sound governance explicitly requires formal alignment between business, portfolio, program and project plans and transparent reporting of status and risks to the Board (Association for Project Management, 2004).

Portfolio management

Many projects and programs take place as part of a portfolio of several projects or programs (Project Management Institute, 2006a, b; Thiry, 2007). It is through portfolio management that an organization clearly links its project and program objectives to corporate strategy, prioritizes projects and programs to share its investment funds. Through its portfolio it can also prioritize the assignment of resources to individual projects.

Program management

Program management is a powerful way of coordinating projects that have shared business objectives and is perceived by some as the most suitable methodology for ensuring the successful implementation of strategies, since it is subtler and more able to respond to emerging data than individual projects. Rodney Turner (2009) suggests that whereas projects should have SMART objectives – they should be Specific, Measurable, Achievable, Realistic and Time-lined – programs may have smARt objectives, that is they may be less clearly defined, and so less measurable and the delivery not so clearly defined. Thus you can implement a program to achieve more emergent strategic objectives over a period of 24 to 30 months, but undertake quite specific projects to deliver components of that program.

Both portfolio management and program management focus on prioritizing resources and optimizing the business benefit. Program management is more involved in day-to-day implementation management than portfolio management which is more periodic and is strongly analytical. Implementing strategy through program management involves continuous updating and adjustment.

Projects

Rodney Turner (2009) advocates the development of a comprehensive definition of a project at the start of the project, in which business plans are aligned with project plans containing key elements of project strategy. The development of business cases and strategic briefs should be considered to be an integral part of the project definition process. In Section 9.2 we dealt with the decision making processes during the early stages of the project to link projects to corporate strategy, and that should be the basis of a project strategy which we consider later in this section.

Competencies, roles, responsibilities and accountabilities
for moving strategy

You cannot translate corporate strategy into project strategy by process alone. Moving strategy through such processes and practices as we have just reviewed requires an extensive range of personal competencies and a clear definition of roles, responsibilities and accountabilities. That highlights the importance of having a clear governance structure. This should be initiated by a corporate policy, such as APM's model (Section 5.3), and then rolled out through governance structures for portfolios, programs and projects, as described in Chapter 5. APM's model states explicitly that it is important to identify people with the appropriate roles and responsibilities, and ensure that they have appropriate competence and authority to undertake those roles effectively. We described the development of project management competence in Section 6.5, and the contribution of the project manager to project success in Section 4.4. In developing a competence model for portfolio, program, and project managers it is important to ensure that their responsibility for strategy formulation and implementation is clearly defined, and that they are given appropriate responsibility and authority to realize their duties.

Developing project strategy

The purpose of a project strategy is to lay the foundations for achieving a successful outcome for our project. Thus the first step is to identify the success criteria and success factors for the project. We dealt with the issue of project success in Chapter 4, and identified two components of project success:

- *Success criteria* are the dependent variables by which we will judge the successful outcome of our project. The success criteria for the project will be derived from the organizational strategy, cascaded down through the hierarchy in Figure 1.5.
- *Success factors* are the independent variables that we will use to help achieve those success criteria, things that we can influence to increase the chance of success.

Thus, in its simplest form, the route to a project strategy is to identify the success criteria for our project, and then choose success factors that will enable us to achieve those criteria.

Peter Morris and Ashley Jamieson (2004) illustrate what they consider to be the components of project strategy. They include:

Context

First you should identify the factors from the project's context influencing the project. The project will be undertaken to solve a problem (the impact in Figure 1.3). You will want to identify what from the project's context creates that need, and what will either support or hinder the achievement of that goal. A PESTLE analysis, the bottom right-hand box in Figure 9.1 will aid in that process.

Organizational strategy and business case

Next we consider what the parent organization expects to gain from the project. The parent organization should have formulated its own strategy, and having followed the concepts above, linked that strategy to the project's goals and objectives. This will also indicate what financial returns or benefits it expects from the project, which will form the first element of the business case. The costs are identified through the following steps are the other element of the business case and from that the value of the project can be determined. The business case is the focus of the bottom left-hand box in Figure 9.1.

Project requirements

We can now turn our attention to the top left-hand box in Figure 9.1, the project definition. The initial element of this is the formulation of the project requirements. Surprisingly, requirements definition is something to an extent ignored by books on project management. It does not receive significant attention in the PMI® PMBoK (Project Management Institute, 2008). For a description of requirements management see McKinlay (2007). The drawing of a benefits map (Figure 1.4) can also assist in the formulation of project requirements, and the subsequent design of the project (Cooke-Davies, 2007; Turner, 2009). With the definition of project requirements you can proceed to designing the new asset and planning the work of the project.

Marketing the project

The fourth element outside the project in Figure 9.1 is the top right-hand box, the attitudes of people towards the project. An essential element of the project strategy (not considered by Peter Morris and Ashley Jamieson, 2004) is the marketing of the project to the parent organization. It is essential that the project sponsor and project manager should define how they intend to win support of key people within the organization (Chapter 7).

We now turn to the elements within the project, the central three boxes within Figure 9.1.

Project success

When discussing project success in Chapter 4, we said that there is a three-step process:

1   First you must identify the success criteria, how the project will be judged successful. The definition of the success criteria will flow from the business case,

statement of requirements and benefits map. At the same time it is useful to identify key performance indicators, measures of those criteria that can be tracked at reviews during the project to keep it on track.

2   Next you must identify the key success factors, those elements of the project you can influence to help achieve the success criteria. Table 4.9 will help show you what success factors are relevant to the success criteria you have identified for the project.

3   Finally, you must identify the tools and techniques relevant to those success factors, to identify those elements of the project management body of knowledge that will be the most use in implementing the identified success factors.

As we said in Chapter 4, you don't assume you are going to use critical path analysis, Gantt charts and all the other paraphernalia because the memes of project management say that is what you have to use. You definitely don't assume you are going to use a mouse because you are persuaded by the advertisements that that is all you need to manage a project. You decide to use those tools and techniques which will have the most impact on achieving your identified success criteria, which themselves will have the most impact on achieving your requirements and business case.

Project model

Now you can develop a relevant project model. There are three components of this, the three boxes in the center of Figure 9.1.

Planning and control system: You define the planning and control system to be used and develop the plans. It is an essential part of governance to define how you will monitor and control progress, through review meetings and in other ways.

Project organization: You define your project organization (Chapter 6), including your procurement and contract strategy to indicate how you will bring resources into the project.

People: You define the roles and responsibilities you want fulfilled (Chapter 6), and find people of appropriate competence to undertake those roles. You also make sure that they have sufficient responsibility and authority to fulfill their governance responsibilities associated with those roles.

As you can see from this discussion, Figure 9.1 is a model of project strategy. Through the bottom two boxes it links into the strategy of the parent organization, as cascaded down through the hierarchy of objectives, and portfolios and programs (Figure 1.5). However, it is not the only possible strategy model. Another is the Project Excellence Model.

9.5 Do all roads lead to Rome?

Perhaps all roams lead to Rhodes. As we have gone through the last eight chapters, we have seen at various stages that different projects need different approaches to their management. However, an overriding legacy of the Optimization School and the systems approach to project management is all about tools and techniques, and any one can apply the tools and techniques to any project. The belief in the project management community is not that all roads lead to Rome but that one road leads everywhere; the only road you need to follow is the memes of project management (Section 1.2). In Chapter 4, we said how a software company in the UK was advertising their project management software by saying, "If you can move a mouse you can manage a project." Any fool can become a project manager with our software. But a fool with a tool is still a fool. Projects are different, and different projects require different tools for their management. They require different project methodologies, they require different project management competencies, including different temperaments from the project manager, and perhaps they even require ideas from different project management schools. In the last chapter of this part we consider the contingency approach to project management.

References

Association for Project Management, 2004, *Directing Change: A guide to governance of project management*, Association for Project Management (APM), High Wycombe, UK. Retrieved on June 15, 2007 from http://www.apm.org.uk/Governance2.asp

Cooke-Davies, T., 2007, "Managing benefits," in Turner, J.R. (ed.) *The Gower Handbook of Project Management*, 4th edition, Gower, Aldershot.

Crawford, L.H., 2005, "Senior management perceptions of project management competence," *International Journal of Project Management*, 23(1), 7–16.

Flyvberg, B., 2006, "From Nobel prize to project management: Getting risks right," *Project Management Journal*, 37(3), 5–15.

Flyvberg, B., Holm, M.K.S., and Buhl, S.L., 2004, "What causes cost overrun in transport infrastructure projects?," *Transport Reviews*, 24(1), 3–18.

Galbraith, J.R., 1977, *Organization Design*, Addison-Wesley, Reading, UK.

Gareis, R., 2005, *Happy Projects!*, Manz, Vienna.

Huemann, M., 2002, *Individuelle Projektmanagement: Kompetenzen in Projektorientierten Unternehmnen*, Peter Lang, Frankfurt.

Johnson, J., 2006, *My Life Is Failure: 100 things you should know to be a successful project leader*, Standish Group International, Boston.

Kahneman, D., and Tversky, A., 1979, "Prospect theory: An analysis of decisions under risk," *Econometrica*, 47, 313–327.

Luhmann, N., 2006, *Organisation und Entscheidung*, 2nd edition, VS Verlag für Sozialwissenschaften, Wiesbaden.

MacDonald, M., 2002, *Review of Large Public Procurement in the UK*, HM Treasury, London.

McKinlay, M., 2007, "Managing requirements," in Turner, J.R. (ed.) *The Gower Handbook of Project Management*, 4th edition, Gower, Aldershot.

Mintzberg, H., Ahlstrand, B, and Lampel, J.B., 2005, *Strategy Safari: The complete guide through the wilds of strategic management*, Financial Times/Prentice Hall, London.

Morris, P.W.G., and Hough, G., 1987, *The Anatomy of Major Projects: A study of the reality of project management*, Wiley, Chichester.

Morris, P.W.G. and Jamieson, A., 2004, *Translating Corporate Strategy into Project Strategy: Realizing corporate strategy through project management*, Project Management Institute, Newtown Square, PA.

244 Part I: The nine perspectives

Office of Government Commerce, 2004, *The OGC Gateway™ Process: Gateway to Success*, Office of Government Commerce, London.

——, 2007, *Managing Successful Programs*, 2nd edition, The Stationery Office, London.

——, 2009, *Managing Successful Projects with PRINCE2*, 5th edition, The Stationery Office, London.

Project Management Institute, 2006a, *Standard for Portfolio Management*, Project Management Institute, Newtown Square, PA.

Project Management Institute, 2006b, *Standard for Program Management*, Project Management Institute, Newtown Square, PA.

Project Management Institute, 2008, *A Guide to the Project Management Body of Knowledge*, 4th edition, Project Management Institute, Newtown Square, PA.

Simon, H., 1957, "A behavioral model of rational choice," in *Models of Man, Social and Rational: Mathematical essays on rational human behavior in a social setting*, Wiley, New York.

Thiry, M., 2007a, "Managing portfolios of projects," in Turner, J.R. (ed.) *The Gower Handbook of Project Management*, 4th edition, Gower, Aldershot.

——, 2007b, "Managing programs of projects," in Turner, J.R. (ed.), *The Gower Handbook of Project Management*, 4th edition, Gower, Aldershot.

Turner, J.R., 2009, *The Handbook of Project-Based Management*, 3rd edition, McGraw-Hill, New York.

Turner, J.R., and Müller, R., 2006, *Choosing Appropriate Project Managers: Matching their leadership style to the type of project*, Project Management Institute, Newtown Square, PA.

Winch, G.M., 2004, "Rethinking project management: Project organizations as information processing systems?," in Slevin, D.P., Cleland, D.I., and Pinto, J.K. (eds), *Innovations: Project Management Research 2004*, Project Management Institute, Newtown Square, PA.

10 Contingency

The project as a chameleon

10.1 Deciding to be different

It is one of the often quoted features of projects that they are unique, although as suggested by the typology in Section 1.3 (runners, repeaters, strangers, aliens), some are more unique than others. However, all organizations are unique, whether temporary or permanent, and so we ought to expect every project to be different. Yet there are people who in one breath will tell you that every project is unique, but in the next that the same tools and techniques can be used to manage every project. They adhere to the fantasy that once you have learnt the tools on one project, you can apply them to every project, regardless of the technology concerned, and regardless of your temperament. "If you can move a mouse, you can use our software product to manage every project you are ever likely to encounter."

There is the question about how much domain knowledge you need to manage a project. There are those who say you cannot manage an information systems project unless you are an information systems professional. On the other hand, there are those who claim domain knowledge is not required. In response, Rodney Turner relates an incident that happened several years ago. He was at a meeting in the UK of an organization called the Major Projects Association. A partner from what was then Andersen Consulting (now Accenture) finished his presentation by saying that only information systems professionals can manage information systems projects, and it would be best if they were an android. Rodney was sat next to a man called Don Heath, a civil engineer, and then project director for a project called Crossrail, to build an East–West railway line under London. The project was then estimated to cost £2 billion. During the next coffee break Rodney asked Don how much of his project was information systems and Don said 10 percent, £200 million. In fact his project was 40 percent civil engineering (tunnels, foundations and railways), 30 percent mechanical engineering (new rolling stock), 20 percent electronics (automatic signaling) and 10 percent computers (driverless trains). As a civil engineer Don had to manage all of that, but of course had lieutenants working for him who had greater domain knowledge of the parts they were responsible for, and also a temperament and leadership style appropriate to that type of project. That of course is the answer; as your career develops, you become responsible for a wider and wider scope of work, and that requires you to develop new competencies – not new technical skills, but appropriate people management and strategic management skills. But you will also have working for you domain specialists to lead the work in specific areas.

As discussed in Sections 4.4 and 6.5, the evidence is now compelling that different projects require different approaches for their management, and different competencies from the project manager. That is not just different technical skills, but different traits, behaviors and leadership styles as well. In this chapter we discuss the different approaches needed for different types of projects.

First, you need to be able to recognize the differences between different types of project, and so we start by describing project categorization systems. Projects are categorized to select projects, to align them with corporate strategy and to develop appropriate methodologies for their management. Just like an organization has a pool of competent project managers for its type of projects, it also develops methodologies for the type of projects it does, rather than choose methodologies project by project. We describe how organizations can design and implement categorization systems for projects. A key component of a categorization system is the attributes used to categorize projects. In the following section we describe attributes of projects that can be used to categorize projects. We base the discussion on the model developed by Lynn Crawford, Brian Hobbs and Rodney Turner (2005). However, we expand their 14 attribute areas to 15. The nine perspectives we have described in this book are themselves attributes for categorizing projects, and so we next describe what guidance the nine perspectives give about the management of our projects, and when each should be used.

10.2 Categorizing projects

We start by considering what we mean by different types of project. This question was investigated by Lynn Crawford, Brian Hobbs and Rodney Turner (2005) in a project sponsored by the Project Management Institute in which they developed a system for categorizing projects. In what follows, we refer to categorization systems for projects rather than classification systems. Classification systems, such as the classification of species, sort things into mutually exclusive sets, whereas categorization systems sort things into sets of items with similar properties. Under a classification system, an item can belong to one set only, whereas under a categorization system, an item can belong to several sets. The latter is what we are trying to achieve in a categorization system for projects.

The need for project categorization systems

Project-based organizations have long been aware of the need to align project delivery capability with corporate strategy. They are well aware of the contribution the project management capability makes to their overall business success. We know that corporate strategy is delivered through projects, and so project management capability is key to our ability to deliver our corporate strategy. To ensure the alignment of project management capability with corporate strategy, managers need to make several choices:

1   They must decide how best to use available resources to achieve their strategic intent. They must decide which projects, programs and portfolio of projects to do to make best use of available resources.
2   They must also ensure they have the project delivery capability to deliver the chosen projects, programs and portfolios.

For both reasons, organizations need to have ways of categorizing their projects. They need to be able to categorize projects to be able to prioritize them, to decide which ones to do, and to ensure they have appropriate skills to do the chosen projects.

The nature of categorization systems

The need to categorize things seems to be an almost innate part of human nature. Language itself is a categorization system, and very little in the world around us is not categorized; it seems to be an unconscious part of our thought processes. There are three challenges in developing categorization systems for a work environment: comparability, visibility and control.

1   *Comparability:* The aim is to develop a system which will enable us to be able to compare projects in some way, so that we can:

  • facilitate communication between people in the organization working on projects;
  • create a shared understanding between them;
  • facilitate knowledge management, drawing on lessons learned from similar projects, and increasing the chance of project success;
  • create a common language for people in the organization, nationally and internationally.

However, the creation of the standard approach creates its own challenges. The standard is inevitability a simplification, and thereby reduces variety, and can lead to people making inappropriate decisions. We have to balance this loss of variety against the benefits of a common language.

2   *Visibility:* Creating a categorization system enhances the visibility of projects. When something is categorized it becomes more visible in the organization. But likewise, things excluded from the system become less visible. This requires us to make certain decisions:

  • Which projects will be included in the system and which excluded?
  • What activities will be categorized as projects and so be included or excluded from the system?
  • Will the system include non-project activities such as operations and maintenance?
  • What makes certain types of projects sufficiently different to merit separate identification?

- What attributes should be used to identify these differences? The creation of a set of attributes is the creation of a language to define different types of projects.

3   *Control:* The design of a categorization system needs to be controlled. You cannot let anybody add or remove categories, so you must nominate people to arbitrate in the gray areas that arise. But, people who have control gain power in the organization. They are the people who interpret the rules. A categorization system is a simplification and so the design and use of the system requires judgment about the creation of categories and rules for assigning projects to given categories. The rules will never be perfect and unambiguous. The people responsible for interpreting the rules gain power over the system, and thence over the application of project management within the organizations. If they also control the definition of categories, it will be easier for them to get their projects into the project portfolio than those who have less control.

These three challenges are pulling in different directions so it is necessary to achieve a balance between them:

- high levels of visibility and comparability reduce control;
- increased control reduces comparability as variance is introduced into the system;
- increasing the number of attributes increases visibility but reduces control.

For a categorization system to work effectively, it must be accepted by the people who use it. Implementing or changing an existing system is an organizational change, and so should be managed as an organizational change project, and all the stakeholders fully involved. The system must reflect the ways the stakeholders perceive projects and enable them to make decisions about project priorities and the selection of appropriate methodologies. This is not always easy as different users may have different perceptions of the system and its fit with work practice. There is often a tension between clear, consistent and scientifically based categories, and intuitive, common sense and well-accepted terminology.

The model

Lynn Crawford and her team (2005) developed a categorization system for projects. The model developed has two dimensions:

1   the purpose for which the categorization systems is used;
2   the attributes used to categorize projects.

Purposes of categorization systems

Any categorization system should define the purpose for which it will be used. That sets the basis for assigning projects to categories. Organizations have three main purposes for wanting to categorize projects:

1   *Strategic alignment:* Organizations need to categorize projects to:

- assign priority for projects within their investment portfolio;
- track the efficacy of their investment in projects;
- create strategic visibility.

2   *Capability specialization:* Organizations need to categorize projects to:

- develop project delivery capability within the organization;
- assign appropriate resources and tools to the management of projects.

3   *Promote the project approach:* The minor need is to:

- decide that the work being done is projects, and differentiate projects from operations;
- differentiate projects, programs and portfolios of projects;
- provide a common language for project management within the organization.

Attributes of projects

Then the system needs to define attributes that will be used to categorize projects to satisfy those purposes. Lynn Crawford and her team (2005) identified that organizations use a large number of different ways for categorizing their projects. However they managed to group the different ways into fourteen broad headings.

- the domain, application area or product of the project;
- the stage of the product or project life-cycle;
- stand-alone or grouped, projects, programs and portfolios;
- strategic importance;
- strategic driver;
- geography;
- project scope;
- project timing;
- uncertainty, ambiguity, familiarity;
- risk;
- customer and supplier relationships;
- ownership and funding;
- contractual issues.

We describe each attribute further in the next section, and what they suggest about the nature of project management processes that should be adopted for different types of project.

Complex systems

In reality, organizations do not use simple one-dimensional models for categorizing projects, but instead multiple-dimensional models. They are of three types:

1   *Hierarchical systems:* Projects are categorized in one way, and then the individual categories categorized further, sometimes in different ways. For instance, at the top level projects may be categorized by size, and then large projects further categorized in one way, medium projects in another and small projects in yet another.

2   *Parallel systems:* Several sets of attributes were assigned to every project. For instance, projects might be categorized by complexity, technology and strategic importance.

3   *Composite attributes:* An example of a composite attribute would be complexity. Many organizations used one dimension for complexity, but some used several classes of attributes to define complexity.

Implementing a system

So how would you go about implementing a project categorization system? Most organizations already have a project categorization system, whether formal or informal. The model could also be used in a green-field site to design a categorization system from scratch. The design or redesign of a system would start with the identification of organizational purposes to which the system would be put, starting at a strategic level and working down to an operational level, aligning capability with strategic intent. The next step would be to select attributes that would be most appropriate for the intended uses. To balance comparability, visibility and control, the attributes should be chosen by working with focus groups of users, and validating the final model with them. Focus groups are a powerful tool for this purpose. The analysis of an existing system would start from the other end, investigating how projects are currently categorized, and the investigating the purposes to which they are put. A project categorization system should be implemented as an organizational change project.

10.3 Attributes of projects

In this section we describe the model of project attributes developed by Lynn Crawford, Brian Hobbs and Rodney Turner (2005). They identified 14 attributes of projects, but here we describe 15, splitting the first one into two: technology and industry. The attributes of projects which can be used to categorize projects, and thereby choose appropriate project management methodologies, and appropriate traits, behaviors and competencies of the project manager are as follows.

Technology used by the project

The first attribute for classification is the technology used by the project. A very simple classification against this dimension involves three categories:

1   engineering and construction;
2   information and communication technology (ICT);
3   organizational change.

In looking at the traits and behaviors required by project managers, Rodney Turner and Ralf Müller (2006) found (Section 6.5):

- the managers of engineering projects should be conscientious, sensitive and good at motivating the team;
- the managers of ICT projects should be self-aware and good at communicating with stakeholders;
- the managers of organizational change projects should be good at communicating with stakeholders and motivating the team.

There was this overriding sense that the managers of engineering projects must be internally focused, conscientious and thorough, working with the project team, whereas the managers of ICT and organizational change projects must be much more focused on the wider sense of stakeholders. Of course any given project may involve elements of all three of these:

- the construction of a building may involve the installation of ICT equipment;
- a computer system may involve the construction of a computer center and the implementation of new operational processes;
- an organizational change project can involve building work, and a new computer system.

Rodney Turner and Ralf Müller found through their web-based questionnaire and interviews that these three categories covered a large range of requirements. A wider list suggested by Lynn Crawford and her team (2005) includes:

1 administrative;
2 computer system;
3 construction;
4 design;
5 engineering;
6 event management;
7 maintenance;
8 new product development;
9 research;
10 other.

They also suggest another categorization where the product can be tangible or intangible and the work intellect or craft, leading to a two-by-two matrix and four categories of projects.

Don Heath's project, described above, involved four types of technology, civil engineering construction, mechanical engineering, technology and information and computers. It also probably involved organizational change.

Industry

The second attribute is the industry that gives rise to the project. Lynn Crawford and her team (2005) treated this and the previous attribute as one. While there is obviously a strong correlation between the industry and the technology used, the construction industry tends to do construction projects, the computer industry tends to do computer projects, and we think it is worthwhile to distinguish between the two dimensions. There are some industries such as the defense industry, the pharmaceutical industry, or research and development, where they do a range of types of project but there are specific features of the projects they do. Likewise there are computer projects in the engineering industry, or organizational change projects in the telecommunications industry which have features both of the technology and the industry.

Lynn Crawford and her team (2005) suggest several categorizations by industry which we have summarized in Table 10.1. Simpler versions of this are possible, with fewer dimensions and categories.

Stage of the life-cycle

Projects can be categorized by stage of the life-cycle. We can identify projects or sub-projects at stages of the project life-cycle or the life-cycle of the product of

Table 10.1 Projects by industry type

Sector	Industry
Engineering and construction	Building
	Infrastructure
	Process plant
	Defense
	Aerospace
	Environmental, waste, sewerage
Information and telecommunications	E-commerce
	Information technology
	Information systems
	Telecommunications
Services	Arts, entertainment, broadcasting
	Recreation and sport
	Business and consulting
	Education and training
	Financial services and insurance
	Health and social services
	International development
Industrial	Automotive
	Electronics
	Manufacturing
	Chemicals and pharmaceuticals
	Food
	Research and development

which the project is a part. In Section 8.2 we described several different types of life-cycle: the life-cycle of the product produced by the project; the life-cycle of the portfolio, program or projects; the management cycle; and functional cycles such as the risk management cycle. Projects can occur at all the stages of of these life-cycles.

Stand-alone or grouped

The next categorization considers whether the project exists on its own or as part of a program or portfolio. Aaron Shenhar and Dov Dvir (2007) consider whether the project is a standalone assembly, part of a multiple assembly or a distributed array.

Strategic importance

Next we consider the strategic importance of the project. The model Rodney Turner and Ralf Müller (2006) used was to consider whether the project is mandatory, repositioning (product development and innovation) or renewal (maintenance). What was unsurprising was they found that repositioning projects are very similar to organizational change projects, but what was interesting was they found that renewal (maintenance) projects are very similar to information systems projects. A related model views the project as mandatory, business critical or business strategic. Paul Dinsmore (1999) developed a model where he viewed projects as strategic, product or market expansion, capital expansion, or operational improvement. Strategic projects are ones that generate little revenue on their own but enable the organization to exploit new opportunities.

Strategic driver

This attribute looks at the relative importance of the objectives of the project, and so is related to the Success Perspective. The strategic driver can be time, cost, quality, people, process or performance. The first three are of course the wretched triple constraint.

Geographical location

We can simply categorize projects by whether they are domestic or international, and if domestic, whether they are in our home region or elsewhere. Rodney Turner (2009) gives an extensive overview of the issues associated with international projects. International projects can be categorized by which country or continent they are in. Roberto Evaristo and Paul van Fenema (1999) take a different view about how distributed the project is. The project can be on one site, or many sites, or it can be part of a program or portfolio on one site or many sites. They were looking at globally distributed projects and virtual teams.

Project size and scope

Next comes the size and scope of the project. There is a significant difference between a project of $50,000, $5 million, and $500 million. But what we mean by a small, medium or large project can be quite variable. Rodney Turner saw an advertisement once for a course about the management of "mega projects," which were described as anything over £1 million ($2 million). For some people those are very large, for others they are very small. Rodney Turner (2009) defines a small, medium, large or major project relative to the turnover of the parent organization. A large project is defined as one with cost equal to about 10 percent of the turnover of the parent organization. A major project is ten times that, so the cost is roughly equal to the turnover of the parent organization, so it is very high risk, as a mistake can sink the company. A medium-sized project is one-tenth the size of a large project and a small project one-tenth in size again. Rodney Turner was looking at port-folio management. So a large project (or program of similar size) will be a standalone entity in the company's investment portfolio. Separate portfolios will be required for medium and small projects (Section 5.3). Major projects may need to be undertaken as joint ventures to spread the risk. Project scope usually considers the number of organizations involved. A simple model views the project as potentially involving:

- a single function within one organization;
- multiple functions within one organization;
- several companies from one industry;
- several industries;
- several countries.

As you move through this hierarchy, projects tend to become larger and more complicated, or even complex.

Project timing

The duration of the project influences the nature of the project. Rodney Turner, Martina Huemann and Anne Keegan (2008) showed that the nature of the human resource management practices are very different depending on whether the project is less than a couple of months duration, between a couple of months and one year, and of more than one year. In fact they say that often the entity of less than a couple of months' duration is not a project, but a temporary task given to the routine organization (Turner and Müller, 2003). Terry Cooke-Davies (2002) has shown that projects are much more likely to be successful if they are less than one year in duration, or split into phases of less than one year in duration.

We can also look at the speed of project delivery. Rodney Turner (2009) categorizes projects as fast build, fast track or concurrent depending on the amount of overlap between the stages of the project life-cycle, and the interrelationship between the components of the project. In all three cases there is overlap of design and delivery, but with increasing risk.

Fast build: the project's output consists of components which can be designed separately. So the second can be designed while the first is built. With a building, for instance, as long as the height and footprint of the building does not change, the foundations can be built while the infrastructure is designed, and the internal fitting designed while the infrastructure is built.

Fast track: there is some overlap between the design of the separate components. This is the case with process plant. So assumptions have to made about the performance of the overall plant, and as long as those assumptions remain correct the components of the plant can be designed and built separately. But if the assumptions are changed, corrections can be very expensive.

Concurrency: the design of all the components of the plant is so interrelated they all have to be signed off together. This is the case with aircraft: changes to the design of the wings, airframe or engines will all influence each other.

Type of contract

Projects can be categorized by type of contract. In Section 5.6, we identified three dimensions of contract strategy, the scope of supply, the form of management, and the pricing. We described different types of contract under each of those three dimensions.

Relationship with the customer

Organizations categorize projects depending on the relationship with the customer. One simple categorization is whether the customer is internal or external to the organization. That can affect the governance structure (Chapter 5). Another is to categorize the customer by market segment. Rodney Turner (2009) in looking at international projects considers whether the customer is in their home territory and the contractor foreign, or the contractor is in their home territory and the customer foreign, or both are foreign to the country where the project is taking place.

Source of funding

Projects can be categorized by source of funding. You can categorize projects simply by which budget they are funded from. That may be capital or revenue, or different business units within the organization. Funding can come from within the parent organization in the form of capital or revenue expenditure, or from external financiers in the form of limited or non-recourse (project) financing (Turner, 1995). The budget allocation will also influence the ownership of the project. Which department within the company owns the project? That is related to governance (Chapter 5); who is the owner and who is the sponsor?

Uncertainty and ambiguity

Lynn Crawford and her team (2005) deal with uncertainty and ambiguity, risk and complexity separately. Under uncertainty and ambiguity they introduce the two typologies described in Section 1.3. One deals with the level of uniqueness, and the extent to which the work of the project is familiar, classifying projects as runners, repeaters, strangers, or aliens. The second deals with where the uncertainty lies, in the definition of the product of the project, the method of delivering the product, or both. Aaron Shenhar and Dov Dvir (2007) suggest a categorization based on the familiarity of the technology, with four levels:

1   Low technology: well known mature technology;
2   Medium technology: adaptations of familiar technology;
3   High technology: first use of new technology;
4   Super-high technology: radical new developments.

Risk

In classifying projects by risk, Lynn Crawford and her team (2005) merely suggest that all the previous classifications point to potential sources of risk. While this is correct, it risks making other potential sources of risk invisible. So in classifying projects by source of risk, you must retain an open mind about where the risk can come from. Yes, all the previous categorizations point to potential sources of risk, but so do other categorizations of risk (Turner, 2009). Risk can also be categorized by whether it is business risk or insurable risk, whether the source is internal to the parent organization or external, whether it is a people risk or technical risk (Turner, 2009). It can also be categorized as to whether the likelihood is high, medium or low, and the consequence is high, medium or low, pointing to different methods of dealing with the risk (Turner, 2009).

Complexity

Lynn Crawford and her team (2005) suggest that complexity arises where several of the project categorizations combine to create risk. Luhmann (1996) suggests complexity arises where three or more nodes interact, and so that would suggest a project starts to become complex if three or more categorizations interact to create risk. Terry Williams (2002) suggested complexity had two sources, uncertainty in the project's goals and uncertainty in the method of achieving the goals (based on the goals and methods matrix, Section 1.5). Kaye Remington and Julian Pollack (2007) expanded that to identify four sources of complexity:

1   *Structural complexity:* arising from the complicatedness of the project's structure and resulting in uncertainty in time, cost and resource requirements;
2   *Technical complexity:* arising from the novelty of the technology, and related to Aaron Shenhar and Dov Dvir (2007)'s fourth level of technological complexity, "super-high";
3   *Directional complexity:* resulting from uncertainty and lack of agreement about the project's goals, and disagreement between the stakeholders;
4   *Temporal complexity:* resulting from uncertainty about the project's context and changes that may occur in the context with time.

10.4 Using the nine perspectives

The nine perspectives are themselves a typology for projects and project management. However, how we suggest you use the nine perspectives is to identify which schools of research are relevant to your project, and then decide what that tells you about how your project should be managed. For instance, you might be relying only on the traditional tools of project management, associated with the Optimization Perspective, to manage your project and find it is not working. An analysis of your project in different circumstances reveals the following:

(a) The Success Perspective suggests you should carefully identify the actual success criteria for your project. From Table 4.1 you identify four key success criteria for your project, and that points to relevant success factors and tools other than the ones you are using. With four success criteria, modeling your project is more relevant than the application of critical path analysis; you need to aim to satisfice the four success criteria rather than optimize them. So you adopt more sophisticated modeling. Table 4.1 also identifies that there are several key stakeholders for the project, so you need to market the project to them to obtain their support, so you adopt the tools from the Marketing Perspective.

(b) In your project you are grappling with complexity and uncertainty. So you decide to adopt the Process Perspective to define the algorithm to help define the process you are going to use to clarify your project. Then you also need to adopt the Decision Perspective, to help your decision making process as you reduce complexity and uncertainty. Governance structures are also important. You need to define key governance roles, the sponsor and owner, to aid in the decision making process and obtain political support for the decisions that are being taken.

(c) A large number of people are involved in the project, with different views of what the project is about. You need to adopt the Behavior Perspective to define the team building and leadership processes for the project. Then you also need to adopt the Success and Marketing Perspective to define the project's success criteria and sell them to the various stakeholders.

(d) Different parts of your project require different methodologies for their management. This was the case with the development of Denver Airport, where different methodologies should have been used for the construction of the airport and for the development of the baggage handling system (Shenhar and Dvir, 2007). In that case a methodology appropriate for the construction of the airport was used for all the work and the baggage handling system ended up delaying the project. Or you might be doing an organizational change project involving building work, the development of a new computer system and the definition of new jobs and the recruitment and training of new staff. Different project management methodologies and leadership styles will be required for those three areas of work.

In each case we suggest you identify two, three or four perspectives relevant to your project, and see what they suggest about how the project should be managed and what approaches they suggest you should use. So move away from the memes of project management, and adopt a wider perspective on how the project should be managed. We now discuss what each perspective would suggest about the wider perspectives you can use in managing your project.

Optimization

We use the Optimization Perspective on simpler projects, when we aim to optimize the performance of the project. We normally suggest that we aim to optimize three parameters, the duration of the project, the cost, and the performance of the outcome, the beloved triple constraint or iron or golden triangle of time, cost and quality. Using most optimization algorithms it is usually only possible to optimize two parameters. So we have to take one of the three, time, cost or quality, as a given, and optimize the other two for that given value of the first. We can of course vary the given value, and so find a range of optimums, but already we are beginning to satisfice and not optimize.

The tools available from the Optimization Perspective are critical path analysis (CPA), bar (Gantt) charts and earned value management. CPA in particular is very linear and deterministic. It is a powerful tool to calculate the schedule of the project and schedule resources when coupled with a resource smoothing tool. However, it works only as long as the project goes according to plan, and as long as it does not involve probabilistic branching, feedback, inductance or capacitance, that is, as long as the project is relatively straightforward. As the project takes on other complexities, we need to look to the other perspectives to give guidance on how to approach it.

Modeling

As the project becomes more complicated or more complex we can no longer use the Optimization Perspective. Terry Williams (2002) suggests that the complexity of projects is increasing and so the Optimization Perspective will become less relevant to the management of projects. Is there a difference between complicatedness and complexity? The current view is that there is. Complicatedness is said to be a function of the technical difficulty of a project. If the design of the output uses advanced technology then that can add to the difficulty of visualizing the project plan. Above we listed Aaron Shenhar and Dov Dvir's (2007) four levels of technological difficulty. At level 3 the project is becoming complicated. But the project can be complicated, and yet still deterministic. Things behave in very predictable ways. With Kaye Remington and Julian Pollack's (2007) four dimensions of complexity, any one on its own make the project complicated. It is as the two or more begin to interact that the project becomes complex. Complicatedness also tends to be a function of the technical difficulty. Human interactions tend to create complexity.

Complexity arises in a number of circumstances, and the more of these that come into play, the more complex the project:

(a) *Multiple parameters to optimize:* As we have said, most optimization algorithms can only handle two parameters to optimize. If there are more to optimize, the best that can be hoped for is to satisfice, that is, to find a solution to the problem that is better than most. But what we tend towards is a local optimum. We can never be sure there is not some better solution far removed from the local optimum we have found.

(b) *Capacitance:* Delays can occur in the project process. Yes, dummy activities can be put in the CPA network to represent a delay. But queuing theory tells us that the length of the queue and the time in the queue is related to the rate at which items arrive in the queue. CPA cannot handle nonlinear variable durations like that.

(c) *Inductance:* What is happening in one part of the project can influence what is happening in another. Again, yes, a dummy activity can be put in the CPA network, but often the influence is not as precise and deterministic as that would suggest.

(d) *Feedback:* We discussed feedback in Section 3.2. Terry Williams (2002) has shown that in some feedback loops that occur in projects applying standard project management actually reinforces the feedback loop, making the situation worse.

(e) *Probabilistic branching:* We discussed probabilistic branching and the associated technique GERT in Section 2.2. Standard CPA just does not allow it.

(f) *Dynamic human interactions:* This is the major contributor to complexity. Some people say it is the only contributor to complexity, all the previous are about complicatedness. We disagree. Where there are three or more components to any of the above, there is a contribution to complexity. But with human interactions, Luhmann (1996) suggests that where there are three or more communication nodes, the system is complex.

Thus where the project has one or more of the above features, the chances are it will have elements of complexity and the Modeling Perspective will be appropriate for its analysis. Soft systems modeling will particularly be of relevance in the case of dynamic human interactions.

Success

Carefully defining the success criteria is important on all projects. But the Success Perspective will be particularly relevant on the following types of projects:

(a) Where it is unclear what tools and techniques should be used to manage the project. Then you need to move through the steps suggested by Wateridge (1995):

- define the success criteria for the project;
- identify the success factors that will help achieve those success criteria, perhaps using Table 4.8;
- identify the relevant tools to enact those success factors.

(b) Where there is a diverse range of stakeholders with different views of the success criteria or success factors. Then you need to work with the stakeholders to define the success criteria and the success factors. In this case you may also need to combine the Success Perspective with the Marketing Perspective, to persuade the stakeholders to buy into the agreed set of success criteria and so support the project, and the Behavior Perspective, to understand what is motivating the various stakeholders.

(c) Where the project is going badly wrong, to identify what targets the project team should be aiming for, and what methods and techniques they should be using.

Governance

Again, the Governance Perspective is relevant to all projects, and roles such as the sponsor, owner, steward and project manager should be carefully defined on all projects. But there are three elements to the Governance Perspective, and so there may be three circumstances where the school may be particularly significant:

1   Where an organization undertakes large projects, it may be important to ensure that proper governance and compliance regimes are in place, perhaps using the eleven principles of the Association for Project Management (2004), to ensure

- the objectives of projects are properly defined;
- the means of obtaining objectives are properly defined;
- control mechanisms are in place, both to ensure projects deliver their objectives, but also to ensure there is a proper audit trail;
- roles and responsibilities are defined and assigned;
- people have appropriate competence and authority to enact their roles.

2   Where transaction costs or the principal–agency relationship are likely to be significant. Then the project can be analyzed as a temporary organization to help identify the impact of those issues.

3   On projects involving contracts, a contract strategy should be developed and appropriate forms of contract chosen to properly motivate the contractor to achieve the client's objectives and minimize agency costs, particularly residual loss. The project should also be viewed as a partnership, where client and contractor work towards mutually consistent objectives to best deliver the client's objectives.

Behavior

The Behavior Perspective is particularly required in three circumstances:

1   On projects where there is a diverse range of stakeholders who need melding into an integrated project team. Then you need to consider organizational behavioral issues such as team building, motivation and organizational design.

In this case the perspective may need to be combined with the Success and Marketing Perspectives.

2   Where it is critical to ensure that the Human Resource Management (HRM) practices support project working, and the motivation and cohesiveness of project team members drawn from different parts of the organization. It may also be critical to consider HRM issues on virtual project teams, or teams with people drawn from several organizations such as on alliance contracts.

3   On a large project with several different areas of activity, it may be necessary to consider the leadership profiles of the sub-project managers to ensure they match the type of work they are doing. It can be possible even on small projects with radically different sets of stakeholders to have different sub-projects suited to communicating with the different stakeholder types.

Marketing

Projects need marketing to diverse sets of stakeholders and to senior management. As we have seen several times, where there is a diverse set of stakeholders, with different views about the project success criteria, it is necessary to obtain agreement about the success criteria and then persuade all the stakeholders to accept the compromise. Also it is necessary to get senior management to buy into the project and accept their project roles such as owner and sponsor. We may also want senior management to buy into the idea that project management itself can provide value to the organization (Thomas and Mullaly, 2008). We need the support of senior management for effective project management. They need to devise appropriate governance structures, and give project managers appropriate support and authority, and they are most likely to do that if they can see the value of project management to the organization.

Process

The Process Perspective is useful on projects involving some uncertainty. The perspective will help us devise a project process to manage the reduction of uncertainty on the project, and take structured and controlled steps towards the solution to the project.

Decision

The Decision Perspective will then help us to develop a project strategy, ensure the project is soundly based at its start, and that we create an audit trail for the decisions we take through the project.

Contingency

We have a repeating reflection in a mirror. The Contingency Perspective should be used with diverse project types.

10.5 Did we achieve the best of all possible outcomes?

As we have moved through the nine perspectives of project management we have tried to move away from the Optimization Perspective and the systems approach. The systems approach has been responsible for the idea that project management is all about tools and techniques: that as long as they can master the tools and techniques, anybody, no matter how otherwise incompetent, can apply the tools and techniques to manage any project. We have shown that the Optimization Perspective does not model enough parameters and the tools adopted are too linear and deterministic. We have shown that both the optimizing and Modeling Perspective of our projects need to be based on an understanding of the success criteria and success factors of the project, and that these need to be linked to corporate strategy. A project is a temporary organization, and that means that there are people involved. We mustn't forget about them, and we need to persuade all the people involved from the most senior to the most junior to buy into the project. Project management is a process to convert vision into reality, desire into memory. We follow a structured process to achieve our end objectives, and help solve problems along the way. As we work through the project process, we process information to take better decisions about what we want to achieve and how to do it. Finally we recognize that every project is different and so we need to adopt different processes to manage different projects. Throughout the first part of this book we have explored the rich diversity of projects and project management.

But at the end of the day, what do we want to achieve through all of this? We want to achieve the best of all possible outcomes for our project, and that takes us right back to the Optimization Perspective. Coda.

References

Association for Project Management, 2004, *Directing Change: A guide to governance of project management*, Association for Project Management (APM), High Wycombe, UK. Retrieved on June 15, 2007 from http://www.apm.org.uk/Governance2.asp

Cooke-Davies, T., 2002, "The 'real' project success factors," *International Journal of Project Management*, **20**(3), 185–190.

Crawford, L.H., Hobbs, J.B., and Turner, J.R., 2005, *Project Categorization Systems: Aligning capability with strategy for better results*, Project Management Institute, Newtown Square, PA.

Dinsmore, P., 1999, *Winning in Business with Enterprise Project Management*, AMACOM, New York.

Evaristo, R., and van Fenema, P.C., 1999, "A typology of project management: Emergence and evolution of new forms," *International Journal of Project Management*, **17**(5), 275–281.

Luhmann, N., 1996, *Social Systems*, Stanford University Press, Stanford, CA.

Remington, K. and Pollack, J., 2007, *Tools for Complex Projects*, Gower, Aldershot.

Shenhar, A.J., and Dvir, D., 2007, *Reinventing Project Management: The diamond approach to successful growth and innovation*, Harvard Business School Press, Boston.

Thomas, J., and Mullaly, M., 2008, *Researching the Value of Project Management*, Project Management Institute, Newtown Square, PA.

Turner, J.R. (ed.), 1995, *The Commercial Project Manager*, McGraw-Hill, London,

Turner, J.R., 2009, *The Handbook of Project-Based Management*, 3rd edition, McGraw-Hill, New York.

Turner, J.R., and Müller, R., 2003, "On the nature of the project as a temporary organization," *International Journal of Project Management*, **21**(1), 1–8.

Turner, J.R., and Müller, R., 2006, *Choosing Appropriate Project Managers: Matching their leadership style to the type of project*, Project Management Institute, Newtown Square, PA.

Turner, J.R., Huemann, M., and Keegan, A.E., 2008, *Human Resource Management in the Project-Oriented Organization*, Project Management Institute, Newtown Square, PA.

Wateridge, J.H., 1995, "IT projects: A basis for success," *International Journal of Project Management*, **13**(3), 169–172.

Williams, T., 2002, *Modelling Complex Projects*, Wiley, Chichester, UK.

Part II
The three case studies

11 Using the nine perspectives

11.1 Taking a perspective

We started Chapter 1 by saying that the aim is to take new perspectives on projects and project management. The perspective that has dominated project management thinking is the Optimization Perspective. This reflects two things:

- The genesis of the field of modern project management as an offshoot of Operations Research and optimization theory. This perspective dominates because people just don't look any further. They are told that is what project management is, and just accept it at face value.
- The substantial investment by software vendors in software to perform critical path analysis and draw increasingly sophisticated Gantt charts (and we mean sophisticated in the original meaning of the word – as used by sophists). It would have a significant impact on their cash flow for them to admit that CPM is of little use and we should use more appropriate modeling tools, and so it is in their interest to keep on persuading us to use CPM and draw Gantt charts, and so we accept that at face value and look no further.

However, we have shown throughout this book that it is possible to take new and different perspectives on our projects, and we have suggested there are at least nine. In fact we could have suggested twelve; we could have divided Behavior into OB and HR and Governance into temporary organizations, governance and contracts. Or we could have limited ourselves to seven (Miller, 1956) by merging optimization and modeling and merging process and decisions. But nine we have.

Our thesis is that by taking different perspectives on a project, we open up whole new worlds of project management methods, approaches and techniques. Each of the perspectives emphasizes different issues relevant to the project and at the same time suggests we should neglect other issues, as with each perspective we can only see what we can see. The value comes by using several perspectives on the project, which helps us create a project management methodology designed specifically for that project, by choosing appropriate project management methods, tools and techniques.

For instance, in the Shuttle Wagons Project mentioned in Chapter 3 (Ackerman *et al.*, 1997; Williams *et al.*, 1995a, b) we might decide that the success, modeling, contingency, and optimization schools are important.

1   We need to decide how the project will be judged to be successful, and what the key success factors are;
2   We need to model the interrelationships between those success factors, and identify any potential feedback loops as illustrated in Figure 3.3;
3   We need to develop a model that reflects the true and specific nature of the project;
4   Our overall aim is to achieve the optimum outcome for the project.

We can then develop a modified version of Figure 3.8 reflecting the four relevant schools and their interrelationships (Figure 11.1), and turn to the four schools to select appropriate methods to develop our methodology for this project.

11.2 Choosing methods

A method is a process or recipe for achieving a specific goal or undertaking a specific task. If we are baking a cake, we follow a recipe, and that is the method we follow. Techniques are specific elements of the method. So if we are baking a cake, there is a technique for beating eggs, a technique for blending flour and butter, and a technique for mixing eggs and milk so that the milk does not curdle. Then we use various tools: egg beaters, wooden spoons, baking trays. A methodology is a collection of methods to achieve a more complex goal or undertake a more complex

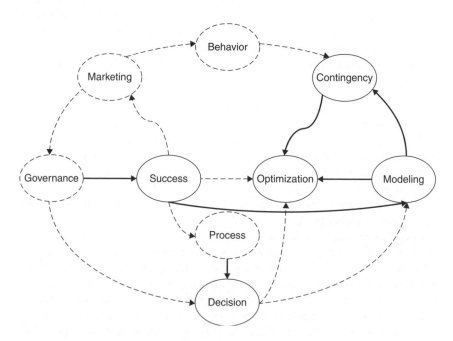

Figure 11.1 Four perspectives on the Shuttle Wagons Project (Section 3.2)

task or tasks. So if we are preparing a meal, we need methods to make the soup, to cook the meat, to prepare the vegetables, and to bake the desert. Put the methods together and they make a methodology to prepare a meal. So for our projects we can draw methods from several schools, based on our perspective on the project, to develop an integrated methodology to meet the needs of that project.

To identify appropriate methods for our project we turn to the fields of research, the schools, that correspond to the perspectives we have taken on the project. Table 11.1 shows some of the methods and techniques associated with each school.

Table 11.1 Project management methods related to perspectives

School	Project management methods	Associated techniques
Optimization	Optimizing time, cost and resource usage	CPM PERT Gantt Chart Resource histogram WBS
	Project simulation	Monte Carlo analysis
	Forecasting cost and time to and at completion	EVM
Modeling	Project simulation	Project modeling Computer simulation Soft-systems techniques Interrelationship digraph
Success	Achieving successful project outcomes	Success criteria Success factors Quality plan
Governance	Managing the temporary organization	Transaction costs Principal–agency theory
	Governance of project management	Program management Portfolio management Project office Project management capability Health checks and audits Benchmarking
	Governance of the project	Owner Sponsor Steward Project manager
	Project contract management	Contract selection and strategy
Behavior	Project organization	Project roles descriptions Team building
	Leadership	Leadership techniques
	Human resource management	Selection and assignment Appraisal Reward Development Dispersal and release

Marketing	Stakeholder management	Stakeholder analysis Communication plan Project homepage Project folder, video, newsletter
Process	Process management	Life-cycle Management process Start, controlling, close down workshops Milestone planning Process-oriented WBS
Decision	Project initiation Project implementation Project strategy	Results based management Estimating End of stage reviews Seven forces analysis Seven forces analysis Project excellence
Contingency	Project categorization Project perspectives	Project attributes The nine schools

11.3 The cases

In the remainder of this book, we describe three projects, to show how the nine perspectives can provides us with a better understanding of our projects to be able to manage them better. One is a construction project, one a computer project, and the third an organizational change project involving international collaboration. Table 11.2 shows the perspectives illustrated by each project. We see that all the perspectives can be appropriate to different types of projects.

Table 11.2 The three case studies

Chapter	Case	Technology	Illustrated perspectives
12	Amsterdam North–South Metro Line	Construction	Governance Decision Marketing
13	Computerization of London Ambulance Service	Computers	Success Decision Governance Marketing
14	Antibiotic Stewardship (ABS) Project	Organizational change	Success Decision Process Behavior Marketing

References

Ackermann, F., Eden, C., and Williams, T., 1997, "Modelling for litigation: Mixing qualitative and quantitative approaches," *Interfaces*, **27**, 48–65.

Milller, G.A., 1956, "The magic number seven plus or minus two: Some limits on our capacity for processing information," *Psychology Review*, **March**, 81–97.

Williams, T.M., Eden, C.L., Ackermann, F.R., and Tait, A., 1995a, "Vicious circles of parallelism", *International Journal of Project Management*, **13**, 151–155.

——, 1995b, "The effects of design changes and delays on project costs," *Journal of the Operational Research Society*, **46**(7), 809–818.

12 The North–South Metro Line

Managing in crowded historic Amsterdam

Pau Lian Staal-Ong and Eddy Westerveld

12.1 A brief history

With an estimated cost of €3.1 billion, the North–South Metro Line currently being built in Amsterdam (NZL: Noord–Zuid Lijn) is one of the biggest infrastructure projects ever undertaken in the Netherlands. The project has already faced many interesting challenges, and many more will follow, with commissioning currently planned for 2017. In this chapter we outline some key events in the life of this large infrastructure project which has caused extraordinary turmoil in both regional politics and amongst local inhabitants living in the vicinity. To introduce the case and the perspectives used for analysis we start with a history lesson.

Around the year 1000, the swampy area surrounding what now is known as Amsterdam was developed into a farming community. When the peat started to set because of draining, dikes had to be built to protect the land, which was now lower than the water. In the thirteenth century, fishermen living along the banks of the river Amstel built a bridge across the waterway near the river IJ. The bridge served as a dam, protecting the town from flooding. Thus the meaning of the name Amsterdam: dam on the Amstel River. The mouth of the river Amstel, crossing the river IJ, formed a natural harbor and became a very busy and important area for trade. This is where the Central Station is currently located.

Throughout the following centuries, Amsterdam became an important pilgrimage town and prospered through beer, grain and timber trade. In the Middle Ages, canals were dug and embankments raised for new buildings. In 1300 about 1,000 inhabitants lived in Amsterdam. A hundred years later, there were 3,000. In the seventeenth century the number of inhabitants grew to 210,000. The town faced many challenges, varying from the plague, the great fire and several wars. During industrialization however, around 1870, a new period of expansion took place. In 1889 the Central Station was opened near the dam, lying on an island which divided the city from the river IJ. Renewed commerce, new types and forms of industry such as financial services, led to a rapid population growth. The city was pushed to its limits and living conditions of workers were bad. This lead to the creation of new districts outside of the seventeenth-century town borders, called the nineteenth-century belt. Economic prosperity occurred through the twentieth century, resulting in a population increase to 757,000 inhabitants by 1930.

In the 1930s plans were proposed to further develop the city. The economic crisis of the 1930s and World War II hindered the development of these plans. After the war, the plans were largely carried out. Due to the building of the IJ-tunnel and other embankment connections, the northern part of Amsterdam was also further developed to accommodate the growing need for housing. In the 1960s city-forming plans were developed focusing on the economic functions of the city. Huge designs for dike bursts and filling in the freed space arose, including the building of an extensive metro network. It was at that time that the local inhabitants first organized resistance to the city council, for example stopping the plans for the building of a main road in the Nieuwmarkt area.

The city was transformed again in the 1970s and 1980s, with urban renewal through demolition, building of new houses and comprehensive renovations. Many families moved out of the city in search of larger houses in the centers of urban development outside the city. Industry and large offices also moved out towards the southern and northern areas, in search of space and accessibility. This is still going on. But even so, statistically the housing density is quite high. In January 2009, Amsterdam counted 756,347 residents. The average housing density in Amsterdam is 2,319 per km^2, approximately 11 times the national average. One out of every three residents owns a car. In 2006, Amsterdam counted approximately 253 million public transport users who traveled 987 million kilometers.

12.2 The Amsterdam North–South Metro Line

Why this history lesson? The reason is that some main elements visible in the historical description are essential in the context of the NZL Project. The following three elements in this introduction characterize the restrictions on the Project:

- very little space to work in – a densely populated area;
- soft soil underground – causing technical challenges;
- citizens who want to be heard – meaning a highly political project.

Based on these characteristics we use the following perspectives to analyze the project:

(a) *The Governance Perspective, which looks at the project as a legal entity:* This is an interesting one to use since it focuses on the beneficial change, in our case the increased mobility, for example, to be realized with the project. The many stakeholders involved, as the result of dense population and active citizens, result in many goals and interests being associated with the project. To achieve this change the City of Amsterdam has set up a project delivery organization. How does this project delivery organization govern the project in order to achieve the beneficial change(s)? In which way are the shareholders and stakeholders within the NZL organized? These are questions we can look into using the Governance perspective.

(b) *The Decision Perspective, which looks at the project as a computer:* This allows use to take a look at the specific elements of decision making within the

NZL Project. On which information was the decision to approve the project based? Here we use the theory presented in Section 9.2, deciding where to go. Did this information include mention of the technical challenges arising from the soft soil? In addition the decision perspective poses some views to look at decision making in complexity – how to decide when the situation is uncertain? How the project delivery organization deals with uncertainty during implementation greatly affects which project strategy is chosen.

(c) *Marketing Perspective, which looks at the project as a bill board:* This illustrates the importance of "selling" the project to its main stakeholders (Section 7.2), something which is of special importance here because of the densely populated area in which the new metro is being built: the citizens need to support the project for it to be executed smoothly. As noted in our history lesson, the citizens of Amsterdam will definitely speak up when they feel they are not being heard and taken seriously. So the marketing and communication of the project to the stakeholders is essential in the NZL.

Project facts and figures

The NZL is a new metro line running between the North and South of Amsterdam (Figure 12.1). Key data is given in Table 12.1. Like any major large infrastructure project, the NZL has several goals. Some of the most important are:

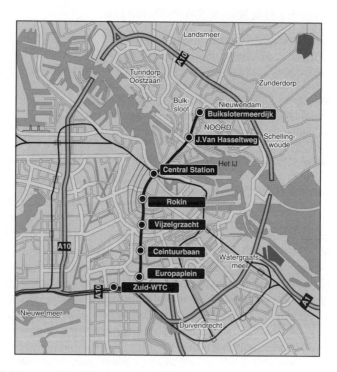

Figure 12.1 Route of the NZL

Table 12.1 Essential figures of the NZL Project

Parameter	Figure
Length	
Total	9.5 km (5.9 miles)
New	9.0 km (5.6 miles)
Underground	6.0 km (3.8 miles)
Bored tunnel	4.2 km (2.6 miles)
Stations	
Total	8
New	7
Underground	5
Cost	
Budget	€3.1 bn
Schedule	
Commissioning date	2017
Travel	
Expected passengers	180,000 per day
Frequency	1 train per 5 minutes
Journey time	16 minutes
Improvement	27 minutes
Speed	35 km/h

- to connect the city center to the developing northern and southern regions; with possible further expansion to other regions in the future;
- to realize an adequate and more efficient transport system required by the increasing number of public transport passengers – the bus and tram network is judged to be unable to transport the 1.2 million passengers per day in a fast and reliable manner;
- to improve the accessibility of the city center, reducing congestion;
- to reduce hindrance of motorized transport in the city center;
- to support tourism;
- to support economic development.

Project delivery organization

Figure 12.2 shows the structure of the project delivery organization for the NZL Project as it was from 2003 to the end of 2007. The NZL is financed by both the Amsterdam City Council and the Dutch Government. The city council provides the majority of the finance and carries the construction risk. Currently their contribution is €2.0 billion. The contribution of the Dutch Government comes through the Ministry of Transport and is fixed at €1.1 billion. The project is executed under the responsibility of the Amsterdam City Council, which serves as the civil principal. Within the city the Alderman of Infrastructure, Traffic and Transport is the politician responsible for project execution. The alderman heads the project organization which is currently placed within the Department for Infrastructure, Traffic and

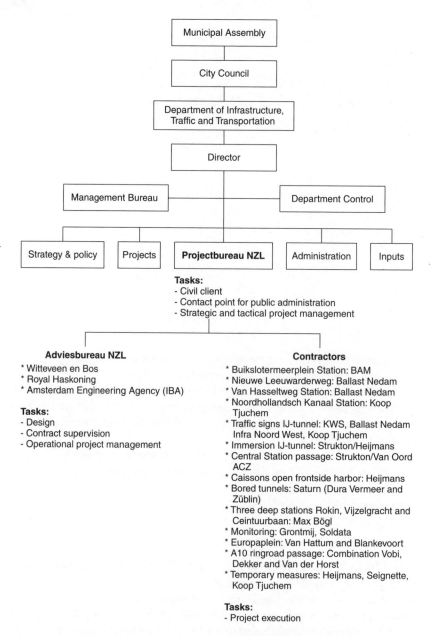

Figure 12.2 Structure of the NZL project delivery organization 2003–2007

Transport (*Dienst Infrastructuur, Verkeer en Vervoer*). This department has installed a separate project delivery organization. This structure, however, will likely be changed, since it is planned to set up a special department within the city organization to deliver the project in 2010. The project delivery organization North–South Line has awarded 16 contracts so far and works with six main contractors that take care of the design and construction of the line.

The main operator of the new metro line after its planned commissioning in 2017 is still unknown, but it is likely that the Community Transport Company (*Gemeentelijk Vervoerbedrijf*, GVB) will play an important role. Since 2002, GVB has been responsible, based on specific contracts, to deliver several public transport services to the citizens and visitors of Amsterdam. This means the community of Amsterdam serves as their client. There have been initiatives to privatize the GVB, but this was blocked by a city referendum in 2002 after the city council had already given its approval.

The civil community of Amsterdam is the parent organization of the project. Within the city of Amsterdam independent city boroughs (*Stadsdeelraden*) have been set up to govern separate parts of the city. Close cooperation with these districts is necessary.

To ensure the project will be carried out well, close collaboration is also needed with other parties such as other municipal services, the police, fire brigade, utilities such as telecommunications and electricity, and of course, the contractors.

12.3 Project history

Decision to build a metro line – 1955 to 1988

In 1955, in a report on the inner city, the Amsterdam City Council suggested the building of an underground rail network, the main reasons being the need for a faster way of transporting passengers and reducing the traffic in the streets of Amsterdam. A feasibility study was conducted, and the resulting report suggested starting by building a metro line for the area with the largest traffic flow, being the connection between the north and the south of Amsterdam. It took until 1968 for the city council to decide to build a metro line, but it was decided to start with the line from the city center to the east, due to the development of the south-east region of Amsterdam, the Bijlmermeer.

The building of the East Line started in 1971. Due to many problems encountered, including large cost overruns and time delays, as well as the social resistance through a well-organized citizen protest to the demolition of houses and buildings resulting in riots, the city council decided in 1978 to discontinue the expansion of the metro network, therefore canning the planned building of the North–South Line. Opponents of the North–South Line were afraid of cost overruns and potential caving-in of the construction works. In addition, they were afraid that there would be more demolition of houses and buildings, which at the time was the only way to construct a metro line. The word "metro" became a politically charged term, one that was avoided for a long time.

But by 1988, the city was becoming more and more overcrowded. Accessibility was terrible and the above ground bus and tram network could not accommodate the approximate 1.1 million travelers per day. The political party D66 ordered research into the building of the North–South Line, resulting in a referendum that took place in 1997. Some 123,198 voters turned out for the referendum of which 79,832 (64.8 percent) voted against the line. However, the result was deemed to be not binding because the number of "no" voters had to be greater than half of the number of voters at the last municipal elections. That meant that a minimum of 154,935 "no" voters was required to stop the project. Since this number was not reached, from a democratic judicial process perspective, the construction of the NZL Project could go ahead.

In the years between the bad experiences of building the East Line and the decision to re-evaluate the building of the North–South Line much had happened. The Amsterdam City Council had experiences with the execution of three large projects. The first was the East Line itself. The second was the Piet Hein tunnel, at that time, the longest car tunnel in the Netherlands. That project was largely successful, being finished on time and within budget. The third project was the Ring Road A4-West, also a largely successful project. In addition, new boring techniques had developed, allowing for the possibility of boring deeply underground in soft soil, whereby the need for demolishing houses could be avoided (one of the major problems during the building of the East line). As a result of these previous experiences, it was thought that the NZL Project could be mainly outsourced and made the responsibility of the city transportation company (GVB).

The start of the implementation of the project – 1990s

The project delivery organization was set up at the beginning of the 1990s according to the principles that were (then) acceptable for the realization of large infrastructural works in the Netherlands, such as the High Speed Line or the Piet Hein Tunnel in Amsterdam.

In 1993 an organizational model for the NZL Project was described in a plan written by the consultancy firm Toornend and Partners. Two aspects were central in their advice:

1   A large civil technical project like the NZL should be realized according to preset operational, technical and financial definitions. The main task of the project organization is to monitor the scope, the predetermined budget and the planning.
2   In order to be able to execute this main task, there needs to be a differentiation between the management of the project (the project directors) and activities for the realization of design, contracting and monitoring.

This organizational advice led to the initiation of a task awarding organization, as Employer for the project (the Projectbureau Noord/Zuidlijn), part of the city Infrastructure, Traffic and Transportation department and the Project Engineering organization responsible for the realization tasks (the Adviesbureau Noord/Zuidlijn). As well as the primary building activities, the realization included activities for facilitating the building process including permits, environmental measures, communication, etc.

The second round of implementation – 1997 to 2002

Because of problems with the environment, namely stakeholders involved in the project and client doubts about the way the project organization was set up, in 1997 KPMG reevaluated the structure of the project delivery organization and suggested the Projectbureau should not only be responsible for building management but should pay extra attention to stakeholder aspects. According to KPMG, the project delivery organization needed to define a second major task for itself, namely stakeholder management. Included in managing the environment were managing several secondary related building projects and attention to accessibility, livability and safety aspects.

In 2002 the Amsterdam Infrastructure, Traffic and Transportation department organized an internal research resulting in a revised description of the project delivery organization (Figure 12.3). Next to building management and stakeholder management, a third main task was introduced, communications. Previously this role had been fulfilled by the Adviesbureau. In addition, new staff functions in the areas of finances and planning and governance and legal matters were introduced.

The third round of implementation – 2002 to 2009

Since 2002 (Figure 12.3) the project delivery organization has focused more on managing and maintaining permits and licenses as well as the corresponding governance and legal processes. In fact, managing the permits and licenses has become a fourth major task of the project delivery organization.

During the history of the project delivery organization, it is apparent that slowly a transfer of activities took place between the Project Engineer (Adviesbureau Noord/Zuidlijn) and the Employer (Projectbureau Noord/Zuidlijn). More and more operational tasks and responsibilities were taken over by the Projectbureau and the

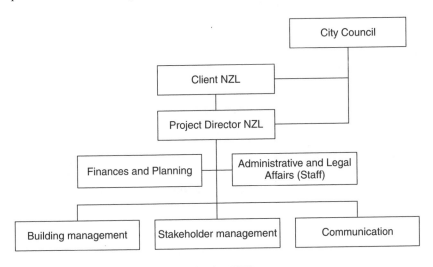

Figure 12.3 NZL project delivery organization 2002

Adviesbureau Noord/Zuidlijn referred back to traditional tasks of an engineering company which provides technical expertise and advice.

The project delivery was based on the principle that the client of the project, the city of Amsterdam, would and could manage the project from distance. All the operational tasks, such as design, monitoring building activities and financial control, were the responsibility of Adviesbureau Noord/Zuidlijn, which was a separate private organization. This organization was set-up as a collaboration between the engineering companies Witteveen+Bos, Royal Haskoning and Amsterdam Engineering Agency (a city department). In the legal entity, the engineering company Witteveen+Bos functioned as the leading partner.

At the start of the implementation of the project, the development phase, this dual model worked very well. In the execution or construction phase of the project, several limitations arose. Some operational responsibilities, such as monitoring permits and licensing processes, discussions with city council boroughs and departments and control of building and consultancy costs, were transferred to the client of the project, the City of Amsterdam. As a result, a mixture between public and private activities began to ensue as well as confusion of the operating building companies and project surroundings.

In 2004, after a reported cost increase of several tens of millions of Euros as well as a further delay in the schedule, the city council requested an external commission, led by former Minister of Justice, Winnie Sorgdrager, to research the project management and financial management of the project and provide suggestions for improvement. In 2005, the commission advised to reorganize the project delivery organization even further. Additional research later supported this advice and in September 2007, a large organizational change was implemented (Figure 12.4). The Adviesbureau Noord/Zuidlijn (the Project Engineer) and the Projectbureau

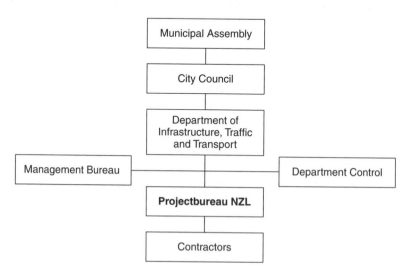

Figure 12.4 Structure of the NZL project delivery organization 2007–2009

Noord/Zuidlijn (the Employer for the project) were integrated. As a result, the responsibility for the realization of the project was now centralized and the focus was put on optimizing work processes.

With an integrated Adviesbureau Noord/Zuidlijn and Projectbureau Noord/Zuidlijn, a better control of the project was anticipated as the distance between the client and contractors was minimized:

1   More direct city council involvement in the management of building projects leads to more insight into costs and risks and therefore a better control of time and costs;
2   A shorter distance between the city and the building sites makes it possible to anticipate and react to signals from the environment quicker;
3   Integrating the two bureaus offers efficiency possibilities.

The city council decided that the new organization should have the aspects of a project organization: in structure, work processes and combination of personnel. This type of organization is formed for one specific goal, has multidisciplinary and often changing personnel and per definition it is a finite, flexible and a one of a kind organization.

The Dutch have gained substantial experience on large infrastructure and spatial projects in setting up effective organizations for the realization phase of these projects. In general, these organizations have the following three-tiered structure:

*   project management (carrying the overall responsibility);
*   staff departments (consisting of specialized functions for consultancy, planning and control);
*   units for the realization of the work to be carried out (Realization Teams or Contract Teams).

This three-layer structure was also chosen for the integrated NZL Projectbureau in 2007. It was in line with the build-up of the Projectbureau and Adviesbureau Noord/Zuidlijn. This organizational structure lasted until the end of 2009.

The fourth round of implementation – 2009 and onwards

In 2009, the city council had an external commission look to the future of the NZL Project and conditions under which it could be continued in a successful manner. Among the reasons for this research were continual nuisance to the environment, several unexpected incidents (failing technique), rising yearly budget (cost increases) and delayed delivery (schedule overrun). The City Council asked the commission: when looking at the scope of the project, to what extent is it still feasible? The Commission reported on June 2, 2009 that stopping the NZL project at this time was not an acceptable option. It is important for the city of Amsterdam to have a Noord/Zuidlijn, but within realistic and controlled boundaries of safety and livability. In order to be able to realize the project successfully, the citizens of Amsterdam and other stakeholders need to regain trust that the realization of the project will take place in a safe and open environment. To achieve this, several organizational changes are needed. All changes were accepted by the City Council, resulting in yet another form of organization (Figure 12.5) to be implemented from 2010.

An important element in the recommendations of the commission was that collaboration between several city departments responsible for the project will need to improve. They need to improve not just physical collaboration, who's responsible for what, but also, cultural aspects, such as "finishing the job together." Most importantly, from January 2010, NZL is an independent city council department (Figure 12.5), reporting directly to the responsible Elderman and fully mandated for achieving the project goal of delivering an integrated working transport system. The name of the organization will be changed to Dienst Noord/Zuidlijn. This is a new organizational model for the city of Amsterdam. The expectation is that the organization will be able to act and respond quicker to situations it encounters and will have a better grip on coordination activities.

A Project Commissariat, consisting three external members, the Directors of the Infrastructure, Traffic and Transport Department and the Environment and Soil Department, will control and advise the Project Director with respect to adequate realization of the project in technical, financial, organizational and societal terms. This Commissariat advises the alderman responsible for the NZL Project about realization of the project in administrative context. They will guard, and influence where necessary, the clarity of roles of the various city department actors. The Commissariat can also be asked by the alderman to be available for consultation by the city council Steering Committee for Traffic and Transport. Along with implementing this organizational change and a thorough reevaluation of risks, the total project budget has been increased to €3.1 billion and the delivery date moved to 2017.

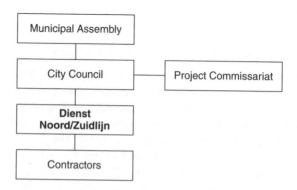

Figure 12.5 Expected project organization from January 2010

Summary

Thus the decision making process for the NZL Project can be summarized as shown in Table 12.2. The most important milestones of the NZL Project are shown in Table 12.3.

12.4 Using the nine perspectives

In the previous section, we outlined the historical development of the project delivery organization which is responsible for the implementation of the NZL Project. This historical overview already gives us some interesting insights into the project which we can use in applying three different perspectives on projects for our analysis. We use each of the three perspectives, governance, decision, and marketing, to analyze the project and draw conclusions (Figure 12.6). In the sections on each perspective, we have added some new case information to provide better insight into the NZL and better apply the various perspectives.

Governance

Realizing the NZL has always been challenging because it is situated in and affected by three major environments:

- social;
- political; and
- (geo)physical environment.

Table 12.2 Summary of the decision making process for the NZL Project

Year	Event
1964	The Bureau Stadsspoorwegen (Office of Urban Railways) recommends improving public transportation in Amsterdam by creating a metro network to supplement the diffuse network of buses and trams.
1971	The construction of the Oostlijn (East Line) starts.
1975	The plan for the metro network is withdrawn in response to major opposition from the general public during the construction of the Oostlijn (due to the demolition of buildings).
1978	The City of Amsterdam decides against any further expansion of the metro network.
1988	The possibilities of using the tunnel-boring technique beneath Amsterdam are brought to the attention of the Chamber of Commerce.
1989	The go-ahead is given for the first NZL study.
1990	The second study phase begins.
1991	City council presentation.
1993	The third study phase begins.
1994	The preparations for the plan and the definition of the project starts.
1995	The City Council orders a partial determination of a definitive schedule of requirements.
1996	The City Council issues a decree in favour of construction.
1997	Referendum on the NZL is held.
1998	The subsidy application is submitted.
1999	The Dutch Lower House of Parliament awards the subsidy.

Table 12.2 (*continued*)

Year	Event
2000	The subsidy package is accepted.
2002	The definitive "go" decision is made.
2003	Construction activities for the NZL start.

Table 12.3 Important project milestones (as per date of writing)

Date	Event
1 July 1994	Schedule of requirements defined.
22 September 1999	Implementation of Temporary Measures start.
12 December 2000	Call for tenders (I).
25 October 2001	Call for tenders (II).
7 November 2002	Contracts for the Central, Rokin, Vijzelgracht and Ceintuurbaan stations are awarded.
7 April 2003	Contracts for tunnels are awarded.
22 April 2003	Construction starts.
August 2008	Construction of the table (tunnel) construction under the Central Station finished.
January 2009	Construction finished on Johan van Hasselt station.
February 2009	Delivery contract 8.1: refurnishing and reconstruction of roads and temporary measures in Amsterdam South.
April 2009	Construction of Nieuwe Leeuwarderweg finished: lowering and reopening of a main road in the North.
2017	Metro expected to start operating.

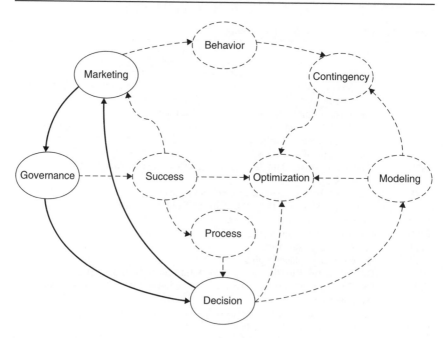

Figure 12.6 Using the nine perspectives to analyze the NZL Project

These three environments have a major effect on the governance structures chosen for the implementation of the NZL Project.

Social environment: Because of the densely populated city, there are residents living in the immediate vicinity and surroundings of the building locations who experience nuisance from the building work on a daily basis. All other stakeholders also experience the effects the project has on the city center. Businesses, entrepreneurs, canal boat companies, schools, tourists, hotels, the RAI (major Congress center) and of course the local traffic of trams, cars, buses, and bicycles are affected by the project. And to complicate matters, the project is taking far longer than was expected and communicated at the start of the project.

Political environment: The NZL Project far outlasts the political environment. There are new city council elections every four years. Since 1989, the project has had eight separate aldermen responsible for it. This means that much time and effort must be spent on informing and updating the politically responsible persons. The political environment is not only visible at the level of aldermen and the city council. Within the City of Amsterdam, as the responsible agency for project implementation, there have been many changes in structure as we noted above. Often these changes also resulted in changes of project personnel. As an example of the political sensitivity in terms of the implementation agency, eight Project Directors have been heading the project within the Projectbureau since 1989.

(Geo)physical environment: Because of the soft soil under Amsterdam, special techniques have to be used during the building of the NZL. The development of tunnel boring machines has meant that underground construction could be implemented. This is fully proven and accepted technology. In addition, new and state of the art technology has had to be designed to face some challenges encountered. One example is the machine that was developed to pull the 2,500 piles out from under the Central Station. Usually, these 30- to 40-meter-long piles can be extracted vertically. In the case of the NZL, the historic Central Station building standing above these piles could not be moved or damaged, meaning that the piles had to be extracted in a different and new way.

Governance structures

Section 5.3 suggests that the governance of projects takes place at three levels:

1   corporate governance;
2   between corporate and project;
3   individual project.

Thus, according to the Governance Perspective, proper arrangements need to be made in order to make sure the right objectives are formulated for the project (level 1) which then need to transferred to the project (level 2) which in turn needs to set specific sub-objectives and determine how to achieve those (level 3) (Figure 12.7).

As we suggested in Section 12.2, the NZL serves a range of objectives. At the highest level, the corporate level, there is a need within society for reduced travel

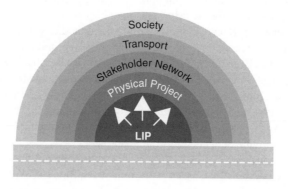

Figure 12.7 Hierarchy of project objectives (after Hertogh *et al.*, 2008)

times, which puts demands on the transport system. In a democracy these demands are then collected and weighed by the responsible politician against the scarce resources available and the interests of involved stakeholders in case politicians chose to fulfill these demands in any way. Within the NZL, the politicians have decided, based on these demands and constraints, to implement an infrastructure facility: a new metro running from the North to the South of Amsterdam. They have installed a specific agency, the project delivery organization, to implement this facility. Here we see how transport and society demands are transferred to the project (level 2). Within the project delivery organization we then see a governance structure which involves the key stakeholder in order to implement the project.

Now how do these three levels of governance compare to the historical development of the project delivery organization? As noted earlier, the implementation of the NZL is characterized by the high number of stakeholders involved and their active participation and attitude towards the project. Within the historical development of the project delivery organization, as the responsible temporary agency for delivering the project output, we have seen how this is incorporated in the governance of the project. The project delivery organization focusing on a specific task towards delivering the NZL, has developed into an independent project delivery organization with integral responsibility for (all) the project deliverables.

In the first phase of the project, the project delivery organization split the responsibilities between the Projectbureau and Adviesbureau. In governance terms, their relationship can be described as a principal–agent relationship (Section 5.2). However, in terms of responsibility, these two agencies could never be held fully independently responsible for delivering the project objectives as their tasks could not be seen as separate packages and these tasks and responsibilities were not defined clearly enough. In addition, in the case of the delivery of rolling stock, essential to fulfill the transport needs and objectives, these were placed under responsibility of another department within the City of Amsterdam. The Projectbureau was responsible for providing the sub- and superstructure. Another complicating factor is that the Projectbureau was placed within a department

(Infrastructure, Traffic and Transport) within the City, causing a large distance between the responsible alderman and the project managers and creating long and bureaucratic reaction times. The dependency on other city departments also caused increased bureaucracy and lengthy reaction times. Finally, one of the problems in the principal agent relationship became more and more visible during the construction phase: the agent (Adviesbureau), consisting of organizations with commercial interests focused on operating within the financial constraints provided by their budgets instead of focusing on the overall objectives as formulated by the responsible politicians.

Using the Governance Perspectives to evaluate the NZL, it becomes clear that the link between the objectives at corporate level and project level was not properly made: interfaces between responsible agencies were ill-defined or lacking, something which was gradually corrected by the interventions of the external committees. In 2010, the project delivery organization will most probably become a separate entity comparable to an independent department within the City of Amsterdam, with full integral responsibility (and necessary mandates) for the project: delivering a running metro between the north and south of Amsterdam. This greatly shortens the link between corporate objectives and simplifies the governance structure of the project. Earlier the responsibilities of the Projectbureau and Adviesbureau were already integrated to synchronize objectives and eliminate the issues mentioned related to the principal–agency theory.

So the Governance Perspective greatly helps to explain the various changes in the structuring of the project organization. After some major intervention, earlier ill-defined governance structures were abandoned and adapted.

Decision

As we saw in the history of the NZL Project, the decision to construct the new line was surrounded by discussions. The decision perspective allows us to take a look at this decision process and how this has influenced the implementation of the project over time. In Sections 9.2 and 9.3, we find some useful views which can help us, in particular:

- the influence of the project context;
- the role of estimating bias;
- bounded rationality.

The implementation process of the NZL can hardly be seen as a straight line running from A to B. Instead it is better characterized as a non-linear process with major interventions and changes and various rounds of decision making. In particular, the political interventions are highlighted: the NZL has been investigated by external committees several times, often leading to changes in the project strategy. Here we see that the process of implementation can never be under the full control of project managers within the project delivery organization. Project managers need to operate in a broad array of connected stakeholders. There are many factors influencing the project success, which fall outside of their control.

Similar issues play a role when discussing optimism bias. The great technical challenges of building a tunnel project in soft soil were highlighted in our introduction. These technical challenges cause numerous risks and uncertainties for the delivery of the project and greatly hamper the making of accurate cost estimates, something which was clearly a factor in the decision making of the new metro line. As is now being researched, the decision making at the beginning of the NZL Project was most probably influenced by a strong and convincing alderman advocating the project. All the characteristics of optimism bias were visible. As a result, a decision to go ahead with the project was taken based on optimistic interpretations of very limited and uncertain information that was available at that time.

The fact that information is limited, biased and uncertain is not something which is exactly new in large infrastructure projects (Hertogh *et al.*, 2008), which often take many years to realize, or something which can be avoided. Complexity theory, building on the work of Herbert Simon (1957) and others, has already outlined some of the consequences of decision making for complex projects. For one thing, decisions which might seem right at the time can turn out to have a completely different impact than intended. In addition, the consequences of decisions in the long term can be greatly different from the consequences in the short term. With the NZL we saw that the decision to build the line based on uncertain and optimistic information has resulted in a project budget and time schedule which was, in hindsight, completely unrealistic, putting great strain on the project delivery organization. As a result, it was very difficult to report more realistic information, based on new insights and more accurate information. The consecutive cost increases and schedule delays, based on this more accurate information as well as the incidents at the Vijzelgracht location, have negatively influenced the image of the project, the credibility of the project delivery organization and the perception of the stakeholders. With the creation of an independent project organization in 2010, integrally mandated and responsible for all aspects of the metro line project, fully implemented financial and control processes, reporting directly to the alderman responsible, monitored by the Project Commissariat, it is expected that the project will be able to meet its newly defined goals more effectively.

Marketing

The marketing perspective, described in Chapter 7, views the project as delivering beneficial change for key stakeholders. In order for the end product of the project to be accepted, the project delivery organization needs to be accepted in order for them to commit to it. In the NZL Project, the extreme importance of stakeholders is clear. Two main reasons for this are the building of the metro line in a densely populated area and the active citizens of Amsterdam who are used to expressing their views and opinions.

Now how has this marketing view been picked up as a management perspective within the project delivery organization? If we look at the earliest stages of implementation, we see that the project only had a minimal focus on stakeholder interests, or getting the project accepted and supported. The dominant perspective was the view of the project as a challenging technical task which could be performed by focusing on the strict boundaries of schedule, costs and scope. This view is illustrated by opting for a split between a strict principal–agent relationship (as we labeled it with the Governance Perspective) between the Adviesbureau and the Projectbureau. In this principal–agent relationship, the elements of stakeholder management and communication, which are at the very center of the marketing perspective, were initially delegated to the Adviesbureau. In a complicated environment, where local knowledge of the stakeholders, the peculiarities of the city structure with its independent city boroughs and the many involved city departments is essential, this system did not work.

During the second phase of the project, the stakeholder management and communication tasks were put under responsibility of the Projectbureau (project delivery organization) to improve them while at the same time the project lacked external visibility and acceptance by citizens and the many local organizations involved. So the marketing perspective relevant for successful project implementation, received more and more attention over the course of the project. The second tier of changes, from a principal–agent model to a more integrated model of organization, also had various reasons, related to communication and stakeholder management. Here the mix between the private entity of the Adviesbureau and public authority of the Projectbureau started to cause confusion when the project transferred from its design phase to construction phase. At building sites, for example, it was unclear to citizens who to approach for questions and complaints and which meetings were organized for whom. For the people working on the sites, it was also unclear what their mandates were. In addition, the permit-acquiring processes needed to be streamlined. So when we noticed in the Governance Perspective that a strict division of responsibilities might be beneficial in terms of technical progress and execution, it might not be fitting in terms of the marketing perspective.

The investigation of the latest commission gave us a final adjustment to the use of the marketing perspective within the NZL. Here two key focal points of the recommendations focused on restoring trust of citizens and enabling an open and transparent approach in project implementation. Future activities within the soon to be fully independent project delivery organization will use these recommendations as the basis for the future activities.

So what are the current activities performed by the project delivery organization which typically fall under this perspective?

Stakeholder management

According to the 2007–2008 annual report of the Communication and Community Liaison department, the task of the Projectbureau Noord/Zuidlijn is to:

> Realize the North South Metro Line as well, as quickly, as cheaply and as safely as possible, with as little possible nuisance for stakeholders (especially citizens living near the building sites) and the rest of the city.

As you can gather, this has not been an easy task. Major challenges for the contractors were that they need to work at very small building sites, calling for very detailed phasing. In addition, working hours are limited, there are very strict rules put on them by the project delivery organization and they work in a "Big Brother" environment. Some sites are only three meters from houses and the Amsterdam citizens are not afraid of complaining if they see something happening they don't like. Figure 12.8 shows workers hoisting a synthetic slurry wall reinforcement for the Ceintuurbaan station. The walls on the head-side are synthetic to allow the tunnel boring machine to pass through at a later date.

State of the art technology alone is not enough to realize the NZL Project. From the beginning, it was clear that managing the stakeholders would be a very important focus point. Once the Projectbureau reclaimed the Community Liaison tasks in 2002, it focused on translating these into four main themes: accessibility, livability, safety and communication, in project terms, known as BLVC (*Bereikbaarheid,*

Figure 12.8 Work at the Ceintuurbaan station, showing proximity of the buildings

Leefbaarheid, Veiligheid, Communicatie). The basis of the BLVC principle is to create cooperation between the Contractors, Supervisors, BLVC-Coordinator, 14 city boroughs (being merged to seven on May 1, 2010), Project Liaison Officers and the project management. Cooperation must lead to safety around the construction sites. As well a monitoring system (monitoring movement of buildings), rules for loading and unloading (not during business hours), fencing, a fire alarm and compensation grouting, with respect to the various BLVC parts, this entails the following.

Accessibility

Accessibility demands that measures are taken and activities are coordinated so that all buildings in the city (houses, shops, hotels), remain accessible during construction. There is a central coordination system in place. All projects, no matter what size, are reported to the person responsible for this system. The coordination system surpasses the city borough boundaries and calls for cooperation with the city boroughs.

Livability

In 2000, the position of Community Liaison Officer was introduced at the Adviesbureau. Since 2002, these are persons working at the Projectbureau for the central Community Liaison and Communication Department, but spend most of their time in and around specific building sites in collaboration with specific contract teams. Their main responsibilities are to:

- guard the livability of the neighborhood;
- organize and manage all communication concerning the construction site;
- solve problems between the construction site and the neighborhood and deal with complaints.

The project organization has a "Livability Plan" in place which describes what can be done to decrease hazard. Basically, it is a folder describing the measures that the citizens have a right to claim and in which circumstances. The plan does not describe the damage compensation procedure – that is the responsibility of the department responsible for damage and claims. The livability plan describes topics such as when people can apply for alternative housing, a stay in a hotel, a substitute workplace, compensation for additional moving costs, cleaning activities in the vicinity of a building site, extra help if you are elderly (such as buying groceries), etc. These measures are financed via the Livability Fund (€4 million for citizens).

Safety

The Community Liaison Officer is involved in all building phases in the contract team work. One responsibility of the Community Liaison Officer, to guard the interests of the environment, sometimes influences the way that work needs to be carried out, sometimes slower or in a different fashion that the contract team would wish! What does that mean? In the design phase the BLVC-measures negotiated have influenced the construction methods chosen, including:

*   tunnel boring in the city center following the street pattern and not under houses and instead of the caisson method, which causes much more nuisance;
*   cut-and-cover method for underground construction: building sheet piling on one side of a street and then moving the building site to the other side of the street to build the sheet piling on the other side, so that traffic can run continuously;
*   silent piling: reducing noise levels;
*   special foundation techniques;
*   size of construction site: as small as possible;
*   to pour concrete at once or in smaller portions.

Figure 12.9 shows that the NZL-route largely follows the route of the street pattern from the North to the South of Amsterdam.
    In the contracting phase, BLVC-measures have lead to the following:

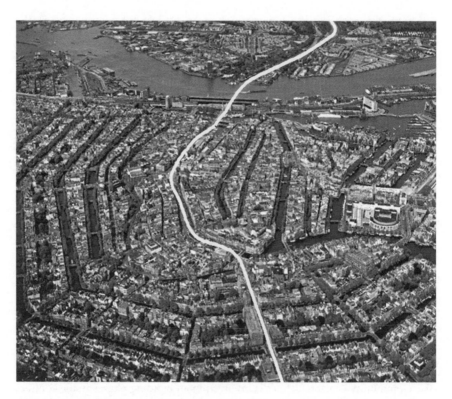

Figure 12.9 Aerial photograph of the route of the NZL

- parking of all delivery trucks outside the city – deliveries to construction sites can only be done after office hours;
- there is no storage of materials at the construction site – in some cases storage of goods is done on the canals;
- existing buildings bought by the city council are used for offices when possible;
- a number of "no-noise days" have been agreed to, especially with the RAI, one of the largest Dutch exposition centers;
- no trucks are allowed to wait on the public roads;
- no radios are allowed on construction sites;

During construction, the following BLVC-measures were agreed on:

- all trucks and other work vehicles must have their engines off as much as possible;
- all construction sites have a large billboard showing a "working hour clock," a large clock which is changed daily to communicate the time that work will end that specific day;
- all construction sites have fence decoration, which allows for (upcoming) artists to promote their work on a large scale, allowing for special cultural promotional activities as well as improving the way the construction sites look;
- only in special cases is limited extension of working hours possible and only after sound checks have deemed the work acceptable;
- small interventions from neighborhood groups will be accepted;
- complaints and questions will be dealt with formally;
- regular neighborhood consultation will take place to inform and discuss project progress;
- individual solutions will be realized when necessary.

In principle, the project and the contractors needs to show and tell the surroundings what they are doing, and do what they promised.

After construction has taken place, a new After Care phase is launched. After Care can mean that something unexpected has happened (there was more noise than expected, work had to go on longer than agreed on, etc.) and something needs to be done to compensate the stakeholders for this. Measures are tailor-made and may include:

- compensation of trees – where trees were cut down and replanted elsewhere, new trees were replanted when possible;
- flowers handed out after an unexpected gas-leakage, requiring people to leave their buildings for a short time;
- theater tickets for active citizens involved in helping the project to be realized;
- free entry cards for archeology museum as an incentive to get interested in archeology, a project phase that has shed light on some of Amsterdam's history through some of the findings.

Communication

From the start of the project, communication has been a topic of increasing importance. The early strategy chosen focused on two communication levels. The first level of communication focused on informing those stakeholders directly affected by the project. The communication consisted of providing reliable information on specific topics. These topics varied from road pollution levels, noise nuisance information, routing, accessibility of roads, etc. The information focused on providing specific stakeholder groups with relevant information – sometimes on a daily basis – and was tailored per building site location. Communication forms varied from information letters, SMS-messages, group information sessions and individual meetings. The community liaison officer plays an important role.

The second level of communication is the corporate communication. The main objective of this level is to provide general project information to anyone interested in the project. For this purpose, an information center was created that combines communication and education, as well as an Internet website, articles and interviews in various media – newspapers, local television, corporate brochures and fact sheets on specific topics such as building techniques, contract forms, etc. This strategy focused very much on the principle that the hindrance level and project duration should influence the communication strategy. At the beginning of the project there are no (visible) results to be communicated, while at the same time the hindrance level is the highest. At some point in time this changes as there are project results to be communicated while the expectation is that the hindrance level should reduce.

As soon as the project entered the building phase however, this communication strategy proved to work ineffectively. The impact of the building sites, the equipment and the building process itself was underestimated. In addition, the hindrance level and results obtained was not balanced. It would take much longer to reach any results the project could communicate about and at the same time the hindrance level remained at a constant high level. With this great hindrance the project organization thought it not timely to communicate any successes. To improve the effectiveness of the communication, new tools were developed. These included financial compensation for extended noise nuisance periods, additional soundproofing of houses, providing alternative working locations for people working from home or locations near building sites, periodical window cleaning and redressing public spaces. A central complaints procedure was organized.

Still, the focus on compensating the hindrance of the project as well as the technical difficulties encountered during building and the cost and time overruns has caused the relationship between the stakeholders, especially the people living and working in the building sites' vicinity in the city center, to be fragile. Since the major incidents in 2008, a new strategy has been initiated in order to regain the trust of the stakeholders in the project and to improve its image. The Project Organization has initiated a "Programma V," "V" standing for trust (*vertrouwen*), consisting of several sub-projects focusing on improving relationships with the major stakeholders. Part of this new focus will be initiated by the end of 2009, and will likely include more timely and direct communication with stakeholders as well as focusing on some project successes – such as the completion within time and budget of several contracts in the North and South of the NZL project.

12.5 Conclusion

The NZL Project is an example of a challenging and complex project that has evolved through many years from its inception to realization. As seen from the governance, decision and marketing perspectives, the project has developed in each of these areas respectively through time. At this time, the project still has some years to go until we can enjoy a ride on the first metro line from the north to the south of Amsterdam. The future will prove to what extent the independent project organization, fully mandated and integrally responsible, will be able to fulfill its objectives successfully.

Acknowledgments

The authors would like to acknowledge Transumo for their support in writing this chapter. Transumo (TRANsition SUstainable MObility) is a Dutch platform for companies, governments and knowledge institutes that cooperate in the development of knowledge with regard to sustainable mobility.

References

Hertogh, M., Baker, S., Staal-Ong, P.L., and Westerveld, E., 2008, *Managing Large Infrastructure Projects: Research on best practice and lessons learnt in large infrastructure projects in Europe*, AT Osborne, Utrecht.

Simon, H.A., 1957, *Models of Man: Social and rational*, John Wiley and Sons, Inc., New York.

13 The LAS story

Learning from failure

Darren Dalcher

13.1 A journey from failure to success

This chapter tells the story of a series of projects to computerize the world's largest ambulance service. The four attempts span 24 years. The first three present different kinds of failures ranging from cancelled projects to total operational failure. In one case, attempts to switch off and re-start failed forcing the operators to resort to a hastily coordinated manual procedure. In contrast, the fourth attempt, which represents a drastic change in approach, was hailed as a great success, and led to the award of a prize. Going from failure to success is a great achievement. The prevailing culture and the financial climate which played a major role in shaping the events that led to the earlier disasters had to be overcome. Multiple stakeholders have their own concerns, perceptions and preferences which need to be recognized. Engaging with stakeholders and understanding the dimensions of success are both crucial to delivering projects in a demanding environment.

Background

The London Ambulance Service (LAS) was founded in 1930 to replace the Metropolitan Asylums Board, and enlarged in 1965 to incorporate parts of eight other emergency services in the London area. In 1974 it became a quasi-independent body with its own board, managed by the South Thames Regional Health Authority under the control of the National Health Service. The service covers a geographical area of 620 square miles with a resident population of 6.8 million people, boosted by commuters and visitors to as many as 10 million. This makes the LAS the largest ambulance service in the world, with an annual budget of £70 million. About two-thirds of the budget and more than half of the staff are devoted to emergency services. The demand for emergency services increases by around 15 percent per year. The service receives an average of over 2,000 calls per day and transports over 5,000 patients, about 1,400 of which are emergency cases. Some 700 vehicles based in 70 ambulance systems attend an average of 1,200 incidents a day. They are controlled from a central control room at LAS headquarters.

The story of the London Ambulance Service's continuing attempts to computerize its operations began in the mid-1980s. The background to the story had two key features. First, LAS was falling short of recently established national standards of performance for ambulance mobilization and arrival times. Second, the introduction of the so-called "internal market" to the National Health Service in the UK, together with chronic shortages arising from long-term under-investment, led to relentless pressure to squeeze budgets while simultaneously improving performance.

The problem

The original manual system used at the LAS headquarters had three major components:

Call taking: Control Assistants at Waterloo would write down the details on a pre-printed form before locating the incident co-ordinates in their map book and placing the completed forms on a conveyor belt transporting all the forms to a central collection point.

Resource identification: Another assistant would collect the forms, scan the details, identify potential calls, and allocate them to one of the four regional resource allocators. The appropriate resource allocator would examine the incident forms, consult ambulance status and location information provided by the radio operator, consult the remaining forms maintained in the allocation box for each vehicle, and finally decide on which (ambulance) resource to mobilize. The ambulance details would be entered on the form.

Resource mobilization: The forms would be passed to a dispatcher who would then phone the relevant ambulance station (if that was where the ambulance was assumed to be) or pass the mobilization instructions to the radio operator, if the ambulance was known to be mobile.

Over time a number of problems and bottlenecks had been observed, including:

- manual searching of the map book often requiring a search for a number of alternatives due to incomplete or inaccurate details;
- inefficient movement of paper around the control room;
- maintaining up-to-date vehicle status and location information as provided by the radio operators and allocators;
- communication procedures and the use of voice communication were slow and inefficient, and could lead to mobilization queues;
- over-reliance on human ability and memory to identify duplicate calls and avoid mobilizing multiple units to the same incident;
- over-reliance on human ability to note and trace all available units;
- call back (callers phoning for a second time) which forced the assistants to leave their post to talk to the allocators, using up time and introducing physical congestion into the control room;
- identification of special incidents (large or extremely urgent) depended on human judgment and memory.

The establishment of the new national mobilization standard, introduced during the early 1980s, required dispatch to be completed inside three minutes. The manual system was too slow and inefficient to comply with the new standard. Performance was degraded further during peak time and large incidents impacting on the average figures. The LAS gradually became convinced that a computer despatch system was the only approach that could automate ambulance call-outs and ensure the meeting of the despatch standard.

13.2 The first attempt: Starting small

It was hoped that the computerized system would handle all major tasks which existed in the manual system. Calling 999 and asking for the ambulance service would connect the caller to a dispatcher who would record details of the call and assign a suitable vehicle. The dispatcher would select an ambulance and the system would transmit details to the selected vehicle. Following a year of delay in awarding the contract, a three-year project to develop the £2.5 million new systems was launched in May 1987 by a consortium consisting of IAL (International Aerdio Ltd., a subsidiary of British Telecom), and CGS (Cap Gemini Sogeti). The key part of the project was the delivery of the Radio Interface System for voice transmission, as there was no requirement for mobile data capability and vehicle location system. In 1989, the specification was extended to include mobile data (without amending the target date or expected budget). The project was terminated in October 1990 after two tests investigating peak load performance failed. At the point of cancellation, the project was severely behind schedule (having already missed the ultimate delivery date) and had already accumulated costs of £7.5 million.

Failure: Post-project review

Following termination, the LAS sought damages from the contractors, claiming they did not understand the requirements. The contractors counter-claimed, alleging that the specifications were ambiguous, lacked clarity and were subject to constant change. An out-of-court settlement was eventually reached. An independent assessment, conducted by Arthur Andersen, recommended acquiring a packaged system on a turnkey basis, estimating a cost of £1.5 million and time-to-field of 19 months. The assessment was based on the original statement of requirements (that is without mobile data and vehicle location systems). If no suitable packaged solution could be found, it warned that the cost and time for developing a bespoke system would be significantly higher.

13.3 The second attempt: Fostering ambition

The LAS evaluated a number of packages, including some operated by other UK ambulance services, but none were judged acceptable. LAS then embarked on specifying requirements for a new bespoke system. The proposed system would automate not only manual tasks but also decision-making. Once information from callers had been fed into the system it would take over, allocating and mobilizing

ambulances, interacting with crews, and monitoring vehicle positions and performance. The control room would no longer communicate with vehicles by voice radio
or with ambulance stations by telephone, as the system would handle all communications. Intervention by controllers would be required only in exceptional cases,
such as failure to despatch an ambulance within 11 minutes, failure of an ambulance
crew to acknowledge a message, or an ambulance going "the wrong way."

The software specification was developed with an eye to saving costs and, perhaps more crucially, time. Insiders report a sense of urgency that pervaded meetings, attitudes, and decisions relating to the computer system. Hardware
components from the previous failed attempt were incorporated into the proposal
as a means of saving time and capitalizing on a previous investment. In order to
fully capitalize from the benefits, it was decided to achieve them as fast as possible
by planning for big-bang rather than phased implementation, switching to full functionality overnight, and to achieve economies by using hardware acquired or
planned during the previous project. The specification was completed in early
February 1991, less than four months after abandoning the old system. It required
the new system to be operational in 11 months (8 January 1992). The document was
very detailed and prescriptive on how the system should operate, leaving little
opportunity for suppliers to incorporate their own ideas and experience, or optimize
the use of technology. Most of the work (and subsequent bid selection) was carried
out by a contract analyst and the systems manager, while a major management
restructuring was under way.

LAS fully realized that the system would require a "quantum leap" in technology. Combining sophisticated allocation and monitoring with judgment and
decision-making tasks involved a major intellectual and technical effort. They
were prepared to attempt this ambitious undertaking despite their stated belief that
the previous project, for a significantly simple system, failed because the vendors
did not understand the complexity inherent in the environment. Indeed, insiders
report that at this time there was a pervasive sense of optimism, excitement and
urgency in the systems team, no doubt fed by the large benefits (operational efficiency and reduced costs) promised by the proposal.

A common factor in successful implementations is that users feel they share the
benefits and have a sense of involvement and ownership. Achieving such user attitudes is often critical, and will almost certainly be so in a "quantum leap" with very
high stakes. Based on recent history of industrial conflicts and attitudes towards
structural change within the LAS, there was every reason to assume another major
change to the organizational culture would require tact and careful management.
The new system would make radical changes to working practices and was bound
to introduce anxiety and possibly conflict. As an example, it was proposed that
ambulance crews could be allocated to incidents away from their home stations:
that would mean that they could spend much of their time covering unfamiliar areas
and that, at the end of a shift, it might take them a long time to drive back to their
home stations – amounting in effect to unpaid overtime.

There was, however, no attempt to sell the system to the users, or in any other
way to reduce resistance to change. The specification and subsequent guidelines on

new working practices were written without input from ambulance crews, control room staff or unions.

Constraints build-up

Standing instructions of the Regional Health Authority required all new systems to be put out to tender. An advertisement accordingly appeared in the *Journal of the European Communities* on 7 February 1991. Thirty-five companies expressed interest in bidding and were sent the requirements specification. Most potential bidders questioned the 11-month deadline for development and implementation. They were told it was non-negotiable. Half the companies did not proceed. The remaining 17 provided proposals for all or part of the system. Several of them proposed implementing a basic system by January 1992, with full functionality available in early 1993. LAS's initial screening eliminated all proposals that did not accept the January deadline for the full system. The overt criteria for evaluating the handful of remaining contenders included quality and performance factors such as resilience, functionality, flexibility and response times. In practice little attention was paid to these: the effective criterion was price, and moreover there was a secret price target of £1.5 million.

The target price seems to have been adopted from the Arthur Andersen recommendations. They were made, however, in an entirely different context, assuming a package solution, without a mobile data capability, and with a 19-month implementation schedule. The absence of any of these factors should have resulted in a serious re-evaluation. The failed first project, for a simpler system, had lasted over three years before cancellation, and exceeded its £2.5 million budget by a factor of three. Experience, analysis or just plain common sense should have made it obvious that the Arthur Andersen estimate was inappropriate in the new conditions. On the contrary, the early commitment (also known as anchoring) to the £1.5 million price tag seems to have infected the decision-making process, so that it was adopted without challenge and then defended by groupthink. This early commitment to a figure, albeit an irrelevant one, and the apparent homogeneity of the group could have blinded them to the relative danger of fixing an initial budget before evaluating the quality and strengths of the incoming bids. Set out in cold print, it is tempting to condemn the team. However it is a recognized phenomenon that collective rationalization, illusions of invulnerability, self-censorship, and the consequent absence of dissent, can lead groups to ignore external opinions and alternative solutions and to adopt positions that are not rationally defensible, leading to significant escalation of commitment.

Selecting a winner

Focusing on cost as the single selection criteria meant that only one bid could qualify. The clear winner was a bid for £937,463 for the complete system to be implemented by the mandated deadline. The nearest competitors came in at £1.6 million and £3 million. The winning bid was from a consortium led by Apricot Computers (a UK hardware supplier owned by Mitsubishi). Apricot would supply networked PCs and a fault-tolerant file server. Systems Options (a small UK software house) would supply the despatch system software, based on their Wings geographical information system. Datatrak would supply the automatic vehicle location system. Solo Electronic Systems would supply radio interface systems and mobile data terminals, which were to have been used in the previous abandoned systems.

The quoted price for the despatch system software, the main hub of the system, was £35,000. The price represented less than 4 percent of the overall price of what was clearly a software-intensive system, a grossly mistaken estimate given the complexity of the requirements. The significance of the software was clearly understood, at least by LAS and Apricot. LAS expressed concern by warning Systems Options that the failure of the previous system was largely caused by the supplier's software house not being able to cope with the complexity of the system. Apricot, who led the consortium at the bid stage, refused to assume project leadership because of the dependence of the entire system on the quality of the software. Under strong pressure from LAS, Systems Options agreed to accept leadership of both the consortium and the project. It later emerged that System Options had been reluctant to bid for the system in the first place, but had been persuaded to do so by Apricot. An earlier bid by the two companies for a far more basic system for the Cambridgeshire Ambulance Service had been rejected because of the lack of technical understanding exhibited in that bid. The required system was significantly bigger and more complex than anything any of the consortium members had handled previously. The main experience of Systems Options was in developing government administrative systems. LAS felt reassured by the fact that they had delivered systems for police and fire services, but those had been administrative systems, and the company had no experience in developing real-time, safety-critical command and control systems. The letters of reference suggested that Systems Options was overstretched on its current contracts and had been having trouble delivering simpler and less demanding software on time. A letter from the Staffordshire Fire and Rescue Service expressed grave concern over the ability of Systems Options to cope with the LAS project. Those claims were not investigated or even acknowledged by the LAS procurement team.

The procurement team was small and inexperienced in terms of both technical knowledge and acquisition procedures. Procurement guidelines for the Regional Health Authority stated that the lowest tender should be accepted unless there were "good and sufficient reasons to the contrary." No attempt was made by the team to investigate whether such reasons existed, why the price was below the internal target price, or why it was so much lower than even the next cheapest. As with authorship of the requirements specification, bid evaluation was undertaken primarily by the systems manager (an ambulance-man who had taken the job temporarily on the understanding that he would be replaced by a qualified systems manager at some point) and the contract analyst (who had five years experience with LAS, largely on the failed original project).

LAS higher management was in the course of restructuring. Normal practice required it to audit the selection process before accepting the recommendation of the internal procurement team. The audit, performed with the involvement of an external assessor, indicated that the process was risky and required close management attention, but the selection was approved. The management restructuring was eventually completed in April 1991. Senior and middle management ranks were slimmed by 20 percent, the four divisions were reduced to three, and a large number of experienced staff left. The rapid changes eliminated any stability within the organization. The remaining managers were unmotivated, stressed, anxious, and oppressed by job insecurity. To compensate for the loss of some high-caliber managers, others were promoted or shifted sideways to new positions. Directors were left with a great span of responsibility and power. The internal climate was influenced by a minimal investment in staff or managerial training and little scope for career advancement. In the absence of consultation with employees and the unions, industrial relations deteriorated, resulting in resentment, lack of trust, low staff morale, and increased absenteeism. The reputation of the new CEO for "sorting out" troublesome employees and interfering trade unions did not help.

On 28 May 1991, with just over seven months to the deadline, the Executive Board ratified the decision on the contract. Learning from the lesson of the previous failure, LAS required the consortium to provide a complete systems design specification detailing how the final system would operate, as a demonstration that they truly understood the requirements and could provide an adequate solution. A small starter contract was awarded for the development of this design specification, which was carried out during June and July.

In developing the design specification, the consortium opted to use Windows 3.0 for the user interface and Visual Basic for screen dialogues. That decision, which was not specified in the design specification, involved a trade-off of time and quality against performance. Visual Basic is essentially a prototyping tool, typically used in small, non-safety-critical applications to generate and test screens rapidly. Code generation, however, is inefficient, and the resulting performance is slow, so that it is often necessary to follow prototyping by fine-tuning to increase speed and reduce memory consumption. In the LAS case that did not happen. Further, the inefficiency of the generated code was compounded by the fact that it was to run on slow 486 machines operating at 25 MHz. The resulting low performance could easily account for the bulk of the mobilization time allowed by the national standard. The allocation algorithm was complex and required high processing speeds to meet performance requirements. An increase in the number of incidents would cause, on the one hand, an increase in the volume of calculations; on the other hand, it would cause a decrease in the number of ambulances available, leading in turn to an increase in the average distance between an incident and the available ambulances, and an increase in the complexity of the calculations. Those increases in the volume and complexity of the calculations caused a slow-down in the system, the severity of which would depend on system processing speed.

Managing the project

While the design specification was being developed, LAS was considering its management strategy. Among concerns that were noted and minuted, but never followed up, were:

- no full-time LAS staff member, and no project review group, had been assigned to the project;
- the draft project plan left no time for review or revision;
- the six-month schedule was considerably shorter than the 18 months that other services had needed for less complicated despatch systems.

The Director of Support Services invited one of the losing bidders to perform independent quality assurance on the project. This was rejected internally, as it was felt by the project team that quality assurance was the contractor's responsibility and not its concern. Rather than have external quality assurance (incorporating risk assessment and audit features), the team devolved all quality assurance activities to Systems Options, the software developers.

The PRINCE project management method was selected to guide the development effort. As neither LAS staff nor the consortium had much project management experience, or knew anything about PRINCE, a special course was arranged to acquaint them with the methodology. Very little use was ever made of this knowledge and nor was any alternative project management approach adopted in its place.

Official project launch

Although there was no formal sign-off of the design specification, and although it contained omissions and undeveloped sections (such as interfaces with other components and systems), LAS accepted it. The full contract was then formally awarded to the consortium on 8 August 1991, leaving exactly five months for development and implementation. The contract with Solo Electronics for communications hardware, the essence of which was to salvage key features from the earlier abandoned project, was not signed until 16 September, four months before the delivery deadline, and three months after the award of the system design contract. During early project meetings it became clear Systems Options was unable to manage the entire project, as it was struggling to manage its own software effort. No experienced project manager was available either in LAS or in the consortium. Despite their inexperience, the LAS Director of Support Services and the contract analyst undertook to add overall project management to their list of duties. The only scant attempt at project management was made by those individuals; none was attempted by any of the consortium members. There was no quality assurance, change control, configuration management or test planning.

Software deliveries were all late. Systems Options blamed the delays on the two months needed to develop the design specification, and on the delay in signing the contract for the communication equipment with which its software needed to interface. LAS hired a new systems manager in October. He promptly arranged a formal project review, which reported the following key findings to LAS senior management in November:

- little time had been allocated for review;
- increased quality management was needed;

- troubling technical problems were occurring;
- the January operational date should be maintained if only to keep pressure on the suppliers.

Publicity and external pressure resulted in parliamentary questions. The government expressed the view that the consortium was fully qualified for the task at hand. LAS management decided to take no action.

By mid-December it was clear that the 8 January deadline was not achievable. The despatch software was incomplete and untested, the radio interface system was yet to be delivered, the design of the data terminals and their positioning in the ambulances required changing, the vehicle location tracking system was not fully installed, the data provided by the tracking system was reported to be neither accurate nor reliable, and no training of ambulance crews or control room operators had been initiated. The second attempt was also a clear failure.

13.4 The third attempt: Cutting up the elephant

Having missed the delivery deadline, the project was radically re-organized. By late December, a new schedule for a three-phase delivery strategy was agreed, with final delivery scheduled for 26 October 1992.

- Phase 1 would deliver the call-taking function. Recorded calls would be printed out for use within the existing manual procedure.
- Phase 2 would deliver an improved allocation function. Allocators would have terminals displaying call information. Ambulance locations would be automatically tracked by the system, which would also issue despatch instructions to vehicle-based data terminals. Decisions on selecting and mobilizing vehicles would still be made by the allocators.
- Phase 3 would deliver the fully automated system. All allocation tasks would be handled by the system, and allocators would no longer be used.

The replacement of big-bang by phased implementation gave rise to additional requirements and problems. For example, the need to print call details in Phase 1 required the introduction of printers – not part of the original "paperless office" vision. Their introduction led to problems such as screens locking up, server failures and, on one occasion, the loss of calls when a printer was switched off, erasing the contents of its buffer memory. During Phases 1 and 2 different system versions were delivered at different times to the three operating divisions and then enhanced in an uncontrolled fashion with different changes. Thus the systems in use in each division were not functionally or operationally equivalent. This led to great confusion and difficulties in the control room.

Meanwhile, a staff attitude survey, commissioned by the LAS and carried out by Price Waterhouse in January 1992, revealed that only 13 percent of staff believed that the LAS was providing a quality service, 10 percent felt they knew what the LAS plans were for the future, and 8 percent believed that management listened to them.

March 1992 was the Phase 2 deadline. It was marked by a major system crash, resulting in a 30-minute delay to emergency calls, delayed ambulances and lost incident reports. Some LAS local area officers ordered a switch back to voice radio communication until the computer was able to match its performance. The union area officer called for an urgent public enquiry. An LAS spokesman reassured the press that these are. "... normal teething problems and no one has anything to worry about." A new review conducted by the LAS systems manager revealed:

- the radio interface system was failing almost daily;
- no volume testing of the whole communications infrastructure had been done;
- there was no way of tracking changes to the system;
- ambulance crews and control room staff were not trained.

No recommendation on future progress or cancellation of the project was made in the review report, which did not elicit any response from LAS senior management.

A number of letters from computer consultancies and safety experts, warning that the system was "totally and fatally flawed," reached the LAS and government ministers. In April 1992 hundreds of callers failed to get through to the ambulance service. LAS management blamed the public for making too many calls and clogging lines. The LAS board was presented with a formal vote of no confidence in the system by staff from one of the three divisions. Additional complaints and expressions of concern throughout the rest of the year were brushed aside by LAS management. The purpose of phased trials, it was explained, was to highlight problems, and there was no need for concern as the final system would work. Some new problems began cropping up at this stage. These included:

- locking up of terminals (prompting an instruction to staff to simply reboot their screens);
- overload of communications channels;
- inaccurate information provided by the vehicle location system;
- crews using different ambulances from the ones allocated by the system;
- slowness of the system;
- failure of the system to identify the nearest available ambulance;
- failure of the system to identify every fifty-third vehicle in the fleet.

As a result, calls were getting lost in the system, while others failed to reach ambulances. Vehicles were being assigned incorrect codes, while others were missing from the system. Call waiting queues and the ever multiplying exception message queues simply scrolled off the top of the screen. At no time during Phases 1 and 2 was the system stable or operational across all three divisions.

In the background intense government pressure was being applied on LAS to reduce its seriously overspent budget. Accordingly it was decided that planned capital improvements and preventive maintenance on emergency vehicles would have to be delayed.

Up and running?

Phase 3 was scheduled to come on line in the early morning of Monday 26 October 1992. At this time the software was known to have two errors that could cause the system not to function, 44 that could cause operational problems likely to affect patient care, and 35 minor problems – 81 errors. No stress testing had been done on the full system. No backup plans were in place in case of system failure. The LAS did not even have its own network manager, having relied on the contractors to rectify all previous problems. The move to the final phase required a move from the existing divisional structure to a centrally controlled "pan London" approach within a unified control room. The control room had to be reorganized and all temporary equipment and temporary solutions, such as printers, dismantled and removed. Once the control room was cleared up, similar groups, such as radio operators, controllers and allocators could be united and positioned in different parts of the room.

By mid-morning callers were often having to wait over 30 minutes to get through. Ambulances arrived late, or not at all, or two at a time. These problems often meant that a single incident generated multiple follow-up calls. The system was slow at logging acknowledgments, and there was therefore a proliferation of warnings that ambulances were not meeting arrival deadlines. These warnings, together with other error and alert messages, and new calls, wiped old calls off the screens, even if they had not been dealt with; the old calls were then lost to the system, again giving rise to follow-up calls. The increasing volumes of system traffic generated by system failures, and the rapidly growing exception queues, were creating overload conditions and slowing the system down. Screens and mobile data terminals began locking up. At one point the exception queue was cleared of its contents, erasing all calls. But that was not all! The map system failed to recognize certain roads, forcing operators to scramble for maps and despatch ambulances by telephone unbeknown to the system – even though staff were under instruction to minimize voice communication. Many indeed felt too threatened to make any attempt to rectify problems by voice communication.

The system depended on radio for data feeds on ambulance location and status. The limitations of radio communication in an urban area with tall buildings were not taken into account. No attempt was made to specify or test the system's response to incomplete or incorrect data, and the consequent need for perfect information at all times proved to be a critical millstone. Frustrated staff, unable to communicate with base, switched to their radios, which used the same frequencies as the data communication system, adding to the already clogged airwaves. The number of ambulances that could be traced by the system declined, resulting in more complex allocations, and in delays which further constrained the system. This constituted a positive feedback loop which in the right circumstances would ensure the situation escalated out of control.

A specific aspect of the poor performance of Visual Basic programs is that filling the screens can easily take several seconds. To overcome this, control room staff preloaded all the screens likely to be needed at the beginning of a shift and used Windows to move between them as required. That added to the demand on memory, slowing system performance, and led to extra clutter on controllers' screens, slowing their performance.

The overnight reorganization of the control room eliminated the familiar structure of the room and split up divisional teams who had worked together. Teams with local knowledge and experience of local traffic, short-cuts and hospital locations who used to share sector desks were thus separated and placed in unfamiliar positions. These changes, together with the new operating procedures, put control room staff under great stress and made it extremely difficult for them to intervene and correct problems. Ambulance arrivals within 15 minutes were achieved in only 17 percent of incidents, against 30 percent under the Phase 2 system, 65 percent prior to phase 1, and the requirement of the national standard of 95 percent. The average ring time for each call peaked at 11 minutes, with many callers waiting 15 minutes. Londoners are lucky that no major incidents capable of stretching the system beyond its limits occurred in the 36-hour period while the system was in a state of total chaos. During that time, over 900 complaints were received, some patients were kept waiting as long as 11 hours, more than 40 patients may have died as a result of delays (depending on which estimates you accept) – and a team of public relations experts were busy promoting the new technological efficiency of the service.

Failure in action

At 2.00pm on Tuesday 27 October, a decision was made to take the Phase 3 system down and replace it with the semi-manual Phase 2 system. More ambulance crews and control room staff were brought on duty in an attempt to cut the backlog. The computer team initiated an attempt to investigate the errors and relaunch the system. On Wednesday morning, LAS claimed that no serious disruptions were caused by the computer system. That afternoon, however, the LAS chief executive resigned. It was later argued that he was under extreme pressure to improve performance by the end of that year and had thus been forced to rush the computer implementation. Following intensive pressure from families of patients, the unions, and a stormy session in Parliament on Thursday evening, the Health Secretary announced an official inquiry into the affair. The unions called for the system they described as a "lethal lottery" to be shut down in the interest of patients. Their plea went unheeded. The reduced functionality system operated for the next eight days. On 4 November 1992, it in turn started slowing down, and it finally locked up altogether at 2.00am. Operators rebooted the system, to discover that it was still frozen. The back-up system (designed to interface with the full-functionality system, but not with the semi-manual system) did not come on-line. There was then no alternative but to revert to the manual methods of the 1980s. Performance figures for mobilization and arrival recorded dramatic improvements, usually by a factor of around two.

Post-project review

The official inquiry report released on 1 March 1993 was scathing (Page *et al.*, 1993). It described the chaotic management and total lack of planning and technical oversight which led to the disaster, and called for a complete revamping of the LAS and the way it conducted its business. During a press conference marking its publication, a member of the inquiry team commented that the LAS "went through every mistake in the book." Following publication, the LAS chairman resigned, saying "We caused a considerable amount of anguish to the people of London. We failed to deliver the service we could." In addition to failings already identified above, the inquiry's findings included the following.

- Despite a claim by LAS management that an excessive number of calls were made on 26 and 27 October, the number was found to be only 6 percent above the average for October. Due to the frequent lack of response, there was a higher-than-usual number of call-backs, but even so the total number of calls was within the predicted upper limit. The total number of patients transported on the two days was less than the daily average for October.

- The LAS management claim that ambulance crews deliberately sabotaged the system was shown to be false. Despite losing the personal touch of having a familiar human voice despatcher, crews seem to have accepted the initiative, albeit reluctantly, and cooperated. Datatrak, the primary contractor for the vehicle location subsystem, stated that resistance at LAS was no greater than they experienced at other organizations.

- The LAS management claim that users and crews had been inadequately trained in how to use the system was supported. Training provision was divided between LAS and Systems Options. In the case of control room staff it comprised just a two-day familiarization exercise. All training was scheduled to be completed by the original implementation date in January 1992. Despite the ten-month delay between that date and the eventual implementation, and the system changes during that period, no further training was given. Operators were thus not in a position to spot problems or be able to override them.

- Eleven causes for a lack of perfect information (necessary for the allocation algorithms to function correctly) included radio black spots, failure to press correct buttons, noise corruption, wrong call signs, and too few operators. No consideration had been given to the possibility that the assumption of perfect information would not hold.

- Delayed and duplicated allocations resulted in a build-up of exception messages, which required personal attention from operators and prevented them from answering new calls. As the lists built up the system slowed down. The linked slowdown of system and operator performance caused an increase in call-backs, and therefore yet further exception messages. The positive feedback effect overwhelmed the system and its operators.

- The complete system had never been performance-tested to predict its behavior under extreme or atypical conditions, such as a disaster scenario, incomplete or contradictory information, operator errors or high volumes of exception messages.

- The demand to reduce costs and budgets was responsible for more ambulances than normal being out of service due to degradation and lack of repairs, compounding the pressure on the system.

- An error in Systems Options software meant file server memory was not released after each ambulance mobilization, leading to the steady consumption of all available memory.
- While Systems Options "rapidly found themselves in a situation where they became out of their depth," it was also judged "within the time constraints imposed on the project and the scope of requirements, no software house could have delivered a workable solution."

13.5 Fourth time lucky

The new CEO started to work on repairing the relationship with the unions. Despite the pressure to introduce a new system quickly to deflect media attention, the CEO recognized the high risks and sought to adopt a more cautious approach (Fitzgerald, 2000). The newly appointed IT director spent the first nine months listening to people and learning about the organization. Realizing the despatch system could not solve all the problems, senior management embarked on a series of "warm-up projects" to sort out ailing infrastructure that had been neglected during years of under-investment. The successful delivery of the smaller non-IT related projects demonstrated it was possible to deliver benefits within the LAS environment and got people to buy into the change management process. The projects attempted were becoming gradually larger. They were also using PRINCE to make sure the project management procedures were understood in a non-IT project context.

The fourth attempt at computerizing the LAS was finally under way. The key decision was to go with a hardware solution that had worked in other emergency services for 20 years. The software system would be developed in-house in small chunks; with the content of each clearly defined and understood. The concept of phased delivery through a well-structured, well-planned series of projects, each delivering some functionality or certain sub-systems was adopted (Dalcher, 1999, 2007). A series of prototypes refined the call taking, gazetteer, call viewing, and management alert system functions. This approach was intended to encourage belief in the value of change and the possibility of ultimate success.

Expectation management was clearly crucial and communication and consultation were essential to success. A key decision was to try to get the computerized system to mirror the manual procedures to further encourage acceptance and familiarity. Open forums were established to discuss any aspect of the project and working groups were formed to gain understanding of system requirements and design procedures. The idea of competing prototypes, where four parallel teams would develop prototypes for the same functionality and then meet to discuss the differences was adopted and was useful in reaching consensus following the discussions. The need to be prescriptive and define the full functionality was thus abolished in favour of an exploratory approach that was not confined to time and cost constraints. True functionality was thus allowed to emerge through a consensual iterative process. The flexibility in the approach meant that the project was not wedded to any particular scope or indeed to the traditional time and cost constraints. Instead, getting the users to respond and design the system around their work needs took precedence. Implementation was further delayed to ensure the training of users was complete and comprehensive (Fitzgerald, 2000).

The call taking project took 18 months to develop and release and went live on 17 January 1996. After a week of successful running, it was moved into the control room itself. Additional functionality is added roughly every quarter and indeed, will continue to be added into the system at regular intervals.

Delivering success

The first staged delivery won a British Computer Society Award for excellence in IS Management in 1997 for obtaining user buy-in, delivering a useful and usable system and improving the efficiency and performance of the service. The prize recognized the turnaround in fortunes at LAS and the improved performance the turnaround has engendered. The system was perceived to be a success in other ways too. The House of Commons Health Committee congratulated the service on the improvements and the change in atmosphere within the organization. Indeed staff now believed in the capability of the service; the new delivery approach had finally managed to break the culture of distrust. In terms of performance, the three-minute activation figure dropped to 35 percent following the failure in 1992 and remained around 40 percent for the next four years. Following the release of the staged delivery the figure improved to 80 percent, rising to the region of 90 percent at the turn of the century. This played a key part in restoring the confidence of the public in the LAS. Indeed, the number of complaints from the public dropped significantly following the release of the new system.

13.6 Beyond success: Looking to the future

The introductory section talks about performance pressures imposed through national standards and a systemic dearth of resources. The pressures identified in the beginning of the story continue to plague the LAS. In 2000 LAS was criticized for poor performance in its standards and blamed for endangering lives. The service was sued for negligence and the CEO left his post following crisis talks with management. Staff complaints focused on chronic underfunding despite increasing demand and the inability to meet target times or find enough crews to respond to emergencies. Regular update projects continue to be implemented. However, an upgrade in July 2006 resulted in repeated system crashes and forced dispatchers to go back to old manual methods used before the introduction of the computer system. Over a period of several weeks the system repeatedly crashed forcing the service to resort to pen and paper. The problem was compounded by staff shortages in the control room.

Increasing demand and limited staffing and funding continue to impact the service. In December 2008 the CEO reported that the service was struggling to cope. Indeed the performance targets for December 2008 dropped significantly below the required average, with significant performance shortfalls in some areas. In February 2009 the LAS limited its responses to life-threatening calls only, an action that was repeated during the heat wave of July 2009. The service provided during most of 2009 has been continuously described as being in a "critical" or "severe pressure" state of operations (where critical is one stage away from potential service failure). Additional pressure comes from the new national standard targets introduced in April 2008 which stipulate that ambulance services are expected to respond more quickly as the response time to patients now begins as soon as the patient is connected to the control. Life-threatening cases should be reached within eight minutes of making contact with all other cases addressed within 18 minutes. The new targets, combined with budgetary pressures and short-staffing are again leading to poor relationship with the workforce and introducing the pressures that existed prior to the first attempt. They may also necessitate the urgent addition of new functionality and scope to the system and can therefore result in new enhancement projects conducted under severe budgetary and timing constraints.

Determining success and failure

It is worth pointing out that this was the first attempt to computerize the LAS and hence the technology and its potential benefits were not well understood. The claims and counter-claims following the disintegration of the first attempt indicate that the clients, let alone the users, had no understanding of how the system might work and what was to be included. Not surprisingly, the first attempt to computerize the LAS was deemed unsuccessful. Indeed, the documentation reveals that the basic starting point for the project was never formally established. Moreover, adding requirements for mobile data and locations represented a significant enhancement to the project which would have required re-scoping (yet the budget and the delivery date remained unaltered). At the point of termination, when the technical tests failed, the project was five months behind schedule with a very significant cost overrun of 200 percent (that is three times over budget). While no success criteria had been formally defined, the triple constraint had been monitored. The basic view of success predicated on the triple constraint indicated that the project was clearly failing and it was duly culled.

A post-project review was conducted by independent auditors and some of the findings were fed into the discussions regarding the next attempt. However, the auditors were looking at delivering the initial reduced-scope specification, assuming that a package could be sourced from elsewhere. Their estimate of the budget and schedule was thus derived from the assumption that only a minimal system was needed. This was to form the constraints, and provide the implicit criteria used to assess the success of the next two attempts.

The second attempt called for an ambitious project that went beyond expected capability in terms of technology and systems. The scope of the system was defined internally in precise and prescriptive terms – however some aspects of the specification were simply not included. The delivery deadline was prescribed at 11 months (note that this would not have been realistic even for a packaged solution, let alone for a solution that required a quantum leap in technology). More crucially a totally unrealistic budgetary constraint was placed on the project. Users were not included in the consultation thus excluding any stakeholders from getting an early glimpse of the intention or participating in designing their own future. The triple constraint was thus established as the criteria used for assessment, as some of the technical criteria were relaxed. When the deadline arrived it became clear that the system could not be delivered on time as major chunks were still missing and others were known to be unreliable. Following the failure to deliver on time, the project was re-structured into three increments. However simply re-structuring the deliverables into three portions was not sufficient as the staggered delivery required additional new interfaces to ensure that each phase would be operational.

Cost remained the primary success criteria as the LAS was being pressured by government to reduce operating budgets. Phase 3 of the third attempt came online on target in terms of budget and schedule. Internally it was viewed as a success. However, in the next few days the system started to slow down with its performance deteriorating gradually until it locked out completely and stopped functioning, thus becoming a clear operational failure. Extending the timescale beyond the point of delivery thus shows the project was a failure in terms of the expected results and delivered performance. A summary of some of the flaws associated with other technical issues appears in Table 13.1.

Safety first

In the financial context of disasters, the third attempt was a minor case, costing less than £1 million. However, despatch systems have safety-critical components. Following the failure there were claims by reporters and the unions that between 23 and 46 people may have died as a result of the delays that occurred (Dalcher, 1999, 2007). The claims were not supported in court as litigants had to prove that the same people would not have died had it not been for special circumstances. Obtaining incontrovertible evidence that they would have survived is close to impossible and hence most of the cases were not pursued. The alleged claims for loss of life associated with this disaster point to more profound implications. Even the cheapest of systems can become a menace and result in loss of life, serious litigation, embarrassment, and loss of reputation when safety-critical components fail.

Safety-critical systems are used in areas where failure can mean risk to human lives, pushing cost into secondary considerations. The results of even a temporary failure are too serious to be ignored. Aside from the technological concerns, the negligence view (which is the principle governing medical malpractice) requires that a product or activity meet reasonable expectations for safety. In the LAS disaster, LAS management and the team compiling the systems requirements specification failed to specify safety-critical software requirements. As a result the delivered system lacked the typical characteristics expected from a safety-critical system. A minimum requirement should have included the implementation of the safety functions necessary to achieve and maintain a safe state for all components under the control of the system. While the number of deaths during this period is disputed by both unions and LAS management, it is clear that service provided to Londoners reached a new low. Reports of critical patients waiting ten or even eleven hours for

Table 13.1 Summary of the fundamental flaws in the London Ambulance System

Issue	Flaw
Concept	The new breakthrough system would have represented a quantum leap in technology. The most sophisticated system of its kind, it was meant to pinpoint positions on electronic maps, calculate ideal mobilizations, and handle all communications and allocations. It was expected that all the benefits and full functionality could be delivered in a single-shot implementation. Inappropriate assumptions were made during the early stages. The level of expectation from an untried system was too high. The apparent overreliance on technology served to freeze out the human element which was vital to the success, or at least the failure, of the system. The high public profile contributed to the overall pressure to succeed.
Management	The incessant pressure to improve performance and response times underscored most management decisions and led to the acceptance of many risks. The nature of the relationship between management and staff deteriorated further when the lack of attention to staff needs was coupled by major overspending of scarce resources on glossy brochures, management consultants, and corporate image. Pressure from regional management contributed to the overall rushed climate. Critical information was withheld, while higher management failed to examine progress and respond to identified concerns and shortfalls.
Industrial relations	The history of the LAS is based on strong internal politics and bad industrial relations. The early system became operational without any consultation on staffing, new duties and responsibilities, health and safety, training, or ergonomics with any user representatives. The lack of consultation with both ambulance crews, control room staff and the unions contributed to the lack of trust in the new system. Staff were simply informed that all critical allocations and decisions would be carried out by the computer. Most members of staff concluded that their skills and experience were no longer needed.
Project management	Lack of project sponsor and experienced project leaders may have played a part in accepting impossible targets and trying to meet them at the expense of quality and reliability. Total lack of project management experience and disregard for the chosen project management methodology contributed to the disorganized development effort. It is common for the software house to take the lead in LAS type projects, but members of the consortium were all too happy to transfer this responsibility. No professional was in charge of managing the project. No configuration management procedures were used and many changes to the system were not recorded. The use of project management on LAS illustrated two sayings: "PINO: PRINCE in name only": PRINCE was nominally being used but nobody was trained or competent in its use, and so "A fool with a tool is still a fool."
Risk management	No account was taken of all the risks. Major assumptions were allowed to proceed unchallenged and group decisions about values and costs were allowed to "anchor" perceptions. The unrealistic deadline should have been challenged and explored. Novel solutions equate to high risk!
Procurement	The cost and time limitations imposed on the effort constrained the development process. An inexperienced team, with no management skills or IT or procurement experience, was asked to use flawed guidelines and was put in charge of selecting the winning bid. No attempt was made to check the track record of bidders or to investigate major inconsistencies.

Table 13.1 Continued

Issue	Flaw
	Nor was there any attempt to explain differences between the bids or why some invited contractors failed to bid. The result was the selection of an inexperienced software house that naively agreed to complete a system they did not understand properly by a totally unrealistic deadline.
Design	The need for perfect information at all times was a critical millstone. The limitations of a communications system in an urban area with tall buildings were not taken into account. Frustrated staff, unable to communicate with base, switched to their radios which used the same frequencies as the data communications system, adding to the already clogged airwaves. Due to the inability to obtain perfect information, the quality and accuracy of the information available to the system rapidly deteriorated. The number of ambulances that could be traced by the system continued to decline. This resulted in more complex allocations and delays which further constrained the system. This positive feedback loop served to rapidly escalate the situation out of control and bring about a rapid disaster. The system was designed to deal with the average number of calls ignoring the extreme bounds that must be "allowable" for this type of system. The user interface design did not allow operators to scroll through the list of calls to ensure a vehicle had actually been dispatched. Overall, the system was riddled with design and technical flaws that collectively triggered its collapse.
Testing	The entire system was never tested under operational conditions! No tests were devised to evaluate the response to incomplete or incorrect data. The hardware was not tested under full load. There was no form of independent quality assurance. The frequent changes to the system were not recorded.
Training	Only basic training was provided, and this was carried out far too early. Many changes to the system took place after the completion of training, while staff had to wait another eight months before they could test out their newly acquired skills.
Operational environment	The LAS severely underestimated the intensive pressure placed on staff in the control room. The overnight reorganization of the control room eliminated the familiar structure of the room and split up divisional teams who had worked together. Teams with local knowledge and experience of local traffic, shortcuts, and positions of hospitals who used to share sector desks were thus separated and placed in unfamiliar positions. The changes made to the operating procedures, organizational structure, and the physical layout of the control room made it extremely difficult for staff to intervene and correct problems. This meant that attempts to override certain features of the system were complicated by the lack of local knowledge.
Back-up	Back-up procedures were totally inadequate. The addition of printers as a temporary solution was mainly responsible for the failure of the only back-up system to come on-line. Contingency measures were never tested. The paper back-up system was discarded that morning.
Release	An incomplete system was released boasting a number of uncorrected, critical, yet "approved" errors. The software was not complete nor was it fine-tuned. The communication infrastructure was unable to handle the volumes of data. The decision on the day was to use only the computer-generated resource allocations despite of all the known imperfections. Neither the system, nor its users were ready for full implementation.

an ambulance filled the press pages in the ensuing weeks. Londoners were very lucky no major incidents capable of stretching the system beyond its limits, took place on those critical dates! The LAS inquiry report suggested that managers had rushed ahead with the high risk strategy of installing a system that was incomplete, with known technical problems, which had not been tested and had insufficient backup. Staff were not trained properly to use the system which was imposed by an over-zealous and misinformed management.

The performance of emergency ambulance services is measured in terms of the speed with which they respond to calls for aid. Continuous under-performance and inability to reach the prescribed target were reported as the underlying rationale for initiating the LAS computerization attempts. Following the implementation, performance targets dropped to an unprecedented level. Response times of less than 15 minutes were only achieved for 17 percent of incidents (compared with the expected 95 percent). The average ring time for each call peaked at 11 minutes, with many callers waiting 15 minutes. In contrast, the response time percentage prior to the first attempt was above 65 percent.

Project trade-offs

The pressure resulting from the need to improve performance and enhance the reputation of the service drove a number of trade-offs as well as the obsession with the power of technology. Charette (1995) noted a number of computer-aided despatch systems vendors approached stated that even given perfect conditions (proper management, unlimited timescale, and full resources), it would have been impossible to achieve the quality and reliability LAS required from the data terminals and automated vehicle location systems. Even the use of new advances such as Global Positioning Systems, inertia navigation systems, and satellite-based communications, would not have provided the level of performance expected. In addition, the despatch vendors pointed out that the development of an allocation and mobilization algorithm is an extremely challenging task. Even very simple cases spanning limited geographical areas struggle to cope with basic assumptions and introduce numerous exception messages. The introduction of the complexities inherent in a metropolis the size of London (such as storms, major accidents, road works, festivals, processions, sports matches, demonstrations) to the uncertainties of the system itself (such as broken down vehicles, staff holidays, missing drivers, equipment, black-spots) and the interacting humans would suggest that the algorithm required to make the allocation may belong to the class of intractable problems (wicked problems that are either impossible to solve, or impossible to solve in at least polynomial time). Indeed, a report published in 1990 by the National Audit Office revealed that of the 62 ambulance services in the UK, 25 had either not attempted or abandoned attempts to computerize route scheduling activities (National Audit Office, 1990).

Quality versus speed

The adoption of a hastily planned schedule allowing very little time for the development of an advanced and innovative system, the like of which could not be found anywhere, meant a rushed development. In order to meet target dates, the natural temptation to take short-cuts could not be resisted. Tests, detailed assessments, and quality procedures became redundant in a furious race to finish on time. The novelty of the system meant that the required knowledge did not exist, but with time running out something had to be developed. A further failure to deliver would simply not do. With no time to run a comprehensive training program and the lack of foresight to test and implement a number of fall-back procedures, the reliability of the system was dramatically challenged.

Quality versus cost

The move towards more decentralized and directly financially accountable management underscored the financial climate. The combined effect of chronic shortages and long-term under-investment with the reallocation of NHS priorities away from London highlights many of the reasons for under-performance. The constant pressure aimed at saving resources coupled with a strong focus on the performance of public services was a powerful incentive for driving agendas. Against this backdrop, the attempt to computerize the system was severely constrained by prevailing attitudes toward cost saving. A major leapfrog in safety-critical technology requires expensive research and adequate funding. This was clearly not available for this project as concerned management anchored on to irrelevant figures and forced the assessment procedure to rely on cost as the defining factor in assessing proposals. In cases where projects rely on a time-critical schedule, it is assumed that major resources will be invested in the project in order to compensate for this shortcoming and allow completion on schedule. The LAS had no reason to make this project time-critical, but once it was decided that the timescale was fixed, ample resources should have been made available to compensate for this factor and make sure a fit for purpose system was going to be released.

Design issues

In order to allow the complex allocation algorithm to run, extreme processing power was needed. The greater the distance between the incident and an ambulance resource, the longer the time needed to calculate the resource allocation due to the need to identify the most appropriate resource. At busy times when the number of incidents increased and the number of resources not already dealing with other incidents decreased, the entire system would slow down due to the volume and complexity of the calculations. The consortium decided at an early stage to perform a trade-off between ease-of-use and performance in order to facilitate a user-friendly interface. The consortium opted for Microsoft Windows 3.0 for the user interfaces and Visual Basic as the development tool for the creation of the screen dialogues. This was not specified in the proposal submitted to the LAS.

Performance versus user interface

The computer screens were designed using what is essentially a prototyping tool. Visual Basic is used in typically small, non safety-critical applications to rapidly generate screens. While the basic screen design can be tested and finalized quickly, the performance of such development tools is slow and inefficient. In the LAS system, the visual basic code was implemented on extremely slow 486 machines operating at 25 MHz. Following their development, such products tend to be fine-tuned to improve their performance and reduce memory consumption. In a safety-critical environment where every second counts, the inefficiencies associated with the screen design tool could easily account for the bulk of the mobilization time allowed by the national standard. When added to other delays, this degrades the overall performance of the system to a dangerous level. When the LAS control room operators started to pre-load the screens to save time, they put other parts of the system under increased pressure (which was not anticipated).

Moving towards success

Attempting to leapfrog to a full system with innovative technology is fraught with risk. With complex systems that are not easily understood, the concept of implementation in phases with each module delivering some useful functionality and building on what is there offers a controlled approach to dealing with risk in small increments. The fourth attempt to deliver a working system for the LAS recognized the need to engage stakeholders and manage expectations. Prototyping was used as a way of creating dialogue and building trust. Following a string of small successes users learned to perceive the process as less threatening and engaged in a creative way while attempting to improve their environment. Through the engagement process the team was effectively creating new success criteria for each small project which went beyond achieving the overall purpose. Users and champions were satisfied, the project team felt they were making a difference and therefore felt a greater commitment to the organization. The overall risk of non-delivery was thus reduced as small, functional, useful components were being delivered at agreed intervals. The overall effort could be assessed based on results to date and it becomes easier to spot trouble earlier, and either adjust or terminate the overall effort. This approach also gave the users a flavour of what the system could do for them and got them enthusiastic and on board, reducing resistance and securing a better fit. More crucially it offered future benefits in establishing working relations that could be drawn upon, in creating new competencies and establishing a deeper understanding, and above all in ensuring that the next increment resulting from the success of current work was always likely to follow and utilize the enthusiasm and team spirit that had already been achieved. By stopping to think, the LAS managed to develop parts of the system successfully. The challenge is to build on the success rather than to pander to the pressures that underlie the environment within which the LAS is operating. Success is never guaranteed. It comes through recognition of the conditions that are needed to secure it and requires a continuous effort to maintain it.

13.7 Using the nine perspectives

There were many factors that contributed to the failure of the first three attempts. But an over-use of the Optimization Perspective, and the disproportionate significance given to time and cost were significant. Figure 13.1 shows how the use of the nine perspectives might have led to a better outcome. We suggest that in this case the four most relevant perspectives were:

1   Success;
2   Decision;
3   Governance;
4   Marketing.

Success

This story is primarily one of success. During the second and third attempt, LAS focused on just the binary constraint of cost and time, and indeed at the third attempt the project was first hailed to be a success because it had been delivered on cost and time, even though the system subsequently failed absolutely with possible serious consequences. The most important element of the triple constraint was the system should perform. The second most important element was cost; the system should have been delivered within a sensible cost. Time was almost irrelevant. An analysis of Table 4.3 would indicate that there are several stakeholders with different views of success, and a balance should be sought between those different stakeholders.

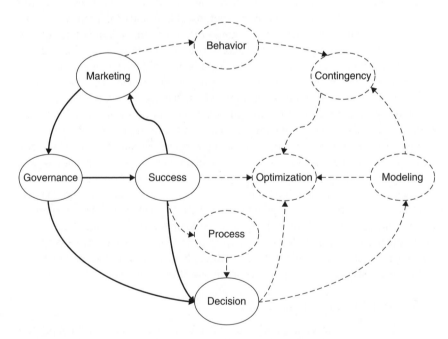

Figure 13.1 Using the nine perspectives to achieve a better outcome on the LAS case

Investor

The investor, in this case the board of LAS and its parent organization, the South Thames Regional Health Authority, were the most important stakeholders. The system should perform, and should have been delivered within cost. It should enhance the reputation of LAS to provide excellent service to the public, and provide them with new competence to deliver that service.

Consumers

The consumers, the people dialling 999, want a service that responds within as short a time as possible, and especially in accordance with nationally defined standards.

Operators

The operators are both the people in the call center and the ambulance drivers. They want a system that is easy to use, that has high availability, reliability and maintainability. It should provide them with new competences to do their job effectively.

Sponsor

On the project there was no sponsor. We will deal with that further under governance. But if they had existed they would have represented the investors' wishes.

Project manager

Again, there was not a clear project manager. But if there was, he or she would want to deliver a system that works within the budget. He or she would want to be treated with respect by the investor and supported by the sponsor. He or she would also hope that the project provided them with a learning opportunity.

Suppliers

The suppliers would look to make a profit, while meeting the investors' needs, and hopefully do a good job so that they can win similar work in the future.

Public

The public want an effective ambulance system to meet the needs of London.

Decision

Decision making was flawed throughout the project. But if the project had been properly established at the start, there would have been more effective decision making throughout. The seven forces model (Figure 9.1) provides a basis for a project strategy.

Context

A PESTLE (Political, Economic, Social, Technical, Legal and Environmental) analysis would set the basis for the project. The system is highly political, meeting essential social needs. The second attempt tried to develop a highly complex, technical solution. We will deal with that further under definition. The system is being developed in the public sector, which imposes economic constraints. We will deal with that under sponsorship. The system delivers an essential social service within the constraints of a large metropolitan city. LAS have legal requirements to deliver the service within nationally defined standards.

Sponsorship

The fact the system was subjected to spending cuts due to budgetary constraints suggests it was being paid for out of revenue. It should be paid for out of a capital budget. It should have a clear business plan, describing the likely cost and expected benefits. A business plan is an essential component of PRINCE2, but that was first issued in 1996. It was not such a clear component of PRINCE which was being used here. The urgency should have been properly defined as part of the business plan and managed. There was probably no urgency.

Definition

The objectives, scope, design, technology and resources should have all been properly defined and managed.

Attitudes

The attitude of staff was critical on this project. Their commitment, motivation, support and shared vision were all essential. We will return to that under the marketing perspective.

Systems

The project should have been properly planned and controlled. Quality was the most important element of the triple constraint. An effective risk analysis might have helped to identify many of the problems and avoid them.

People

Even though the intention of the computer system was to replace much of the manual operation, it still depended critically on the support of the staff and their attitudes. LAS management fell short on leadership and influence.

Organization

The most critical element of project organization was the contract strategy. We will return to that under governance.

Governance

The two most critical elements of governance that were missing were the governance roles and contract strategy. The roles of project manager and project sponsor should have been clearly defined, and would have been had PRINCE2 been followed (but it was not yet published at that time). A senior manager should have taken responsibility for leading the development of the project, defining the desired impact and outcomes, and hence enlightening the design of the system. A competent project manager should have been identified and appointed, and used an effective project management methodology.

Marketing

The support and attitudes of staff was essential to the success of this project, so a stakeholder management and communication plan would have provided considerable benefit. Part of the communication plan would be to seek feedback from the staff, to gain their contribution to the design of the system and support for its operation.

Apology

It is very easy to be critical. But many of these ideas have only come to the fore since the failure of the project. Peter Morris and George Hough (1987) began to develop success criteria of projects, but the real development in thinking only dates from the early 1990s (Wateridge, 1995). A version of the seven forces model appears in the first edition of Rodney Turner's book (2009), but that didn't appear until 1993. Indeed it derives from a model in Peter Morris and George Hough's book (1987), but it was not well known. Concepts of contract strategy go back to the 1930s, but there have been substantial advances since the mid-1990s. Also the work in the 1930s related to the construction industry, while contract strategy in the IS industry is still very developmental. The concept of the project sponsor was suggested in the first edition of David Frame's (2003) book, which appeared in 1987. But it is only in the last five years that thinking in that area has truly advanced. PRINCE had been published, but PRINCE2 first appeared in 1996. And we are still fighting the battle of project marketing.

Acknowledgments

The author wishes to thank the numerous contributors and correspondents who volunteered information in various formats.

References

Charette, R.N., 1995, "No one could have done better," *American Programmer*, **8**(7), 21–28.

Dalcher, D., 1999, "Disaster in London: The LAS case study," *Proceedings of IEEE Conference on the Engineering of Computer Based Systems, ECBS*, 41–52, IEEE.

——, 2007, *Successful IT Projects*, Thomson Learning, London.

Fitzgerald, G., 2000, *IT at the Heart of Business: A strategic approach to information technology*, British Computer Society, London.

Frame, J.D., 2003, *Managing Projects in Organizations*, 3rd edition, Jossey Bass, San Francisco.

Morris, P.W.G., and Hough, G., 1987, *The Anatomy of Major Projects: A study of the reality of project management*, Wiley, Cichester.

National Audit Office, 1990, National Health Service: Patient Transport Services, July, National Audit Office, London.

Page, D., Williams, P., and Boyd, D., 1993, *Report of the Inquiry into the London Ambulance Service*, South West Thames Regional Health Authority, London.

Turner, J.R., 2009, *The Handbook of Project-Based Management*, 3rd edition, McGraw-Hill, New York.

Wateridge, J.H., 1995, "IT projects: A basis for success," *International Journal of Project Management*, **13**(3), 169–172.

14 ABS International

Sustainable project management

Roland Gareis and Annegret Frank

14.1 Sustainability and projects

Over the last 20 years sustainable development has become a recognized integrative component of political and entrepreneurial decision-making. In societies and companies sustainable development receives widespread attention. However, in temporary organizations, that is in projects and programs, it is rarely considered. In projects, the concept of sustainable development can be related to the success of a project as well as to the design of the project management process. In this chapter we describe the application of the concept of sustainable development to the ABS International Project.

Sustainable development

Originally, sustainable development was as a political concept (Jacobs, 1995; Lafferty, 1995). For the general public, the concept of sustainable development acquired wide attention following the publication of the Brundtland Report by the World Commission for Environment and Development in 1987. The Report defines sustainable development as "development that meets the needs of the present without compromising the ability of future generations to meet their own needs" (World Commission on Environment and Development, 1987). In the subsequent 20 years, sustainable development has found application in organizations. Recently the concept of corporate social responsibility has received increasing attention. While sustainable development is a normative societal concept, corporate social responsibility can be seen as a strategic management approach aiming at increased competitiveness and building the bridge between the societal demand and the success of an individual company (Steurer and Martinuzzi, 2005). Sustainable development can be defined by seven guiding principles:

1   holistic approach (integrated consideration of the economic, ecological, and social dimension);
2   long-term orientation;
3   large spatial and institutional scale;
4   risk and uncertainty reduction;

5   values and ethical considerations;
6   participation;
7   capacity building.

Sustainability and project success

A content-related understanding of sustainable development applies to the project results, while a process-related understanding applies to the project management process. The temporary nature of projects seems to contradict the long-term orientation of sustainable development. But projects initialize investments in new products, markets, organizations, or infrastructure. Therefore projects contribute to the realization of long-term business objectives. The long-term orientation of sustainable development is to be taken care of in project management by considering the post-project phase and the business case of the investment initialized by the project (Figure 14.1). So both project success, measured at the end of the project, and long-term business success should be considered.

Sustainability and the project management process

Sustainable development is to be considered in the design of the project management process, that is in designing the sub-processes of project starting, project coordinating, project controlling and project closing-down (Figure 14.2). Sustainable development is of relevance for the objects of consideration of project management, including project objectives, project scope, project schedule, project costs, resources, and project risks, project organization, project culture, project personnel, project infrastructure and the project context.

Project and Investment

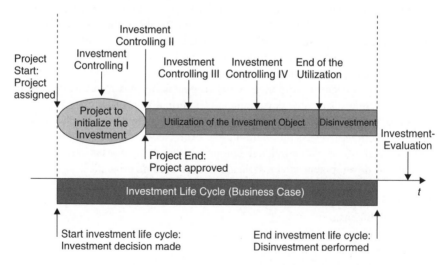

Figure 14.1 Relationship between a project and an investment (after Gareis, 2005)

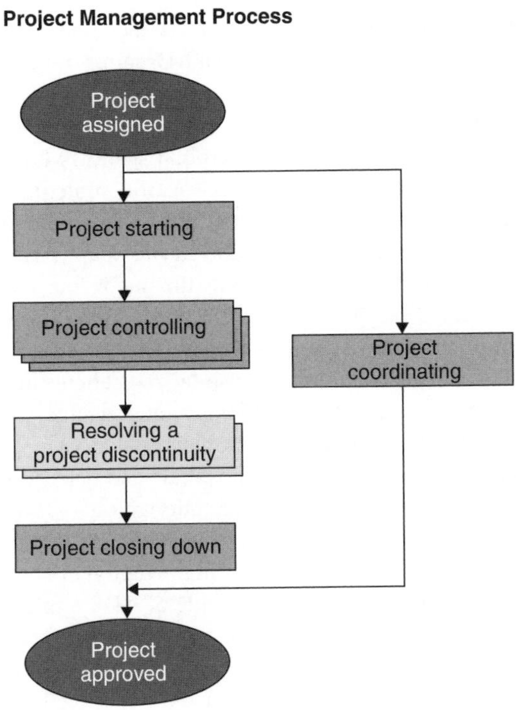

Project Management Process

Figure 14.2 Project management process (after Gareis, 2005)

In the definition of project objectives, economic, ecological and social interests can be considered (Figure 9.1), and that leads to the internalization of external interests. Relationships to relevant project environments are a context dimension to be managed in projects. Based on a participatory and holistic approach, the quality of the project environment analysis can be improved. In designing the appropriate project infrastructure travel times can be limited by working virtually and using video conferencing. New organizational approaches for the design of project organizations consider integration (such as the representatives of suppliers and customers in the project organization) and the empowerment of the project team members and of the project team. Sustainable development increases the complexity and dynamics of projects. On the other hand it might speed up the decision processes in projects, because of a more cooperative project culture.

14.2 The ABS International Project

We start by giving an overview of the ABS International Project describing the project context, the project objectives, the WBS, the project milestones, the project risks, the project organization, and the relevant social project environments. Then we analyze the success and the project management processes adopted.

Project context

The increasing incidence of antibiotic resistance represents a serious, worldwide, health problem. In 1998, the World Health Organization (WHO) issued an "urgent" recommendation that all countries should ensure measures are taken to develop national guidelines for antibiotic therapy. The recommendation of the EU Council in 2001 on the prudent use of antimicrobial agents in human medicine calls upon EU member states to make sure that specific strategies for the prudent use of antimicrobial agents are in place and are being implemented. The problem of antibiotic resistance requires antibiotic stewardship (ABS) at the European level. Long-term sustainability is found to be the major focus of antibiotic stewardship programs. Conan MacDougall and Ron Polk (2005) formed the formal definition of antimicrobial stewardship as an ongoing effort by a health care institution to optimize antimicrobial use among hospitalized patients in order to improve patient outcomes, ensure cost-effective therapy, and reduce adverse consequences of antimicrobial use (including antimicrobial resistance).

Traditionally, ABS is related to hospitals and departments of hospitals. But it also applies to regions, nations and international healthcare systems. At the regional and national level, ABS-related strategies and measures do not address only single hospitals, but all hospitals in the region or country, as well as community care and veterinary care. An example of ABS implementation at the international level is the EU-financed project, ABS International, in which a consortium of representatives from nine EU Member States cooperated in implementing European antibiotic stewardship objectives at a national level. This project was co-financed by the European Union, DG Health and Consumer Protection through the Community Action Program for Public Health (2003–2008). The project started in September 2006 and ended in February 2009.

Project objectives

The overall aim of the ABS International Project was to implement the sustainable use of antibiotics in nine European countries. It was a project with the aim of producing a sustainable outcome. To achieve this aim, its objectives were:

- to develop standard templates for AB prophylaxis, AB therapy and the ABS organization of hospitals;
- to analyze the ABS culture in each partner country;
- to prepare and perform a training program for ABS trainers and ABS consultants;
- to perform ABS training and ABS consulting in cooperating hospitals of partner countries;
- to develop and validate process measures and quality indicators for antibiotic use;
- to establish an international network of ABS experts.

The underlying business objectives were:

- to develop the organizational tools and qualified capacities for identifying and distributing best practice on the prudent use of antimicrobial agents in human medicine in hospitals;
- to enhance and implement specific strategies for the prudent use of antimicrobial agents in hospitals;
- to elaborate methods for evaluating the applied antimicrobial strategies;
- to disseminate the project results across the European Union and candidate countries.

Work break-down structure

The ABS International Project was broken down into eight project phases ("work packages" in the EU language) as shown in Figure 14.3. The major work packages were as follows:

Work package 1: Project management

This work package formulated the management of the project start, project co-ordination, project controlling and project close-down processes, as well as the financial and administrative management between the European Commission and the partner countries.

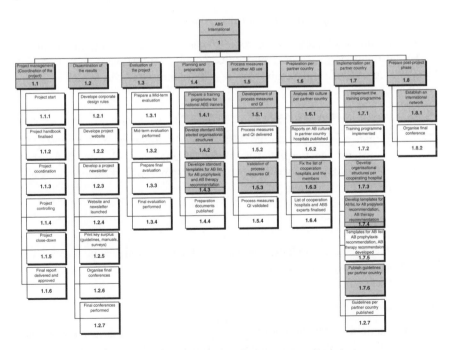

Figure 14.3 Work breakdown structure for the ABS International Project

Within work package 2: Dissemination of results

The key results of the project were disseminated EU-wide via project website, newsletters and publications. A final international conference took place, as well as final national conferences in each partner country.

Work package 3: Evaluation of the project

This was a work package pre-determined by the EU, to submit the interim and final project reports, both technical and financial.

Work package 4: Planning and preparation

This included the development of templates for ABS Tools (AB list, Guide for AB treatment, Guide for surgical prophylaxis, AB consumption controlling) and the development of standard AB-related organizational structures (AB-related communication structures for a hospital, role descriptions for AB-officers, etc.).

Within work package 5: Process measures and QI for AB Use

Process measures and quality indicators were developed and subsequently validated in cooperation hospitals.

Work package 6: Preparation per partner country

The ABS culture of each partner country was analyzed with the questionnaire "ABS hospital nature." Using the results, country reports were published. The cooperating hospitals and members of the ABS trainer team were settled on.

Work package 7: Implementation in partner countries

The performance of the "Train the ABS Trainer" programs and the subsequent ABS trainings for the hospital teams was undertaken in this work package. Additionally, the ABS tools were adapted and implemented in the cooperating hospitals of the partner countries.

Work package 8: Preparation of the post-project phase

This had the objective to obtain sustainability of the achieved results. A web-based network of ABS experts was established.

Project milestone plan

The milestone plan for the project listed the due dates of central events in the progress of the project. The milestones were spread over the project duration of two and a half years. In the project start process for each milestone, planned dates were determined, which were subject to adaptations during project controlling. As an example, Milestone 1.6.4 "List of cooperating hospitals and ABS trainers fixed" was originally planned for 31 May 2007 (Table 14.1). In the project controlling meeting that took place in March 2007, representatives of each partner country reported that they would not be able to obtain all cooperation agreements signed by the medical directors of the cooperating hospitals in time. The date was therefore changed to 20 June 2007. The actual date where all signed cooperation agreements were sent to the project office was 6 July 2007.

Project risks

The project team identified possible risks in a brainstorming session on the basis of the work breakdown structure during the project start process. Risks were defined as a negative or positive deviations from the project objectives regarding project scope, project schedule and project costs. The identified risks were described, and measures were planned to manage the identified risks. No monetary evaluations and no estimations of occurrence probabilities were made (Table 14.2). As an example, within work package "1.6.1 Analysis of AB culture per partner country" the risk of a low responsive rate on the questionnaire survey on AB culture was

Table 14.1 Milestone plan for the ABS International Project

Code	Milestone	Planned date	Revised date	Actual date
1.1.2	Project handbook finalized	22 Sep 2006		22 Sep 2006
1.2.4	Project website and newsletter launched	30 Nov 2006		31 Dec 2006
1.4.4	Preparation documents published	29 Dec 2006	25 Jan 2007	25 Jan 2007
1.6.2	Report on culture in partner country hospitals published	30 Apr 2007		30 Apr 2007
1.6.4	List of cooperating hospitals and ABS trainers finalized	31 May 2007	20 Jun 2007	6 Jul 2007
1.5.2	Process measures delivered	31 Jul 2007		31 Jul 2007
1.3.2	Mid-term evaluation performed	28 Sep 2007		28 Sep 2007
1.5.4	Process measures validated	8 Jan 2008	15 Dec 2008	2 Feb 2009
1.7.5	Templates for AB lists, AB therapy & AB prophylaxis developed	31 Mar 2008		31 Mar 2008
1.7.7	Guidelines for partner countries published	30 May 2008		30 May 2008
1.8.3	Final national and international conferences held	1 Sep 2008	17 Oct 2008	17 Oct 2008
1.3.4	Final evaluation performed	23 Sep 2008	31 May 2009	28 May 2009

Table 14.2 Risk analysis for the ABS International Project

WBS Code	WP/Phase	Risk	Response
1.6/1.7	Preparation in partner countries Implementation in partner countries	English, the project language, is not understood by all experts	Interpreters provided if needed
1.6.1	Analysis of AB culture in each partner country	Response rate to questionnaire low	The questionnaire will be sent to more than the required number of hospitals Project partners contact hospitals direct
1.6.3	Define members of national expert teams	Key ABS experts cannot participate	List of experts drawn up as early as possible to compensate for loss of expertise
1.7	Implementation in partner countries	Progress behind schedule	In quarterly meetings work plans will be reviewed and corrective action taken as necessary For serious problems the project manager will draw up a discontinuity plan for appropriate action
1.7.1	Implement training program	Hospital staff don't have sufficient time to participate	It is desired that three hospitals per partner country should participate, but a list of four to five will be maintained

identified. As a risk management measure, it was planned to address the questionnaire to more than a sufficient number of hospitals per partner country, and more importantly, each project partner was encouraged to contact the hospitals directly in his/her country to submit the questionnaires.

Project organization

The project partners were recruited from nine member states of the European Union, namely Austria, Germany, Belgium, Slovakia, Italy, Poland, Hungary, the Czech Republic and Slovenia. They represented universities, public institutions, national and international expert groups, etc. The main partner of the project was Roland Gareis Consulting, an Austrian company that provides training and consulting services in project, process and change management, and that also had broad experiences in managing health-related projects. The project organization chart depicts the organizational structures of the ABS International Project (Figure 14.4).

The project roles, both individual and team roles, and their relationships are illustrated. The ellipse around the project organization gives it a boundary and symbolizes the relative autonomy of the project as a social system. The project team consisted of the project manager and the national coordinators of each partner

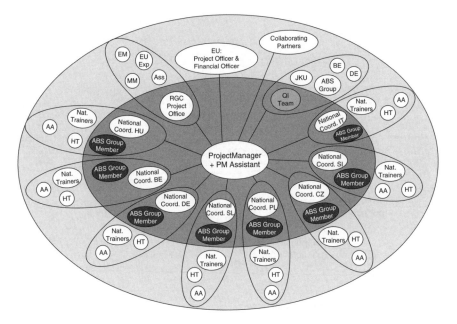

Figure 14.4 Project organization chart

country. Each national coordinator was assisted by a member of the Austrian ABS GROUP and lead a sub-team composed of the national ABS trainers/ABS consultants, the hospital teams (HT) and administrative assistants (AA). The project owner team consisted of the technical and financial project officers at the EU Commission.

The project team met regularly every six months for project controlling workshops that lasted one to two days. Otherwise, project communication took place "virtually" by e-mail, telephone and with the help of a project collaboration platform.

Project environment analysis

During the project start process, the relevant project environments and the relationships between the project and the single environments were analyzed by the project team. A "relevant" environment was defined as a group, an organization or an institution that could influence the project success (Figure 14.5). Initially, all relevant environments were listed and clustered, such as the EU, public authorities in each partner country, hospitals and hospital owners, etc. Next, the team described result- and/or process-related expectations of the relevant environments toward the project. Based on an analysis of potentials and conflicts in the relationships, concrete measures to manage the relationships were planned (Table 14.3). As an example, it

Figure 14.5 Project environment analysis

was assumed that the national ministries of health would have positive expectations about the project. Thus, they would be interested in the project results and would be a potential sponsor of national ABS activities after the end of the project in order to ensure sustainability of the project. Therefore, measures planned were to keep them informed about the project progress (such as via project newsletters) and establish a good basis for communication for further cooperation after the end of the project.

14.3 Sustainable success

As we have seen, the ABS International Project had the aim of producing a sustainable outcome. There were several contributing factors to this.

Success for different relevant project environments

The different relevant (social) environments of the project had different expectations toward the project and its results. Most of them shared the interest in sustainable project and business case results. A few examples are given:

(a) The EU Commission DG SANCO expected that the project brought added value to the existing public health knowledge allowing the practical use of that ABS knowledge in the field. It was also expected the project would contribute to EU policies. The project should have a positive implication for the health of EU citizens. Moreover, the project had to demonstrate that the reproducibility

Table 14.3 Relationship to relevant environments

Environment	Relationship	Response
Project organization	Gain experience of international EU projects	Professional project management documentation Document lessons learnt
Roland Gareis Consulting	Interested in good project results: image, PR	Effective project marketing and dissemination of results
ABS Group	Daily routines and additional projects may affect purpose	Efficient planning of work packages Early communication of delays
Associated partners	Daily routines and additional projects may affect purpose	Efficient planning of work packages Early communication of delays
Collaborating partners	Provide scientific excellence to the project Not considered in the project budget	Keep informed Invite to final conferences
EU	Co-finance the project Contractual and financial constraints	Keep informed Regular reports Ensure all participants understand contracts
Country hospitals	Profit from project	Establish AB teams to ensure success

and transferability of the actions had been planned, so to cover the whole concerned population in the future.

(b) The national partners had the interest to build capacities for future ABS services in their respective countries by developing ABS trainers and ABS consultants. Some of the national experts (project team members) wanted to use the data generated in the project, such as the defined ABS quality indicators, to publish in scientific medical journals. By this they contributed to their recognition as researchers.

(c) Most of the partners appreciated the cooperation in the project as a basis for long-term networking contacts. Actually a proposal for a subsequent EU-funded project was developed during the performance of the ABS International Project. Even some of the suppliers (such as graphic design and printing companies) expressed their interest in a continuing cooperation.

Many expectations of relevant environments related to the sustainability dimensions of "long-term orientation" and "capacity building."

Project results and business case results

Projects funded within the European Commission's health program are expected to contribute to solving problems in the long-term at the European level, and should not duplicate existing initiatives, but provide an added value at EU level. The projects should not simply duplicate actions that can be taken at member state level but rather enable to address problems that would otherwise not be sufficiently addressed by the Member States. This requirement relates to the sustainability dimension of "large spatial scale."

When applying for an EU-funded health project, the EU asks for "specific" and "general" project objectives in their application form. Looking at the EU's definition of specific and general objectives one can notice that specific objectives relate to project results and general objectives relate to business case results.

> The specific objectives are concrete statements describing what the project is trying to achieve in order to reach its general objective. They should be matched to the problem determinants identified in the problem analysis, and should be written at a level which allows them to be evaluated at the conclusion of the project. They should also be specific, measurable, acceptable for the target group, realistic, and time-bound.
>
> A general objective is a general indication of the project's contribution to society in terms of its longer-term benefits (e.g., contribute to the reduction of cancer mortality; reduce social inequality in population's health). The general objective has to correlate with the different specific objectives.

The "business case" results therefore represent the contribution of the ABS International Project to society in terms of its longer-term benefits, such as the improvement of patient safety, the assurance of cost-effective therapy, and the reduction of antimicrobial resistance.

Sustainable success through dissemination activities

When applying for an EU-funded health project, applicants must clearly illustrate a dissemination strategy in order to ensure transferability and sustainability of results. Dissemination refers to the process of making the results and deliverables of the project available to the stakeholders and a wider audience. In the ABS International Project, a dissemination plan was elaborated, explaining how the project plans to share outcomes with relevant environments, stakeholders, and other relevant institutions and individuals. The main dissemination tools of ABS International Project were the project website and regular project newsletters. The project provided:

1   general information about the ABS International Project (objectives, partners, the involvement of the EC, planned activities and outputs);
2   access to all project results, in particular ABS tools, ABS training programs, manuals on ABS process measures and quality indicators, etc.;
3   access to best practice examples in the prudent use of antibiotics;
4   access to a database of ABS experts in the European Union;
5   related links to project partners, the EC, other international projects and other ABS information sources;
6   the possibility of facilitating a dialogue with the general public.

The project regularly issued project newsletters to inform about activities and output produced during the project as well as related information from the project partners.

14.4 Sustainable project management

The ABS International Project also used sustainable project processes (Gareis, 2005).

Sustainability and the project start process

The main objective of the project start process in ABS International was to establish the project team and to communicate the "big project picture" to all members of the project organization. A two-day project start workshop took place in September 2006 in the Austrian Federal Ministry of Health. Objectives of the project start workshop were:

- getting to know each other;
- establishing the project as a social system;
- developing trust in the cooperation;
- learning about the ABS status of the cooperating countries;
- informing about the structures of the project;
- planning the next steps in the project.

The 25 participants of the project start workshop included the EU project officer from the EU Commission DG SANCO, the project owner, the project manager and all project team members. The project team members consisted of the national coordinators of all involved partner countries (Germany, Belgium, Slovakia, Italy, Poland, Hungary, the Czech Republic and Slovenia) and the ABS Group. Selected representatives of relevant environments (such as the Austrian Federal Ministry of Health) also took part. After the first day of the project start workshops a social event was organized for the participants to meet and network in a more informal way. As a follow-up to the project start workshop the minutes were prepared and all project plans were finalized based on the agreements achieved during the workshop. As a result of the project start process sustainable structures for the performance of the ABS International Project were created.

Sustainability and the project co-ordination process

Professional project coordination in the ABS International Project required the use of an appropriate ICT infrastructure. Especially in an EU-wide project, with project team members working at different locations, project coordination had to take place virtually. Travel times had to be minimized. So the appropriate software and telecommunications media were defined. The use of common project management software and of office software was ensured. It was decided to use project collaboration software, and to perform telephone conferences and video conferences. The web-based project collaboration platform was installed. It should provide the following advantages:

- one communication platform accessible from everywhere (Internet);
- information about the project status always available;
- easy handling of reporting;
- support of the day-to-day management.

Unfortunately this project collaboration platform was not extensively used by the members of the project organization. Many project team members continued to send emails with attachments. This might be because many project team members were doctors, not used to downloading and uploading documents on collaboration platforms. As the benefits of the platform were not obvious, telephone and e-mail were the preferred ways of communication.

Sustainability and the project controlling process

In the ABS International Project, a formal project controlling was performed periodically, on average every two months subject to the long project duration of two and a half years. Each project controlling cycle included a project team meeting and a project owner meeting, as well as the control and adaptation of the project plans and the agreement on directive measures. Reporting methods were the project progress report and the project score card (Figure 14.6). The project score card was used to describe, visualize and communicate the project status at each controlling date. It provided an holistic view of the project status considering the following dimensions:

- project environment relationships;
- project progress, project schedule, project costs, project resources;
- project objectives and context;
- project roles, project communication, project culture, project teamwork.

The draft of the project score card was prepared by the project manager, the scoring was performed in a participatory approach by the project team. The constructions of common holistic project realities by the project team and communicating the project status to the project owner contributed to a sustainable project management process. Besides these periodic project-internal controlling cycles the EU Commission carried out a review halfway through the project. An interim technical implementation report as well as an interim financial implementation report had to be delivered and accepted.

Sustainability and the project close-down process

The formal closing-down of the ABS International Project served to dissolve the project as a social system, as well as to dissolve the project environment relationships. Moreover, remaining tasks had to be completed and the post-project

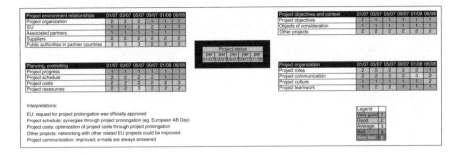

Figure 14.6 Project score card for the ABS International Project (June 2008)

phase had to be planned. Know-how gained in the project needed to be transferred to the respective organizations of the project partners. The quality of the project close-down process was assured by using the project plans developed during the project start process and updated during the project controlling cycles. For example, the project objectives plan was used to evaluate the project success, and the project environment analysis was used to plan the dissolution of the project environment relations. As formal communication structures of the project close-down process, a project close-down workshop and a final international ABS conference were performed. The objectives of the close-down workshop were:

- to present the project results and the close-down report;
- to reflect on the learning experiences;
- to plan remaining work and first activities for the post-project phase;
- to plan the dissolution of the project environment relationships and the establishment of new environment relationships; and
- to evaluate the project success.

As an example, the implementation plan for the post-project phase was prepared (Table 14.4). As the EU wants to ensure long-term sustainability, this implementation plan was an important deliverable. After the close-down workshop a final "social" event was organized in order to close-down emotionally, too.

14.5 Using the nine perspectives

The ABS International Project took place much more recently than the LAS Case and so has incorporated much modern good practice. It used at least five of the nine perspectives as illustrated by Figure 14.7. The perspectives are:

- success;
- decision;
- process;
- behavior;
- marketing.

Table 14.4 Implementation plan for the post-project phase

3) Implementation plan for the post-project phase
National • Organization of periodic national conferences • Development of national action plans
International • Dissemination of follow-up publications • Networking between project partners • Cooperation in ABS related activities at an EU level • Project Proposal 2008; Project Proposal 2009

Success

The success criteria for the project were clear, especially the desire for the sustainability of the project process and the project solution.

Decision

The foundation of the project had to be clearly established at the start. The context was analyzed and sponsorship provided by the EU. Then the objectives of the project were clearly defined, and good attitudes developed by marketing the project. An appropriate project process and project organization was developed, and the partners to the project clearly led and guided through the project process.

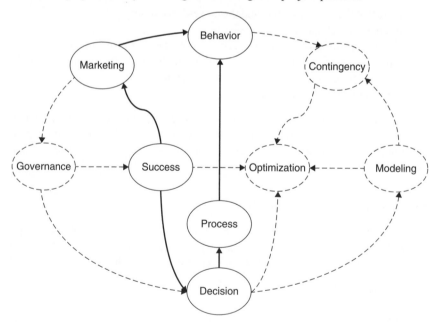

Figure 14.7 Using the nine perspectives to achieve a better outcome on the ABS International Project

Figure 14.8 Logo for the ABS International Project

Process

Having developed the foundation of the project, the project process was defined (Figures 14.2 and 14.3).

Behavior

The project process was supported by a clear project organization structure (Figure 14.4). But the support of the project partners had to be obtained, and this was done by working closely with them through the project organization, but also by marketing the project. A key part of the project organization was that the project had a name – the ABS International Project – and a logo (Figure 14.8) which was made the banner of all the project planning documents.

Marketing

There were two clear points of focus of the project marketing: one was to obtain the support of the project partners, and the second was to disseminate the knowledge of the project after it was complete. Several of the milestones relate to the early marketing, particularly "1.2.4: Project website and newsletter launched." Several elements of the close-out plan also relate to the post-project marketing, including the need to train the trainers and the national and international conferences.

References

Gareis, R., 2005, *Happy Projects!*, Manz, Vienna.

Jacobs, M., 1995, "Sustainable development, capital substitution and economic humility: A response to Beckerman," *Environmental Values*, **4**, 57–68.

Lafferty, W.M., 1995, "The implementation of sustainable development in the European Union," in Lovenduski, J. and Stanyer, J. (eds), *Contemporary Political Studies: Proceedings of the Political Studies Association*, Political Studies Association, Belfast.

MacDougall, C., and Polk, R.E., 2005, "Antimicrobial stewardship programs in health care systems," *Clinical Microbiology Reviews*, **18**(4), 638–656.

Steurer, R., and Martinuzzi, A., 2005, "Towards a new pattern of strategy formation in the public sector: First experiences with national strategies for sustainable development in Europe," *Environment and Planning C: Government and Policy*, **23**, 455–472.

World Commission on Environment and Development (WCED), 1987, *Our Common Future*, Oxford University Press, Oxford.

Index